WARDS IN THE SKY

THE RAF'S REMARKABLE NURSING SERVICE

MARY MACKIE

For all the women and men who have so faithfully served, in war and in peace, as members of the Princess Mary's Royal Air Force Nursing Service.

Original hardback edition published 2001 (Robert Hale, London)
This edition updated and revised 2014

The History Press
The Mill, Brimscombe Port
Stroud, Gloucestershire, GL5 2QG
www.thehistorypress.co.uk

British Library Cataloguing in Publication Data.
A catalogue record for this book is available from the British Library.

ISBN 978 0 7509 5956 8

Typesetting and origination by The History Press
Printed in Great Britain

Contents

Acknowledgements

Twelve years after publication of the original version of this book I was delighted to have the opportunity to update the text. My thanks to everyone who co-operated in the preparation of three new chapters and updating of details and lists, including current DNS Gp Capt Phil Spragg, who kindly checked the new material; also Wg Cdr Mike Priestley, CO of Tactical Medical Wing, for correcting some errors concerning his unit. Special gratitude goes to WO Debbie Meikle, who arranged for me to interview a variety of RAF nurses, senior and junior, female and male, at MDHU Peterborough (and kept me supplied with coffee and moral support), with the help and permission of the unit's then CO, Wg Cdr K C Mackie (now Rtd), who also acted as initial editor. Thanks, too, to the current PMs who generously spared me their time and shared their experience. It was a privilege and honour to meet you all.

Finally, to Chris, my long-suffering husband and unpaid assistant, for help too varied to detail, for being a strong shoulder when the going got tough and a supportive cook and bottle washer over many months when my computer screen saw more of me than he did!

Thank you, all.

Acknowledgements to first edition, 2001

This book could not have been written without the contributions of many people. My gratitude and appreciation extend to all of them: in particular to Air Cdre Robert H Williams (Rtd), who as Director of Defence Nursing Services and first male MiC of the PMRAFNS determined to have a history of his Service brought to print, for allowing me the privilege of being the one to write it and for his unfailing support and assistance.

To Wg Cdr Annie Reid OBE ARRC (Rtd); to my tireless ally Wg Cdr (Rtd) Angela Scofield; to Air Cdre (Rtd) Valerie Hand, for her own stories and her eagle eye for factual and grammatical accuracy; and, not least, to Mrs Marion Donaldson (PMRAFNS Rtd) for her personal support and encouragement and, in her role as editor of the *PMs' Magazine*, source of invaluable information and assistance.

To all members of the PMRAFNS, past and present, who allowed us into their homes where they recounted their own amazing stories. Special thanks to Gp Capt (Rtd) Liz Sandison, RRC, for being such a wonderful hostess over two days when a squadron of PMs gathered at her home to share their experiences with us.

To the many, many other PMs, their husbands and families, to RAF doctors, patients, WAAFs and medics who responded to my appeals for information and bombarded me with photos, cartoons, maps, menus and wonderful stories that made me laugh out loud or brought a lump to my throat. Sometimes both. Lack of space has forced me to leave out much that I had hoped to include. However, all the material has been added to the official archive.

To all at the RAF Museum at Hendon; to Jean Buckberry, College Librarian at RAF Cranwell; Sandy Gilbert-Wykes, CRO at RAF Coningsby; Mr Stankus at the Royal Signals Museum, Blandford; to all at Air Historical Branch, London, and Personnel Records, Innsworth; and to the staff of the Imperial War Museum and the Public Record Office (PRO). My work at the latter was immensely aided by a list of relevant files compiled by Enid Zaig, and Jean Holmes generously shared her research into the youngest VC, RAF Sergeant John Hannah.

Introduction

A history of the Princess Mary's Royal Air Force Nursing Service (PMRAFNS, or the PMs) was first envisioned in 1930, when the first matron-in-chief began to gather anecdotal material. Her rough jottings, and letters with stories from early sisters, waited in the archive like diamonds for me to bring to light. Other researchers, over the years, had gathered bits and pieces of material, which I inherited and gratefully incorporated in this book. Meanwhile, time has been galloping on and every year has added yet more stories to be told.

As I discovered to my dismay and disbelief, even in books which purport to cover the whole RAF, little or no mention is made of the PMRAFNS. Huge and busy hospitals fail to merit so much as a footnote in tomes giving minute details of airfields and squadrons, and even the *History of the RAF Medical Service for World War Two*, in three huge volumes, spared the PMs only ten pages. One history of RAF Halton, whose hospital is regarded as the wellspring of both the Medical Service and the PMRAFNS, adds insult to injury by mentioning the hospital in passing but getting its name wrong: Queen Mary's RAF Hospital instead of Princess Mary's – an entirely different lady!

I was, therefore, delighted to be asked to set matters right and produce a book telling the story of the RAF'S own nursing service, not as a dry and dusty record of facts and figures but as a human tale with plenty of personal anecdotes. I confess that when I accepted the task I was not fully aware of the mountain I had to climb; despite the hard work and moments of hair tearing, however, it has been a journey of discovery, full of interest, excitement and fascination. It has also made me aware of the courage of the thousands of women and, latterly, men who, for nearly a century, have been proud to call themselves 'PMs'. I hope that the result will please all members – retired, serving or prospective – and perhaps provide 'a good read' for anyone interested in nursing, or in the air force, or simply in a true story of human beings with all their virtues, faults and foibles – and a wonderful sense of humour.

Writing for a wide audience, I have tried to avoid nursing or service jargon. A 'fainting fit', for instance, is understood by all, whereas 'vasovagal attack' would send most people rushing for a dictionary. In most cases I've settled for plain English.

Contributors other than PMs are fully identified within the text: 'Jimmy Brown, RAF Sgt' or 'Corporal WAAF Polly Perkins' or 'patient Mrs Johnson' speak for themselves. Any name without such explanation is, or has been, a serving member of the PMRAFNS. To avoid complications caused by changes of rank and, in the case of the ladies, by maiden and married names, I've settled for the simple approach, referring to nearly every lady by her maiden surname, adding her married name, as appropriate, in brackets. So someone identified as 'Joan Smith (Mrs Bloggs)' will mostly remain Joan Smith, or simply Joan, during the rest of that segment. If we meet her again in a later chapter she will be re-identified as 'Joan Smith (Mrs Bloggs)' for clarity. The men, too, you'll generally find as 'Sam Jones' or simply 'Sam', whether they were Aircraftman or Group Captain. Occasionally, for variety and flavour, I've slipped in a 'Sister Joan Smith' or 'PM Sally Spigot' or 'Flight Lieutenant Sam Jones'. For anyone interested in discovering more about these contributors – when they served, what rank they held and where I gleaned their stories – an Appendix list details all PMs actually quoted in the text. I have not included awards and honours against these names, there being no time to check every single one; rather than risk making a mistake and causing offence, I've compromised by leaving them out. In fact, very many PMs have been awarded honours such as the Royal Red Cross or the Order of St John of Jerusalem, as is made clear in the main text.

Another problem in a book of this kind is the preponderance of acronyms, which can make a page unreadable to the layman. Everyone knows what RAF stands for but other terms such as NBC or MDHU are less familiar and may have different meanings in different contexts. I've endeavoured to keep them to a minimum or, where necessary, to write the words in full; if anyone gets really lost, an alphabetical list of acronyms appears in the Appendix section.

Among the Appendices you will find the main dates and details of all RAF Hospitals, one list for the UK, the other for overseas – I am particularly pleased with these as they appear to be the first-ever such lists on record. In one or two instances exact opening and closing dates of these units have eluded me, which is regrettable, but some records no longer exist.

Spellings of foreign place-names provide another area for error – where there's an anomaly unsolvable by recourse to atlases and libraries, I've settled for the most widely used spelling.

Writing a book of this kind, there is a minefield of possible misinformation and opportunities for error. I have done my best to check my facts and members of the PMRAFNS have provided invaluable technical and editorial help, but no doubt some mistakes remain. For these I take full responsibility. In spite of them, I hope you will enjoy reading this celebration of Princess Mary's Royal Air Force Nursing Service.

Mary Mackie,
Heacham,
Norfolk

PART I

Nothing Shall Deter Us

Nec Aspera Terrent

Motto of the PMRAFNS

I

Hurricane Hattie

It's 1961. Yuri Gagarin rides through space. A dance called 'the Twist' arrives in Britain. The Beatles are still unknowns and *Coronation Street* has been on British screens for just a year. In the Soviet Union, Nikita Khruschev holds the reins of power, while over in Washington, DC, the charismatic young president, John F. Kennedy, is newly settled in the White House. Political tensions keep armed forces alert, ready to respond at the first sign of aggression.

Britain's Royal Air Force patrols the skies from airfields across Europe, the Middle East and the Far East. And, equally far flung, members of Princess Mary's Royal Air Force Nursing Service (PMRAFNS) carry out their daily duties: in the Mediterranean, Flight Officer Joy Harris is enjoying 'trooping' aboard HMS *Devonshire*, and Flight Officer Jane Stott is in Singapore, at RAF Hospital Changi. Not so very long ago, Changi endured horrors during Japanese occupation: now, when a Royal Navy vessel passes, merry midwives wave nappies in greeting from louvered windows. At home, at RAF Hospital Cosford, Shropshire, Flying Officer Eileen Smith is beginning a romance with Flying Officer David Dodds. The same unit welcomes young Bob Williams, a boy entrant to the Medical Branch, to begin eighteen months' training as a nursing attendant; he will emerge, in due time, as Warrant Officer Boy Entrant and Head Boy of the School, ready for the next stage in his air force career.

On 30 October of that same year, the latest Soviet atomic bomb test, a massive 60 megatons, provokes worldwide protest.

On the following day, Flight Officer Dorothy 'Hutch' Hutchins was in a cinema enjoying a film when a message flashed up on the screen summoning her immediately back to her unit. A stir of curiosity rippled through the cinema as she hurried out. Arriving at RAF Hospital Wroughton, she found that she and her colleague Flying Officer Iris Rawlings, both on call for aeromedical evacuation duties, were ordered to RAF Lyneham. They and the rest of the aeromed team were to gather their equipment and fly to the Caribbean, where Hurricane Hattie had devastated British Honduras, flattening its capital, Belize. Iris Rawlings (Mrs Kerse) takes up the story:

> Within a couple of hours we were at RAF Lyneham meeting the rest of the team and being issued with what was to be our uniform for the next two weeks – men's khaki drill shirts and trousers. The rest of the team consisted of a medical officer,

> about a dozen technicians, and an adjutant, Flight Lieutenant 'Pinkie' Pinks, whose home was in Belize and who was to prove invaluable to us.

The team boarded a Britannia and flew 6,000 miles across the Atlantic, to find the town of Belize wrecked and the airfield flooded. Their landing was tricky, on an airstrip marked out by lamps. Iris explains:

> HMS *Trowbridge*, a RN vessel, had been first on the scene. We were met at the airport by some of her crew and guided, through knee-high water, to the town library, which they had made their Mess. They gave us a meal and afterwards, since we had brought stretchers and blankets, we were invited to choose our bed space. We elected to sleep beneath a sign saying 'Unusual Hobbies'.

Next morning, borrowing wellington boots from the navy, Iris and Hutch went out to survey the damage:

> The shore was only about a foot above sea level and the tidal waves had removed the roofs from all the houses and completely wrecked the less substantial ones (the majority). The church, one of the few brick buildings, had been used as a refuge and its subsequent collapse had resulted in the highest death toll, running into hundreds.
>
> It was decided that we should rehouse and tend the patients from the local hospital, which had been totally demolished. We commandeered the remains of the house of a local dignitary. This was the largest house in the area and, having been two-storeyed, still had one floor with a ceiling …
>
> Once the patients were comfortably installed (two to a bed!), we had to prepare the upper floor for our occupation. The technicians fitted a tarpaulin roof, we unpacked the stretchers and blankets, and there was our 'home'.

Dorothy Hutchins recalls:

> Sanitary arrangements consisted of a bucket which, for lack of other means of disposal, had to be emptied into the sea. There was a nightly curfew because of escaped prisoners and looting, a fire watch duty because of hurricane lamps … and the US Air Force dropped emergency food packs of tinned goods, including tinned bread, tinned butter, even tinned Smarties.

Unexpected horrors imprinted themselves on Iris Rawlings' memory:

> Next to the hospital there was a water storage tank, where people would queue with their receptacles. Hutch and I would sometimes go out on what remained of

the veranda and watch. One day we were told that a body had risen to the top of the tank.

One of our patients died and an army truck came round to collect the body. I talked to one of the soldiers, who couldn't have been more than 18 years old. It seemed their daily task was to go round collecting bodies and taking them for cremation on pyres by the sea shore. The ground was too flooded for burial – sheer volume of bodies apart – and the bodies could not be kept. I asked the young soldier how they coped and he said they were given a bottle of whisky each day to see them through. I imagine the memory must haunt him for life – it does me, and I only heard about it.

Eventually it was decided that we had done all we could and it was time to leave. We were to spend a day or two in Jamaica, as guests of the QAs [Queen Alexandra's Royal Army Nursing Corps]. Imagine our joy when we were met at the aircraft by their Matron and told she had made hairdressing appointments for us that afternoon. Only a woman would think of that! We were also told that no female help was being allowed into Belize – we had rather jumped the gun. How glad I am that we did because it was an adventure I wouldn't have missed for anything.

As a result of this 'adventure', Dorothy Hutchins was awarded the ARRC and Iris Rawlings received an AOC-in-C's Commendation, for 'meritorious service'. Just two of the many awards earned by members of the PMRAFNS.

2

Introducing the PMs

Once, long ago, arrow, sword and shot sufficed to despatch an enemy. The twentieth century has added the sophisticated niceties of mustard gas, the fighter plane, the doodlebug, the nuclear bomb, napalm, the 'smart' bomb, chemical and biological weapons … All of these enable us to wage more impersonal war, with human targets obscured by distance and technology. Fortunately, our capacity for inflicting pain and death has obliged us also to learn better ways of soothing and healing not only the wounds caused by our warfare but also illnesses which have plagued humankind for generations. Many of these medical advances have been pioneered and perfected with the help of the Royal Air Force Medical Service (RAFMS) and its twin, the Princess Mary's Royal Air Force Nursing Service (PMRAFNS). Members of this latter Service refer to themselves affectionately as 'PMs'.

The story of this elite and specialised group mirrors the political, military and medical story of the twentieth century. Born out of the horrors of the Great War, 1914–18, in the following two decades the Service spread to aerodromes across Britain and put down roots in the turbulent Middle East. As another World War shattered yet more bodies and minds, the service's supportive tendrils reached across three continents, from Iceland to Japan. It held steady as Korea erupted, as Cyprus revolted, and as hurricanes howled. Through the Falklands Conflict, in the Balkans, through Iraq and on to Afghanistan, and during thousand upon thousand of individual dramas in between, PMs have answered the call for nursing aid.

Their main claim to uniqueness lies in their mobility. Wherever an emergency arises, even halfway across the world, specially trained aeromedical teams can fly to the scene within hours, using the most up-to-date planes and carrying the latest equipment. Their expertise in in-flight nursing has been honed and perfected over ten eventful decades.

Those years have seen many changes in the Service. Nurses are no longer simply ministering angels, offering little beyond soap and water, tender smiles and the touch of a soft feminine hand. PMs enter the third millennium as highly qualified, multi-skilled professionals, male and female, officers, warrant officers, NCOs and students. They work closely alongside naval and army nurses, as part of the Defence Medical Services. But they proudly continue to proclaim and defend their identity as members of the PMRAFNS.

The legacy of Florence Nightingale

The history of nursing, both civil and military, has been chronicled in detail elsewhere. Suffice it here to say that until comparatively recent times nursing was the province of amateurs and/or ill-paid incompetents. In warfare, while steel and shot killed a good many fighting men, far more died of wounds gone rotten through well-meaning ignorance and lack of hygiene. Not until the mid-nineteenth century did nursing become first a respectable occupation and eventually a fully trained profession, thanks largely to the post-Crimea efforts of Florence Nightingale.

By the time Miss Nightingale died, in 1910, she had established the basis of a system of nurse-training that was to be adopted throughout the world. Its military ethos spawned all those terrifying Sergeant-Major-style matrons who have been parodied down the years. But out of those schools came the women who were to form the nursing services of Britain, the various civilian branches as well as those of the Royal Navy, the British Army and, as the early years of the twentieth century drew half the world into war, the Royal Air Force.

Genesis

In 1900 powered flight was in its infancy. Few people imagined that those first flimsy aircraft and the daredevils who piloted them would ever prove as effective in war as a cavalry charge or the bombardment from a battleship. But some visionaries thought the possibilities worth exploring. An air battalion of the Royal Engineers came into being on 1 April 1911. It comprised two companies, one working with balloons and airships, the other with aircraft. In May 1912 this Battalion became the Royal Flying Corps (RFC), divided into a military wing and a naval wing later to be titled the Royal Naval Air Service (RNAS). With the arrival of 1914, intrepid young pilots swiftly improvised new techniques for waging aerial war.

In those early days, medical and nursing care for members of the RFC and RNAS came from whatever source lay closest. Sick or injured flyers, treated initially by unit medical officers and orderlies of the Royal Army Medical Corps, were passed on, as necessary, to the nearest military or naval hospital and the care of doctors and nurses of the army or navy. However, this state of affairs rapidly proved impracticable, mainly because flying stations (as they were then called) had to be situated on level uplands, with ample room for take-off and landing. Most of the airfields which sprang up during the Great War lay deep in the countryside, well away from large concentrations of population and established hospitals, whether army, navy or civilian. Clearly, special medical arrangements had to be made to serve the needs of flying stations.

A sick bay for flyers of airplanes, airships and balloons was opened at the RNAS training station at Cranwell, Lincolnshire, in 1916. Around the same time, a fund was launched to establish a hospital for officers of the Royal Flying Corps; the unit opened that same year at Bryanston Square, London, with twenty available beds. Shortly afterwards, thanks to the generosity of voluntary contributors, the fund was sufficient to open a larger unit, at Eaton Square. A third RFC hospital, at Mount Vernon, appointed its first medical specialist, a bacteriologist, on 11 October 1917, and soon a convalescent home was established in a large hotel with 200 acres of grounds, at Shirley Park, Croydon. These facilities were staffed by nurses 'borrowed' from either the army or the navy – Queen Alexandra's Imperial Military Nursing Service (QAIMNS), as it was then called, or Queen Alexandra's Royal Naval Nursing Service (QARNNS). As yet, the embryo flying services had no separate medical or nursing branch of their own.

On 1 April 1918, under the command of Major General Sir (later Lord) Hugh Montague Trenchard, the two wings of the RFC merged, assuming their new and enduring title of the Royal Air Force. Just three weeks later the new service won its first famous victory when one of its pilots shot down and killed the top-scoring German fighter ace, Rittmeister Manfred Freiherr von Richthofen, the 'Red Baron'.

On 1 June that same year, the fledgling RAF acquired its own (temporary) nursing service. Qualified civilian nurses might apply, and army and naval nurses could elect to leave QAIMNS or QARNNS and become members of the Royal Air Force Nursing Service (RAFNS), at least for the duration of the war.

Four women

Looking back at those days of early 1918, we find a world in turmoil. At the front, young men were still fighting and dying, knee-deep in mud, while at sea U-boats menaced great iron-clad warships and, in the skies, the new, fragile flying machines augmented the senior forces. Meanwhile, in the background, millions of people toiled in support. They included many women, who turned their soft hands to painting and doping, to carting artillery shells, butchering meat rations or, in the more traditional way of women through the ages, tending the hurts of those who returned from the front.

Among those carers were four particular women – Margaret, Kate, Marion and Mary. Differences of age and rank separated them, not to mention geography, but each of the four was involved, in her own way, in the war effort and in nursing. Three were well-experienced nurses: Margaret was based in India, Kate in London, Marion close to the front in France. Mary, the youngest of the four at only twenty, had for some time been deeply involved with volunteer war work in England. None of them had met any of the others as yet, nor did they suspect the roles that awaited them. Their only connection, in early 1918, was the vocation that had called them.

Margaret: Joanna Margaret Cruickshank, known to her family as Margaret, was born on 28 November 1875, the second child of William Cruickshank. Her father, a Scotsman from Aberdeen, ventured out as a young man first to try life in Australia and later to settle in India. His five children were all born in India and grew up as part of the Raj, in an era when the British Empire was still a powerful force in the world.

It is thought that Miss Cruickshank's interest in nursing began in India, perhaps through working with Lady Minto's Indian Nursing Association (INA). She eventually returned to the UK to take professional qualifications, starting as a probationer nurse at Guy's Hospital in 1907, at the somewhat advanced age of 31. After completing a general nursing course she gained extra diplomas in massage and midwifery and, around 1912, travelled back to the east to rejoin her family and become a sister with Lady Minto's INA.

In 1917 she joined Queen Alexandra's Imperial Military Nursing Service. The Great War was at its height. In the mountains and deserts of the north-west frontier and the Middle East, Indian soldiers fought beside their British comrades. Margaret Cruickshank was one of the army nurses who cared for them amid the heat and the dust – and the mosquitoes. In common with many of her patients, she contracted a malignant form of malaria. Stricken by recurring fevers which depleted her strength and left her unable to work, she sought relief in the Punjabi hills, whose cooler air might restore her health. But sadly, in March 1918, she was invalided home to the more temperate climate of Britain.

The journey proved an eventful one, especially for a sick woman of forty-two. She recalled her voyage from India as being fraught with:

> delay, difficulties and dangers. The culminating point was when the ship was torpedoed in the Mediterranean. We had, of course, been aware of the danger, but none of us realised just what it would feel like. Even now … that moment when the ship was struck is as vivid in my memory as when it happened. We had to take to the open boats and after a few hours at sea we were picked up by a Q-boat and sent home overland through Spain. We expected at any time to be detained as prisoners of war.

Fortunately, she arrived home safely.

Kate: During July 1918 the Air Ministry launched its nursing service by advertising in the nursing press for a matron-in-chief and four matrons, plus forty sisters and staff nurses. This first quota was filled mainly by army and navy nurses, but some civilian nurses also applied. When the first Director of Medical Services (DMS) for the RAF, Lieutenant-General (later Sir) Matthew Fell, asked the authorities at Guy's Hospital, London, to recommend suitable candidates for his new service, among the names put forward was that of Kate New.

Kate had started her general nurse and midwifery training at Guy's Hospital in 1908 at the age of twenty-five. Once qualified, she stayed on at the same hospital. As soon as war was declared she volunteered to join the forces, but was persuaded that her talents were more urgently needed at Guy's. However, in October 1918, when the air force nursing service offered her a post, she readily accepted.

Marion: Another early recruit to the new service was Marion Welch, who celebrated her thirtieth birthday in January 1918. Trained at Huddersfield, where she won a Gold

Medal, she too became a qualified midwife, with an extra diploma, in dispensing, from Apothecaries Hall. She worked at hospitals in England and later served in France with the British Red Cross Society, in a tented hospital not far from the battlefield. In the year before she applied to join the RAFNS, she had been nursing at the War Hospital in Chichester.

<u>*Mary:*</u> As for young Mary, on her twenty-first birthday, 25 April 1918, her parents agreed to allow her to apply to one of the London hospitals to become a probationer nurse. Persuading them to grant her this dearest wish can have been no easy task. Girls of her station did not, as a rule, take up a profession of any kind. But the war had changed many things. When Victoria Alexandra Alice Mary Saxe-Coburg Gotha became a trainee at the Hospital for Sick Children in Great Ormond Street, the matron was advised that her new recruit was to be 'treated as one of the nurses under all circumstances'. The order came from Buckingham Palace. The new probationer was the only daughter of King George V.

First members

If His Majesty had no objections to his daughter's working as a nurse, he did have reservations about allowing her to be named as Royal Patron of the newest nursing service. The Air Ministry considered her the perfect candidate, young and fresh, modern and caring, the very personification of the RAFNS. But when her father was approached, as early as October 1918, with requests that his daughter's name might be linked with the new service, he chose to withhold his consent until the RAFNS was fully established – probably a wise decision, as it turned out.

Even in this first inchoate 'temporary' incarnation, the new service took time to organise. To begin with, an 'Acting Principal Matron' had to be appointed. The successful applicant was Miss L.E. Jolley, another product of Guy's Hospital. She had lately been a matron at the Royal Southern Hospital in Liverpool and then a sister/acting matron in the QAIMNS Reserve. Being forty-eight at the time of her appointment to the air force nursing service, she was already well over the upper age limit for military nurses – owing to the urgent needs of 1914–18 this had been raised to forty-five – but the matter of age was waived in her case. Her officially stated role was to act as adviser in the formation of the new service, with a salary of £300 per annum but with 'no guarantee of permanence in the post'. In common with all other members of the early RAFNS, Miss Jolley was appointed for the duration of the war only. On those terms, she began work at the Air Ministry in July 1918.

Later that month, the Assistant Medical Administrator (AMA), Lieutenant-Colonel Heald, asked her to draft a document setting out conditions of service for the RAFNS. He added that 'this will be very simple as it is merely a question of putting down the pay and conditions of service of the QAIMNS'.

On 4 September Miss Jolley rather testily memoed (on economical brown Air Ministry paper, in a flourishing script and flamboyant blue-green ink!), 'Can I be informed, please, as to what units are likely to be opened and when, also of any vacancies to be filled by nurses, as I want to give applicants some idea when their services will be required.' The answer came that 'Matlock may be ready within 2 or 3 weeks – an asst matron, two sisters and three nurses, with one masseuse, will be required.' Another two weeks later, the AMA advised Miss Jolley not to engage more nurses than they were likely to need, but 'the three nurses for whom you have no immediate billets … can be absorbed on to the Matlock establishment'.

As summer turned to autumn, air force sisters and staff nurses replaced army and navy nurses at the small hospital units in London and at Cranwell; others went to Women's Royal Air Force depots at Glasgow, Birmingham and Sheffield; to the convalescent centres at Matlock in Derbyshire, and at Hastings; and to station sick quarters at the recruit training camps around Salisbury Plain. With them went members of the equally new RAF Medical Service, whose personnel included male and female doctors and dentists, with male nurses and medical orderlies. Women of the Voluntary Aid Detachment (VADs, trained in first aid and home nursing) acted as ward orderlies, cooks and general assistants. Later, in October 1918 and January 1919, air force personnel replaced army staff at existing hospitals in Blandford and Hampstead. From 1919 these places begin to appear in the records as RAF Hospitals.

The black 'Dick'

One aspect of uniform (one that holds memories for every nursing officer who ever wore it) made its debut very early on. For some it was the bane of their lives, for others a dear friend, but to all it became a close companion. This item was, and still is, the formal black highwayman-style headgear worn by female nursing officers with their blue-grey outdoor uniform, and fondly referred to as a 'Dick' (as in Turpin). Its distinctive quatrecorne shape came into being in September 1918.

An early proposal that the new service should adopt a black tricorne head-dress caused consternation in the Women's Royal Naval Service (WRNS), whose Deputy Director Miss Crowdy wrote to protest that 'since officers of the WRNS have already adopted such hats, the (D)WRNS deprecates this shape being used by another service'. In a memo, Medical Administrator (RAF) Major-General R.C. Munday noted, 'It is considered desirable to avoid any ill-feeling with the WRNS and I therefore propose adopting a four-cornered hat for the RAF Nursing Service … The Matron in Chief is in favour of the four-cornered hat.'

All subsequent PMs who had problems with that darned hat now know who to blame! Still, it was to be some time before the exact shape and style were agreed, and the hat continued to evolve over the years – sometimes officially, by order of matron-in-chief, sometimes by individual and less orthodox methods, as we shall discover.

While outdoor uniform was, as yet, a type of military motley, for members of the RAFNS indoor ward dress was simple: light blue ankle-length cotton dresses, white caps and long white aprons, with black shoes and stockings. In winter, as one sister remembers, some added Burberrys and gumboots. Conditions which demanded such practical clothing were to arrive, along with the killer flu, later that first year.

First hospitals

Some postings led those early RAF nursing sisters to comfortable billets in picturesque areas. Others, as Marion Welch observed, 'worked under greater hardship and difficulties than many on active service during war'.

One of the more desirable postings was Matlock, the spa resort in the Derbyshire hills of central England, which became the site of the RAF's No 1 Health Centre. Before 1914 the building, set on a steep hillside with terraced gardens, had been the luxurious Rockside Health Hydro, and it would become so again once the war ended. But now it was turned into a convalescent hospital for air force officers. Its matron, Miss W. Charlesworth, left a report which paints a happy picture:

> Most of the Hydro furniture was removed and stored in a building at the bottom of the hill and was replaced by barrack and hospital equipment. The patients admitted were all walking cases and usually required treatment such as massage and medicated baths. The Hydro contained a small swimming pool where the patients used to take a cold plunge before breakfast. There were also most types of medicated baths. A PT instructor used to give exercises and games to the patients in the ballroom. There was a tennis court attached to the Hydro and the golf links were quite handy.
>
> The Hydro had one of the best ballrooms in Matlock and many a gay evening was spent there by the patients as they were allowed to hold a dance there about once a fortnight. The civilians had a hospital at the Royal Scotch Matlock Bath and the civilian Sisters were always invited to the patients' dances at Rockside. In those days the RAF Nursing Staff were not allowed to dance with the patients so they had to be onlookers.
>
> The Rockside Cafe adjacent was a popular rendezvous for the patients as delicious home-made cakes were served there.
>
> There was quite a lot of talent among the patients and one or two very successful concerts were given … We were asked to give this concert and play at the civilian hospital (which contained quite a lot of Tommies) a few days later and Sister Rees and I had a very nice box of chocolates each, presented to us by one of the Tommies.

In Hastings, on the south coast, however, things were not quite so rosy. One of the early sisters, recalling her experiences, wrote to her matron-in-chief:

> We arrived at Hastings on a cold winter afternoon, and went straight to the hospital, the Hermitage. We were met by a very worried CO: 'So sorry, Sister, no accommodation for you. Hospital not opened yet, or equipped. No room for you at all.'
>
> But, having received a wire that afternoon announcing our impending arrival, he had gone over the road to a YWCA Hostel, and they would put us up. Like shop-

> girls we shared cubicles in a large dormitory; but for the Matron, Miss Nicholson, we managed to get a tiny room, so small that when she pulled her trunk from under the bed the door wouldn't open! It was bitterly cold … Most days we spent there were meatless.

This same Sister (whose name, alas, is not recorded, though her writing tells vivid tales) soon moved along the south coast from Hastings to Blandford Camp in Dorset:

> Then I was posted to Blandford … colder than ever … camp about four miles from the town. When we took over the hospital from the Army, conditions were really awful … where we slept at night, by day became the operating theatre. They got us billets in Blandford, and about 7 a.m. daily we were taken for the day to the camp by ambulance or lorry (most of them on their last legs – or wheels!). We always took with us a huge churn of milk, and where the road was very rough it would splash over us in spite of the lid … We had to balance it most carefully when we went in one old ambulance that was so decrepit that we all had to sit on one side or it would have collapsed. The churn seemed to take up all the room.
>
> Night duty in those days was eventful – it always seemed pitchy dark and we had to walk endless distances to our hutted wards, over rough tracks and duckboards (mostly missing) – and mud – with rats running everywhere … Sisters going round two- or four-hourly to do their treatments by the light of hurricane lamps. And the gales! One night I was hopelessly lost – lamp blown out – and suddenly out of the black darkness a voice: 'Halt! Who goes there!'
>
> Knowing there was a bayonet not far away, I gasped, 'Sister!'
>
> 'Pass, Sister!' and the sentry relighted my lamp for me.
>
> Then the disused railway cutting! If one missed it and slipped over, one could get a nasty fall.

Blandford Camp, Dorset

Blandford Down, outside the town of Blandford Forum, plays a brief but interesting role in the history of air force nurses. Located on open uplands rising out of pleasant green woods, the area had been used by the military for some 200 years.

The first winter of the Great War saw a vast hutted camp of the Royal Naval Division spread across the downs, its wooden billets, ablutions huts and stores all linked with duckboard walkways to save the boots of thousands of recruits from miring in the mud. Other huts held a YMCA, a Methodist mission, a Church of England church, a post office with telegraph facility, canteens for the men, ward-rooms for petty officers and messes for officers. The camp also boasted a Divisional medical area, with a hutted hospital unit not far away – a hospital that was soon to become very familiar to members of the RAFNS. From this sprawling base on the wind-swept South Downs, men went out to the trenches of Belgium and the carnage of Gallipoli. Among them was the young Sub-Lieutenant Rupert Brooke, soon to become famous as one of the best of the Great War's poets.

By 1916 Blandford Camp had expanded further with the opening of two separate detention centres for German prisoners of war (PoWs). These men might be employed on duties within the camp or hired out to local farmers. They were not allowed to sit idle.

As the war ground on, the huge training camp was adapted for use by the Royal Flying Corps, which in April 1918 metamorphosed into the RAF. That summer, Blandford Camp became an RAF Recruits Wing. A 3-mile extension of the railway link with Blandford Forum boasted a platform 200 yards long. In September the RAF Record Office came to the camp, followed in November by WRAF Records. Blandford developed into a huge hutted city, where recruits and other personnel of both the RAF and the WRAF rubbed shoulders with German PoWs going about their chores. The hospital was busy, army nurses soon giving place to new arrivals from the air force. They coped with the usual crop of illnesses and accidents, plus a bad bout of summer flu which no one realised was a mere foretaste of things to come.

Members of the WRAF at Blandford turned their hands to whatever work arose. A WRAF butcher, who had been a milliner in civilian life, handled huge carcasses which supplied meat rations to the troops. WRAF electricians worked two shifts in the power house, which supplied all the power for the great camp and brought light to the busy, hutted hospital. Going to and from work on wintry nights, nurses of the RAFNS and members of the WRAF trekked across the downs through wind, hail and snow, with wet skirts swishing about their ankles and hurricane lamps swinging.

That November, when peace was finally declared, on the eleventh hour of the eleventh day of the eleventh month, Blandford became a repatriation camp. Personnel from overseas came there to be demobilised, many of them shattered both mentally and physically. A line from one of Marion Welch's letters strikes a chill down the spine: 'That suicide wood at the back of the hospital lines was a grim reality and not a piece of newspaper fiction exploited by "John Bull".'

As winter set in, with rain and freezing winds, hospital staff had their hands full. Reporting to matron-in-chief ten years after the events, Marion Welch recalls:

> The winter was a severe one … Much of the camp was under canvas and the war huts set aside for the hospital wards were far from weatherproof, and a considerable distance apart. So limited was the accommodation available for sisters' quarters that several had to sleep in the operating theatre at night, and day [staff] and night staff had to use the same quarters. After the first couple of months, billets were found in the old market town of Blandford, some five miles from the camp. A great debt of gratitude is owing to some six or eight residents for their unfailing care and kindness to those Sisters of the RAF who were privileged to live in their homes.

> [But] the really interesting tales could never be published in the press. Who would credit the fact that we had to nurse men on stretchers in empty huts without any hospital equipment? The weather was so appallingly wet that even though we kept in gumboots and Burberry coats we were drenched going from hut to hut and constantly held up by armed sentries when on night duty.

On occasion, these night-duty excursions had hilarious consequences. The unnamed sister tells how:

> When the ambulance deposited us at the camp we had quite a walk along the disused railway line to our night quarters and tiny duty room – which we often saw little of on busy nights. There were three or four of us walking along the line one night, and I was carrying the PUDDING – Matron had an idea we didn't need any food at night (we often used to buy food for ourselves) but as a concession we had been allowed to make the rice pudding! In the dark I caught my foot on a railway sleeper, and down I came! Away went the pudding, but so solid was it, it just hopped out of its dish whole! By the light of a lamp we found it. It had lost nothing, but gained a good quantity of coal- (and other) dust. We put it back carefully in its enamel pie dish. Cook (we had a good cook for the patients) washed it – it made three puddings! But it was the last time I was allowed to carry the pudding.

A little later, she adds, 'Then came the awful pneumonia and flu …'

First uniforms

Inevitably, in those first few months the various branches of the new air force comprised a merry mix of army and navy flyers and ancillary personnel, plus a few former civilians. A month after the air force had formed, authorities decreed that khaki should be worn as service dress during the war; when peace came a new light blue uniform would be introduced as standard. However, while war lasted, this new light blue could be worn as mess dress if desired. Most air force personnel continued to wear versions of their old army and navy uniforms, but a few invested in the new light blue. A letter in the archive, from Mary Edwards (Mrs Sellors), recalls, 'those officers who had been in the Army wore their khaki uniform until they got the pale blue uniform of the RAF. This uniform had gold rank markings. I only saw one Sqn Ldr wearing this uniform, and I thought it most unserviceable and rather theatrical.' This 'theatrical' pale blue was, presumably, the same as the 'light blue colour adopted for the RAF' which is specified in an order for '3,000 yards of blue whipcord' to make uniforms for the RAFNS in October 1918. Little hard evidence remains of this early colour, but later files mention a 'new' air force blue which was introduced around October 1919, so one may guess that the pale blue was swiftly superseded by the more practical and now familiar blue-grey. Thousands of RAF personnel down the years must have been grateful for the change of mind!

Spanish flu, 1918–19

In June and July, that summer of 1918, a brief outbreak of flu had claimed the lives of two young RAF recruits at Blandford. Now, as autumn became winter, a great flu pandemic swept across the world.

At the time, viruses were beginning to be recognised as such, but nothing could counter the strain of Spanish flu which struck in the winter of 1918–19. In particular it attacked healthy young people, such as the thousands of recruits and repatriates who crowded the camp at Blandford. Victims died within two or three days, with haemorrhage and fluid on their lungs. Unable to breathe, they drowned in their own bodily fluids. Some sources suggest that this particular virus came from birds, transmitted direct from avian to human. Worldwide, it claimed even more lives than had the recently ended war.

From the Air Ministry, Medical Administrator R.C. Munday reported in October to the Secretary of State:

> In order to cope with the urgent needs at Blandford, rendered still more serious by reason of the recent influenza outbreak, the immediate taking-over of the Workhouse has been effected … and the cleaning and equipment of five huts as an hospital extension. A statistical report on the epidemic is in course of preparation.

Kate New, recently recruited to the RAFNS, was appointed matron of the 200-bedded auxiliary hospital in the old workhouse at Blandford. Pausing only to collect her uniform from an outfitters in Westminster, Kate caught a train to Blandford Camp. She found the old workhouse under-staffed, ill-equipped and filthy. She and her assistants – a handful of male nursing orderlies and general-duty chaps – had only ten days in which to turn the place into a hospital. They set to and started scrubbing the place out, exterminating weevils from the walls and evicting mice from every nook and cranny. The mice were especially well-settled in the old cheese store, which was to be Kate's office and bedroom.

Just as the first patients arrived, reinforcements appeared in the shape of three trained nurses; then five more arrived. Soon there were fourteen members of the RAFNS working at Blandford's old workhouse. They were badly needed. In this second flu outbreak, between September and December 1918, twenty-four RAF men died, mostly youngsters from the Recruits Wing, along with six German prisoners of war. The anonymous sister adds:

> many of the patients died after but a few days' illness. The old workhouse in Blandford had been taken over, but its accommodation – or lack of it – was even worse. [We were] understaffed – patients pouring in, lying on the floor on mattresses and stretchers – not enough of anything with which to cope. Fifty SI [seriously ill] or even DI [dangerously ill] patients to one Sister, and one orderly between two

> Sisters. When I took over from a Night Sister, she pointed to the [duty] bed and said, 'I found those sheets left by the last Sister, 'fraid you'll have to use them, there aren't any more.' Any that could possibly be used had to go to the patients. We were short of hypodermics, utensils, everything.

Amid the grimness, however, lighter moments did occur. As matron at the auxiliary hospital, Kate New was responsible for the catering for her nurses. The RAF cook objected to being told how to do his job by a 'mere nurse' and refused to speak to her for ten days after she suggested he might bake the sausages rather than serve up what she describes as 'nasty grey things boiled in water'. Another airman cook had learned his trade 'by watching my wife, miss'.

Rations of bread and meat were doled out by the RAF – 'you took what you were given and were grateful for it,' said Kate New – but other items of food had to be bought by matron, with a daily cash allowance of *2s 6d* [12.5p] for each nurse. Even in 1919 this called for frugal and ingenious shopping.

Blandford has one final claim to fame in the annals of RAF history – its personnel formed one of the early RAF bands. Kate New well remembered hearing, over and over again, the new march that was to develop into the famous, stirring, tingle-down-the-spine theme known to all as the *Royal Air Force March Past*. The unnamed sister adds:

> Those early days are hard to describe, now. All was so terrible and difficult. But when I left Blandford some months later, it was with sadness. There were many happy times, and as things improved we were able to look after the patients better. Transport back to billets often there was none, but it was a lovely walk if the weather was good.

The emergency auxiliary hospital at Blandford closed in 1919 and Kate New went as matron to the hospital at RAF Old Sarum (Salisbury). Slowly the whole huge camp on the Dorset Downs wound down, soon to be demolished and revert to downland and arable, until needed again for military purposes in 1939. Blandford is now the home of the Royal Corps of Signals.

Last to leave in early 1920 were four members of the WRAF. The main hospital had closed. The recruits had all gone home. RAF Records had moved on. Auditors had drawn a final line under WRAF records – indeed, the entire Women's Royal Air Force had been found surplus to requirements and was ordered to disband; the Service officially ended on 1 April 1920, having been in existence for just two years. (Like Blandford Camp itself, the women's branch of the air force was to rise again in 1939, renamed as the wartime WAAF.)

But back in 1920, in the rationalisation of affairs after the Great War, the future of the Royal Air Force itself was in question. What hope of continuation had the temporary, wartime-only Royal Air Force Nursing Service?

3

After the Great War

From 1919, British military planning worked on the premise that there could not possibly be another major war for at least ten years. Britain's most powerful enemies had been silenced and the few remaining problems in the Middle East and Bengal were, by comparison, merely minor skirmishes. What was more, the struggle against Germany had left the country in turmoil and in debt. British people, weary of war, wished only for life to return to normal.

A regime of steady demobilisation returned men and women of the reserves to their thankful families. Men gladly rejoined factories and mines; most women turned with relief to hearth and home. They were happy to believe that the recent conflict had indeed been 'the war to end all wars'. That being so, what purpose could be served by maintaining a separate air force? Better to save money by reabsorbing the flyers and their equipment into the two long-established services. This idea pleased both the navy and the army.

The Admiralty urged the immediate return of its flying wing: it was planning to build more ships capable of carrying and launching aeroplanes; naturally it wanted the whole operation under its sole control. For its part, the War Office knew itself perfectly capable of organising its own air battalions; they were, after all, only glamorous and rather showy extras, playing a supportive role to real fighting men – thus reasoned the army chiefs of the day.

Taking the opposing view, Sir Hugh Trenchard, who had once led the RFC and was now Chief of the Air Staff (CAS), strongly argued air power as the key to future military greatness. The air force must be nurtured as an independent entity and allowed to develop its full potential, with the highest standards demanded of all its personnel: *Per Ardua ad Astra* ('through adversity, to the stars') was, is and always will be the axiom of every branch of the RAF. Trenchard's belief in the effectiveness of air power was soon confirmed by events.

In 1920, a single squadron of DH9s quelled uprisings in Somaliland, largely by swooping over the heads of the so-called Mad Mullah's riders and carrying out bombing raids on pre-warned and therefore empty villages. Later, on the north-west frontier of India and in Mesopotamia (modern Iraq), the RAF flew effective sorties in support of army operations. These successful 'side-shows' proved far less costly, in terms of both money and casualties, than long, arduous ground campaigns. The voices raised against the air force grew fewer. Trenchard was vindicated. He held his appointment as CAS for ten years, during which time the RAF flew many more successful campaigns. And, despite his professed dislike of the tag, he is still best remembered as 'Father of the Royal Air Force'.

But, if the RAF itself had established its right to exist, in Whitehall the question of its maintaining separate medical and nursing services continued to create controversy.

Arguments for a separate medical service

During the war, medical problems peculiar to the flying service had revealed themselves. Aerial activity posed new problems for the human body and mind: improved artillery defences forced planes to fly higher, where lack of oxygen caused what was then called 'mountain sickness'; higher speeds brought increased stresses on bone and muscle and nerve; and spending hours alone in a cockpit could do strange things to a man's mind. A report from the Medical Administrator to the Secretary of State, dated November 1918, notes that seaplane pilots require especially strong nerves: 'the long, lonely patrols over the sea are not to be entrusted safely to a man with an imagination'. Aircrew selection committees, and medical officers responsible for the health of airmen, were obliged to develop new methods to cope with these new challenges. They would obviously require the support of a specialist medical and nursing service. As an Air Ministry memo sharply observed:

> It appears to be quite illogical that the air force should have no medical service of its own while not only the Navy and Army but the Indian Army, the Prison Service, the Police Service, the Post Office, the Home Office, the Local Government Board, the Board of Education and every other Government Department each has its own medical service.

Memos flew back and forth between the War Office, the Air Ministry and the Secretary of State for War and Air (a certain Winston S. Churchill). The Army Council, foreshadowing events of eighty years in the future, took the view that an effort should be made to 'initiate an Imperial Medical Service providing jointly for the needs of the Navy, Army and Air Services'. The Director General of Army Medical Services asserted that 'We can supply all that is required … As regards nurses, QAIMNS can be used in the Hospitals where Air Service Officers and men are admitted …' His Quartermaster-General added waspishly, 'in war … when the Air Force comes down out of the sky, [it] must clearly have its territorial requirements provided for by the Army'.

In response, the Chief of the Air Staff observed that the War Office seemed to assume that the air force existed solely to co-operate with the army. His lengthy and impassioned memo sums up by saying:

> I strongly deprecate the continuous efforts … of the War Office to say what services ought to run for the benefit of the Air … the Army Medical Service know nothing about the diseases of the Air, or the peculiarities of the Air from a Medical point of view … If this goes on, I cannot see why we should not state that it would be better and more convenient for the Air Service to run the Army Tanks.

Miss Cruickshank joins the fray

The original acting principal matron of the RAFNS, Miss Jolley, resigned after only six months in office. She had, after all, been appointed in an advisory capacity, for the duration of the war only, and she was no longer a young woman. Given the contentious atmosphere that swirled about Whitehall in the wake of the war, she may have been glad to retreat. The RAFNS appeared in danger of being swallowed whole by the much larger and older army nursing service. If it were to survive, it obviously required a Head Nurse of strong mettle and feisty character. Fortunately, just such a woman waited not far away.

We have met her before: Joanna Margaret Cruickshank, who earlier that year had enjoyed an adventurous voyage home from India while suffering from malignant malaria. She joined the RAFNS in October 1918, as a matron attached to Miss Jolley's staff at the Air Ministry, and she became acting matron-in-chief on 25 November, just three days before her forty-third birthday. Her nieces and nephews remember her as 'Aunt Margaret', but to her nursing colleagues she is best known by her first Christian name and her later-awarded title: Dame Joanna Cruickshank.

Whatever the history books may say, it can be argued that the defining moment for the RAFNS – the moment when the bedraggled fledgling first stretched its wings, stuck out its scrawny neck and pecked those who threatened it – came on Friday, 5 July 1919. On that day the redoubtable Miss Cruickshank, matron-in-chief of (temporary) air force nurses, came face to face with the equally formidable matron-in-chief of (long-established) army nurses. They were members of a committee of ten, comprising five representatives of the army medical and nursing services, three from the Air Ministry (including the then Brigadier General Sir Matthew Fell, Director of Medical Services for the RAF) and two senior matrons from civilian hospitals in London. On that fateful Friday the committee convened 'to consider the administration of the RAF Nursing Service as a branch of QAIMNS'.

Asked to state his views, Sir Matthew Fell said that the Air Ministry would prefer the two services to remain 'entirely distinct', with members of QAIMNS seconded, initially, to the RAFNS for a period of three years. That, said the army, would cause problems with promotion, and what about the expense of providing a second uniform? Also … moreover … and what of …?

The crunch came when the lady who ruled army nurses learned that nursing sisters of the Royal Air Force would be stationed not only at the main hospitals but at station sick quarters on airfields set in remote areas right across the land. Indeed, some were already working at these scattered units, as far afield as the wild reaches of Salisbury Plain. 'But who is in charge of them?' cried she, appalled by the idea of young women working so far from the supervisory eye of an older matron.

Miss Cruickshank replied crisply, 'They're grown women. They don't need a nanny.' Or words to that effect. As she later observed, in her opinion the nurses she led were 'of discretionary age and … quite capable of looking after themselves'. Women had grown beyond the need for chaperonage: she herself was ample proof of that.

The head nurse from the War Office vehemently objected. She would never allow any of her ladies to work under such conditions. Good heavens, the very idea!

It was a moment Joanna Cruickshank never forgot. As her writings reveal, she decided then and there that air force nurses could not and would not return to the old-fashioned, matriarchal regime that governed the army fold.

Something of the acerbity of the discussion lingers between the lines of the draft minute of that July meeting. Setting out army objections to the proposal, it notes that nurses would 'have to serve in sick quarters, RAF hospitals and in WRAF hostels, under conditions possibly at variance with the matron-in-chief of the War Office's views [!] and under officers not under the control of the Army Council'. What was more, 'Matron-in-Chief of the War Office could no longer control the posting and movements of the nurses.' Interestingly, these phrases are omitted from the more formal draft of the report.

As ever with government policy, the question of finance formed one of the main arguments for amalgamation. It soon became evident that no appreciable saving would result. Indeed, given the strong opposition, and the unique medical needs of the air force, a move to enforce a merger might cause actual harm. As Joanna Cruickshank (quoting W.S. Gilbert) charmingly puts it, the representatives from the Air Ministry '"took heart of grace", and decided, come what may, to go for a Nursing Service of their own'.

In view of the cut-backs in the post-war RAF (a total of over 180 operational squadrons had dwindled to a mere twenty-five by March 1920), the Air Ministry and the War Office agreed that hospital accommodation and treatment for air force personnel in most areas should be provided, pro tem, by existing army establishments. Exceptions were RAF Halton, home of the Aircraft Apprentice School; RAF Cranwell, where the Royal Air Force College was being established; and the RAF's Central Hospital, then located in Finchley, Middlesex. These three centres, already established, should continue. Overseas, too, the army foresaw no medical difficulty except possibly in Egypt, Palestine and Mesopotamia, where special arrangements might be necessary. Given these parameters, the RAFNS could now decide how many nurses it needed.

Official figures for membership of the RAFNS at this period differ wildly: for 1920 alone, one authoritative source quotes forty, another seventy-eight, another a hundred and one. Some figures include VAD nurses, others are vague about exactly who they include. Evidently great fluctuations occurred, month to month, as the Service settled down in the wake of the war years. However, order was about to be restored.

A permanent branch of the RAF

The first official terms and conditions of service were presented to Buckingham Palace in January 1921. On 21 January, King George V granted the RAF Nursing Service a Royal Charter and established it by Royal Warrant as a permanent branch of the RAF.

Candidates for membership were required to be twenty-five to thirty-four years old, and to have completed at least three years training in a large civil hospital. On entry they became staff nurses with the princely annual salary of £60, facing six months' probation before their appointment could be confirmed. Promotion was by recommendation. They wore a prescribed uniform but remained civilians, and though they enjoyed officer status they did not hold military rank – they were addressed by their professional titles, such as staff nurse, sister, matron.

Dame Joanna Cruickshank, writing after the Second World War, explains the problem of status more fully:

> Should nurses rank as officers? – this question arose early. Though nurses in the British Services did not hold commissioned rank, it was already common form in both the Army and the Navy that they should be accorded the respect and obedience due to officers. Should they become officers in fact and in law?
>
> This question had been raised before and was revived by the arrival in this country of USA Army nurses during the 1914–18 war. Australian Nursing Sisters, too, throughout the war, had worn on their shoulder straps the same stars or crowns as the men. But, despite this precedent, after the war the proposal for officer-status of British Forces Nurses was not accepted … in 1919 the Services were not ready for such a change: most members of the Nursing Services felt that their old titles of Matron, Sister and Staff Nurse conferred all the authority they needed. In fact … the majority felt that the granting of military rank might take away rather than strengthen their status as women devoted to selfless vocation.

This situation obtained until the Second World War demanded changes, but that time then lay in the unforeseeable future.

By 1921, many military nurses had retired or gone back to civilian hospitals; some who now wished to join the permanent service found themselves well over the required upper age limit of thirty-four. Indeed, Joanna Cruickshank herself would have been excluded had the new parameters been strictly applied. She pleaded the cause of her older nurses, pointing out their excellent record, their loyal and satisfactory service and valuable experience. As a result, in certain cases the appointment board agreed to waive the age limit rule.

Matron Kate New was one of the older nurses. Since the three remaining RAF hospitals already had matrons established, the only post available to Miss New was as a senior sister at the isolation hospital at Halton. Feeling that the RAF no longer offered a real career, she chose to return to civilian nursing. She became one of the first District Nurses, a vocation in which she continued until she retired at the age of sixty-five.

Meanwhile, with the RAFNS now 'thoroughly constituted and working on a sound and efficient basis', as His Majesty had once desired, when the Air Ministry approached him again the King agreed that his daughter might be formally associated with the new Service.

The original PM

We left Her Royal Highness the Princess Mary beginning as a probationer nurse at the Great Ormond Street Hospital for Sick Children, in spring 1918, when she was twenty-one. But her interest in caring for others began long before that.

Born on 25 April 1897, at York House, Sandringham, amid the woods and fields of Norfolk, Mary was the third child and only daughter of the Duke and Duchess of York. Her great-grandmother, Queen Victoria, still ruled a vast empire, and for paternal grand-parents the little princess had the flamboyant Bertie, Prince of Wales (soon to be Edward VII) and his beautiful, long-suffering wife, Alexandra of Denmark.

When Edward VII died in 1910, Mary's father succeeded to the throne as King George V and her mother became Queen Mary. As for her two older brothers, familiarly called David and Bertie, the first is better known to history as the romantic figure who gave up a throne for love – the uncrowned Edward VIII, Duke of Windsor – and the second as the stammering, self-effacing George VI, reluctantly obliged to take the throne in his older brother's stead. Three younger brothers completed Mary's family: Henry, Duke of Gloucester survived into his seventies; George, Duke of Kent was killed in an air crash while serving with the RAF in 1942, and the youngest, John, born in 1905 and afflicted with epilepsy, died at fourteen. All four of her surviving brothers, as they grew to manhood, learned how to fly aeroplanes. So it was hardly surprising that, when the chance came, Mary eagerly associated herself with the newest of the armed services.

When war broke out in 1914, the royal family responded with vigour. King George and Queen Mary helped to maintain morale by showing themselves in support of their people: they attended parades; they visited hospitals, mines and factories; and, as food and goods grew scarcer, owing to German attacks on sea-borne supply convoys, the King introduced strict rationing into his own household, ignoring the occasional grumbling of his royal offspring. His two eldest sons actively participated in the conflict: young Bertie was already in the navy despite his poor health, while David, Prince of Wales, heir to the throne, insisted on going out to the front to see for himself the horrors that faced the boys of the British Expeditionary Force. For her part, the King's only daughter plunged into the war effort with dauntless spirit. She accompanied her mother on visits to factories, hospitals and children's homes, and in spare moments she knitted for the mud-bound troops such invaluable comforts as socks, scarves and balaclava helmets. Her handiwork added to the tens of thousands of warm garments which went out to the fighting front via the collecting point at St James's Palace.

Not content with these efforts, the seventeen-year-old princess conceived a scheme whereby she might send a personal Christmas gift to every British soldier and sailor. When advised that her own allowance would not stretch to this end, she launched a fund which, aiming to raise £100,000 pounds, exceeded that figure magnificently, totalling £162,000 by the time it closed – a massive sum in those days. She succeeded in sending to each of over 500,000 fighting men a small brass box embossed with her portrait. Each box contained a card, inscribed 'From Princess Mary and friends at home, With best wishes for a Happy Christmas and a Victorious New Year,' and a gift of smoking materials – cigarettes or a pipe and tobacco, with a flint lighter. Non-smokers received chocolates or sweets. The young princess's thoughtfulness touched many hearts. It was a sign to 'the boys over there' in that bitter winter of 1914 that they had not been forgotten, and many an old soldier kept his 'Princess Mary' tin long after the contents had been put to good use.

Across Britain, voices had declared hopefully that the war would 'all be over by Christmas', but, despite a brief truce between front-line soldiers on Christmas Day, the war dragged on, and on. Women began to clamour for something useful to do in support of their courageous menfolk and, in response, Queen Mary founded her 'Work for Women' Fund. Across the country, women of all ages, from terraced back-street or country mansion, earned callouses and cuts by turning their hands to manual labour, from chopping down trees to loading barges to toiling in salvage depots or driving horses to plough fields.

The teenage princess joined her mother in the fund-raising effort. Journeys to inspect and bring heart to troops provided interludes in a diary filled with visits to hospitals, soup kitchens and munitions factories. On one occasion, watching her chat with soldiers about to embark for France, Lord Kitchener remarked to General Haig that the princess's example 'has done more than anything to rally the women of England to the colours'. She became a member of the Voluntary Aid Detachment (VAD), attended a course of first aid lectures at the palace and sat the required exams. She served meals to workers in a munitions factory canteen, or sorted reports and files at Devonshire House. She worked with the Girl Guides, the Women's Land Army, the Needlework Guild and the Red Cross.

On her twenty-first birthday, as we have seen, rather than indulging in the customary 'coming out' ball, which might have been thought frivolous in those austere times, she chose to begin work as a children's nurse. Granted her royal sire's permission, she earned the respect and affection of other staff for her willingness to roll up her sleeves and set to, however menial and messy the chore. Bed-making, nappy-changing, bottle-feeding, applying poultices, feeding by nasal tubes and bathing by water, vapour or hot air failed to daunt her. Having mastered the basics of the medical wards, she went on to offer tender loving care to young surgical patients.

Perhaps her brother David had told her of the makeshift hospitals and first-aid tents he had seen on his visits to Belgium and France. There, VADs with only minimal training served as assistants to the more professional sisters of QAIMNS, while women of the First Aid Nursing Yeomanry (fondly known as FANYs) emulated the legendary Valkyries by riding horseback into inaccessible spots to bring back the wounded. Where sailors needed nursing care, QARNNS sisters leapt into action, and locally the Territorial Army Nursing Service gave help.

As hostilities lessened, Princess Mary visited the front lines in person, taking 'a message from the Queen' to all women serving in France. She saw how nurses shared the privations – wet, muddy conditions with few comforts; basic food, and not much of that; water that had to be boiled before it was fit to drink; beds of straw, in draughty wooden huts, where one slept fully clothed both for warmth and for decency. All of this the nurses endured while caring for men badly wounded by battle or simply made sick by conditions. Soldiers living in trenches, up to their shins in freezing, muddy water, suffered horribly from trench foot and frostbite; diphtheria and secondary infections such as tetanus and septicaemia added to the toll of misery. Of the nurses she encountered, the princess later commented, 'I am glad to know how the girls really lived. I used so often to think of them and wish I could have joined them earlier in the war.'

After the war, the King decided to allow his children to seek marriage partners among the British aristocracy. Many eligible suitors flocked round his only daughter, but it was Viscount Lascelles, heir to the Earl of Harewood and fourteen years her senior, who won her heart and hand. They were married on 28 February 1922, and a year later Princess Mary, Viscountess Lascelles, bore her first son, George.

In response to the request that she might consider lending her name to the RAFNS, Her Royal Highness expressed her pride and pleasure in 'being associated with such a magnificent Service as the Air Force'. On 14 June 1923 she became president of what was proudly renamed in her honour Princess Mary's Royal Air Force Nursing Service.

So began the fully fledged PMRAFNS, an all-female branch of qualified nurses, whose members worked beside doctors and male nurses of the RAF Medical Service. The medical service also supplied nursing orderlies, nursing attendants and theatre assistants, all male until the women's service reformed in 1939. Together, these personnel staffed sick quarters on flying stations scattered across the south and east of Britain. And in larger numbers they worked at the first three permanent RAF hospitals, Finchley in Middlesex, Cranwell in Lincolnshire, and Halton Park in Buckinghamshire, all of which had their origins in the very early days of military flying.

First permanent hospitals

Central Hospital Finchley

The first small scattered hospitals of the RFC, RAF and WRAF which existed in the London area between 1917 and 1920 had mostly been situated in individual houses (see Appendix B). Among them was the Officers' Convalescent Hospital at Avenue Road, Finchley. As the Service consolidated, these units all merged into one, Central Hospital, at East End Road in Finchley, not far from RAF Hendon (scene of the first 'RAF Tournament' in July 1920 and now the home of the RAF Museum). What was then a pleasant semi-rural location with room for a grassy airfield is now lost amid the sprawl of Greater London.

Finchley was the smallest of the three post-First World War RAF hospitals, employing a matron and seven RAFNS sisters. Opened in 1919, it was the first RAF hospital graced by an official visit: Princess Mary, the new president of the PMRAFNS, visited in April 1924. But it was also the shortest-lived of the original hospitals – it closed in June 1925, when it moved to Uxbridge to become the RAF Officers' Hospital.

RAF Hospital Cranwell

RAF Cranwell lies 5 miles from the market town of Sleaford, in Lincolnshire. Well-known as the home of the RAF College and Basic Flying Training School, it can claim to be one of the very first flying stations. As early as 1915 the site was chosen by the RNAS as a training centre for officers and men destined to serve in and with aeroplanes, balloons, airships and kites.

Princess Mary's second brother, 'Bertie' (Prince Albert, later George VI), had been stationed at Cranwell as officer-in-charge of one of the navy squadrons. When the RNAS dispersed into the RAF, the prince transferred with it. Four years later Cranwell was designated as one of the three main RAF hospitals.

In common with most of the hastily erected units flung up during the first war, early Cranwell was a sprawl of wooden huts connected by duckboard walks. The RAF College officially opened in February 1920. Its cadets endured a regime that was strict, spartan and physically demanding, but after two years they emerged fully equipped to be officers of the RAF. Amid a landscape of rolling fields and wide, windswept skies, each man learned how to fly his aircraft to its limits – and how to recover it if he stretched it beyond those limits. Between 1920 and 1925 only two men died in air accidents at Cranwell, which says much for the skill of the young pilots and their instructors.

Staff at the hutted hospital coped with all injuries sustained by Cranwell personnel, whether from flying or some more mundane cause. Led by a matron and ten other members of the RAFNS, they also dealt with the usual illnesses prevalent among young men, and cared for pregnant RAF wives.

Princess Mary paid her first official visit to Cranwell Aerodrome in April 1925, to see both the RAF Hospital and the Cadet College. She was greeted by Matron-in-Chief Miss Joanna Cruickshank, among others, and, after inspecting a guard of honour formed by cadets, she went straight to the hospital where some of the nurses were presented to her. The *Daily Telegraph* noted that she spoke to almost every one of the eighty patients in the hospital, but spent most time in the female ward, 'where she stopped by the bedside of the wife of an RAF man at Cranwell, and chatted with her about her baby boy, born only six days ago'.

The same article later tells of emergency procedures for accidents on the nearby aerodrome:

> An officer of the watch is always on duty, and at the least accident he gives telephonic warning to the hospital, when motor ambulances, and a motor fire engine to cope with any outbreak of fire that may occur, are rushed to the ground, while beds in the special accident ward are, at the same time, instantly warmed by electricity.

The report reminds us how new and exciting it all was then – an aerodrome, with aeroplanes overhead, and on the ground motor vehicles, telephones and electricity!

Louise Hardy, one of the sisters who worked at Cranwell in those days, remembered that Princess Mary also paid less formal visits, when she ate lunch in the sisters' mess:

> On these visits, Princess Mary thought of herself as one of us … when seated at a table she would kick off her shoes … When taking coffee, she filled her cup with sugar crystals and these she ate with a spoon. On one occasion she produced a cigarette case – this was handed round, one noticed, with a rather mischievous smile: smoking at this time was allowed, but not approved … The conversation was about members, and especially those serving overseas; Princess Mary knew all members personally. We numbered 105.

Halton Park, 'cradle' of the PMRAFNS

Set amid the rolling hills and woods of beautiful Buckinghamshire, RAF Halton had glamorous origins. The estate was owned by the super-rich Rothschild family, and during Victorian and Edwardian days the big house – which was to become (and still is) the officers' mess – saw its share of gaiety.

In the early days of the First World War, bachelor Alfred Charles de Rothschild offered the use of his estate to the army, which cleared vast areas of timber and erected hundreds of tents for recruits summoned by the sternly pointing finger of Lord Kitchener with 'Your Country Needs You' booming from the posters. Then in 1917 the RFC took over and opened its Boys' Training School, where apprentice fitters and riggers, known as 'Trenchard's Brats', learned their trade – most of the wooden workshops of the Aircraft Apprentice School were built by German PoWs in the latter years of the Great War.

In January 1919 the RAF Medical School opened at Halton. More wooden huts, set on a hillside, contained the new hospital. Long wooden corridors connected the huts, with the wards set in pairs either side – medical and surgical wards, a theatre and all facilities, plus a separate isolation wing. They had beds for officers, for families and for maternity cases, but with 1,000 young apprentices on the camp, prey to accident and illness, the boys' ward was busiest of all. By the end of 1920, male nurses and orderlies (many of whom had served through the late war) tended their patients with the help of thirty-five sisters and staff nurses of the RAFNS, all under the guiding eye of an experienced matron.

Halton Park quickly established a reputation as the main RAF medical centre. The Central Pathological Laboratory set up its business there; the first pathologist transferred from the earlier RFC Hospital at Hampstead and his particular interest, in tropical diseases, led to the development of the famous Institute of Pathology and Tropical Medicine. The Medical School became the RAF Medical Training Depot (later the Medical Training Establishment and Depot), which produced orderlies, medics, theatre assistants, laboratory technicians and other allied trades.

Of the three early hospitals, only Halton survived in its original location. It grew from strength to strength, pioneering a wide range of medical and surgical techniques. It also provided an introduction to service life for generations of PMs. Many of them still regard Halton as their Service's true home.

Early privations

Life in those early wooden huts was often hard, especially during the winter when Britain's climate turned the ground into either deep squelching mud or frozen ruts. Nurses trudged from ward to hutted ward on rotting duckboards, clutching their great-coat collars about their throats, trying to keep their long skirts from trailing in the wet, and lofting their feeble lamps to guide their way through storm and sleet. Little wonder that some, like Kate New, retreated to more civilised conditions.

Younger and more hardy souls stayed on, among them Marion Welch, who reports a moment of black farce: 'Shall I ever forget the night when that mad orderly Jones tried three times to set fire to the camp and hospital? The AOC's car dashing up at 2.30 a.m. and cutting the only decent length of fire hose we possessed …'

She adds:

> Halton's early days were rather grim – huts that let in all the weather. I have seen patients pulling wool from their dressings and stuffing it into holes in the boards to keep out the draughts. One might have to hoist an umbrella over one's bed in heavy rain, and I used to be fascinated watching the snowflakes coming [between] the boards of my bedroom to form a lovely little heap on the floor. We had a bathroom to each hut, the stove of which we often had to stoke ourselves.

> Two lines of the hutted wards were joined by an open passage we called the 'dark hole of Calcutta'. It was floored with cinder dust. Later it was roofed in and properly floored, but for months it was a horrible alleyway. The wards were all old Army huts which had had their day, but they served their purpose, they lasted on, and stood many years of patching up.

One or two of the older matrons had also 'had their day but lasted on'. Mary Edwards (Mrs Sellors) remembers a certain Miss Cameron:

> [She was] matron of Halton when I went there in 1922 before going abroad [Mary was posted to Basra, Iraq]. She was most particular that our rooms were tidy, so much so that she threw out [a box containing] a white hat which had been specially made for a sister going abroad as she had a very small head!
>
> [Miss Cameron] was to be matron of Baghdad hospital. We were in huts then and she met me on the duckboards and asked me if I wouldn't prefer to go to Baghdad with her. It was rather difficult for me to say, 'No, thank you,' but I did.
>
> She rather annoyed us by calling us by our surnames.

Over the years to come, more than one matron acquired the habit of addressing juniors by surname alone. As a result, through the second war and beyond, sisters themselves hardly knew one another's forenames. Sister Higgins became eternally 'Higgie' and Sister Thomas became 'Tommy'. At reunions one still hears these affectionate nicknames on many lips as old friends meet. And the story goes that one formidable senior matron so far forgot herself that she addressed a surgeon by roaring his surname down the ward: 'Jones!' Stung, he turned and bawled back, 'What do you want, SMITH?!'

Dame Joanna Cruickshank summed up the early days:

> The new Service came to birth in critical times, when neither was the 1914–18 war ended nor victory assured. Under the forced incubation of hard struggles that lay ahead, its growth was rapid, though the new Service was soon to experience the pangs of under nourishment when the aftermath of war brought the campaign for economy and the Committee known as the 'Geddes Axe'.
>
> PMRAFNS, as it is now termed, is unique in that it was born and grew up with its parent Air Force as one of the family – cherished, but not spoiled – and, as the story of its work will show, it has never failed its parent, working hand in hand with the Medical Branch – for doctors and nurses own the same calling.

The oft-repeated tradition of sixty original sisters in the Service is difficult to pin down to an exact date. By August 1923, according to official files in the Public Record Office, the PMRAFNS counted 101 permanently appointed members, but, as we have seen, recorded numbers varied bewilderingly. They would continue to do so, with minor fluctuations and a slight but steady overall increase, until 1937, when the war reserve began to form. However, in 1923, there were indeed about sixty sisters on duty at home in Britain. By that time, the other two-thirds of the total 100-odd had been posted overseas.

They had gone out to the mysterious Middle East – to Mesopotamia.

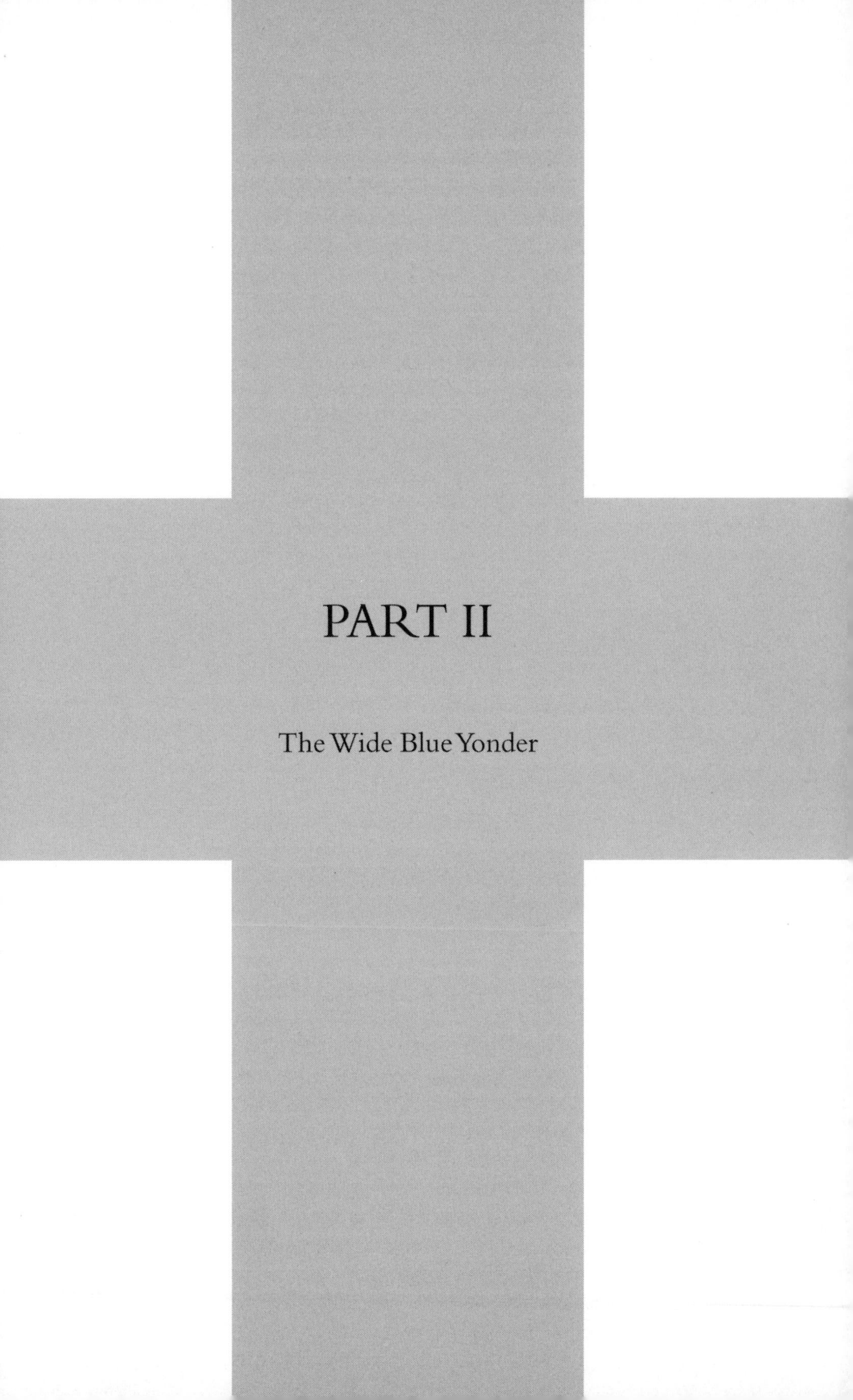

PART II

The Wide Blue Yonder

4

'Mespot'

The land of Mesopotamia, nicknamed 'Mespot' by British troops, encompassed parts of Persia (Iran) and much of present-day Iraq. Watered by the ancient rivers Tigris and Euphrates, and peopled by diverse tribes and itinerant desert peoples, it once formed part of the mighty Ottoman Empire. Britain's interests in the area had increased with the opening, in 1869, of the Suez Canal, which made the trading route through the Red Sea to India so much shorter. It was important to keep the canal and its environs in friendly hands.

Having allied themselves with Kaiser Wilhelm during the Great War, in 1918 the Turks shared his defeat. Their empire crumbled, leaving the Middle East in danger of descending into chaos, with rival factions fighting each other for supremacy. As a preventive interim measure, the League of Nations decided to govern the area by mandate – that is, they gave control of the ex-Turkish territories to the European allies, each country to administer its given areas, for the benefit of the inhabitants, until the emergent nations grew stable enough to govern themselves. Britain's particular areas of responsibility were Mesopotamia, Palestine and TransJordan (now Israel and Jordan) but it had also independently established Protectorates, including that at Aden, along the south-east coasts of Arabia. These territories were originally administered as part of the Indian Empire, garrisoned with British and Indian troops to safeguard trade routes with the Far East.

Humiliated by their defeat in the war, the Turks encouraged unrest among the area's indigent tribes, some of whose leaders resented the imposition of foreign rule. Tribal clashes and anti-British uprisings caused nearly 3,000 British casualties by the end of 1920.

In the following year, the League of Nations created an Iraqi kingdom whose first monarch, Faisal I, had been an ally of Lawrence of Arabia. To allow Faisal time to establish his authority, his country remained under British mandate, which caused political ferment and unrest. RAF squadrons went out to support the peace-keeping efforts of British and Indian troops. Often the mere sight of an aircraft swooping over the desert was enough to give the rebels pause, though some warriors became deadly accurate using rifle-fire against the airborne enemy. To friendly tribes, however, RAF crews proved to be helpful allies; on occasion their aeroplanes flew seriously ill Bedouin sheikhs to British service hospitals for emergency treatment.

Such mercy flights did much to increase the friendship between Britain and the people of 'Mespot'. They also added to the RAF's ever-widening expertise in evacuating casualties. Indeed, the RAF's first major 'cas-evac' was to take place in Mesopotamia before long. Fortunately, by that time a brand new RAF hospital, staffed by members of the PMRAFNS, had been established beside the River Tigris, at Hinaidi.

The interrupted voyage of the Braemar Castle

With trouble escalating in Mesopotamia and more squadrons being posted to the area, the RAF's Director of Medical Services proposed that some of his nursing sisters should take over from army nurses already established in desert areas. These first overseas postings took ten PMs to Iraq.

On 13 September 1922, a matron and nine sisters sailed aboard the troopship *Braemar Castle*. Among them was Mary Edwards (Mrs Sellors), bound with one or two others for Basra, while the rest were posted to Baghdad. The voyage was not to be a pleasure cruise; as their ship sailed towards Gibraltar, trouble brewed at the far end of the Mediterranean.

For some time, Turkish forces under the leadership of Mustapha Kemal Bey (Ataturk) had been threatening the peace of the mandated territories. In mid-September 1922 these rebels arrived at the neutral zone surrounding Gallipoli and set up camp outside the town of Chanak (Cannakale), whose fortifications commanded the narrows of the Dardanelles straits. They seemed intent on shattering all peace treaties and sweeping aside the European forces that barred their way to Constantinople. As the crisis deepened, the French and Italians withdrew, but British Prime Minister Lloyd George resolved to hold Chanak: Britain and Turkey stood on the verge of war.

In response to the crisis, the *Braemar Castle* diverted to the area and anchored outside Constantinople. The PMs remained on board, but the RAF contingent went ashore to join the defending troops. The seaplane carrier HMS *Pegasus* sailed closer to add its weight to the argument, and more RAF squadrons set out from the UK. However, with the onset of winter floods and frost the tension ended and a peace pact was drawn up.

Hinaidi Hospital, Baghdad

For the PMs, after ten days' delay their long voyage continued, through the Suez Canal and the Great Bitter Lake, down the Red Sea, round Aden and the Arabian peninsula and up the Persian Gulf. Mary Edwards remembers transferring to a British Indian ship in the Shatt-al-Arab (the confluence of the Tigris and Euphrates) for the last few miles up to Basra. But at Basra the army hospital was not ready to receive air force nurses, so all the PMs went on to Baghdad. There they took over at No 23 British Combined Services Hospital.

Within weeks, Mary Edwards was sent to work at the Indian sick quarters at nearby Karradah. She did not take up her original intended post, at Basra, until the following year, when the RAF opened a Combined British and Indian Hospital in that city.

Soon, other PMs joined those first few. Twenty sailed for Mespot around the turn of the year and by midsummer 1923 another nine had arrived in Palestine. Early that same year, the staff at the old army hospital in Baghdad moved to a splendid new purpose-built RAF British General Hospital at Hinaidi, on the banks of the Tigris, some 8 miles out of Baghdad.

As described by Marion Welch, who was twice matron there, the hospital at Hinaidi comprised seven or eight large buildings containing wards with high, cool ceilings and wide verandas to alleviate the heat, with space for 500 patients of both the air force and the army and benefiting from all the latest equipment.

Louise Hardy, posted there in 1926, remembers:

> a superb building, the wards named after the Air Aces of the 1914 war ... Our Mess and living quarters were also on the grand scale, and the ante-room very attractive and comfortable, the floor covered with beautiful Persian carpets. Our bedrooms were very large, each with its own bathroom. On the flat roof above was a second bedstead where one could sleep in the hot weather.

Over fourteen eventful years, Hinaidi was to be home for many PMs. They enjoyed the services of a domestic staff of Assyrian bearers, hospital assistants both Indian and Hindu, and leisure facilities including two fine tennis courts and stabling for fourteen horses. 'It was customary to ride in the early morning before breakfast,' writes Louise Hardy. 'In accordance with the social etiquette of those days, we had to pay calls and receive callers. We were also elected to membership of the British Club ... the centre of social life for the British Community.'

Despite these apparent luxuries, it was not an easy life. Nurses and troops alike endured the heat, the dust and the flies, for what was then an overseas tour of a full five years, far from home and, for most of the men, far from wives and families, too – only a few privileged officers had their wives with them.

By 1923 there were eight RAF squadrons based in Iraq – three at Hinaidi, two at Baghdad West, one at Shaibah and two further north among the hills at Mosul. Aircrew continued very active, flying sorties against rebellious tribes and Turkish forces. Death and injury stalked every flight over craggy gorges, inhospitable mountains and baking deserts, in climate and conditions never foreseen by the manufacturers of those early 'string-and-sealing wax' aircraft. Since ageing planes often obliged their crews to make forced landings in hostile territory, the aircraft usually flew in pairs, so that the second one could land nearby and lift the stricken crew to safety, often under attack from tribesmen intent on mutilation, murder and pillage. Parachutes were not a regular part of equipment until the late 1920s and few accurate maps existed.

With the practice of tropical medicine still in its early stages, endemic diseases took their toll and the climate added its own punishment – men could die of simple heatstroke. Nor were recommended precautions always effective – regulations obliged the wearing of a four-inch wide pad of felt which hung down the back suspended from a cord round the throat; this 'spine pad' was deemed necessary to protect a man's backbone from the 'deleterious rays of the sun'!

The then-commander of Hinaidi-based 45 Squadron, later Sir Arthur 'Bomber' Harris of Second World War fame, in his book *Bomber Offensive*, wrote that he would 'never forget the appalling climate, the filthy food, and the ghastly lack of every sort of amenity that our unfortunate men were compelled to put up with in "peace time"'.

The first major 'casevac' by air

Aerial evacuation of casualties began as early as 1870, when, during the siege of Paris, 160 patients were successfully lifted away from danger, courtesy of a hot-air balloon. The RAF's experience of casualty evacuation – 'casevac', as it became known – began in 1918, at Helwan in Egypt, when a patient strapped firmly to a stretcher and swathed like a mummy against the dust was loaded into a cut-out section of the fuselage of a De Havilland 6 'Dung Hunter' for the 15-mile hop to the Stationary Hospital at Cairo. A couple of years later, during the war with the Mad Mullah, three patients, lying on stretchers fixed inside the fuselage of a DH9, were flown 175 miles to hospital.

At RAF Halton, in Buckinghamshire, the first air ambulance service, using specially fitted aircraft, began and ended in the mid-1920s. A similar service lasted longer in the Middle East. However, purpose-built air ambulances proved unnecessary since most troop-carrying planes could easily be converted to carry casualties, and in real emergencies almost any aircraft could make shift as an ambulance.

In Mespot at this time, rebel Turkish leaders Kemal Ataturk and Sheikh Mahmud had vowed to reclaim large areas of upper Iraq, including Kurdistan. This northernmost part of Britain's mandated territories was, like the Persian Gulf, blessed with 'black gold', which made it contentious ground. The Turks, with their eyes on the oil, claimed that the Kurdish people were actually Turkish nationals, who must be protected from exploitation by the British. The Kurds (then as now) regarded themselves as an independent people with a right to self-determination.

In February 1923 British Intelligence discovered that Sheikh Mahmud planned to spark a general uprising in northern Iraq. In response, RAF detachments flew to Kirkuk, Mosul and Erbil, to reconnoitre and make bombing sorties in support of the ground-troops. They also supplied rations and other necessaries to inaccessible areas; and, as had become a regular habit, they evacuated sick or wounded troops back to the hospitals and sick quarters.

However, casevac skills were put to their first real test when a severe outbreak of dysentery struck in the remote, arid mountains of Kurdistan. Original plans for evacuation had involved the use of river rafts, but the stricken troops had penetrated far into the mountains, beyond the river's navigable limits. The only available means of ground transport were mules and donkeys, an impossible method with life-threatening disease felling scores of men. Back in Baghdad, emergency plans swung into operation and soon the largest casevac yet seen was under way.

Over four days, using twelve aircraft and covering a total flying distance of nearly 10,000 miles, the RAF conveyed a total of 359 patients some 200 miles to the splendid new hospital at Hinaidi and the tender loving care of PMRAFNS sisters. Without this prompt air action, many lives would inevitably have been lost. The operation conclusively proved the vital role which the RAF could play in future transport of the sick and wounded.

Social life in Baghdad

But work, war, danger and disease provided only part of the picture. Mespot had its fair share of social life, too, most of it centred on the capital, Baghdad, where the large British community, which included many civilians, enjoyed cricket matches, dances and teas, church outings, film shows and horse races. Romance also blossomed in a community where single men far outnumbered the few marriageable women. Inevitably, several members of the PMRAFNS joined the ranks of blushing Baghdad brides.

Sister Kathleen Isobel Sweeny, for instance, met her future husband in Mesopotamia. He was Flight Lieutenant Fairweather of No 30(B) Squadron, RAF Kirkuk. The wedding took place at RAF Kirkuk, in the north of Iraq.

Their son, John Fairweather, says that his mother was known fondly as 'Sister Sunshine' because she was 'not at her best first thing in the morning'. Being a fever-trained nurse and the only one in Mespot with such qualifications, she had found herself in charge of the fever ward at Hinaidi. There she came up against a formidable matron who insisted on pristine neatness and cleanliness on the ward, particularly in areas behind the bed head, and who had been known 'to go on her knees and personally check these areas with her white gloves'. One day, just before matron's rounds, the ward admitted a new patient who needed an injection, which was administered by Sister Sweeny. When matron arrived to find the bedside locker still littered with kidney bowl, hypodermic and so forth, she declared it:

> a disgustingly filthy ward almost unfit for human habitation. She then went on her knees to check the skirting behind the bed head and, being of ample proportions, displayed a rather large and well-corsetted posterior. A soldier in the next bed, who had 'taken a bit of a shine' to Sister Sunshine … leaned over, grabbed the syringe and jabbed it straight into matron's derrière.

Mr Fairweather adds that his mother 'swore that Matron's shrieks could be heard three wards away and her false teeth were picked up three beds further down!' The soldier was put on a charge and sentenced to detention:

> The Doctors, however, considered him unfit to undergo punishment, so he served his sentence in my mother's ward in the company of a Military Policeman … the Doctors discharged him as fit for duty coincidentally on the day he completed his sentence!

Kathleen Sweeny left the PMRAFNS when she married her dashing aircrew officer. Married women were not allowed to remain in the Service in those days.

Mary Edwards tells of her friend Miss Oliver, who:

> was matron at Finchley when I was there and was posted to Basra … She married out there: one Colin Macpherson. I was her bridesmaid.
>
> Before she married, I went to Baghdad with her in an oil tanker which tied up at the Maud Bridge. One night I was awakened by a coolie who came into my bunk. I dashed up and caught hold of his coat, but he wriggled away from me. I got such a fright that I went to Miss Oliver's cabin and told her. She was most sympathetic and told me she had never seen me so frightened before.

Occasionally, naivety caused even more hair-raising incidents. Louise Hardy and a friend, having just completed a three-month stint of night duty with no time off to keep in touch with local affairs, went into Baghdad to buy film for their cameras. Unaware that it was the final week of Ramadan, a month of fasting and one of the five pillars of Islam, they were persuaded to go in a taxi to see an interesting mosque in a nearby town, 'the third holy city of Muslims'. The mosque had a courtyard paved with blue and white mosaic glimpsed through gateways, but:

> across these were heavy golden chains. Fortunately we only wished to see and not go in … We saw pilgrims praying, kneeling on glorious Persian rugs … We walked round to look through several gates … We were very impressed and realised fully that it was a very holy place to the Muslims following us.

Evidently they didn't realise quite fully enough. As the growing crowds around them began to talk ever more loudly and heatedly, a man drew the two women aside and warned them in English that they must leave at once. He told them to have money ready to throw into the crowd, as a distraction to allow them to gain the safety of their taxi, which by this time was 'covered with Arabs sitting on the roof and the bonnet … the driver slumped over the wheel quivering with fear.' They threw the money, the men leapt down to squabble over it, and the taxi shot off: 'he drove like a maniac. We bumped and rolled along until in sight of Baghdad. By this time the radiator was boiling and we were bruised from being thrown around …'

Later that week they heard that there had been a riot in the town they had visited, with 200 headless bodies found outside the walls. The problem seemed to have stemmed from anger roused by the visit of 'two Christian women earlier in the week'.

When Louise and her friend confessed that they had been the two women involved, they were questioned by their own matron, by the hospital CO and then by the British Chief of Police. Finally they were called before the Air Officer Commanding, who said that if they had read 'Daily Routine Orders' they would have known that Baghdad and all other towns were out of bounds until the end of Ramadan.

Presumably the truth of this particular escapade did not reach the local press. As a rule, news of the British community, including details of cricket scores from the UK and reports of the social whirl of Mespot, appeared in at least two English-language newspapers: *The Iraq Times*, printed and published in Baghdad, vied with *The Times of Mesopotamia*, which in June 1924 claimed to be 'the oldest established British newspaper in Iraq'. It was printed in Basrah (or Basra, Busrah or even Busra; all four spellings are to be seen on the front page).

Marion Welch had been matron at Hinaidi for just over eighteen months when, in May 1926, she fell ill and had to be invalided home to England. She spent three weeks in hospital and was then granted a week's sick leave before returning to duty as matron of the RAF Officers' Hospital at Uxbridge, Middlesex. In August, however, she was taken ill again and underwent a major operation. Happily, this time she made a good recovery.

Having been at Uxbridge for just over a year, she was given a plum appointment – first matron at the newly built hospital at Halton, Bucks. We shall join her there shortly.

Aden

Legend claims that the name Aden derives from 'Eden', that it is the place where Cain and Abel lie buried and also the site of the building of Noah's Ark. It lies in South Yemen, clustered around the edges of a vast bay which came under British control in 1802. After the opening of the Suez Canal, trade expanded rapidly and Aden, strategically placed near the entrance to the Red Sea, became not only one of the largest ports in the world but an important stop for passenger ships sailing between Europe and the Orient. In its rocky, mountainous, desert hinterland lay several small states collectively known as the Aden Protectorate: Britain protected the local rulers and in return those rulers levied a quota of soldiers to help British forces keep the peace.

Turkish incursions into the Yemen called for military vigilance, but RAF squadrons based in Aden also helped patrol other problem areas such as Sudan, Kenya and British Somaliland. The first squadron went out in February 1927, to a place named RAF Khormaksar, which in the men's eyes replaced Iraq as 'the pits', as far as postings went.

RAF Khormaksar lay on the northern, inland side of the port of Aden, flanked on the western promontory by army encampments and the oil refineries of Little Aden. To the east, RAF Command Headquarters at Steamer Point clustered on hilltops with the main town below. The narrow confines of the inhabited coastal strip are surrounded by the famous 'barren rocks of Aden'.

The hospital, high over the bay at Steamer Point, benefitted from thick walls which minimised the heat. It was said to have originated as a Turkish prison. The RAF took it over from the army in April 1928, re-equipped the wards and built a new operating theatre. Five members of the PMRAFNS arrived there in June 1928 – a matron, two sisters and two staff nurses. Others were to follow.

Aden's climate made life particularly trying. The warm 'winter' was bad enough but during the high summer season, from May to September, temperatures rose to 100°F and more. The only air conditioning came via great wooden fans that merely circulated the hot air and stirred up the dust. With humidity at 80 per cent, sisters spent their days drenched in their own sweat, sometimes changing their ward dresses four or five times a day.

With no natural water available, only tepid water could be had, and that needed boiling before you dared drink it. Vegetation such as small gardens and patches of lawn had to be watered every day, otherwise it withered and died, blending into the uniform sere dusty brown of the landscape. Rain was so rare that when it did come it sent people out fully dressed to enjoy a soaking; unfortunately it usually arrived in torrents that broke walls and washed roads away.

The nursing sisters' mess lay almost at the top of the hill, separated from the town by a tortuously winding road. White-washed walls edged rocky ridges where the hospital buildings perched, each one higher than the next. Near the top, a tall and airy building with verandas shaded by slatted blinds remained much the same during the forty years it served as a mess for PMRAFNS sisters. It commanded magnificent views over the town to the vivid blue of the bay, where visiting ships – cruise liners, yachts and cargo vessels – lay at anchor with Little Aden on the further headland, below a horizon of misty mountains which on home-sick days might resemble the Cuillins on Skye.

Spectacular as the setting may have been, the hospital at Steamer Point was no place for idle dreamers. Nursing sisters looked after cases of dengue fever, sand-fly fever and malaria, skin conditions such as prickly heat and dhobi itch, and the slow healing of septic wounds got by all the usual causes, plus sea urchin spines in swimmers' feet, and bites of such local inhabitants as ants, scorpions and tarantulas. There were sharks in the sea, too. Not surprisingly, Aden was classed as an 'unhealthy' posting.

Palestine and Egypt

Policing the struggle between Palestinians and Jews was, for Britain, a thankless task, and difficult to perform in a relatively well-developed, well-populated country. Anti-Jewish riots began in earnest with massacres in 1920, after 40,000 young Zionists arrived and established kibbutzim, and Hebrew became the official language of Jews in Palestine.

As the bloodshed and unrest continued, RAF squadrons dropped supplies and flew reconnaissance missions. Operations included the first use of wireless/telegraph packs mounted on camels; where aircraft might be ineffective, the RAF even used armoured cars. One of these, as reported by PM Mary Gall, had once belonged to a gangster and was, reputedly, both bullet-proof and mine-proof. Happily, the truth of this was never tested.

PMs first went out to Palestine in 1924, to take over the army hospital at Ludd (Lydda), which was replaced by a new hospital at RAF Sarafand, opened in 1926 and visited two years later by Princess Mary. Sarafand remained a posting for PMs until 1940.

Neighbouring Egypt had been under British control for many years. It was peaceful, regarded as a kind of 'Clapham Junction' of the air, within easy reach of probable centres of unrest both east and west, and therefore a good location for a small RAF force to train and wait in reserve. Since many army troops were stationed there, army hospitals provided care for most British personnel (the same was true of the north-west frontier in India). Two PMRAFNS sisters did briefly staff a station sick quarters at RAF Aboukir, on the Egyptian coast, from September 1924, but riots forced the place to close in 1925, the sisters being transferred to Palestine. PMs returned again from 1928 to 1931, but were withdrawn owing to lack of patients.

However, the Second World War would bring them back in force to the land of the Pharaohs.

5

The New RAF Hospital Halton

The scheme for constructing a permanent hospital at RAF Halton had been approved in 1923 but it took four years for the new brick buildings with their Nightingale wards – long, wide rooms with a row of beds on each side – to be completed. In 1927, vacation of the old wooden huts took place in stages. First the offices, X-ray unit, dispensary and ancillary departments moved to their new premises. Next the new kitchens were equipped and stood ready for use. Lastly came the transfer of the wards, accomplished in a single day. By that time most of the patients had been discharged or sent on sick leave; only a few remained, some still 'bed' cases, others 'up' and reasonably mobile.

Marjorie Ells, then sister-in-charge of the ear, nose and throat ward, remembers it well:

> The great move began with the surgical and medical wards the first to go, and the huts began to feel strangely empty. None of us had seen the new hospital or the wards, so it was an exciting occasion. My ward was the last to go, at about 8 pm. All my patients were mobile, fortunately, for on arrival, to our horror, we found bedsteads and mattresses awaiting making up and, in the middle of the ward, a pile of bricks and rubble left by the builders. I gathered the staff together with the patients and we all got together to remove the debris, find buckets and form a team to scrub the place out.

A later PM, Lesley Cornwall-Jones (Mrs Howat), was actually born in the old First World War huts at Halton. Her father Richard, a member of the Works Directorate, was involved with the building of the new hospital:

> Father used to tell the tale that when the hospital was opened and the first patients were wheeled in on stretcher trolleys, they couldn't get into the lifts! Only the length of the stretchers had been calculated and not the longer stretcher poles. In the usual manner of the English, the problem was soon overcome, when the carpenters were sent for and round holes were cut in the wooden walls of the lifts, to accommodate the ends of the stretcher poles! ... They were [still] there in the 1950s.

Despite these problems, the new Princess Mary's Royal Air Force Hospital Halton, and the new sisters' quarters, were officially opened on 31 October 1927 by HRH the Princess Mary, Royal Patron and President of the PMRAFNS. One may imagine the excitement of the young apprentices forming the guard of honour, with the band playing and several VIPs, including Matron-in-Chief Joanna M. Cruickshank, lined up to greet Her Royal Highness. Later, Matron Marion Welch conducted the princess around the new wards.

At this point an ambulance arrived containing PM Louise Hardy (she who had started that riot in Iraq). She writes of being invalided home from overseas and rushed straight to Halton, arriving 'as Princess Mary was doing her inspection, and I had to wait outside until it was over. I had the distinction of being the first sick sister at Halton.'

A case of shingles

Though as yet the PMs had no RAF rank, their professional status was declared by stripes set on braid on the shoulders of capes or at the wrists of jacket sleeves. Staff nurses wore plain dark blue braid, sisters the same but with a single pale-blue stripe; senior sisters and above had maroon braid with pale blue stripes as appropriate – wider stripe, higher status. The old blue ward dresses had been replaced by white cotton, worn with white linen collars, cuffs and aprons, plus a yard-square traditional 'veil' of white lawn fashioned into a deep triangle down the back and wings framing the head. Black stockings and shoes continued for a while but they too were soon replaced by all-white. An RAF blue cape, with a medical badge at each front corner, covered the shoulders when appropriate.

Walking-out uniform was the familiar Royal Air Force blue-grey, made to a 'sealed pattern' as cut by service tailors. Some wealthier PMs had tailors or seamstresses make their suits; others gave the task to a deft-fingered amateur (often mother), hence the variations in styles of lapel, numbers of buttons, etc., in early photos.

For formal evening occasions in the mess an elegant long blue satin dress might be worn, though it had to be acquired at the wearer's expense. This mess dress had self-covered buttons down to the waist, with Swiss lace at wrist and collar and a matching satin shoulder cape. A delicate organdie veil with blue wings at the back corner adorned the sister's head.

A veil was worn also with the grey-blue dress and shoulder-cape which made another option for mess and fairly formal wear. Or nursing sisters could go out and about in grey-blue jacket and skirt, white shirt and black tie, black shoes and stockings. This uniform suit was worn either with a double-peaked storm-cap or the four-cornered black 'Dick Turpin'.

That formal four-cornered hat created problems for the more fashion-conscious sisters in those days of 'flappers' and dropped waists. At a meeting of the Medical Advisory Board in February 1928, Miss Joanna Cruickshank informed her colleagues that matron after matron had approached her, on behalf of their nursing staff, with a request for a change in the style of the uniform hat. The sisters complained that the present style could not be worn neatly, or comfortably, on a fashionably shingled head, with hair cut severely short at the back. The company who made the hats had 'recommended the re-blocking of the hat to a shape that would meet all objections'. A sample of the new shape was shown, but the committee 'agreed that a change was undesirable. Matron-in-chief undertook to see whether the firm supplying the hat could offer further suggestions about making the hat suitable with either type of head, without in any way taking from the distinct character of the hat.' Happily, by the time the committee met again in June, the hatters had produced an 'altered hat which in no way alters its character'. A close call for the 'Dick'.

Miss Welch and Miss Watt

Marion Welch remained in post as Halton's first matron for only a few months. The following April saw her promoted to the Air Ministry to work with her friend Miss Cruickshank. Her place as matron at Halton went to Katherine Christie Watt.

Kate Watt had begun her RAF career in 1919, nursing at WRAF hostels in Glasgow and then at Great Yarmouth; she had worked at various RAF hospitals in Britain, including Old Sarum, Halton and Finchley, where she had been acting matron. When Uxbridge first opened she filled in as matron there, too, until the appointment of Marion Welch. She had worked with Miss Cruickshank at the Air Ministry, and then been sent to Baghdad to replace Miss Welch when the latter had to be invalided home.

In fact, Kate Watt and Marion Welch had danced an intricate *pas de deux* through most of the important postings in the Service, with Miss Watt just that small step behind all the time. By 1929 they were both highly experienced, well-respected senior matrons of the PMRAFNS. And, as everyone knew, Miss Cruickshank was nearing retirement age. A new matron-in-chief would be needed. Which one would it be? Miss Welch or Miss Watt?

Airships

Despite earlier disasters, trial flights with airships continued. One of them caused a commotion at Halton Hospital when most of the patients on the orthopaedic ward (the single exception was a poor chap in traction!) ran out to stand on the lawn and watch the R100 'floating gracefully across the sky'. Charles James was one of 'Trenchard's brats' at the time, in hospital with a damaged spine, treatment for which called for him to lie supine with the small of his back supported by two sandbags. He associates the airship's arrival with the smell of Sunday breakfast kippers, and great excitement, until 'a loud voice from the doorway ordered, "Get back to your beds!"' It was matron, a woman of considerable size and vast authority. She was not amused.

In October that same year, news of the trial flights of the latest airship, the R101, reached even the high seas. Marion Welch, now aged forty-one, was in the

Mediterranean on board the *Nevasa*, bound once more for Iraq and another stint as matron of Hinaidi. On notepaper headed 'British India Steam Navigation Co Ltd', she penned a letter to her friend Miss Cruickshank:

> The Nevasa is a terrible ship for rolling even in a moderate sea. We should reach Port Said on Friday and have to coal there, so most people will take the opportunity to go ashore for a few hours. I shall be very glad when we reach the end of our journey.

A day or so later, she added:

> 17.10.29. Another storm last night and most people had a return of mal-de-mer. Hope we shall find it calmer in the Red Sea. Miss Hards lands at 8.30 a.m. tomorrow, Port Said. Only herself, one Medical and one Flying Officer and forty-seven men to disembark for Egypt. The MO does not know his destination in Egypt until he reports at Cairo. Must finish my mail. So glad to see by wireless news that the R101 trial flight was so successfully carried out. Did you get a view of the airship when it passed over London? With all good wishes …

The 'Miss Hards' she mentions was another long-serving member of the PMRAFNS. One wonders how she must have felt at the prospect of disembarking, for destinations unknown, as the only woman with forty-nine men!

She flies through the air …

On a summer day in 1930, at Grosvenor House on Park Lane, London, Matron-in-Chief Joanna Cruickshank held an 'At Home' attended by many leading members of the nursing and medical services of all three forces. Guest of honour was the Princess Mary, Countess of Harewood. At this charming social event the nursing press reported that attending PMs 'were daintily and tastefully attired in afternoon dress, and wore on the left shoulder, as a distinguishing mark, a badge in crepe de chine resembling a flower in the three Royal Air Force colours'. Some guests had come from long distances, especially the matron of the Palestine hospital, who 'had actually travelled from the Holy Land – not, as the uninitiated might think, by air, for that species of locomotion is forbidden to RAF nurses when on duty, but by the ordinary route'. The 'ordinary route' was, of course, the sea.

Back in 1920, Kate New had tried flying. While nursing at Old Sarum she had her one and only 'flip' in an aeroplane, suitably attired in a pair of serge 'bloomers' (as popularised by Mrs Amelia Bloomer, of New York, for use while bicycling). Kate New thought these garments more suitable than 'pretty panties' for clambering into the front of a two-seater Avro, but before they set off she admonished the pilot not to get up to 'any tricks like looping the loop'. Hearing of this escapade, DMS Sir

Matthew Fell was not amused. He made a special trip to Old Sarum to advise Miss New that 'nurses did not fly in service aircraft'.

The intrepidity of these women is exemplified by Mary Edwards, who on her second tour in the Middle East, in 1929, found herself at Hinaidi, from where:

> we were allowed to fly to Egypt in training flights … On the return journey – fortunately outside the hills of Amman – I noticed oil pouring out of the engine; so we came down in the desert in mid-July. There was another plane with spare parts following us. It came down beside us; so we transferred to it.

Two years later:

> I was transferred to Sarafand to do matron's duties … I went by aeroplane in which was ex-King Ali – brother of King Faisal. We had a terrible journey. As I was sitting beside the King I thought it better to move down to the tail and put my head down. When we reached Amman King Ali waited for me and said to me, 'Vous étiez tres malade, madame' [You were very ill]. He passed me a bottle during the journey. I opened and smelt it. It was ether! So with thanks I returned it.

Perhaps the Middle East allowed for a certain licence in such matters. In England, the combination of women and wings was still anathema. Dame Joanna Cruickshank, in later life, pondered the question:

> Should nurses be allowed in the air? It seems odd, now, to think that though they were in a Flying Service, in those early days it was only in very exceptional circumstances that the nursing sisters were permitted to be passengers in official aircraft on duty. It was argued that they were civilians, and they might be killed! Whether killed or injured, questions might be asked in the House – always a bugbear to Ministers and their Civil Service henchmen. And how about compensation, even though the victims should have signed a certificate that they took the air at their own risk?

Writing after the Second World War, she merrily admits to having personally defied the ban:

> On one occasion, the RAF hospital at Cranwell was being inspected by the then-so-called Director of Medical Services (since just before the last war, this title has been Director-General of RAF Medical Services). For obvious reasons, the Matron-in-Chief PMRAFNS, Miss (now Dame Joanna) Cruickshank, wished – indeed, was expected – to be there to meet him. Owing to some unforeseen combination of accidental circumstance, she found herself unable to reach Cranwell in time if she travelled by train. She determined to fly, and managed somehow or other – not

> without perseverance – to get round the official taboo. However, she did not arrive by air! After the second of two forced landings she would still have gone on, but her pilot thought that he would 'call it a day'. So Matron-in-Chief had to proceed – in the Services one does not 'go', one 'proceeds' – ignominiously by car! And late!
>
> Now it is but a 'normal occasion' for Sisters to travel on duty in Service aircraft, and the day may not be far distant when a Matron-in-Chief pilots her own light aircraft on an inspection tour.

Fifty years after Dame Joanna scribbled this spirited account of her own adventures, the present (1999) matron-in-chief would no doubt be only too delighted to be awarded use of his own personal light aircraft.

A successor for Miss Cruickshank

With Miss Cruickshank due to retire on reaching the age of fifty-five in November 1930, two candidates appeared eminently qualified to succeed her – Miss Marion Welch and Miss Katherine Christie Watt. Miss Cruickshank wrote references for each of these ladies, including details of their training, careers and her own recommendations on their suitability:

> In addition to holding very good professional qualifications, Miss Welch possesses outstanding administrative and organising abilities. She has the power of maintaining a high standard of efficiency, has a wide range of knowledge, general and professional, a generous outlook, possessed of sound common sense and a sympathetic understanding of human nature. I have no hesitation in recommending her as my immediate successor.

Of Miss Watt, she concludes, 'Miss Watt's professional, administrative and moral qualifications equal those of Miss Welch, but she has not Miss Welch's wide range of general knowledge and experience.'

Air Ministry evidently agreed with these conclusions. In July 1930 they wrote to Miss Welch in Iraq to inform her that she had been selected to succeed Miss Cruickshank – on the understanding that she would retire in 1936 after completing twenty years' service: evidently they did not want her to think she, too, could hang on until her fifty-fifth birthday, thirteen years on!

What must have been their reaction when Miss Welch turned them down flat? She informed them that she was resigning the Service. She had communicated her reasons to Miss Cruickshank.

A clue to those reasons lies in a delightful letter written from Hinaidi, dated 21 November 1930:

> Writing this letter, the last to you as our Matron-in-Chief, is a very sad event … I hope and pray that the next part of the road may be even more interesting though

> less arduous to travel … Miss Watt takes over when most of the spadework is done, though there will be plenty of battles to be fought in the future …
>
> I look forward to seeing you when I come home next year. Have not made any final plans about the wedding yet, but expect to get married about March and spend the summer in Europe.

Romance had belatedly blossomed for Senior Matron Miss Marion Welch, then aged forty-two.

This same letter gives some amusing sidelights into everyday life and attitudes in British Baghdad:

> The Bazaar last week in aid of the Civil Chaplaincy Fund was a great success … Mrs Ludlow-Hewitt gave her first dinner party last Tuesday and Miss Walker, Adamson and I were the only ladies invited. She had to give it in the AOC's Staff Mess as her domestic trials with servants at present are very acute …
>
> Last night we had several health films shown in the hospital, one on Malaria, another on Hookworm and two comics called 'Giro the Germ' issued by the National Health and Cleanliness Council in London. The portable cinema apparatus was lent to Mr Lampard by the Ford Motor Co. On Saturday we are to have the latest Ford films on production of cars and farming implements. The men are always so interested in anything mechanical.

'Giro the Germ' sounds fun. I'm not so sure about 'Malaria' and 'Hookworm'! The gentleman who operated the 'portable cinema apparatus' was her intended, Mr Lampard, resident in Baghdad as secretary of the Young Men's Christian Association. He and Miss Welch were married in the spring of 1931.

And so Miss Katherine C. Watt became the second matron-in-chief of the PMRAFNS. She remained in post until 1938.

Sour grapes?

Prior to Miss Cruickshank's retirement, Air Ministry requested that the Treasury might grant her a special rate of pension:

> Miss Cruickshank was the first Matron in Chief. To her fell the onerous task of building up the Royal Air Force Nursing Service from its beginning and the efficiency of the Service today is due in no small measure to the good work that she has done.

The ensuing discussion is on file only in scribbled memos between two writers whose identity is not clear, but some of the comments are revealing. One of them says that Miss Cruickshank's efforts at setting up the RAFNS were rewarded by her getting the CBE – that, he implies, should be sufficient, without giving her extra retirement pay too (which makes one wonder how he felt when she received the DBE in 1931).

Another minute adds a bracketed PS concerning another senior nurse (Matron in Chief of the Ministry of Pensions): 'She has been a bit "troublesome" … in the last year or two, but I suppose most of them get a bit that way; Matrons-in-Chief are so used to being autocrats with the staff they control.'

The other chap replies, 'Miss Cruickshank was no doubt glad to get such a post as MIC at an age seven years above the usual maximum. One cannot expect to enter a Service late in life and derive the same benefits as regards pensions as if one entered at the normal age.' He seems to forget that during the First World War nurses were gladly accepted up to the age of forty-five.

Not surprisingly, in view of these hostile male witnesses, the appeal for a special rate of pension was turned down. However, minutes of a meeting of the Nursing Service Advisory Board record:

> high appreciation of the way in which Dame Joanna Cruickshank had discharged the duties of Matron in Chief during her long tenure in office. She had the responsible task of creating the Nursing Service, and the Board consider that its present state of high efficiency is largely due to her ability, guidance and example.

Nor was she about to sit with her feet up. As the Second World War began, Dame Joanna accepted the demanding post of matron-in-chief of the Joint War Organisation of the British Red Cross and the Order of St John of Jerusalem; she designed a special cap for nurses, a simple shape over which a gas mask could be fitted with ease; but she was no longer a young woman and perhaps she had taken on too much – ill-health forced her to resign her position in 1940. That same year she assumed the duties of Commandant of the Alien Women's Internment Camp on the Isle of Man, but again her health obliged her to relinquish this work in 1941.

Now aged sixty-five, she at last contented herself with a back seat and, some years later, turned her mind to writing a new and more personal history of the PMRAFNS. It would, no doubt, have been a lively read, but sadly only a meagre twenty typed quarto pages of a first rough draft survive – some of the highlights have enlivened this present account. What else might she have written, memories that only she could have told? Lost forever, alas.

Right up to her death in August 1958, aged eighty-two, Dame Joanna maintained a keen interest in the nursing services to which she had been attached. She was particularly pleased to renew acquaintance with old friends of the PMRAFNS, at reunions and at the annual inter-hospital tennis tournament which is named after her. The Dame Joanna Cruickshank Tennis Tournament is still played today, a happy summertime occasion. The trophy is a fluted silver rose bowl presented to the PMs by their first matron-in-chief in 1930.

Days of sunlight

The early 1930s brought tranquil times and an increase in social functions. The PMRAFNS 'Dinner Club' held its first reunion dinner in 1931 and later an 'At Home' reception took place in the ballroom at Claridge's. In the New Year's Honours List for 1932, the Service's Royal Patron received a new title when her father King George V created her Princess Royal. This honorary title may only be conferred by the sovereign on his or her eldest daughter and its last holder before the Princess Mary was her aunt, Princess Louise, Duchess of Fife, who had died in 1931.

The RAF's new hospital at Halton flourished and new buildings for the RAF College Cranwell were soon to be opened by the Prince of Wales (later Edward VIII, Duke of Windsor).

The third hospital, located at RAF Uxbridge, served a huge depot where adult recruits entered ground-support trades. In those days all RAF personnel worked closely with aircraft and in order to win his 'props' (leading aircraftman insignia) a man, whatever his trade, had to prove himself physically capable of turning a real aircraft propeller.

PMs employed at the RAF Hospital Uxbridge had at last vacated their old wartime quarters and set up home in a new sisters' mess, built along the same lines as those at Halton and Cranwell, centrally heated with a whole suite of rooms for matron and for each sister a separate bedroom with hot and cold water on tap. These luxuries must have brought some comfort after an epidemic of cerebrospinal meningitis (spotted fever) hit the depot: 200 patients were isolated, half the camp quarantined and special precautions taken, including armed guards on the gates, to prevent the disease from spreading to the nearby town. Even so, six recruits died, despite their being rushed to Halton Isolation Hospital.

Elsewhere, other young patients had happier outcomes. In Ireland, the family of sixteen-year-old Aircraft Apprentice R.J. McQuigg received an alarming telegram informing them that their son was in PMRAFH Halton suffering from something called nasopharynxitis. They rushed to consult their GP, who assured them this polysyllabic terror was nothing more than a feverish cold. Mr McQuigg says drily, 'Thanks to a week of care from Princess Mary's Nursing Sisters, and the strict discipline of Matron, I made a good recovery.'

Another young apprentice, Charlie Chapman, developed rheumatic fever and spent six months in a ward at Halton. He particularly remembers the kindness of the staff, and also 'an import of victims of the Quetta earthquake disaster'. Quetta (Pakistan) was then in British Baluchistan and had long been an army outpost. When the earthquake happened, on 6 May 1935, an estimated 30,000 lives were lost. This was the first occasion when an entire medical unit moved by air, when a team of army doctors, nurses and equipment flew from Karachi to the scene of the disaster. Evidently some of the victims ended up in the care of PMs at Halton.

The RAF's medical and nursing services continued to thrive and grow, developing expertise in specialist fields, particularly aviation medicine. Flying remained a dangerous occupation. However, interesting statistics from 1932 reveal that for every man killed or injured by flying in that year, twenty-seven were injured whilst taking part (often compulsorily) in games or physical recreation. Happily, none of the sisters entering for the Dame Joanna Cruickshank Cup had their names added to the list.

As reported in the nursing press, at this time the tennis tournament took place in 'the lovely gardens of the Officers' Mess at the RAF depot, Uxbridge'. It developed into 'a delightful social function as well as a reunion of members of a very scattered service. On every side one could hear such names as "Basra", "Baghdad" and "Karachi" mentioned as casually as one ordinarily hears "Hyde Park" or "Oxford Circus".'

On another occasion the *Nursing Times* reporter observed the presence of 'umpires perched on a chair set on a table, "ball-boys", stalwart hairy-legged Air Force lads, spectators, nurses in mufti with friends and officers. The stage was set … for the semi-final and final singles match …' That year Miss Helen Cargill won the trophy with Miss Veronica Ashworth as runner-up (both went on to become matrons-in-chief post-Second World War). Naturally air force nurses had their share of admirers. The report adds, in a bracketed aside, 'There is always a very masculine element about the RAF nurses' functions …'

After years of complaints of a general shortage of good nurses, August 1936 brought a rise in pay and allowances, with a chance for swifter promotion. A new member of the PMRAFNS, joining as a staff nurse, could now expect promotion to the rank of sister in one year rather than three. Maximum pay for a sister could be achieved, by annual increments, in nine years rather than seventeen as previously. Along with improved pay for special qualifications, an increase in allowances and a greater number of substantive appointments in the grades of matron and senior sister, the opportunity to travel and work abroad made the PMRAFNS an attractive career for an ambitious young woman. Entering at the minimum age of twenty-four, she could hope to be earning £125 per annum by the time she was thirty-three, always supposing she didn't succumb to the urge to get married. Marriage still meant enforced retirement for women in those pre-war days.

'Coming events cast their shadows …'

In a cuttings book kept by Dame Joanna, alongside snippets about the tennis tournament, with teas and parasols and happy chatter amid glorious summer weather, there is a column clipped from *The Iraq Times*. It reports an incident at RAF Hinaidi when a British civilian engineer was shot dead by an infuriated Iraqi mechanic. On the back of this cutting, only the last part being legible (the rest is glued down), is a piece which reports a military review in Germany, in the presence of:

> the former 'Corporal Hitler', now Supreme Commander of the German forces. Herr Hitler, alongside General von Blomberg, reviewed 6,000 troops at the

Zeppelin Meadows. Over 60,000 political leaders, Storm Troops and Guards were ordered to attend the demonstration. Though only a small part of the army took part, the military technique was 'a revelation'.

Meanwhile, in Mespot

In the Middle East the RAF and its hospitals continued to deal with victims of skirmish, disease and accident. Between 1919 and the end of 1938, a total of 2,806 casualties were moved by air, across hundreds of miles of inhospitable desert and mountain.

On one flight, from Egypt to Iraq, PMs Hards and White were among the passengers on a Vickers Victoria aircraft when something forced their pilot to head for an emergency landing, in the middle of the desert, at night. According to Service instructions, a certain door had to be opened on such occasions, but the airman who performed the duty slipped and fell from the plane, some 700 feet above ground. 'The machine landed safely, and the remainder of the party were rescued at dawn by a "plane from Baghdad"', said the *Daily Telegraph*. The unfortunate airman was buried with full honours at Hinaidi.

In August 1931, cholera broke out among the population of southern Iraq and queues formed outside the dispensaries at Basra. According to *The Iraq Times*, 'Thousands of Arabs from the desert, marshes and river villages for miles around are swarming in for inoculation, the value of which they fully realise. When the dispensaries close, crowds patiently sit outside waiting through the night'. As the epidemic began to abate, 633 cases had been reported, with only 300 surviving. But many others had been prevented from catching the disease. A dispensary orderly held the men's record of 1,500 injections given in one day, but a 'British girl nurse' had established a record for women – in one day she inoculated no less than 1,000 desert Arabs.

Habbaniya

Under an Anglo-Iraqi treaty of June 1930, the RAF agreed to withdraw from Hinaidi and Mosul within five years of Iraqi independence, which was due in September 1932. A reduced RAF force was to reside at Sin el Dhibban, 60 miles from Baghdad. Construction work for the new camp, named RAF Dhibban, began in 1934, flying squadrons were based there from 1936, Squadron HQ took up residence the following January, and the hospital completed its move from Hinaidi in December 1937.

The camp lay in the flood-plain of the Euphrates, only a few miles from a treeless plateau where Lake Habbaniya rippled on dusty, gypsum-saturated shores. A rest and leave centre grew up near the lake, and a yacht club flourished on waters where Empire flying boats landed. The big, airy RAF hospital had 500 beds, including some for the Iraqi levies – troops enlisted from local tribes to serve beside British forces in their area.

The unit was officially renamed RAF Habbaniya from 31 May 1938. Some pronounced it HabBANiya, some HabbanEEya, some preferred the shortened 'Habb' and others went on calling it Dhibban. Most personnel loved it.

However, PMs in Iraq did not permanently sequester themselves within the safety of their hospitals and the comfort of their well-staffed messes, nor even within the confines of the camp and the British community. Throughout their long acquaintance with the country, from 1922 to 1958, nursing sisters often travelled long distances to treat tribesmen and their families in remote villages. They also accompanied RAF personnel to their summer 'rest and recreation' camp at Ser Amadia, high and remote in the cooler climate of the Kurdistan hills.

Ser Amadia

Initially a summer training camp for Iraqi levies, Ser Amadia opened each summer, from the early 1930s to 1954, with a break during the war years. PMs sent to work there dispensed first aid from a makeshift, tented sick quarters to which tribesmen from miles around would flock. Some came from beyond the Turkish and Persian borders. These men and their families might travel for days in order to camp nearby and await medical attention from these much-admired ladies and the doctors and medics who worked with them.

Among the sisters involved was Louise Hardy, who explains that 'each year in May an advance party … composed of officers, airmen and two nursing sisters … left Hinaidi with tents and other portable equipment. The only fixtures remaining [at Ser Amadia] from one year to the next were the rifle range and a fine swimming bath.'

The medical team left Baghdad at sunrise, flying in a Vickers Victoria aircraft to a small village north of Mosul, where they landed in a bumpy field of grass. Lorries took the main party on but the adjutant brought his car to convey the sisters:

> by a shorter but more precipitous route … a typical mountain road, very steep and with exciting hairpin bends which had to be negotiated with care for flocks of goats and groups of horsemen might be met around any corner. The horsemen were fierce-looking Kurds … each carried a rifle across his saddle bow.

By early afternoon they had reached another mountain village where 'having changed from uniform to jodhpurs, we mounted mules for the final climb … no defined path, but the mules picked their way very cleverly over great boulders and up steep paths until suddenly the camp came into view'. It was seven o'clock in the evening. Tired and hungry, they were shown to their tents by a bearer who had gone ahead with the advance party. 'Our quarters were very comfortable, and we liked particularly the leafy hut known as a *caprana*, which had been erected at the entrance to the tent. It was a cool and pleasant place to sit and have one's meals.'

Official morning sick parade took little time, the men being generally fit, but afterwards the sisters and the medical officer, Flight Lieutenant Bellringer, would walk across to the camp of their Assyrian guards:

> where an Indian doctor prescribed for local people. [He] was grateful for our help with the women patients, and Flight Lieutenant Bellringer, an experienced surgeon, performed remarkable operations, using only a set of ward instruments and a kitchen table ... We could not send the very sick to their homes, so gradually a small tented hospital grew up around the sick quarters. These hardy, mountain people recovered quickly from conditions which in those days, without the use of penicillin, would have killed a European. Their material needs were cared for by their own relatives, and goats, being 'rations on the hoof', wandered around everywhere.

On one occasion Louise and another sister rode for four hours on mules to attend an Arab woman in difficult labour. Having overseen the delivery of a healthy boy, they set out for the four-hour ride back, escorted by the child's father and a party of other men, with a bright full moon silvering the mountains. When they passed other riders the new father would shout the news of his son and the men all fired their rifles in salute – 'which startled us a little the first time it happened', Louise Hardy admits. She had many adventures in Iraq but she particularly recalls those 'exciting periods of beauty in Ser Amadia'.

Farewells

When Matron-in-Chief Katherine Watt retired in January 1938, the press announced her intention of going on a travel tour to visit, among other places, 'Iraq, where she hopes to see over the new Royal Air Force Hospital, opened last December, at Dhibban.' It was still called Dhibban at the beginning of that year.

By July, when Marion Welch, now Mrs Lampard, paid her last visit, the hospital had become Habbaniya. *The Iraq Times* tells the story:

> We much regret to announce the death of Mrs Lampard, the wife of the Secretary of the Young Men's Christian Association in Baghdad. Mrs Lampard had been indisposed for only a few days. On Tuesday she went to Habbaniya where (as a former Matron of the Royal Air Force) she was admitted to the hospital. She died yesterday from the effects (we believe) of septicaemia.

She was fifty years old and had been married for seven brief years.

Gwen Butler's sojourn in Iraq had a dramatic ending, too. While holidaying at Ser Amadia in August 1939, she and other RAF personnel took lunch with the Regent of Iraq and his ministers, a rather glamorous occasion. On their return to the rest camp, they found it rife with 'desert rumours' of war and news of an immediate recall, though no one knew anything for sure. They had all been aware of growing political tension in recent years: a reserve force for the PMRAFNS had been started in 1937; the Munich crisis had occurred just twelve months earlier; back in the spring Germany had annexed Czechoslovakia, then Italy invaded Albania. Had the crisis escalated beyond all hope?

They set out at 4 a.m. to ride down the mountain, their mules picking a way down sheer hillsides amid scenery made breathtaking by the rising sun. And when eventually they reached the nearest RAF airfield, they discovered that war had not, after all, been declared. 'We learned with relief that Mr Neville Chamberlain was on a fishing trip,' Gwen Butler recalled.

Their relief proved premature. A week later, Britain was again at war.

Part III

The Sternest Days

Do not let us speak of darker days; let us rather speak of sterner days. These are not dark days, these are great days – the greatest days our country has ever lived.

Winston S. Churchill,
speaking at Harrow School
29 October 1941

6

Preparing for War

In 1937, responding to the growing threat from Nazi Germany, the Air Ministry began to recruit a war reserve for all branches of the air force, including the PMRAFNS. Fully trained SRNs aged between twenty-four and forty-five were invited to sign on and stand ready to be called up for service should a national emergency arise. That first appeal brought in two hundred immediate enquiries.

The following year, on 25 October, four PM sisters were part of the 1,000-strong force of RAF personnel which gathered aboard the troopship *Nevasa*. This is believed to have been the largest RAF contingent ever sent overseas in one ship, with personnel destined for such postings as Malta, Aden, the Sudan, Iraq and India.

Meanwhile, at home, two new RAF general hospitals were under construction, one at Wroughton, near Swindon in Wiltshire, the other at Ely, near Cambridge. These large, brick-built hospitals would provide full medical and surgical facilities for patients, plus refresher courses for medical officers and training for medical airmen and women. While Ely hospital was being built, beds for RAF personnel in East Anglia were provided at a former convalescent home of the Transport and General Workers' Union, at Littleport, just outside Ely. This facility later continued as an annex for the new hospital, which boasted the most up-to-date equipment and facilities. Its operating theatre, built to be blast-proof, was the first in the RAF to have twin air-conditioning.

Across the country, at hastily erected RAF and WAAF recruiting stations, large hutted station sick quarters (SSQs) – mini-hospitals, equipped for swift expansion as needed and all with nursing sisters on their staffs – looked after the health of thousands of young trainees. By the end of 1939, SSQs at Padgate and Cosford had been upgraded to station hospitals, with St Athan to follow suit in 1940. More station hospitals opened wherever numbers of personnel required them and before the war ended the RAF had over forty large medical units in Great Britain. Overseas, there were many more (see Appendices B and C for full lists).

PMs were also posted to sick quarters at Initial Training Wings, Recruit Centres and Schools of Technical Training; some found themselves quartered in seaside boarding houses in Blackpool, Bournemouth, Newquay, Scarborough and Yarmouth.

At all locations, nursing sisters worked in tandem with men and women of the Medical Branch and Dental and Psychiatric trades, of all ranks from medical officers to what was fondly known as 'AC Plonk' (aircraftman second class). As yet, the PMs themselves held no service rank, but, as one merry recruit put it, 'we were saluted by all and sundry and we gave back a gracious smile (or grin)'.

Bog rats and battleaxes

The influx of hundreds of modern young women with new ideas came as a shock to some of the long-established sisters, who heartily disapproved of the 'giddy young things' now joining up.

When 'Jenny' Jenkins first joined the service, 'new members were unofficially referred to as "Bog rats" and we thought the Senior Sisters very old. They were about forty, possibly younger.' Iris Jarred (Mrs Bartram) had the impression that new recruits were 'very much looked down upon – "little whipper-snapper" sort of attitude. [We kept] coming up with new ideas, whereas "they" were still nursing in their day.'

The Halton matron frowned upon too much lipstick and short skirts. She required new members to bend over and demonstrate that their popliteal space (the back of their knees) wasn't showing. And new member Rona Black (Mrs McAlpine) felt sorry for Principal Matron Gladys Taylor:

> Poor Miss Taylor … dealing with all these non-conforming volunteers. You would have seen one little curl peeping out from under the beautifully laundered caps, then a gradually increasing quantity of curls … I wouldn't say we were received with open arms – at best we were tolerated. I suppose my worst offence was to be seen in the Sergeants' Mess, where was the only piano, practising my songs for a concert.

It was, of course, not done for a nursing sister to be caught fraternising with NCOs.

With five or six other applicants, Kathleen 'Kay' Cranston (Mrs Slim) appeared before the appointments' board at Adastral House in October 1938. After registering, she remembers being led 'right to the top of the building, over the roof, all among the chimneys' and down into what might have been the same or another building, for a medical examination. 'They treated us as if we were pilots and they spun us round, jumped us up and down, made us breathe into all sorts of things … evidently they had never examined Sisters before.'

New recruits also brought their own ideas about fashion. Sister Cranston had acquired her indoor dress, but still needed her outdoor uniform. As instructed, she reported to:

> the special tailor's shop which had what they called the 'sealed pattern' of the outdoor costume … I was horrified. It had not been changed since the 1920s … a type of Norfolk jacket with a waistline way down round your bottom … awful. So, being a tailor's daughter and knowing what was right, I said, 'I'm not wearing that.' With this nice tailor we devised a very smart (for those days) fitted jacket and skirt. Well, there was mayhem when I wore that back at Halton. The Matron-in-Chief was sent for.

> I paraded in front of them all like a mannequin, but they all liked it and said, 'Oh, we'll change it.' So everybody had the new uniform.

In those early days each new member received a copy of the 'sealed pattern' and took it to her own tailor to be made up. Close examination of photographs reveals that Kay Cranston was not alone in making adjustments. Particularly variable features were the position of the belt and the length of lapels.

Finding itself with two vacancies for regular (permanent, as opposed to temporary reserve) members, in June 1939 the PMRAFNS interviewed twenty hopeful applicants. Most of them were well-qualified sisters, trained at big London hospitals, and Welsh-born Iris 'Fluffy' Jones (Mrs Ogilvie, later Mrs Bower), from St Mary's, Paddington, felt rather overawed to be in this company. She was twenty-four years old but looked much younger, being only 5ft 2in and slightly built, with a halo of fluffy golden curls which had earned her her nickname. Confronted by a board which included Matron-in-Chief Emily Blair and the Director-General of Medical Services (DGMS), Air Marshal Sir Victor Richardson, she did not feel she was doing particularly well. When the board asked if she spoke any languages, Fluffy hesitated to mention her schoolgirl French but declared instead that she spoke Welsh. She fancied that the Air Marshal gave her a very odd look. Convinced that she had blown her chances, she went to sit outside and await the verdict. To her astonishment and delight, she was chosen. Her Welsh connection had done the trick – the DGMS's mother was Welsh, too.

But for her accident of birthplace, she says, 'my whole life would have been different'. The story of the PMRAFNS would have been different, too. 'Fluffy' Bower, who died in her nineties, remains one of the service's best-loved and most distinguished heroines.

Tension grows

The reality of war came nearer when station orders called for exercises to test out air-raid and blackout precautions. During air raid practice at Halton, all personnel – except nursing sisters – wore gas masks. As one Flight Sergeant Peach drily explained to young Sister Kay Cranston, 'Lethal gas goes round Matrons, Group Captains and Wing Commanders, but not Sisters!'

After a few days' leave, Kay Cranston came off the train to find the village of Wendover in total darkness. Bewildered, she walked the lanes to the darkened hospital, groped her way to her room and lit a candle to see her to bed. Next day the CO sent for her to ask why she had been showing a light – and such a bright one, too. When she explained that she had not realised there was a blackout practice, and that all she had used was one small candle, he said, 'That's amazing. That little light could be seen for miles!' A good demonstration of the need for total blackout.

Despite growing tension in Europe, the minutiae of nursing life went on. Minutes of a matrons' meeting at the Air Ministry in March 1939 record matron-in-chief's reminder that two days off per month should be taken to mean per calendar month and not one day per fortnight. A nice distinction. But in those days off-duty time was a precious privilege and with only two free days allowed every calendar month, each minute counted. That was the norm. No nurse complained. And the patients seemed happy.

Wilfred Gooch had nothing but praise for the care he received in Halton when, as a young airman at Upper Heyford, he had been badly burned by an old field-kitchen boiler which had exploded. He commented on the number of boy apprentices who would come into the hospital 'trying it on' to get away from parades over at the training school. But the sisters' remedy of 'a dose of cod liver oil and a charcoal biscuit' soon sent the truants back to work.

As Germany continued its provocative march towards confrontation, the recruiting drive for nurses grew urgent. The nursing press reported how the administration class of the British College of Nurses had paid a visit to RAF Halton, where the hospital stood in beautiful grounds among the Chiltern Hills. In the sisters' mess, a sitting room with a sunny bay window overlooked 'what is to be a glorious garden … when the demolition of the remaining huts of the original camp is completed'. The windows of the second floor boasted:

> a view of Halton Camp Airport, extending for miles … Workshops, where thousands of boys are in training for the Force, the Schools, the Barracks, married men's houses, and finally, situated on a rising eminence … Halton House, once the home of a member of the Rothschild family and now the Officers' Mess.

Articles such as this tempted more young women to sign up.

Early in 1939, Jessie Higgins was happily nursing on the private wards of Queen Charlotte's Hospital in London. Disturbed by events in Germany, she decided to apply to join the PMs. Her aunt had nursed in the First World War, in the reserve of QAIMNS, but had advised, 'Whatever you do, don't go in as a reserve – join the service!' Jessie Higgins took that advice, launching herself into a career that was to last for thirty years and see her rise to be a well-loved and respected senior matron. However, that career had a somewhat anticlimactic beginning: recruits signing on in April 1939 were told to go home and wait to be called. This was mostly because of insufficient accommodation.

To counter this problem, as we have seen, a huge building programme had begun.

Station hospitals

The first RAF station hospitals (RAFSHs) grew up at three recruit reception and training centres which opened in western Britain. At Cosford, in Shropshire, a large station sick quarters with a capacity of ninety beds had a senior sister in charge and five sisters among the staff. It opened in September 1938, dealing with recruits of the RAF and the WAAF. A year later it became a station hospital, with extra sections opening as builders finished erecting more huts.

By June 1940 Cosford was large enough to be designated a Royal Air Force general hospital (RAFGH). It developed into one of the largest and busiest of RAFGHs, including a rehabilitation centre for technicians and an important burns unit, staffed by ten doctors, twenty-seven nursing sisters, twelve VADs and eighty-three airmen and airwomen.

Another wooden-hutted hospital, at the recruit reception unit at Padgate, near Warrington in Cheshire, opened in May 1939. On arrival, many recruits proved unfit for service despite their initial medical clearance; they had to be treated, in or out of hospital, before taking up their duties. The hospital also ensured the fitness of personnel drafted overseas when RAF Padgate became one of the main Personnel Despatch Centres, and later when it served as a quarantine centre for suspected smallpox contacts disembarking from troopships at Liverpool – its latrines being inadequate, buckets were provided and emptied into the local sewer.

At the new, wooden-hutted recruit-training camp of RAF St Athan, Glamorgan, the SSQ was still under construction when, in January 1939, measles broke out. At first the nearby civilian hospital provided beds, but it couldn't cope when six more cases occurred among men on a Flight Riggers' course. Two sympathetic PM sisters hurried to get ready what beds they could, with the result that the patients, much to the ribald appreciation of their mates, found themselves in what would become the maternity ward. Alfred Thorne, one of the six men involved, says that he was admitted again, later, with toxaemia, which a medical book informed him was a condition of pregnancy. At which point he 'began to wonder if I was having a sex change'!

St Athan SSQ was upgraded to a station hospital in 1940 as the opening of more RAF stations nearby called for extended medical facilities. The increased complement of staff included fifty-six PMs, led by a matron and four senior sisters. As with many wartime units, the St Athan hospital was a sprawl of wooden huts linked together by walkways, some covered and some open to the elements. The old SSQ turned into an infectious diseases centre and annex for the busy new hospital whose patients came from RAF stations throughout Wales and across the Midlands.

'I have to tell you now …'

On 3 September 1939, Prime Minister Neville Chamberlain's sombre broadcast announced the end of all hope for a peaceful solution to the problem of Nazi Germany. Within minutes air-raid sirens sounded across the south-east of England and people headed for newly built public shelters beneath a sky devoid of German aircraft – that first air-raid warning, and many more that followed in the early days, turned out to be a false alarm.

The PMRAFNS had, at this time, 400 women on its strength – 184 regular members plus reserves and a pool of VAD nurses. Many of the VADs had been trained at

RAF hospitals at Halton or Cranwell, forming a valuable addition to the reserve. On declaration of war, 6,000 volunteers applied for 460 vacancies. 'The Royal Air Force, youngest of the services, is, with the Navy, most active at the present stage of the war, and the life of the Sisters in PMRAFNS has become hazardous and full,' observed the *Nursing Times* that October.

The wartime PMRAFNS

Once the Second World War had begun, no new members were appointed to the regular service: each new recruit entered as a member of the reserve, and remained in her civilian post until called to duty, at home or overseas. On call-up, she began a six-month probationary term, at one of the three main RAF hospitals, where she learned about service routine and practice, ward administration, and what one new recruit called 'those wretched forms'. This initiatory period could include specialist training in areas such as infectious diseases, burns treatment, rehabilitation, electrotherapy and thoracic surgery – the RAF offered its nurses a wide range of experience.

From her training hospital the new PM moved on to wherever need arose. It might be a station hospital or a sick quarters, in rural Wales or on the south coast, or up in the windy wilds of north Scotland; it might even be, and increasingly was, some overseas spot that she had never heard of and possibly couldn't spell, let alone pronounce.

At home, PMs based in station sick quarters looked after the day-to-day health of serving men and women, while at the big RAF hospitals they prepared to accept casualties brought from the front by flying hospital units staffed by men of the RAF Medical Service. These units were equipped with blood transfusion equipment which could be taken right to the front line and even used in transit, as necessary. The nursing sisters, their equipment, their hospital beds, all waited – and waited …

By day silver barrage balloons decorated the skies; by night silver searchlights stabbed up at the clouds. School-age evacuees left London in their hundreds. People carried gas-masks and responded to the wail of air-raid sirens, expecting hourly the first assault from German bombs. But the bombers failed to arrive. The country had entered a deceptively quiet period, often called the 'phoney' war.

The 'phoney' war

During eight long months, while the enemy's attention focused on eastern Europe and Scandinavia, British involvement in the war remained peripheral. A handful of bombs dropped in the far north of Scotland, but the most violent encounters occurred at sea, including the sinking of the *Royal Oak* in the harbour of Scapa Flow, Orkney, and the scuttling of the trapped *Graf Spee* in far-off South America. In response the convoy system began, to guard supplies across the Atlantic from prowling U-boats. Certain provisions grew scarce and the government issued ration books, but the war itself seemed unreal. Evacuees returned to the cities, gas-masks began to seem an unnecessary encumbrance and, with every quiet night that passed, feet trailed more reluctantly to air-raid shelters. In France the British Expeditionary Force played cards along the Maginot Line, and the RAF, prevented by the rules of fair play from attacking any but military targets, had to content itself with dropping not bombs but millions of propaganda leaflets over Europe.

At RAF hospitals, too, staff watched and waited. Geared-up to expect hundreds of war casualties, they found themselves dealing instead with the usual run of health problems.

The wartime nurse worked long hours without complaint, despite hardship and sometimes personal danger. In the blackest days she tended the wounded, learned how to heal burns and shattered jaws, taught crippled men to walk again or to function without hands, and comforted those whose psychological wounds lay too deep for the surgeon's knife. But mostly, and especially during those quiet early months of the war, she confronted old familiar foes – infections of eyes, ears, nose and throat; stomach upsets of all kinds; hernias, cuts and grazes, varicose veins, blisters and, of course, the common cold. In fact, as records reveal, over the whole six years of conflict disease caused far more casualties than did bombs and bullets.

When modern central heating began to be installed in RAF premises, hospitals took priority. Personnel lodged in hutted billets took comfort against winter weather by huddling round a coal or coke stove. As a result, colds and other respiratory infections spread happily. At RAF Hednesford, in the bitter winter of 1940/41, scarlet fever, flu, mumps, measles and meningitis rampaged through huts each heated by a single 'tortoise' stove, with fuel severely rationed. Two-thirds of the camp's 6,000 men fell sick and a nursing team was seconded to Hednesford to tend them. John Limmer, one of the medical orderlies on the team, writes of 'all the water pipes frozen, ambulances immobile [because of] two feet of snow … we had to carry the worst cases into sick bay by stretcher. Most huts had the skull and crossbones chalked on the door, putting them in quarantine.'

And when germs took a break there were other hazards – boots, for instance. Long hours of drill on hard parade grounds took their toll of tender feet accustomed to softer civilian footwear, and many a keen drill-instructor failed to understand the damage that could be inflicted by foot-stamping and heel-clicking (both were officially banned). At depots for the now-titled Women's Auxiliary Air Force (WAAF), too, recruits complained of blisters and sore feet caused by heavy shoes.

Increasing numbers of airwomen on all stations created problems for the relatively inexperienced WAAF sick quarters' attendants (later called nursing orderlies). Early in the war, PMs were sent in to improve the quality of care for airwomen and ease demand for female medical officers. On stations where large numbers of WAAF required an SSQ of more than fifty beds, two sisters were assigned, while home stations employing more than 350 WAAF had one sister added to their strength. These experienced nursing sisters helped in the training of both male and female sick quarters' attendants; they were able to visit WAAF who lay sick in billets; they gave lectures in hygiene and conducted the infamous FFI (free from infection) inspections, which did wonders for the incidence of head lice and for standards of personal hygiene. In general, they acted as friends and advisers to young airwomen who were often far from home and in need of wise counsel. Nursing sisters also discovered the inevitable cases of venereal disease, along with the allied problem, endemic among naive young women suddenly plucked from home and facing an uncertain future – the unplanned pregnancy.

Innocents on the loose

The call to arms took thousands of young men and women away from their homes and families and plunged them into strange situations, unusual occupations and, often for the first time in their lives, into one another's company without benefit of chaperons. Joan Metcalfe, who joined the service after the war and stayed on to become matron-in-chief, well remembered her own days of innocence: 'Our schooling was limited … [We had] no television, and there were only two radio programmes. We were not as knowledgeable as they are today …'

Not as knowledgeable in geography, history, dealing with heat and dust and snakes – and certainly not in sexual matters. Some late developers had not even been told about menstruation, let alone warned of the dangers of intimacy, as Jessie Higgins discovered after being posted to Cosford:

> They put me on to what they called WAAF Welfare, that was looking after 'naughty girls'. We had the main STC – Special Treatment Centre (in other words VD) – unit at Cosford, a separate hospital completely, and the girls that were diagnosed with it were sent to a hospital at Evesham. When they were taken off the treatment, whatever it was – in those days we had no penicillin, of course – they were sent to me.
>
> There were about 2,000 WAAF there – not all of them naughty girls! I was posted from the hospital staff to the station staff and I had a nice Warrant Officer's married quarter as a little sick quarters. I was also responsible for seeing the WAAF had their FFI inspections. It was just nits – and spotting pregnancies, of course. The WAAF Officers couldn't cope, didn't know what they were looking for.
>
> Well, I did this FFI and it took me about a fortnight to get through them all. I reckoned there were twenty-two girls pregnant amongst all this lot – all stages, from six or seven weeks to a good, what I call nine and a half months. Half these kids didn't know what was happening. So of course I had to tell the WAAF officer, and of course she went running to the CO … I was hauled up there – phone call – CO's Adjutant – 'You will be here within fifteen minutes, sistah!' – so I hops on my bike … went in, WAAF Officer, CO … he says, 'What's this I hear? Twenty-two girls pregnant on my station? You've got a dirty mind, sister!'
>
> So I said, 'Well, time will tell, won't it?' … Anyway, they all had babies.

The RAF hospital which opened in 1940 at Evesham, Worcestershire, developed special wards where discreet women doctors dealt with cases of venereal disease and pregnancy among members of the WAAF. With women by the thousand stationed nearby – at Bridgnorth, Innsworth, Gloucester and the WAAF Officers' School at Loughborough – during its six years' existence Evesham treated women of all types. Gossip renamed the place 'Eve's Shame' and made it a source of grievance among the local community. Any WAAF found to be pregnant would, of course, have been discharged 'on compassionate grounds'.

Evesham also had the usual medical and surgical wards. Pilot Officer William 'Dutchy' Holland, injured when his Whitley crashed near Stow-on-the-Wold, was rushed to Evesham Hospital, where he met his future wife, Sister Ethel Littler. He remembers a Sister Fanny Baldwin, a pre-war regular who, he says, epitomised the 'Sarah Gamp' type of nurse. She would:

> enter the mess, line herself up with one of the red leather armchairs and flop with a whoosh into it, legs akimbo, displaying blue issue bloomers! But she had a heart of gold. She specialised in working on 'VD' wards for WAAFs, to whom she gave unstintingly not only of her compassion and care but also much of her meagre pay to buy clothes and necessities for their babies.

The end of the 'Sitzkreig'

During that first winter, 1939/40, the war centred on Scandinavia. Finland fell to the enemy; then Denmark and Norway. Suddenly, shockingly, war came home to England when the first bombs dropped on Canterbury. The next day, Panzer divisions invaded Holland, Belgium and Luxembourg, sweeping through the Ardennes to bypass the Maginot Line where British and French forces waited. Caught out, British troops were obliged to withdraw in haste to the French coast.

Only the bravery of the navy and the crews of a fleet of individual little boats saved the British Expeditionary Force from decimation at Dunkirk. Some of the men brought back nothing but the clothes they wore. Some were so exhausted they came home and slept for two solid days, cared for by willing nurses. But such had been their haste that they left most of their equipment – tanks and guns and lorries – behind them. Much of it they had destroyed themselves to prevent the enemy from using it.

Holland fell. Belgium surrendered. The Luftwaffe raided Middlesbrough and Italy allied herself with Germany. Within days, France had fallen; then German troops took the Channel Islands. Since America remained aloof, refusing to be drawn into the conflict, and Russia maintained a treaty with Germany, Britain stood alone. Ever the rhetorician, Churchill declared it our 'finest hour'. But in truth it was probably the most desperate, desolate period of the war, for the Prime Minister as well as the British nation.

Hitler again offered peace – on terms that Churchill found unacceptable – so the German Chancellor decided he would batter this arrogant little off-shore island into submission. He planned to start by destroying her airfields.

First bombs at Cranwell

That spring of 1940 the RAF College Service Flying Training School, Cranwell, was filled to capacity with new recruits and trainees all eager to join the aerial defence of Britain. But after the long lull of the 'phoney' war they had relaxed their guard. According to Kay Cranston (Mrs Slim), Cranwell at that time did not observe any blackout:

> Lights were on all the time, there were no curtains and the flare paths were lit up because they discovered they had accidents with the boys who were learning to fly, and the blackout meant more accidents. So they gave them every light they could and occasionally a German plane would come in at the tail end of their exercises.

The 'boys' had begun to regard the war as a bit of a bore and they longed for something exciting to happen. Their wish was granted on a night in June, as Kay Cranston reports:

> We had our first air raid there and the bombs fell right down the runway – which was lucky, for had they gone a little more to one side they would have hit the Officers' Mess, the Sisters' Mess and the Hospital. As it was, it didn't cause much damage. All they did was fill in the holes and all was right again. Three bombs did not explode and the naughty Officers put them in front of their Mess in the garden and were having bets on which one would go off first.
>
> All the bits of bomb, shrapnel, etc., which were lying around were gathered up by everyone as keepsakes. Little did we know that everyone could get a bit of bomb eventually, but at that time it was all new and everyone wanted a souvenir. When the bomb disposal people came down they were furious because there were no bits of bomb left for them. They were angry with the Officers for treating the unexploded bombs so casually …
>
> I remember after the raid asking one of the Officers if anyone had been hurt and he said, no, only one casualty, and that was the Padre – his knees were sore because he had been down on them praying all the time.

This attack, the first of many in the area, took place at 10.30 p.m. on the evening of 6 June 1940. One German aircraft flew across the aerodrome and dropped thirty bombs, of which only fourteen exploded. Of those, nine dropped ineffectually in fields; only five hit the runway.

The authorities had already decided to move the RAF hospital. Cranwell offered too tempting a target for the enemy and, besides, once the war began in earnest the concentration of Bomber and Fighter Command bases in Lincolnshire would call for larger medical facilities than the training station could offer. Even as those first bombs fell, plans were in hand for transfer to a less vulnerable site a few miles away, at what had been the Rauceby Mental Hospital.

The building at Rauceby was already in use as an annex for Cranwell. Kay Cranston had helped with the cleaning:

> The place smelt horrible, stale urine, horrible pictures drawn on lavatory walls … We soon had it cleaned up. But it was great fun at first because, as we got the wards ready, making up beds, etc., the self-locking doors would lock us in the wards and we couldn't get out. Fortunately there was a telephone!

When the building was ready, and all the locks had been changed, an ambulance convoy transferred patients and stores the few miles from Cranwell:

> But we kept losing some of the patients. We discovered they were having a whale of a time locking each other in the padded cell and not telling anyone! The inmates of the mental asylum, who worked in the hospital laundry and on the farm, still remained. Our CO gave us a talk and said we were to be polite and considerate to these men and women. He concluded … 'These people have certificates to say they're sane, which is more than any of you lot have!'

Iris Jarred (Mrs Bartram), who worked on the burns and orthopaedic wards at Rauceby, remembers that 'They kept a few inmates and the more normal ones ran the laundry. There used to be a little man pushing a trolley and whenever he saw you – "Ooh, little blue eyes! Dear little blue eyes." He used to totter around the grounds …' She describes the hospital as a huge place with several detached buildings, holding 400 beds:

> The private wards we had for Officers and burns were across the garden. The rest was very dour, long corridors with padded cells at the bottom of all of them, it really was awful. Yes, grim … they'd got what I thought were rhododendron, but they were laurels – the place was smothered in laurel … The only redeeming feature was a golf course across the road, but then it was a question of just knocking a ball around on your own, more or less, the only time we could get into mufti.

While stationed at Rauceby she was desolated to learn of the death of her brother, a test pilot for Vickers-Armstrong.

Some aircrew patients, having recovered from their wounds, needed psychiatric care. Kay Cranston adds, with sympathy, 'they were just tired and wanted a rest and understanding and a chance to recover. We used to send a lot of them down to Devon, to Torquay.'

Shelter for the shell-shocked

The RAF Officers' Hospital had moved from Uxbridge to Torquay, on the balmy south coast of Devon, a location considered to be relatively safe from the threat of German bombs. Along with convalescent and rehabilitation facilities, it provided neuropsychiatric wards for those suffering nervous disorders. And in central England a similar haven, this one for non-commissioned aircrew, nestled among the beautiful Derbyshire hills at the spa resort of Matlock. The luxurious Rockside Health Hydro, with its ballroom, tennis courts, croquet lawns and bowling green, had once again, as during the First World War, been requisitioned by the RAF.

Patients with notes marked 'NYDN' (not yet diagnosed, query neuropsychiatric) came to such centres to rest and be assessed. John Limmer served as an orderly at Matlock, working with nursing sisters and doctors in a small unit of about forty personnel whose CO, Sir John McIntyre, had been physician to King George V. John Limmer remembers the place as 'very impressive, very luxurious … taken over complete with staff i.e. lady cleaners, waiters, gardeners, boiler man, receptionist … three chefs and a masseuse … Patients were encouraged to record their dreams and hypnosis was also used a lot.' Sisters' quarters lay in another small hydro at the bottom of the driveway with the main building on the hill above, built of stone in five storeys. Its facilities offered mostly single rooms, not ideal for nursing but appreciated by some patients who, under severe stress after terrible ordeals, enjoyed their privacy.

More and more such patients began to need treatment.

Innovative new treatment for burns

Prior to 1939, records show only thirteen non-fatal burns cases among RAF personnel. From 1940 they became all too common.

That summer, the blue skies over England staged a terrible aerial ballet accompanied by the rattle of gunfire, the drift of smoke and the death-dives of burning aircraft. The young pilots of the RAF defended their aerodromes with skill and courage, but at terrible cost. Burning planes fell out of the skies, flaming with an intense heat that virtually melted human tissue. Those who survived suffered dreadful disfigurement. Doctors tried all manner of ointments and unguents but, whatever method they used, still the unavoidable changing of dressings caused patients the most terrible pain and left them badly scarred.

At PMRAFH Halton, a VAD nurse walked into a side room one day and discovered two men engaged in a strange ritual: one of them, wearing what appeared to be a pair of cellophane trousers, lay in a pool of water on the floor while his colleague knelt over him. The men turned out to be two young RAF doctors, Bunyan and Stannard. They were experimenting with coverings designed to contain an antiseptic mixture of Milton fluid and saline solution which would keep burned flesh constantly irrigated and prevent dressings from sticking to the wounds. As more aircraft went down in flames, and ships and tanks caught fire, the Bunyan–Stannard Irrigation Envelope, as it came to be called, was soon being used on hospital wards all over Britain.

Not all of the burns victims were aircrew, or even servicemen. At Halton's Burns Centre, a woman was brought in with 75 per cent burns on her body. A barrage balloon had been shot down in flames and engulfed her. Joan White (Mrs Cool) was on duty, but 'I can't describe how she looked. It was awful, tragic.'

That patient did not survive, but many did. The RAF's chief consultant in plastic surgery, Mr A.H. (later Sir Archibald) McIndoe, won acclaim during the Second World War for his treatment of badly burned aircrew, for whom he formed the Guinea Pig Club. Working out of the Queen Victoria Hospital at East Grinstead, Sussex, he pioneered the use of saline baths to replace treatment by tannic coagulation. The new method – constant-temperature immersion in brine combined with the new relatively pain-free dressings – aided healing and greatly reduced the severity of scarring.

As an accessory to their general training, PMs attended brief training courses at East Grinstead to observe these new techniques. Those who were to specialise in 'plastics' went on to complete their training, in resuscitation and the principles of early skin coverage and healing by skin grafts, at the new burns centres which opened at Halton, Rauceby, Cosford and the brand new RAFH at Ely.

Sergeant John Hannah

Films and TV programmes depicting the war often give the impression that all pilots and navigators were commissioned officers. On the contrary, a great many of our gallant aircrew were non-commissioned officers – sergeants and flight sergeants. And the majority of them were very young men. The story of one of them will exemplify them all.

At Rauceby, eighteen-year-old Sergeant John Hannah, a wireless operator and air gunner, was admitted with burns to his face and hands. He had used his bare hands to battle the flames in a stricken Hampden bomber, which he and his Canadian skipper were nursing home to RAF Scampton. Later, promoted to Flight Sergeant, John Hannah wrote to the *MTE Journal*, a magazine published by the RAF Medical Training Establishment, saying that he used to have a dread of hospitals and everything connected with them. Now, however:

> I have come to regard with admiration and profound thankfulness the wonderful work of the surgeons, and the devoted attention of the Sisters and nursing orderlies … I was fortunately afforded the opportunity of earning the Victoria Cross on one of my return trips from Germany – this time over Antwerp in September 1940 – by extinguishing a number of fires which broke out in the bomb compartment and rear cockpits, and thereby, I understand, I 'saved the aircraft'. I was severely burned as a result and spent two months in RAF Hospital 'R' … The painstaking care with which I was attended on that occasion has been equalled only by similar instances on a subsequent occasion … in RAF Hospital 'Y' …
>
> I should like to be allowed the privilege of here expressing my heartfelt thanks … in particular to Wing Commander Handley and Sister Marshall.

The hospitals whose identities he shields because of wartime security were Rauceby and Yatesbury.

In October 1940 the press published pictures of Sergeant John Hannah as a patient at Rauceby, standing beside Sister Marshall and holding the telegram which told of his award. He was the youngest man ever to win the VC, being still a few weeks short of his nineteenth birthday when he went to Buckingham Palace to receive the medal from the King. Because of his injuries he was never able to fly again. He became an instructor but was discharged as medically unfit in December 1941 – his lungs had been affected by the smoke and heat. He developed TB, from which he died in June 1947, aged twenty-five.

By August 1940 the Battle of Britain had been won. But the Blitz was only beginning. Before the end of the year, London itself would be in flames.

7

Air Raids

As the months went by, every centre of industry, every port and every railway came under attack. No one in Britain could sleep easily. Not even while lying in a hospital bed. RAF Hospital St Athan, in South Wales, found itself too close to the docks of Cardiff and Swansea. Four bombs struck in July 1940, causing one fatality and some damage to the infectious diseases annex. In August two more raids occurred. The first hit outside the station perimeter. The second …

Iris 'Fluffy' Jones (Mrs Ogilvie, later Mrs Bower) was a junior sister at the time:

> but it so happened that on this particular night I had been detailed to be in charge … Suddenly we heard bombs dropping … the siren started wailing in the darkness. I heard Nurse Traherne shouting, 'Don't run!' In a few seconds I had reached a ward full of patients and found the entrance vanished. It was pitch black; shouting, moaning and rushing water could be heard. Suddenly I seemed to be falling into a deep hole – a bomb crater. I climbed out pretty fast, and the first patient I came to was still sitting on a lavatory seat. All the walls had disappeared. I could see by the light of my torch that blood was streaming down his face. He was shocked, but by some miracle was not badly hurt. In no time at all, we could see the funny side to the situation, that he was still sitting on the 'loo'.

Groping her way in the darkness, wading through water from fractured pipes, Fluffy Jones found other patients who were:

> injured and in obvious pain. Fortunately most had minor injuries, only due to the fact that the wards were wooden huts and there was no heavy masonry. The most menacing sound in the darkness was that of rushing water … Ghostly figures running about and the ambulances coming and going made it a hectic night … We were all glad to see the dawn.

The 'Nurse Traherne' she mentions was, in fact, Lady Rowena Traherne, a Red Cross member of the VAD. Her impression, quoted in Dillwyn Rees's history of St Athan, *Twenty-One Caring Years*, was that, 'On a quiet evening in August a lone German plane came over Glamorgan and stupidly dropped all its little 250lb bombs on our Hospital. We were all furious …'

Although, miraculously, human casualties were few, so much structural damage occurred that the entire place had to be evacuated, patients being transported to civilian hospitals at Whitchurch, Llandough and Cardiff. But as soon as essential repair work had been completed RAFH St Athan reopened for business.

Over on the south coast of England, the resort town of St Leonards on Sea, near Hastings, lay in a far more vulnerable area: it faced the Channel, with only a few miles separating it from the coast of Nazi-occupied France. The town itself had become a prohibited zone, its residents dispersed to other counties and forbidden to return except by official permit. Only a few essential services, including those at the Buchanan Hospital, kept the place ticking over.

A huge block of luxury flats dominated the promenade. Shaped to resemble the liner *Queen Mary*, painted white and nick-named 'the skyscraper', Marine Court had been commandeered in 1939 by the Air Ministry for use as an Initial Training Wing (ITW). As the name implies, it housed fresh recruits, turning them from raw civilians into airmen fit for more specialised training elsewhere.

The windows of No 14 ITW commanded wonderful views across the Channel, sea and sky ever changing with season and weather. Conversely, viewed from that sea, and from those skies, the tall white mass beckoned the eye like a beacon. It made a tempting target for 'tip and run' raids by enemy aircraft.

At the sick quarters up on the sixth floor, Mary Moultrie (Mrs Nicholson) experienced her 'most exciting posting'. While making her morning rounds of the wards, she 'heard the unmistakable sound of an aircraft very close by. I was at a window by one of the beds and, looking out, I saw, almost directly above, a German aircraft, probably a Heinkel, the Swastika large and menacing … the pilot literally staring into my face …'

A deafening explosion rocked the building and she rushed out to see smoke and flames belching along the hallway. Several of the maintenance staff were 'seriously injured, I believe two died, and the airmen doing physical training were also machine gunned … The male orderlies were a source of strength.' Those orderlies evacuated the sick quarter wards, transferring patients from the sixth floor down to the basement:

> The lift only took three people at a time so it wasn't too efficient … The Buchanan Hospital was able to admit some of the many injured. Sqn Ldr Mitchell and myself worked all day … stitching wounds went on well into the night, and extra emergency beds were lined up along the floor.

After this, No 14 ITW moved to less exposed quarters at Harrogate in Yorkshire.

Some nursing sisters came under fire even before they joined the service. In autumn 1940 civilian matron Noelle Horrocks completed a contract in Cyprus and travelled back to England aboard the troopship *Empress of Britain*, intent on joining the PMRAFNS. The western Mediterranean being closed to Allied ships, the liner had to go round the long way, via Suez, down the Red Sea and all round Africa. Finally, on 26 October 1940, she was sailing off Donegal, only hours away from home, when a German plane attacked. Incendiary bombs set the *Empress* hopelessly afire.

When the call went out to abandon ship, Noelle Horrocks was having breakfast in the dining room, five decks below sea level:

> As a staircase had collapsed and all the lights had gone, we only got out … by a miracle. General Legentilhomme (the Fighting French leader), who was also a passenger, happened to come along with a torch when we were being stifled by the smoke and had almost given up hope

On deck, fire and smoke cut them off from the lifeboat stations, 'there was nothing for it but to slide down a rope to the sea below … There had been no time, of course, to return to the cabins … so of course we lost everything we possessed.' Having made it to a lifeboat, they were eventually picked up by a destroyer. 'We felt very chilly and inadequately clad standing on Greenock quay at the end of October … However, we had much to be thankful for.'

One small step for woman …

Nursing sisters enjoyed high respect and privilege simply because of their calling. What better title could they have than the time-honoured 'Sister', or 'Matron'? 'In the early days,' recalls Marianne Galletly (Mrs Hollowell), 'we were just proud of being Nursing Sisters and not expected to salute. We wore our smart "Dicks" when in restaurants, etc.'

Even so, their exact status had become more and more anomalous. Their curious blue and maroon rank markings, allied with their unusual quatrecorne hats, caused speculation in the streets. Because they were not officially commissioned officers, they did not return a salute but acknowledged it with a spoken greeting – 'Good morning', or whatever time of day might be appropriate – this 'really confused the Americans', says Joan White (Mrs Cool). She heard people wondering whether she and her friends were in the Fleet Air Arm or something even more exotic. One particular waitress took her for an 'Aircommodoress'!

This confusion was about to end.

Under Defence (Women's Forces) Regulations published on 25 April 1941, all members of the WAAF and the PMRAFNS – and VADs who worked with them – became legally part of the Armed Forces, subject to King's Regulations. At the same time, officers of the WAAF won the right to hold the King's Commission. Although the Director-General of Medical Services requested that members of the PMRAFNS should receive the same privilege, not until March 1943 did the authorities agree to grant emergency (wartime) commissions to nursing sisters.

However, one concession was made in July 1941: since too many excellent young women were being forced to leave simply because they fell in love and got married, the ban on married members was lifted. The change took some time to be effective – in those days it was still 'not done' for a married woman to go out to work – but eventually more nurses did choose to stay on in the Service after they became 'Mrs'.

Overseas, 1941–2

When the RAF hospital in Palestine closed, in 1940, only Habbaniya and Aden remained as overseas postings for PMs. But they too saw their share of troubles in the early years of the war. Reaching these outposts could be quite an adventure. Lurking U-boats and vigilant German planes made voyages out from Britain slow and hazardous and after Italy's entry into the war the Mediterranean became highly dangerous. Wherever possible, merchantmen and troopships avoided what Mussolini liked to call the 'Italian lake' and, travelling in convoy, went round the long way, via the Cape of Good Hope. A voyage to Cairo, for instance, instead of taking a week or two could go on for months. Joan Botting (Mrs Peake), posted to RAFH Aden in autumn 1941, was at sea for nearly eight weeks.

Together with Senior Sister Alice Lowrey and seven other nursing sisters, Joan Botting had been sent to RAFH Wilmslow to await embarkation. Annual pay in those days was, she recollects:

> £117 a year. We were given £20 … to supplement our indoor uniform by six. White shoes – extra shoes because the tropics rotted them – a white felt hat … plus a white topee and two poplin dress uniforms …. We also had to provide ourselves with two suitcases and a tin trunk.

On a Friday morning they rose at 4.30 a.m. to catch a train for Liverpool, where they had breakfast aboard the ocean liner-turned-troopship *Empress of Australia*. Personnel of officer rank had cabins, but below decks the ship carried 2,500 troops. They were part of one of the largest convoys yet to sail, 3 miles long and guarded by forty naval vessels.

This huge convoy split as it plied south, some of the ships heading off westward towards America, looking, as Joan Botting puts it, 'like elephants on the horizon', while the others continued south, into warmer weather. Within a week the PMs 'went into whites for dinner'. Social life was good, with officers of all three services mingling over quoits and cards and cheap drinks, with plentiful food served by the liner's stewards. A leading aircraftman had volunteered to 'look after our buttons, which were brass, all our uniforms, plus cleaning our shoes … it got him out from below decks!'

They paused for a few days in West Africa, anchoring in the river at Freetown, Sierra Leone. The passengers did not go ashore, but extracts from Joan Botting's diary give a flavour of what ship-board life was like:

> Monday. Up 6.20 a.m. … clouds enveloping mountain tops, with sunlight sparkling on water, flying boats round and taking off, it's good to be alive. Sat on deck and wrote. On deck all morning and slept all afternoon. Chatted with Hancock and the Navy after dinner. Drinks with Young later … Wonderful sunset. Molten gold stretching over the sky, turning to flames. Large and little ships as objects against the horizon. Battleships, food-ships all as a silhouette …

> Thursday – leaving Freetown … Going out into the bay one passes charge ships, passenger, warships and hospital ships, all waiting their turn to venture forth … little peninsulas with odd temple-like buildings and palm trees against a vivid green background, till outside the boom nothing remains but a memory of mountains … with European houses at their feet – heat of about 90 with 80 per cent humidity.

After another week or so they rounded the Cape and turned north, pausing again at Durban where they were able to go ashore and do some shopping. Since some of the ships were heading off east, the PMs, bound for Aden and Iraq, transferred to the smaller mail ship, SS *Llandaff Castle*, which took them up round the horn of Africa, into the Gulf of Aden.

At this time Aden provided a base for troops and aircraft opposing the Italians in Ethiopia and British Somaliland. Minutes of the Advisory Board in 1941 record that 'RAF sisters are employed in the hospitals at Steamer Point and Sheik Othman (500 beds)'. These hospitals served personnel from the colony, from RAF Khormaksar and from Sheik Othman, where more RAF squadrons were based; they also took in patients among South African and Polish troops passing through Aden on their way to the western deserts of North Africa.

At Steamer Point, says Joan Botting, the complement of staff 'was supposed to be nineteen, but if we were fourteen we were very fortunate and usually one or two of those were off sick'. The sisters' mess was very comfortable, two sisters to a room with a bearer to look after them, but … 'no sanitary drainage … the bathrooms were large and in each bathroom there were two commodes. You had your own commode …' Hot water came via buckets carried by the bearer. Ants were a problem, so furniture legs stood in tins of kerosene. But the food was good, with fresh vegetables and salad crops brought by camel train every day from Lehej, about 30 miles away. And with so few women among so many men, social life could not have been better!

Ships came through carrying troops towards Suez to join the fighting in Egypt and Libya, and RAF pilots stopped off to learn how to fly Hurricanes before they too went north to the desert. Joan Botting remembers many funerals:

> they either acted the goat and they got killed, or crashed the plane and got killed, or they got some complaint and died. There was no sanitation, either at the hospital or at the camps … at one stage I had about four typhoids in a ward. Well, in that

> climate, at that stage, they just died … Also you got the ships going up to Suez and anybody sick on board, they loaded them off onto the Air Force hospital. All burials were at six o'clock in the morning because [later] it was so hot.

The RAF hospital at Habbaniya, in Iraq, came under siege in 1941 when pro-Hitler rebels led by Raschid Ali surrounded the vast desert base. Chief surgeon at the time was Lewis Mackenzie Crooks, the 'father of orthopaedics in the RAF'. Heavy shells bombarded the camp for several days and some of the flying school's aircraft were hit, student pilots being among the casualties rushed to the hospital. Despite the fact that the light British planes – Airspeed Oxford trainers and Fairey Gordon bi-planes – were vastly inferior to Iraqi air force fighters, the RAF eventually drove off the attack.

Dope

Back at home, while the Luftwaffe rained daily destruction, less expected hazards lurked for those engaged behind the scenes of Britain's defence. Barrage balloons, for instance, not only erupted in flames on occasion but in high winds their steel guy ropes could whip through the air like swords, or foul high-tension grid wires and become electrically charged. Even when brought to earth and under repair, the huge balloons caused problems.

At RAF Chigwell, in Essex, young WAAFs and airmen worked in vast hangers rigging and doping barrage balloons. The rubber solution used for cementing patches was made up in benzol, whose fumes could cause fainting and dizziness, or even death, especially when working in a confined space. The dopers sometimes had to clamber right inside the balloon to effect repairs. It was hard, physical work. For the nurses who worked at Chigwell SSQ, preserving the good health of these essential personnel was a priority.

Florrie Buck, a corporal nursing orderly in the WAAF, recalls that, 'The girls had to be especially cared for … The paint for doping the fabric had a lead content and the girls had to be given extra milk ration and have a chest examination once a month. I would accompany the MO out to Balloon sites to mete out inoculations, etc.' The camp was somewhat isolated, with buildings set far apart to allow balloons room to manoeuvre. Personnel had to walk long distances from the hangers to their billets and messes. 'Some of them were very young, rather scared. Some of them acquired dogs to make them feel safer.'

Around the hospitals

By 1942 twenty-six full-sized RAF hospitals had opened in Britain, with nine more established overseas. Princess Mary continued to do her bit to raise morale and foster esprit de corps among 'her' nurses by visiting as many of them as she possibly could. In one period of four months she managed to visit seven separate RAF station hospitals. Nor was she alone. Many other members of the Royal Family went along hoping to brighten the spirits of both patients and hospital staff.

A visit by the Duchess of Gloucester to RAFH Henlow, however, caused one patient to feel less than happy. WAAF Sergeant Edith Francis, fresh out of theatre after an appendectomy, proudly displayed by her bed a vase of fresh flowers, a wartime rarity brought some distance, by bus, by her young husband. Since they were the only flowers around, a nurse appropriated them to decorate the hospital foyer for the royal visitor.

Mrs Francis was:

> Feeling very low after the op … and when HRH stopped at my bedside to enquire how I was, I dissolved into floods of tears and sobbed, 'The nurses have taken my flowers.' The lovely RAF Nursing Sister, in her blue-grey cape and white head-dress, came to console me after this embarrassing episode, and from then on she was always so kind, and sat beside me during the night. But I didn't get my flowers back!

Nevertheless, Mrs Francis retains fond memories of the 'super ladies who were in that branch of the Service'.

The Duchess of Gloucester may have thought she was jinxed when, as she left after paying a visit to another RAFH, at Ely, loud and clear from the tannoy came the call for 'Three cheers for the Duchess of Kent!'

Answering the call to 'Dig for Victory', PMs at Cosford decided that the land around their mess huts should be ploughed up and sown with potatoes. Minutes of their mess meeting, dated 6 May 1941, note that this will cost £4 15*s* – £2 for ploughing, the rest for seed potatoes. Called to economise in the use of electricity and water, the sisters decided to restrict themselves to having breakfast toast only once a week; and bath water would be just 4 inches deep, as advised by the government, the level to be marked on the baths.

Amid economies, hard work and grim routine, many lighter moments occurred. Valerie Blackwell (Mrs Cornford) attended a dance at Ely hospital, at which the hats of three group captains went astray, to be found next morning in the lavatories at the sisters' mess. On another occasion, she accompanied the CO on his rounds of the hospital at Locking. While inspecting the toilet facilities he observed, 'No toilet paper in this one.' From the next cubicle came the answer, 'Coming over!', and a flying toilet roll just missed the CO's hat.

From the sick bay at RAF Weston-Super-Mare, Aircraftman P.R. Richards, recuperating from double pneumonia, was transferred to RAF Hospital Locking where the sisters were 'charming, very efficient "no nonsense" young women'. He and the other 'Up-patients' helped out with buffering the polished ward floors, distributing food, even with turning patients to alleviate bed-sores. Up-patients had to wear a uniform of 'hospital blues' with white shirts. They also wore pink-red ties whose shape suggested they might look well done in a bow. One day, playing a joke on their popular day sister, the patients all tied their ties as bows, but:

> … before the Day Sister had time to see us, Matron called a snap inspection of the ward … as she swept in with her entourage of Senior Staff, Up-Patients stood to attention at the foot of their beds, whilst the Bed-Patients tried as well as they could to lie to attention. The Matron inspected us all, gazing with horror at our Bow Ties, said not a word to any of us and swept out. We could hear her haranguing the Sister in her office for over ten minutes. Later our Sister returned very upset and holding back tears … The Matron had threatened to demote her and post her to another hospital.

The patients wrote to matron to explain; every man on the ward signed the letter. Nothing was ever said, but the sister stayed on. However, the chaps did notice that for three weeks the tannoy didn't play the usual popular records, and the orderly who took blood samples (they referred to him as 'Dracula') came four times in a fortnight instead of once a week!

At another Initial Training Wing full of new recruits, RAF Bridgnorth in Shropshire, the station hospital became a posting for Barbara Rampton (Mrs White), who often worked on night duty:

> The Isolation ward was well and truly isolated across a field and had to be visited at least twice a night, which could be a little scary, particularly if the mist was rising from the River Severn and the owls were hooting. The staff there had surreptitiously adopted a cat and used to add him to the Ward report, on a separate form, under the name of A/C Tibbles … Once, when taking the Day Report from matron, prior to going on duty, I was shocked to read a report on A/C Tibbles, but said nothing. On going on my first round of Isolation I was relieved to find that there actually was a patient by the name of Aircraftman Tibbles.

Staff at Bridgnorth loved to play practical jokes on the Duty Medical Officer, whose bed was in a room next to matron's office. One night he climbed into bed only to shoot out again on coming into contact with a wet frog. While the duty room was being redecorated, the Duty MO used a twin-bedded en suite side ward, except on one occasion when no spare beds could be found in the officers' mess for two visiting senior officers. The side ward was allocated to them, the MO being told to sleep in his own room in the mess. Barbara Rampton came on night duty and discovered that 'the day staff had already prepared an "apple pie bed" with Prickly Spinach seeds under the bottom sheets'. The guests arrived before she could change the beds, but she did manage to warn the more junior visitor that he had better use the 'apple pie bed' himself and perhaps remove the offending seeds while his superior used the bathroom:

> Imagine my horror the following morning, when I took them a cup of tea, to find the more Senior officer in the 'apple pie bed'. The pair of them roared with laughter … and said that they'd never had such a trick played on them so innocently before.

> In spite of all my efforts the Junior hadn't done as I had suggested, but left his Senior to get into the bed … and had thoroughly enjoyed seeing what happened – those seeds have really sharp spines.

Those days of almost sixty years ago seem imbued with charming innocence, despite the horrors being perpetrated all around.

At Church Village, in south Wales, the hospital had been taken over by the RAF from Glamorgan County Council while still under construction. The brand new building, two-storeys high and made of bricks rather than wood, was an airy place with big windows overlooking lovely countryside. One of the sisters stationed there was herself a patient, in a side ward on her own, when her friend John Rees paid a visit. 'Within a very short time,' Mr Rees recalls, 'the ward sister stormed in and reprimanded me for visiting a female patient unchaperoned. She reported me to the CO …'

And poor Cliff Hardy, an aircrew trainee with tonsillitis, was whisked into RAFH Bridgnorth delirious with fever. Having led a very sheltered life, he was horrified to find himself 'waking up in the middle of the night absolutely soaking wet and trying to fight off a young woman who was trying to take off my pyjamas'. Worse awaited next morning when two young nurses descended on him to give him a blanket bath, 'the most embarrassing moment ever, for me'. Yet he and many other young lads were being trained to fly into enemy flak.

A Sergeant Pilot Sharp, aged twenty-one, walked into the blade of an idling propeller on his Whitley bomber and suffered a terrible injury to his head. Colleagues helped him to the nearby dispersal hut, from where he was taken to RAFH Rauceby. Fellow patient Hugh Aitken recalls how, at night, Sergeant Pilot Sharp was put into a small isolation ward where he would 'sing and whistle, to help him through his great pain and suffering'. Though swathed in bandages with holes for his nose, mouth and one eye, Sergeant Sharp still managed to plague the nursing sisters, especially one young Irish girl. When she told him to lie straight instead of with his knees up, 'he replied, "Sister, it's not my knees!"', which set the other men roaring with laughter while the sister walked out pink-faced.

Was Sergeant Pilot Sharp tended by surgeon Squadron Leader Fenton Braithwaite? PM Maureen Lumley, then nursing at Rauceby, remembers a patient who had walked into a propeller and received a terrible brain injury. She says that Sqn Ldr Braithwaite 'a marvellous surgeon', patched up the damage 'with a bit of placenta from the maternity ward'.

Air ambulances

Civilian hospitals readily accepted RAF aircrew casualties forced down in their local area, but the injured men were usually transferred as soon as possible to RAF hospitals. Since the most speedy method of achieving this transfer was by air, early in the war the RAF established an air ambulance service.

In 1940, Princess Mary, the Princess Royal, presided at a ceremony to receive the first two specially designed Airspeed Oxford Air Ambulances, a gift presented by 'The Girl Guides of the Empire'. Two years later a squadron of seven air ambulances, of various types, covered the whole of the United Kingdom from their bases at Hendon (north London), Abbotsinch (Northern Ireland) and Wick (Scotland). The aircraft all bore the identifying mark of the Red Cross but, being small, could carry only a few stretchers at a time. To cope with greater numbers, it became the practice to modify normal troop-carrying aircraft so that most of them could convert to air ambulances within ten minutes.

Selected orderlies of the RAF Medical Service undertook a course which taught them how to load and unload aircraft with stretchers and medical necessities, and how to prepare patients for air transportation. It also gave them a chance to familiarise themselves with the effects of air travel.

Pioneering work

As yet, no members of the PMRAFNS flew on casevac missions, but in many other areas their expertise expanded hourly. Health problems created by the war forced the evolution of new techniques to deal with them and departments dedicated to the treatment of burns, shattered limbs and specific diseases developed at most of the RAF hospitals. The larger hospitals became centres for many areas of specialisation.

Halton, for instance, specialised not only in burns and plastic surgery but in cancer therapy and renal medicine. It pioneered the use of radiation as a means of locating foreign bodies in the eye. As more personnel went overseas and contracted exotic diseases, their treatment greatly widened the knowledge of Halton's Institute of Pathology and Tropical Medicine (IPTM). When it became evident that the health of troops in foreign climes depended greatly on the efforts of individual medical officers in the field, the Halton IPTM inaugurated courses in tropical medicine and field hygiene for recently qualified doctors. In turn the doctors passed on their new skills to nursing sisters who later worked with them in the desert or the jungle.

The war produced so many jaw injuries that specialisation became imperative in that field too. At Ely the RAF's first maxillo-facial (jaw injuries) centre opened in summer 1942, employing the first dental officer to be specifically trained for such work.

Nervous disorders – another problem – affected two-thirds of WAAF members who were invalided out of the service; but men suffered almost as badly from these illnesses. In the eastern area alone, six neuropsychiatric centres treated operational personnel, while another eight or nine units opened in other hospitals. Before being posted to these units nursing sisters were, of course, required to hold qualifications in psychiatric work.

Similarly, rehabilitation centres at Halton, Ely, Cosford, St Athan, Wroughton, Weeton, Yatesbury and Torquay employed sisters with orthopaedic qualifications. These essential units might be described as the most up-to-date human repair shops in the world, every amenity designed to restore patients to their operational posts with all speed.

On Halton's orthopaedic wards, WAAF nursing orderly Joyce Hooper came to know the long-term patients very well. She hurt her back while lifting a patient and was put on light duties in the occupational therapy department. She loved it there:

> teaching men with hands like shovels to do embroidery … make belts from macramé twine, and soft toys … One patient even knitted a beautiful layette for the baby his wife was expecting, and some of the long-term patients made beautiful regimental badges with silks.

In the welfare field, sixty-three sisters were appointed, some to large WAAF SSQs and some with a peripatetic role covering smaller outlying units in remote areas. They helped to supervise nursing orderlies and acted as health confidantes to WAAFs. As doctors all agreed, the right type of nursing sister could prove invaluable; the wrong type could do more harm than good! However, after D-Day the welfare scheme was to be abandoned; those well-experienced sisters were needed for more urgent duties.

First use of penicillin

WAAF clerk Biddy Spencer (Mrs Wilson), working as secretary to the ophthalmic surgeons at Halton, enjoyed some varied duties, including conducting colour-vision tests for 300 Polish boys who had endured 'a very arduous trek from the Russian-occupied part of Poland'. She also helped to choose the colour of artificial eyes. But perhaps her most unusual task was 'collecting empty face-cream jars for despatch to Professor Florey (Sir Alexander Fleming's assistant) in Oxford, who returned them filled with precious penicillin, still in its trial stage, for use in the Ophthalmic Ward. Progress reports would be typed weekly and returned to Oxford with the next batch of jars.'

Although Sir Alexander Fleming had discovered penicillin in 1928, its full value only became clear eleven years later, when Australian Sir Howard W. Florey and German Dr Ernst B. Chain, working at Oxford, isolated and purified the active ingredient of the mould. The first precious drops, made available by the Medical Research Council, went to RAF doctors who, only hours later, used it to save the life of a soldier with septicaemia.

Joan White (Mrs Cool) first used penicillin 'in the form of a drip, intramuscularly at three drops a minute. This was a nightmare as the apparatus was very hard to regulate …'

Halton also conducted experiments using penicillin in burns creams, under the supervision of consultant surgeon Archibald McIndoe. Fran Keech (Mrs Judson) worked with this 'great character who would always sit on the bed to talk to his patients. Matron's strict rule did not really allow such frivolity, but he was a law unto himself.' McIndoe's ward at Halton was intensely busy:

> treating aircrew who had suffered horrific injuries. Faces were rebuilt, as were ears and eyes, etc, by the formation of pedicle grafts which needed daily injections of penicillin. Penicillin had only just been discovered and was as precious as gold dust. Two staff were needed to measure out the appropriate drops and double check – not as today, where popping the pill is commonplace.

Their work with penicillin earned Fleming, Florey and Chain the Nobel Prize for Medicine in 1945.

Sunday horror at Torquay

The Officers' Convalescent Hospital now flourished at Babbacombe, just outside Torquay, in the former Palace Hotel, with east and west wings flanking a large central block. By the end of 1939 it had achieved its full capacity of 249 equipped beds. After minor alterations, four bedrooms on the second floor became an operating theatre.

Torquay's staff, numbering almost 200, included RAF doctors and dentists, administration and supporting personnel, and around eighty civilians, most of whom were former hotel employees. Matron W.M. Coulthurst led a nursing team of twenty-one members of the PMRAFNS – four senior sisters, ten junior sisters and some VAD nurses – plus a number of nursing orderlies. Having patients in twos and threes in hotel rooms, rather than grouped in large wards, proved a slight inconvenience but generally the hospital was a happy and lively place.

BBC correspondent Macdonald Hastings, writing in October 1941 in *London Calling*, the Overseas Journal of the BBC, described it as being like a country club, but with incomparable amenities: 'wooded grounds with velvet lawns, tropical trees, luxurious flower beds … golf course, tennis courts, squash courts, swimming pool, archery butts, and gymnasium'. In the mornings the gymnasium and its milk bar, run by officers' wives, provided a popular rendezvous. Other facilities included a cinema where the latest films were shown, a concert hall where patients and staff put on shows, a dance floor, sun lounges, writing rooms, libraries, and a fully licensed bar:

> the essence of these RAF establishments is [to] presume that a man who is old enough to fight for the rest of us is old enough to decide how he will comport himself when he himself is in trouble … a man who has been accustomed to shooting down Messerschmitts before breakfast won't take kindly to being tucked up in bed with a jig-saw.

As director of games, RAFH Torquay had the famous tennis player (later a well-known tennis commentator) Dan Maskell. His athletic presence must have inspired the men to get fit again, and his wife did her bit by acting in shows. Mrs Edith Payne, who met and married theatre assistant Fred 'Blondie' Payne while he was working at the hospital, recalls that Mrs Maskell 'nearly brought the house down with her dress, or should I say lack of it?' while 'taking off' the exotic South American film star Carmen Miranda.

Among the nursing sisters was newly-wed Iris 'Fluffy' Ogilvie, nee Jones. In April 1942 she had married one of her patients, a Squadron Leader flyer of heavy bombers. Thanks to the new regulations permitting married women to remain as PMs, Fluffy Ogilvie stayed at her post when her husband, recovered from his wounds, returned to his squadron.

Patients were encouraged to take as much exercise as was good for them, to enter tournaments and races, to entertain wives and girlfriends if they wished, to go off for a walk if solitude seemed beneficial, or to join an outing to some local beauty spot or theatre. Fluffy Ogilvie and her colleagues would take the convalescents on country rambles and occasionally accompany them:

> in a coach lovingly known as 'the drunks' bus', which had been donated by the Dewar Whisky family. The bus would take us down to the Imperial Hotel. I still remember how some of the guests would, understandably, look away when they saw the badly burnt faces.
>
> I remember, too, the good-looking young pilot whose legs had been badly injured … saying to me, 'When we get to the bar, Fluff, sit me up on a stool … I want to chat up the girls, but watch their faces when I get off the stool!' These young men had such wonderful spirit and courage.

The Torquay area seemed an ideal location for such men to recuperate. It was easily accessible; it had swaying palm trees, lovely views of the sea, a balmy climate, and it was relatively well away from the 'bomb alley' that invisibly linked London with occupied Europe. At least, that was the theory. In reality, as Mrs Payne remembers, 'we used to get the German planes coming over … flying low over the front, gunning along the coast. Other times … if they had not dropped all their bombs on Plymouth they would discharge them over Torquay …'

Disaster struck on the bitterly cold, wet morning of Sunday, 25 October 1942, around 1100 hrs. Most of the patients were in their rooms, shaving, dressing or reading the Sunday papers. Domestic staff tidied up, kitchen hands prepared Sunday lunch, and nurses readied themselves for doctors' rounds. Fred 'Blondie' Payne, gowned and masked, was assisting in the operating theatre. Fluffy Ogilvie was on the first floor, with her friend 'Tinkle' Bell, 'a very young, delightful, pretty Australian VAD … A Medical Officer asked me to accompany him to see four patients in a nearby room. I told the VAD that I would join her as soon as I could.' As Fluffy and the MO went into the patients' room, they 'both saw, through the large windows, German planes, with their Swastikas clearly visible. There was no time to be brave or heroic, we dived under the bed …'

After preliminary machine-gun strafing, the enemy dropped high-explosive 500kg bombs. The first scored a direct hit on the east wing. The second landed in the road, its blast shattering windows, doors and partitions in the west wing and severely damaging the operating theatre. Lamps over the operating table fell on to the unconscious patient and a door flew across the room and knocked out Fred Payne.

The room where Fluffy Ogilvie had taken cover lost its door and windows. Rain and cold air rushed in, but all four patients, plus doctor and nurse had survived. The latter pair dashed out into the hall to find:

> dust and rubble everywhere and, where there had been a further room, just one big gaping hole … The first body we came to was that of 'Tinkle' Bell. I saw her hand and arm sticking out beneath the heavy masonry. I also saw … two bodies which seemed to be hanging from the girder. The bomb had gone through all the floors down to the basement.

Two platoons of the local Home Guard had been carrying out exercises close by. Two of their number died in the attack but the rest came to help, along with local Air Raid Precaution volunteers.

Since the most obvious gathering place – the ballroom – had been badly damaged, the CO ordered that casualties should be taken to the sisters' mess. Through the rubble and dust, shivering against the cold winds that swept through shattered windows and gaping holes in brickwork, men carried laden stretchers to where doctors and nurses made rapid diagnoses, applied dressings and splints, and administered what drugs they could; amid such chaos and destruction they could offer little more than first aid. Fortunately they found ample blankets and hot-water bottles to combat shock, and the kitchens still functioned sufficiently to provide hot drinks, so vital on that bitter day.

Nineteen people died, one was missing, another forty-five suffered injury. Had it not been a Sunday, casualties would have been even worse because many patients would have been in the basement gymnasium and its milk bar, which had been flattened. The Torbay hospital took the more serious cases; others went to RAFHs Wroughton or Melksham, and uninjured patients were sent home wherever possible. Within four days the Officers' Convalescent Hospital was empty.

Fluffy Ogilvie, like many of the nursing staff, spent the night after the bombing with a kindly Torquay family. Next day she accompanied a group of patients on their journey to Wroughton:

> I had the unnerving experience of feeling the closeness of the little VAD 'Tinkle' Bell. Her presence was with me everywhere I went for about three days, then it seemed to leave me suddenly. I have never in my life experienced such a feeling …
>
> What a sadness it was to all of us involved. The Palace Hotel had been such a happy place.

The battered hospital remained in the care of maintenance staff until another air raid three months later, in January 1943, destroyed part of the central block. The building was considered beyond repair. The work of the RAF Officers' Convalescent Hospital moved to Cleveleys Hydro, in Blackpool, Lancashire.

And the war ground on, spreading its evil tendrils across Europe, and beyond.

8

Faraway Places

The Blitz went on. Over occupied Europe, RAF planes flew deadly sorties. Everyone's geography improved as they studied newspaper charts of events taking place in the Balkans, Greece and the deserts of north Africa. Most of the news was bleak. But subtle changes began when Russia changed sides in the summer of 1941. In December, Japan made the mistake of attacking Pearl Harbor, drawing the United States into the war. As the first GIs arrived in England, conflict began to spread across the Far East, drawing in Malaya, Burma, Borneo and others. By the autumn of 1942 total war, by air, sea and land, engaged much of the world. Newsreel commentaries tried to bolster morale, remaining relentlessly optimistic despite terrible loss of life, appalling barbarity and the continuing toll taken by disease.

Some PMs were posted overseas within days of being called up from the reserve. For days, and sometimes weeks, they waited at personnel holding units such as Blackpool, before embarking at Liverpool, or going up to Glasgow by train to sail from Greenock. Most had never been outside England before: some had hardly stirred from their home towns; few knew exactly where they were heading. Their emotions can be imagined: apprehension, excitement, curiosity. Amazingly, most of them remember it as being, overall, 'great fun', a chance to travel and share an adventure which many could never have experienced in normal life.

Iris Jarred (Mrs Bartram), still nursing at RAFH Rauceby, was sent for and asked if she was prepared to go abroad – 'India, they were talking about. I said I didn't think it was fair, with elderly parents, in Norfolk, to go all that way. So, for my sins, I went to Wick – in Scotland!'

Windswept Wick

Units of all three armed services, dotted about the north of Scotland and across the Western Isles, enjoyed a relatively mild climate, thanks to the benevolent lapping of the Gulf Stream. But, however mild it might be, the weather was habitually wet and windy. Sister Jarred found it trying: 'You've never known such wind. You couldn't walk without something in front of your face. It never stopped! In fact, you walked backwards to get your breath.'

The sick quarters at RAF Wick, only a few miles south of John o' Groats, expanded when an operating theatre with X-ray opened in 1943; then in January 1944 a nearby cottage hospital became Wick Station Hospital. It lay about half a mile outside the camp, obliging staff to walk to and fro, often soaked to the skin despite being swathed in oilskins and rubber boots. To add to their troubles, they had no proper drying facilities.

Nursing sisters based at Wick would visit outlying stations and offer treatment and advice, but during Iris Jarred's posting the hospital was never really busy:

> Somebody would come down from Shetland, or Orkney … They'd say, 'No, both my men are quite well.' We had to take civilian people in. One drunkard walked off the end of the jetty … It was supposed to be a 'dry' town, too.
>
> And one of the WAAFs suddenly produced this tummy-ache in the middle of the night, and next morning there was the baby. That rather put the cat amongst the pigeons because the two medics we had hadn't dealt with a baby since training days … I [had done] orthopaedics – 'midder' [midwifery] never appealed to me. We didn't know where to put it. I think we found a linen basket.

The RAF squadrons based at Wick occupied themselves 'chasing the battleships in the Norwegian fjords. We had two or three squadrons, and Catalinas coming in from Reykjavik. Of course,' she adds, 'that was a home posting – no, not Wick – Reykjavik!'

On the edge of the Arctic

In Iceland, even the summer is cold and damp. In winter, for months at a time, a thick coat of snow and ice covers a landscape of low, scrub-covered hills, hot springs and mud ponds.

The bleak, windswept bay outside the island's capital of Reykjavik provided anchorage for merchant ships of many Allied and friendly nations. Every ten days convoys set sail, laden with raw materials such as jute, tin and rubber destined for Russia's manufacturing plants. Others plied the Atlantic, bearing cargoes of refugees and raw materials and bringing home crated aircraft and munitions, and food. Royal Navy ships rode escort, on watch for German U-boats.

In order to offer better aerial cover for the convoys, RAF presence in Iceland grew until it stood at 3,000 personnel. The original army hospital, adapted from part of the university buildings, was taken over by the RAF early in 1942. It had 100 beds but could double its capacity if needed. Staff included several doctors, twelve members of the PMRAFNS, and around twenty male nursing orderlies – their numbers went up as the months passed and workload increased. Patients came not only from the British air force and navy, but from Dominion and Allied services, including a Norwegian float-plane squadron.

If prowling U-boats were a menace, Arctic storms provided another. A particularly violent hurricane, reaching 133mph, swept over Reykjavik in 1942. It sank five American flying boats, smashed many smaller craft, destroyed the RAF station workshops and damaged other buildings. Nursing orderly John Limmer witnessed this storm and reported that 'the Aerodrome Log Book records a Nissen hut proceeding in a northerly direction, height approx 60ft, in spite of being fastened down with a steel cable and earthed up halfway'.

For insulation, the huts were buttressed with earth and their entrances draped with tenting or given make-shift porches to keep out the cold. Long and gloomy nights created huge demand on small electric generators and, with both fittings and light bulbs scarce, paraffin lamps came back into their own. Their light reflected from walls lightened with lime wash to alleviate the gloaming. John Limmer writes, 'in spite of a tortoise stove going night and day our boots were frozen to the floor each morning … This was where I had to identify my hut-mate, killed with eight others in a Liberator crash …'

But PM Noelle Horrocks remembers it rather fondly: 'Nissen huts can be made quite comfortable … [but] once the stoves went out, the huts got cold very quickly, so that when we got up in the morning our sponges and face flannels were frozen and all water in the jugs or tumblers turned to ice.' However, despite years spent near the Equator, she:

> did not feel the cold very much … Some days the air was like a tonic. One would go for a walk on crisp snow that crunched under one's feet [and] come in with glowing cheeks. Of course, we got blizzards and sometimes … one would lie in bed at night and feel that the roof of the hut would blow away any minute [or] one would be greeted by a hut thick with smoke and black smuts … But, on the whole, I loved my year in Iceland.

To combat freezing winds and driving snows, issues of special clothing saw PMs clad in hooded duffle coats or waterproof great-coats, clumping about in rubber knee boots, their hands kept warm by lambs-wool gloves covered in waterproof material. But, off duty, they had cinema shows, mountain climbing, whist drives, concerts, bus trips, sports, hobbies' workshops and a library. Hot springs provided a venue for bathing parties all year round, and winter added the delights of skating and skiing.

A party of twelve PMs set out for Reykjavik in March 1943. They included Mary Allen and her friend Barbara Burgess, both Red Cross nurses of the VAD, attached to the PMRAFNS. Since only four VADs had been selected, Mary and her friend:

> thought it marvellous to be two of the four … We could not believe our luck as we travelled by sleeper from Euston to Greenock … Four new PM Sisters accompanied us, plus a few hundred RAF personnel. The voyage to Iceland took about three days. Corvettes accompanied the ship for the first part of the journey … [It] was rough, with mountainous seas and stiff winds. We approached our destination thankfully.

Nursing sisters' accommodation consisted of eight Nissen huts, connected with the hospital via a corridor whose walls:

> were forever papered by a thin sheet of ice. Our sleeping huts (we four VAD nurses shared one) were heated by Tortoise stoves, the living rooms by large fires, and a team of leading aircraftmen came in handy for domestic duties … The huts contained a very comfortable bed each, a chair, rug and wooden box, contraptions for bedside locker and hanging space, and of course a mirror. With the purchase of some printed cretonne, we added curtains to our packing-case furniture.

Apart from sleeping quarters, the eight Nissen huts each had a sitting room and dining room, but no plumbed-in ablution facilities. The twelve PMs had to share a single lavatory, wash-place and bathroom:

> We did have an alcove for washing effects, but as most items in our quarters became frozen, we generally used the bathroom at the entry to the hospital, which had been designated for our use. Oh, lovely hot water to wash, to bathe, to launder – it was precious to the extreme. It was quite usual when I was taking a bath to hear a gentle tap on the door and a 'Let me in, Allen, please, I've got a little washing to do.'

When two of the VAD nurses were replaced by PM sisters, Mary Allen and Barbara Burgess became the only VADs at Reykjavik:

> The patients were principally RAF personnel and sick and injured from passing ships. At one time, apart from British Navy personnel, we had a Norwegian, a Russian woman, a Lascar seaman, and even a Chinese. Once we received three Icelandic fishermen – having wrecked themselves on one of the small islands in the harbour, they were suffering from severe frostbite …
>
> Long days of light and long days of dark were all new and strange to us. I shall never forget the joy of being on duty to see the sun rise, perhaps about 10.30 a.m., in a blaze of glorious colour, with Sunderland flying boats taking off on patrol, soaring overhead like giant white birds.
>
> Duties were inflexible – we were off-duty for half a day every third day, with a whole day off once a month. But the most important day of the month was 'Boat Day' … New personnel arrived and equal numbers left for home and leave, and of course the sick went home. Then, apart from the necessities of life, the mail too arrived. The day was a continual buzz of excitement before, once again, we were left in isolation and our own little world …
>
> As the Sisters' Mess was the one female unit in Reykjavik, you can imagine we were at a premium … for dances at the Officers' Club, for films, and of course for the more formal parties … One really memorable moment was at our Christmas party, I believe on Boxing Day … The Admiral of the Island was Matron's guest and we each had our invited guest. It was puzzling to us that they all seemed to be arriving late, but however at last we were all happy and ready to enjoy ourselves. An LAC

> came into the dining room and asked if a marine might be allowed to enter with a message for the Admiral. Surely nothing could happen to take him away? But with a big smile he rose, saying, 'I think we should all drink a toast to the Royal Navy. The *Scharnhorst* has just been sunk and you are hearing this news three minutes before BBC London.' This explained our guests' late arrival as the air force base was on the alert to go to the aid of the Royal Navy if their manoeuvres had not succeeded.

The *Scharnhorst*, Germany's only remaining battle cruiser, was sunk by HMS *Duke of York* on 26 December 1943.

RAFH Reykjavik continued to function until 1945, when it was reduced to the status of a sick quarters. Three PMs remained on its strength for the few months before the need for the RAF's presence in Iceland ended.

Warmer climes

While some nursing sisters worked amid ice and snow, others headed for the equator. During 1942, two more RAF hospitals opened overseas, the first being at Takoradi on the Gold Coast (now Ghana).

With the enemy dominating southern Europe and fortunes fluctuating in the western desert, Mediterranean supply routes remained hazardous. West Africa had, therefore, become a vital link in the transport chain. Essential supplies bound by sea for the Middle East – including new aircraft, sectioned and crated – by-passed the Straits of Gibraltar and went south, to a spot tucked away under the western bulge of Africa. There, at RAF Takoradi, technicians assembled and tested the new planes before ferry pilots flew them east via staging posts across Africa to the Sudan, and then north to join the squadrons engaged in Libya and Egypt. Transport planes took stores and equipment along the same 4,000-mile supply route via Khartoum, while other RAF squadrons, based in the Gambia, Sierra Leone and Nigeria, flew ocean-reconnaissance missions in support of Atlantic convoys. As numbers of personnel in British West Africa increased, a full-scale RAF hospital opened at Takoradi early in 1942.

The town has a good artificial harbour backed by fertile heath and bush, but the hot and humid climate can be uncomfortable for Europeans, with a wet season lasting for more than half the year. Frequent squalls and rain-storms lash the coast and low cloud obscures the jungle-clad hills inland – perfect conditions for the mosquitoes and other flies that carry malaria, dysentery and yellow fever. In Takoradi endemic disease was the worst enemy: 80 per cent of personnel went down with malaria, decimating whole sections whose efficiency might mean the difference between operational success and disaster. Preventive measures included the use of the drug mepacrine, which turned one's skin yellow and caused unpleasant side effects such as colic and nausea, but was highly effective in combating the disease itself.

Tropical sunlight added to difficulties. Godfrey Jones, a civilian-trained member of the VAD, tells how the hospital overlooked the beach – handy for cooling off when off duty, but 'one chap who had just come out from UK went to sleep on the beach and at 6 p.m. at night was on the operating table for treatment of burns'.

The main two-storey part of the hospital had wide mosquito-proof verandas on both floors. Matron Miss Meikle led a nursing team of fourteen PMs, with appropriate numbers of male orderlies in support. Each nursing sister had her own bedroom and sitting room, a welcome haven from the busy hospital wards. With such a vast area to cover, and with members of all three services as patients, by 1943 the hospital bed-state had increased to over 300. Because of the health risks, nursing sisters stayed for a maximum of eighteen months, and they too had to take mepacrine. Malaria was no respecter of persons.

The Azores

Out in the Atlantic, the steep, fertile, Portuguese-owned islands of the Azores provided a staging post for Allied forces from September 1943. The first tented SSQ and a later larger medical centre at Lagens, on Terceira Island, were both badly damaged by hurricanes in December 1943 and October 1944. In between, staff coped with an outbreak of poliomyelitis. Urgent rebuilding saw a more substantial RAF hospital, of 150 beds, functional by November 1944. Seven PMs, under Matron Gwen Butler, the first British women posted to the Azores, arrived aboard an armed merchant ship, part of a convoy, in January 1945.

Sister Dilys Palmer (Mrs Bore) remembers a good social life, with lots of picnics. A serious outbreak of typhoid added to the workload, but mostly nurses dealt with common illnesses. With sport providing a popular pastime, some patients came in with leisure-induced problems, and gossip suggested that many a fearless rugger tackle was prompted by a desire to 'indulge in the comforts of the hospital and receive the sympathetic attentions of our sisters.'

RAF Hospital Lagens was handed over to Portuguese authorities in October 1946.

Egypt

Before the war, the few RAF personnel stationed in Egypt had been treated by army hospitals. As war loomed, tented sick quarters opened at Heliopolis (Cairo) and at Alexandria, and from 1939 RAF medical facilities in Egypt expanded, adjusting to serve the needs of the hour as war swept across north Africa. Cairo provided military headquarters for British forces fighting what troops ironically dubbed the 'Benghazi Handicap' – the tug of war in which Wavell and Rommel alternately led advance and retreat in the deserts to the west. The history of those years still resonates with the names Tobruk and El Alamein.

No 5 RAFGH, variously referred to as 'Cairo', 'Heliopolis' or 'Abbassia', opened in March 1942 in a new maternity hospital and welfare centre, an elegant white building resembling a big hotel. It was still in the final stages of construction when the RAF took it over, but before long new fences went up and grass-seed sprouted, spreading a cool green sward between the hospital and the main Cairo–Heliopolis road. Shortage of living accommodation obliged the matron and thirty-four sisters, most of them coming straight from the UK, into quarters half a mile from the hospital.

Hardly had they caught their breath than the first patients arrived and in the ensuing days the flow of casualties and sickness kept them well occupied. For a time, as the tide of war surged and fell, they lived in constant readiness to evacuate, but by the summer the Allies had begun to drive the enemy back. Step by step, the desert campaign gained ground. In its wake, dotted along the southern shores of the Mediterranean, temporary front-line RAF hospitals opened. No 5 RAFGH Cairo settled down to its primary task of acting as a base hospital for flying personnel from all the Allied forces.

Ranking officers – on paper, anyway

After three and a half years of war service, PMs finally received a measure of official recognition. From March 1943, they wore regulation rank insignia and enjoyed what the Air Ministry Order called 'the compliments and respect due to an officer of equivalent rank in the WAAF'. Since the title 'staff nurse' had been abolished in 1941, equivalents were:

PMRAFNS	***WAAF***
matron-in-chief	air commandant
chief principal matron (a post established in 1944)	group officer
principal matron (of an RAF general hospital)	wing officer
matron (of an RAF station hospital)	squadron officer
senior sister	flight officer
sister	flying officer

However, appropriate braid on sleeve or shoulder was the only outward sign of this change; in all other ways, PMs were still known by their time-honoured professional titles. Rona Black (Mrs McAlpine) writes:

> I was very proud of my stripes. At that time I was Sister Black, Lady of the Air Force – as such I had licence to resign from the service if I wished – but suddenly we became Commissioned Officers subject to King's Regulations … We soon discovered the reason for the change – a fairly large draft of nursing sisters was required to staff Middle Eastern and African hospitals …

Defying the U-boats

As the war spread, more and more RAF squadrons flew out of more and more overseas airfields. Each squadron required many supporting staff, both RAF and WAAF, and the only means of transporting them was the sea. As a result, many of the larger ocean liners were called on to act as troopships. First to come under sole RAF control was the *Queen Elizabeth*. From May 1943 her crew included two PMs whose work the Nursing Service Advisory Board commended as outstanding. So successful was this initial venture that the RAF were given responsibility for two additional ships, *Mauretania* and *Nieu Amsterdam*, with more nursing sisters on their medical teams. Later the *Pasteur* and the *Andes* also came under RAF control.

As more and more WAAF sailed for duty overseas, separate parts of the troopships' hospital accommodation were allocated to their needs, with WAAF nursing assistants to help the PMs. The authorities, somewhat chauvinistically, expected girlish moans and whinges about cramped conditions and lack of privacy, but the women proved just as tough, resilient and good-humoured as the men when faced with adversity and discomfort – not to mention danger, with U-boats hunting below and German planes circling above.

The Cunard White Star cruise liner *Mauretania*, even when stripped of its most luxurious furniture and fittings, offered a desirable posting. She plied the Atlantic from Liverpool to New York and to Halifax, Nova Scotia, carrying thousands of troops to Europe and bringing British families of American and Canadian servicemen home to their new countries. She was staffed by half RAF and half US Army officers, with a complement of medical orderlies of the RAF Medical Service. The two nursing sisters, Beryl Chadney and Lucy Woodward, covered most eventualities, one being a children's nurse and theatre sister, the other a midwife – 'although a number of the wives were pregnant we managed to get them all on dry land to have their babies!', Beryl Chadney reports with relief.

Each time they left Liverpool, and on their return, destroyers escorted them for two days – the Atlantic crossing took six or seven days each way. The PMs attended occasional dances 'in the beautiful ballroom, when all female personnel were pressed into service for what could only be called "excuse me" dances, since we were totally outnumbered'.

Lucy Woodward had charge of a ward for women and children, with an RAF medical officer, while Beryl Chadney had the men's ward, with American army doctors. Daily clinics and sick parades confronted them with the inevitable sea-sickness and infectious diseases of childhood, and of course there were endless boat drills. At night the two PMs took turns to be on call and, since a night seldom passed without some small emergency arising, they were usually desperately tired by the time they reached port.

On arrival in New York, medical staff disembarked a day later than passengers and came aboard again a day in advance. Since the ship 'turned around' in about five days, this gave them three days' shore leave, staying at the Governor Clinton Hotel and visiting nightspots such as Roger's Corner, opposite Madison Square Gardens in down-town Manhattan. Or they went shopping, armed with long lists of goods unobtainable at home – 'mainly cosmetics and nylons, though I remember having to buy a pair of wellington boots on one occasion', Beryl recalls.

The story of the great liners' involvement could not be told until after the war ended. In September 1945 the *Evening Standard* revealed how the security blackout had been even more important for *Mauretania* than for:

> the famous '*Queens*'. Their greatest protection throughout the war was speed. The *Mauretania* was … eight knots slower … I have seen a list of her war-time ports of call. Hardly an important name is missing, yet the ship moved like a phantom over the oceans, rumour and report never catching up with her …

Light on the horizon

The war dragged on into a fourth year, but events encouraged the Allies to hope for eventual victory. Russia slowly turned back the German incursions on her frontiers; in the Pacific the USA won victories over Japan; and in the Middle East the Desert Rats and their comrades, under Lieutenant-General Bernard Montgomery, had Rommel, the 'Desert Fox', on the run. This was the moment for which the medical branch of the RAF had long been preparing.

As the Allied advance pushed further and further, driving the enemy westward from Cairo, through Libya and eventually out of north Africa altogether, right behind them moved small medical units called mobile receiving stations. These in turn moved on, to care for the immediate needs of the wounded, leaving behind a succession of temporary RAF general hospitals. At the first of these, at Benghazi, PM sisters found the old civil hospital badly damaged by bombs and shells, but they soon had it fit to receive the Allied casualties which poured in. The second RAFGH opened at Tripoli, the third on the site of ancient Carthage (modern Tunis). Rumour has it that, when the hospital in Tunisia opened, a signal came from Air Ministry asking, 'Carthage? Where's that?'

Sisters sailing out to join the three new hospitals, and other units that opened in the Mediterranean area, faced a variety of weather and terrain, from north Africa with its 110°F heat, dust and sandstorms – not to mention plagues of flies – to torrential rains turning battle-scarred land to mud, and deep winter snows in the Italian mountains. In impossible conditions they cared for the sick and wounded of both sides, battling endemic disease such as malaria, typhoid, infective hepatitis, dysentery and, not least, all the varied types of venereal infection. As one of those doughty ladies remarks, 'You didn't worry about that until afterwards. You had a job to do so you rolled up your sleeves and got on with it.'

Mobile hospitals

Mobile receiving stations (MRSs) were conceived at the start of the war, to be a primary link in the chain that sped sick and wounded men directly from the fighting front to the safety of base hospitals. Originally only male nurses worked with these units, but in March 1943 they were joined by PMs, wearing their new honorary rank insignia. From that date, too, to avoid the ambiguity of the initials MRS, the units became known as mobile field hospitals (MFHs).

As their name implies, these tented medical units were designed to move from place to place at short notice, either by air or by road, their equipment loaded onto a transport plane or a convoy of trucks. Where possible they set up close to a forward airfield; otherwise they chose a site convenient for evacuation of casualties by sea, rail or river. As wounded men came in, straight from battle, the MFH offered treatment to stabilise their condition ready for the journey back to the nearest base hospital. The units were designed to cater for up to fifty patients at a time, though on occasion – after D-Day, for instance, as we shall see – they coped with very many more. Nor were the patients all Allied troops; many sick and wounded prisoners of war also owed their lives to the front-line field hospitals.

Staff of an MFH included medical officers and surgeons, dental officers, medical orderlies and medical assistants, plus non-medical support from numerous drivers, cooks, clerks, carpenters and electricians. These men were skilled in the swift packing and unpacking of their unit. Indeed, at a post-war demonstration at Farnborough, a tented 100-bed hospital – 9 tons of it – was flown in aboard a Beverley aircraft; it became functional, a mile away from the airfield, just twenty-five minutes later.

In some locations, once the MFH had established itself under canvas, its staff commandeered local buildings to increase bed spaces and offer more security. Then, with more medical staff posted in, the unit, however make-shift and temporary, might be designated an RAF general hospital. The original MFH might stay, or move on, or split into two separate teams. Even an RAFGH could relocate if necessary. The field hospitals were fluid in both form and function, their work of vital importance, both to the men and women actually engaged in the war and to local civilians who needed medical aid.

Twenty-six MFHs formed during the war years, the earliest in August 1939. They served in all theatres of war and lasted variously from a few months to several years. The last of them disbanded in October 1946. Not all of these units had PMs with them: the choice depended on the senior medical officer (SMO) involved. Some SMOs preferred to lead an all-male unit, especially under more adverse conditions in the desert or the jungle; others, appreciating the benefits of a female presence, found nursing sisters invaluable. When requested, at least two sisters would be attached to each MFH. Some went to North Africa, from where some of them followed the troops into Italy, arriving by landing craft, under enemy fire, at places like Salerno. Others sailed for India and Burma. Meanwhile, back in England, four PMs stood by as part of two mobile field hospitals whose destination was, as yet, unknown – back in 1943, D-Day was only a gleam in Churchill's eye.

The adventures of Number 30 MFH

The variety of life with an MFH is demonstrated by the story of two particular PMs, Senior Sister Jessie W. Atkinson and Sister Helen Jones. They were with

30 MFH from the day it formed, in March 1943 at RAF West Kirby, Lancashire, until it disbanded in Italy in June 1945. The unit comprised eighty-one personnel, with four medical officers, a medical quartermaster, the two nursing sisters, a warrant officer nursing orderly, twenty-seven medics of NCO and airman rank, and supporting staff. They sailed from the Clyde and landed twelve days later, on 23 April, at Algiers, where they had to wait a couple of weeks for their equipment to be delivered. In the interim the sisters helped out at RAF Blida sick quarters while the men found duties elsewhere. When their medical equipment eventually arrived, they formed into convoy and drove east to Tunis, just as the enemy were withdrawing back through Sicily and into Italy. Thousands of Italians and Germans remained behind as prisoners of war.

No 30 MFH opened for business on the seashore at a place named Hammamet. A few weeks later medical reinforcements arrived and took over a school and a convent in Carthage. There, PMs Atkinson and Jones were joined by their colleagues Naughton and Ashworth. Clad in khaki shirts without ties, divided skirts made of khaki drill, khaki stockings and black shoes, worn with wide-brimmed white felt hats sporting a 'flash' of ribbon in RAF colours, they helped to establish a busy base hospital, officially No 1 RAFGH, Carthage.

Contemporary reports from the *MTE Journal* (a wartime magazine produced by the RAF Medical Service) confirm the success of the scheme to evacuate casualties by air via MFHs in the desert:

> The huge transport aircraft … have been carrying as many as thirteen or fourteen stretcher cases in addition to sitting cases which, on treatment at base hospitals, have had a surprising recovery rate.
>
> A British pilot flying over Sollum was attacked and severely wounded in the shoulder and thigh, crash-landing his aircraft. Within four hours he was two hundred miles away receiving the blood transfusion which put him on the road to recovery … Another pilot … was severely burned. In grave danger of dying from shock, he was given intravenous plasma, and in a few hours was speeding by air to base, where a blood transfusion saved his life …
>
> A mechanic was blown up by an exploding petrol tank and tore his side severely. Weak from loss of blood, he was brought into the desert SSQ, straight onto the operating table where his pulse was thought to have stopped. The RAF surgeon worked on him and … after two hours his radial pulse returned to such a degree that he was considered fit to survive a fifteen-mile journey to hospital.

As the Allies launched their offensive across the hundred miles or so of Mediterranean which separated them from Sicily, 30 MFH gathered its personnel together again. Sisters Atkinson and Jones left the relative safety of the Carthage hospital, staff loaded the equipment and, side by side with the fighting troops, sailed for Sicily in landing ships tanks. They came ashore at Lacati and drove in convoy to Lentini, south of the volcano Mount Etna, setting up camp not far from the airfield.

Leslie Moore, NCO in charge of 30 MFH's orderly room, writes:

> On the 11th August, it had been a very wet day but the night was as clear as daylight with a full moon. The RAF aircraft were unable to take off in the mud … The Germans came over in force and dive-bombed the airfield. They also dived on the hospital, but did not drop any bombs. We felt certain that they saw the Red Cross on the ground in the centre of the camp …

German forces pulled out of Sicily the next day and the Allies pursued them into Italy. No 30 MFH followed: 'The beach was still under fire and we drove about a mile inland and set up the hospital in a field, with our two Sisters supervising.' Italy had surrendered but German troops in the country fought on.

Having worked their way across Italy, 30 MFH settled in for the winter in Foggia, just south of the spur on Italy's heel. Here they tended the wounded who came back from the front and airlifted them back to the hospitals in North Africa, or to the new RAFGH which established itself near Naples that December. The next June, as D-Day dawned and the Allied assault on Normandy began, 30 MFH moved on again. Behind it, No 4 RAFGH, sited in an old folks' home with more PMs on its staff, took over medical care in that area.

Through the summer of 1944, 30 MFH travelled in stages up central Italy to Siena, then across to the east coast to spend the winter in a school at Termoli. Extra nursing sisters were sent to help the team at various times during the winter. Then, with the Balkans more involved in the war, Leslie Moore remembers that 'In April 1945 we crossed to Zara in Yugoslavia, where we provided medical cover for the RAF ground crews who maintained the aircraft flown by Tito's pilots … We celebrated VE Day in Yugoslavia but were evacuated back to Termoli in a few days.' And from there they headed back to Naples where the MFH disbanded: 'we packed all our equipment for despatch to the Far East and Senior Sister Atkinson and Sister Jones left us for a Base Hospital.'

In the twenty-six months which had passed since their arrival in Algeria, they had witnessed the liberation of North Africa, Sicily and the rest of Italy; they had travelled, in convoy, 3,571 lurching, rolling, back-breaking miles; and they had lost count of how many times they had packed and unpacked those life-saving tents.

The war produced twenty-six MFHs, but they were not numbered 1–26. The smaller numbers, 1–11, were used for temporary RAFGHs which set up shop in disused schools, convents, etc. Of the others, Nos 21, 24, 30 and 31 went to North Africa and then into Italy; No 50 followed the troops into Normandy; No 52 went to Holland; Nos 60, 61, 62 and 63 sailed for India; Nos 65 and 67 went to Burma; No 80 was in Hong Kong and No 81 in Singapore. The remaining one, number unknown, was operational in Ceylon.

Mediterranean memories

Many PMs were caught up in the unfolding drama, thirty-two at the Benghazi hospital, another forty or so at Carthage, thirty-five at Naples and more at Algiers. From England forty-six of these had sailed aboard the Orontes, in a huge ninety-six-ship convoy which departed in August 1943. They left Liverpool, bound first for the Clyde, on Friday the 13th, and, when Elizabeth Mansell (Mrs Ogden) discovered that she and another sister had been given a berth in Cabin 13, 'we tried to change it, but nobody would change – it was, however, the Bridal Suite!'

Personnel and stores crammed the convoy to capacity, bound for destinations in the Mediterranean, Africa and the Middle East, Iraq, Aden, India and Ceylon. As so often happened during the war, personnel on board had little idea of where they were heading. *Orontes* alone carried almost 4,000 troops, plus 22 tons of petrol for Algiers and Malta. Enemy U-boats menaced the ships and depth-charges boomed from time to time.

Off Gibraltar, the convoy split into two: *Orontes* and others sailed into the Mediterranean, arriving as the Allies were invading Sicily. In the harbour at Algiers, Elizabeth Mansell saw 'two big battleships, the *Howe* and *George V*, waiting to go into the Sicily attack'. Because of the risk of bombers attacking the two battleships, *Orontes* remained outside the harbour all night, to dock next morning to the sound of 'God Save the King'. The PMs took over a boys' school which had recently been occupied by Headquarters, North-West African Air Force. The burns treatment centre was located in the former linen store of the school, into which locally made concrete baths were installed. The place was designated No 2 RAFGH but, Sister Mansell says, 'it was filthy, filthy. Flies, flying into your mouth … we had to do away with the flies … We got some special stuff from the Americans.'

Elizabeth Smallwood (Mrs Andrews) had once danced with legless air ace Douglas Bader to celebrate when his new improved 'tin pins' arrived. Now she found herself where:

> conditions were very bad, flies galore and a shortage of water. We lived on Spam [tinned, processed meat] for one year – breakfast, dinner, tea and supper! We had a canvas bucket half-filled each day by the Water Bowser, in which we washed, and then had to wash our 'smalls' in the same water. We were allowed a small flask of drinking water … one gulp, but it had to last all day.

Later, posted to Tunis, she:

> ended up in the ruins of Carthage, in an old and very dirty monastery, which we had to scrub and clean ready for the wounded … We sisters were put in a Nissen hut, with temperatures of 100 degrees and it was very difficult to sleep. The sea was near so several of us used to go down behind a large rock and bathe, and also wash our hair. My family sent out some salt-water soap.

With few women around, the PMs were in social demand, often dated by Americans. They even attended a party given by General Eisenhower. In January 1943, when 'Ike' and the other Chiefs of Staff met with the British Prime Minister and the American President in Casablanca, Elizabeth Smallwood encountered General de Gaulle, Air Marshal Sir Arthur Tedder and Field Marshal Montgomery. She actually nursed Winston Churchill, who:

> became ill with pneumonia. [We] treated him with one of the first antibiotics – M&B 693 … I was in charge of the hospital on night duty when an Army Sergeant came to my office and asked for a bedpan. I asked who it was for and he replied that it was top secret and he could not tell me.

She persisted and, discovering that the needy patient was Churchill himself, she 'picked out the best of [her] rather battered collection'. Next day she learned that the 'great man' had taken one look at the item and growled, 'Take that damned thing away!'

As the invasion of Italy gathered pace, No 1 RAFGH Carthage handed over to No 31 MFH and packed up to follow the troops, just two days after Christmas 1943. A full complement of PMs went with it. Jean Ponsford (Mrs Howell) remembers being seen off at the airport by Lord Tedder, who had just bidden farewell to Winston Churchill, off to convalesce in Marrakesh. 'We landed at Capo de Chino airport in Naples and were then taken to our mess in the village of Torre-del-Greco. It consisted of two villas, the main one had been four flats, and the other was situated in its own grounds, totally different from N Africa …'

The hospital's advance party had taken over a convalescent home on the lower slopes of a mountain, with 3 acres of grounds in which stood several villas now employed as both extra wards and accommodation for staff. It was not at all a bad posting, with plenty going on – after the army repaired the bridge above, the road was busy with convoys going up towards Cassino. But the PMs did face a few difficulties. To begin with, a typhus epidemic raged through Naples that winter, so the city was put out of bounds to off-duty personnel.

And then there was the volcano!

Torre del Greco stands on the lower slopes of Vesuvius; the town had been laid waste when the volcano erupted in 1800. Even as the PMs arrived, the mountain was rumbling again. It grew ever more active as the weeks passed. At one o'clock in the morning of 22 March 1944, when the hospital was busy with over 300 bed-ridden patients, Vesuvius blew its top. Those whose rooms looked out on the mountain witnessed a spectacular display of boiling smoke, sparks, flying red-hot boulders and rivers of molten lava glowing in the darkness. Fortunately the wind blew most of the cinders and ash in the opposite direction, but a blanket of hot ash descended on the roof of the hospital, making evacuation a necessary precaution.

Mary Drew (Mrs Mitchell) was on night duty that night:

> The battle for Cassino was on when the volcano erupted, and after a difficult night with windows falling and a minor earthquake, it was decided at 6 a.m. that we should evacuate … I instructed my 100 patients to fill one of their pillowcases with their belongings and stay by their beds … (They were all taken to Army hospitals, so the War Department owes the RAF 100 pillowcases!) Matron and all sisters [went] to a transit camp in Naples … Everything was covered in thick dust, and the village of San Sebastiano was destroyed. The lava flow finished at the wall of a house and the ground was very hot for weeks afterwards.

In the windward direction, ash and cinders blocked the roads for 25 miles.

While working at Torre del Greco, Sister Elizabeth Mansell received permission to marry her fiancé, Pilot Officer 'Mickey' Ogden, based in North Africa. They arranged to be married in the British church at Algiers, then Elizabeth returned to Naples, where:

> the Catering Officer made a great big wedding cake. It was in a big wooden box with 'British Red Cross, Wedding Cake' and I had to take it to the airport – the Americans were in charge at that time. They said they 'couldn't put it down the chute, Ma'am!' I had to get four of the crew to carry it on to the aeroplane … The wedding day was held in the mess … twenty-five bottles of champagne at 2*s* 6*d* [12.5p] a bottle, which Mickey got direct from the factory! The food was only like you would have at a coffee morning.

Later she returned to No 1 RAFGH in Italy and 'Mickey used to fly over in a Beaufighter, circling Vesuvius'.

Romance flourished, despite the war.

9

A New Theatre of Care

Just one day after the bombing of Pearl Harbor, on 7 December 1941, Japanese troops invaded Malaya. Within weeks they seemed to have a foothold on every island and peninsula in the area. The early months of 1942 saw the fall of Singapore, the Allied defeat in the Java Sea, then the loss of Rangoon and the long bitter trek back via Mandalay as British, Indian and Chinese troops withdrew behind the Chindwin river into India.

The Japanese were in trouble, too. With supply lines stretched to breaking, they halted to regroup. For eighteen months the Chindwin formed an uneasy boundary between British and Japanese forces. General Slim, commander of the Burma Corps, used the time to prepare a base, at Imphal, from which to mount his counter-attack, while the US fleet kept the Japanese occupied in the Pacific.

Successes in North Africa enabled Britain to direct more of its naval and air forces to the Far East. By June 1943 over fifty RAF squadrons were based in India, with modern aircraft replacing old, antiquated machines and more coming in all the time. At last they were in a position to counter the challenge along the border between India and Burma. This 1,000-mile frontier (which now defines the border between Bangladesh and Assam) runs through impenetrable jungle, among steep mountains traversed by narrow passes, across mosquito-ridden plains and paddy-fields. Roads, where they exist, tend to be swept away or turned into thick mud by the monsoon season which lasts from June to November every year.

This difficult and dangerous country was to be the next theatre of care for the PMs, not that any of them knew it as they waited for the call to embark.

In July 1943, Rona Black (Mrs McAlpine) was at RAFH Innsworth, Gloucestershire, on standby to go overseas. Writing to her mother, she felt able to hint at a possible end to the waiting:

> I may get some leave suddenly … as soon as I know I will let you know - but let there be no panic! It's a great life! … Have been to the hairdresser and have a glamorous style – bags of curls, frightfully natty! I'm sure you will understand this letter but keep your hopes and fears under your hat. Life is uncertain at the moment. We have been warned.

Later that month, she joined 62 Mobile Field Hospital, under canvas at Chislehurst in Kent.

Jessie Higgins, by now promoted to senior sister, had also been told to be ready for overseas duty by June. She ruefully remembers that:

> The list of requirements for the posting included tropical kit and, of all things, mosquito boots! No one had heard of these … I spent two whole days of my embarkation leave searching all boot and shoe shops in London. Eventually, at a great cost of £5 I discovered a pair! Made of thick white canvas and reaching right up and over the thighs, they were the most awful uncomfortable things imaginable and, needless to say, eventually were useless.

Along with Sister 'Tommy' Thomas (Mrs McGregor), Jessie Higgins went to join the staff of 61 MFH, who gathered to begin experiencing life under canvas in a remote area of Essex:

> Getting used to this kind of life was not easy, especially trying to bath in a large canvas bowl … We still had no idea where we were going. Rumours ran riot, but we never considered the Far East and knew nothing then of the 14th Army in Burma.

The Med reopens

With the Allies in command of the Mediterranean, the Suez route to the Far East again became safe for trooping and cargo vessels. The first convoy through, in August 1943, carried with it four mobile field hospitals (Nos 60, 61, 62 and 63), each with two PMs on its staff – the first RAF nursing sisters to go to India.

The call came suddenly. One evening the CO of 61 MFH informed his staff that they were to dismantle their unit, pack up and be ready to leave by midnight. 'Panic stations!' is how Jessie Higgins recalls it. They boarded a train and next morning found themselves at Liverpool. The ship was full, five of the PMs sharing a one-berth cabin, but Jessie Higgins thought this 'terribly lucky, as we had a shower and loo of our own!' The former cruise liner had been stripped of all comforts:

> no chairs anywhere so we had to use our life-jackets as cushions … We sailed that night not knowing to where. Seasickness was bad … The sea seemed to be so huge and rough. We were in a very large convoy escorted by destroyers … quite exciting as depth charges were frequently dropped into the ocean, hopefully to keep away the German submarines.

For Rona Black, it seemed:

> A pioneer expedition! I'd always wanted to be a pioneer so this was just up my street! … Setting out from England we zigzagged across the Bay of Biscay. (The

> second convoy was not so lucky.) I was so seasick all I wanted for my birthday on the eighteenth of August was a torpedo amidships.

The eight PMs – along with a few other servicewomen, including army nursing sisters and VADs – formed a small female contingent among thousands of men. One of those men was Fred 'Blondie' Payne, whom we last met during the bombing of Torquay; as with Rona Black and her friend Jay Gardner, he was attached to 62 MFH.

Rona's letters reveal that she had

> thought of writing a little every day, but the writing of diaries is not permitted as it would give away valuable information … I feel rather like Granma sitting on the leeside with great-coat on and a net over my hair – my knitting is the only thing I haven't got, and that's in my cabin.

One big anxiety was the mail, whether hers was getting to her family at home and why none was coming in. However, women being in a minority on board ship, she and the other sisters had plenty of 'dates', many admirers, even some proposals. 'It's amazing being so popular, we have had a laugh out of it ourselves. The chaps congratulate themselves on getting a word in or a seat beside us, as we are rather tending to be monopolised – at least, three of us are.'

After a week or so, having sailed through the Suez Canal watched by crowds of Egyptians curious to see this first convoy in three years, they reached Port Said and had to change ships, transferring from their cruise liner to a small Atlantic steamer, 'which was dreadful!' Jessie Higgins recalls. 'The heat and discomfort through the Red Sea were awful … and the drinking water so chlorinated that it became a nightmare to keep ourselves hydrated.'

Rona Black, writing soon after the event, remembers:

> We had to change ships at one stage … You have no idea what that entailed. It was a boiling hot day with not a breath of air and a haze hung all around. We were to have trans-shipped at 6 a.m., everyone was up and ready to go. At 8 a.m. we were all browned-off, so we started a pontoon school. They didn't get moving until 11 a.m. But the new ship is much more comfortable, except for the bread, which always tastes bad. We have 100 per cent better food including melons, dates, grapes, bananas, really lovely! Fruit salads are superb.
>
> We got a fresh supply of water at the last port of call, which tastes simply awful … We are lucky to have an open bar … the great drink is brandy squash, which goes down very nicely, in moderation … Though the sky is blue the sea ain't so good and I have felt a bit under the weather. I'm taking belladonna after meals, which is making quite a difference, and a drop of scotch before meals is just keeping my head above water. I don't think pleasure cruising is at all in my line.

When they reached Aden and turned east they must have suspected where they were heading, and as they approached Bombay the smell of the land – the spices, the dust, the amazing aroma that is peculiarly India – came wafting to meet them. Lists of postings went up, finally, twenty-four hours out.

First impressions of the Orient

Staff of the four mobile field hospitals arrived in Bombay on 15 September 1943, eager to begin their work. However, to their dismay their equipment had been delayed leaving England and, since for some reason it went round the long way, via the Cape, it did not reach its destination at Calcutta until mid-December. In the meantime other duties were assigned to the MFHs' personnel.

Bombay proved 'interesting, certainly a shock after UK in wartime!' as Tommy Thomas comments, but the transit camp at Worli just outside the city was even more of a revelation. Jessie Higgins describes how they had been told to dress up for their arrival in:

> special white tricoline dresses and white Dicks [that is, thick silky cotton-poplin with smart tropical quatrecornes] only to find ourselves being helped up into lorries for the drive out to the transit camp at Worli. Never will I forget it. The camp was for hundreds and I think we were some of the first women to arrive there. The huts were of wood and very dark, and had charpoy beds … every door and drawer one opened, huge cockroaches ran everywhere, and the chairs and mattresses were full of bugs.

Jessie Higgins hated bugs. And snakes.

Having waited at Worli for about ten days, they were sent by train to Calcutta:

> four days and three nights of dirt, dust, sweat and tears, four of us to a compartment, which fortunately had a loo and hand basin en suite. Food was arranged whenever we stopped at a large station and it was brought to the train – mostly greasy fried eggs and bread, and fizzy drinks and tea … We left the train at Calcutta, where the troop Officer informed us we were not expected! No one knew what to do with us, so another transit camp for a short stay.

Eventually the PMs were attached to the army hospital in Calcutta, which was crowded with patients. At that time the army provided most medical services for the RAF in India and the PMs looked forward to rectifying that state of affairs – as did the airmen: 'If we appeared in a ward when there were RAF chaps we received a big cheer!'

They stayed in Calcutta until December when their equipment arrived. At last something was happening. At last they were going to establish their own mobile hospital encampments. Or were they? Let Rona Black tell it:

> Christmas Eve, 1943. We were told to be ready early in the morning. We set off by river and train for Chittagong, arriving early the next day. We sang carols on the boat, convinced that the 'big push' was beginning, only to discover we'd had to travel then because no one else would! There was no one to meet us. Our hopes were dashed. Once again we were seconded to the army.

She and Jay Gardner were supposed to be with 62 MFH, but one delay after another kept them from fulfilling the role they had been assigned. The frustration of it all comes vividly to life in one of Rona's letters to her mother, written on 29 December 1943 from 61 MFH, at Chittagong:

> We have moved again as you will see, but unfortunately this is not the last move. There has been such an awful upheaval, I have felt so browned off I have not dared write home. I see from my book it's thirteen days since I wrote. As far as my health is concerned, I'm fine, but the bloody RAF has let us down badly. We all planned Xmas, as you know, and on the 21st they said we were to move at 5 a.m. Xmas Eve, arriving here at 5 a.m. Xmas Day. That we did. The others went to a party on the 23rd and didn't go to bed … At 3 a.m. I was wakened, dressed, had eggs and bacon and off we went. The train journey wasn't too bad. Then at midday we went in a boat, and then back on the train …
>
> When we got here, no one to meet us and eventually, when the CO arrived, we found we were reposted to another army hospital. Were we mad! The next bombshell, Gardner and I, not belonging here, were put to work the next day on the wards. We found when we got here we really weren't expected … our patience is exhausted and we all let everyone know who mattered, from Air Cmdres to S/Ldrs (we don't deal in anything less). Of course we were all terribly tired after the journey, so after a drink of rum I went to bed and slept solidly until 3.30 p.m.. When I woke I felt like I used to on night duty – rather sick and really stupid …
>
> What's more, when we got here we discovered they had no idea where we were going to live … they expected us to sit down quite cheerfully and live here with the QAs. That, of course, is a damn lot of nonsense and we aren't going to do it … Today I'm recovering from the blow of being uprooted for Xmas unnecessarily, and the thought we are annexed by the b–– army medical corps …
>
> Anyway, we have a flat now, very nice room each and every comfort. We have tin pots for lavs and canvas baths … We are moving in on Monday, after the place is clean.

Having let off steam, she soon calms down, writing in January:

> We're settling down here now and have practically recovered from our depression and gloom that settled over us at Xmas … our living quarters are wizard now, we have had the whole place painted and we have acquired furniture, rugs and curtains,

> and really it's going to look wizard. Six rooms in the top flat of a house. It isn't very large but it gives us a room for a lounge ... We are hoping to join our unit very soon. Work is very plentiful here. We are certainly seeing life ... My dress at the various parties from now on, unless specially informed, will be bush shirt and khaki slacks. The mosquitoes are bad and it's more comfortable not being bitten.

It took considerable courage for young women raised in Britain to travel at short notice out to snake-ridden jungles where they were obliged to live and work in primitive, makeshift conditions. Faced with downright squalor, each one of them rolled up her sleeves, swapped her white ward dress for khaki slacks and shirt and, by sheer hard work, brought a semblance of home comfort to cheer her patients' blackest hours as they fought the horrible symptoms of dengue fever, dysentery, typhus, hepatitis and – always and above all – malaria.

The smallest enemies

Hundreds of hastily built airfields, landing strips and RAF stations had spread across India and Ceylon. Unfortunately, owing to the speed of their construction, not enough attention was paid to proper siting or to using building materials suited to the climate and conditions; so huts leaked in the monsoon, campsites flooded and many personnel found themselves living next to mosquito breeding-grounds. Dysentery and malaria became the two arch-enemies, engaging everyone in a never-ending war against the ubiquitous mosquito.

The worst problem with malaria was its ability to lodge in the human system; an apparent cure would be effected, only for the disease to break out again weeks later. Prevention being preferable, items for malarial control were issued: metal gauze screening for doors and windows; camouflage netting, khaki or green, for beds and sundry openings; protective clothing – slacks and long sleeves to be worn from sundown, also the detested 'mosquito boots' for the PMs; insect repellents, though these were unpopular and not very effective; and drugs – when quinine became scarce, mepacrine hydrochloride, which turned skin yellow and irritated the human stomach, was introduced. The most effective malaria preventative was discipline – taking the proper precautions – but many men couldn't be bothered with all that.

Given the benefit of hindsight, the liberal use of DDT, sprayed not only on stagnant ponds and vegetation but in living quarters, kitchens, sometimes on skin, or sewn into the seams of clothes, looks ill-advised, to say the least. *The History of the RAFMS* (published in 1954) speaks casually of 'Paris green', DDT and pyrethrum solutions, being 'spread by hand-held sprayers of poor workmanship, cheap material and parts liable to corrosion in the hot, moist atmosphere of the tropics'. Official anti-malarial control units were generally efficient and well-organised, but all too often these spraying devices were in the hands of squads of untrained service personnel or 'mechanically unskilled coolies', who merrily squirted gallons of poisonous insecticide, directly and daily, virtually everywhere their sprays would reach. But such was the threat of malaria and other diseases carried by insects that eradicating them was of paramount importance and, at the time, DDT and its cousins provided the best weapon.

Some relief and relaxation came from sun-bathing and, if your unit was near the coast, sea-bathing provided a popular form of recreation and did wonders for morale. The benefits far outweighed the possible dangers of sunburn, jellyfish and sharks. But inland lakes and rivers were often forbidden because of the ever-present risks of infection.

This miniature war, with the need for constant vigilance, twenty-four-hour precautions, and personal hygiene – with clean water in desperately short supply – provided an added trial for everyone involved.

Chittagong

By the end of 1943, all four of the RAF's mobile field hospitals had settled in what was then East Bengal and Assam, which remained the main location for RAF units at this stage of the war. For a while, as Rona Black implied above, personnel of 61 and 62 MFHs combined to establish a hospital in the village of Chittagong. The CO and his doctors went to look for a suitable site, while Jessie Higgins, being the senior nurse, took charge of the nursing team of sisters and male orderlies. They took over a derelict girls' school and for extra wards built basha huts, described by Jessie Higgins as:

> bamboo buildings with just a roof of bamboo, no windows or doors, but better than canvas tents as at least we had a little breeze. Latrines and a washing area were built for the men.
>
> The equipment we had was nothing! Because, of course, everything that was supposed to arrive in the Far East never did, they were torpedoed so much. We had one set of so-called theatre instruments, and we had to sterilise with methylated spirit lamps to heat the water. As a field hospital, of course, we only used the operating theatre for emergencies – tiny little room at the end of this old school that we took over … and of course we had the snakes, scorpions, every sort of creepy crawly.

Snakes and bugs became the bane of Higgie's life.

No sooner had the hospital set up than patients came in, soon filling the 150 beds. 'So much sickness', is what Jessie Higgins remembers:

> Dysentery, malaria, jaundice, typhoid, and even smallpox … very few surgical cases … mostly abscesses – very common – appendix, leg fractures, and occasionally a real casualty such as gunshot wounds, flying accidents and crashes …
>
> One thing that brought it home to us was … we had an air-raid and [Japanese pilots] were shot down. They brought two of these Jap boys in to us. Neither of them were badly wounded, just broken legs and things, but they had to be guarded … We only had charpoy beds. Exactly the width of a body between the beds, and

> all these damn mosquito nets and of course the two guards had to sit either side of the bed …
>
> We had awful problems getting ill boys to eat and drink because the food was absolutely ghastly and of course you couldn't get any oranges or lemons, the only thing you could get was limes. We used to barter them for pilchards in tomato juice … We had a lot of boys with minor heart conditions, a result of dysentery or typhoid.

They used the precious limes to make squash to add vitamin C to the diet of the very ill patients, but since the two Japanese pilots were not seriously ill they had only plain water. One evening, as Sister Thomas poured drinks by the light of hurricane lamps, one of the Japanese reared up and threw his water into her face:

> Of course the two guards jumped on him [says Jessie Higgins] and I think even the illest patients in those wards were out of bed. How he wasn't lynched … It was the most frightening thing! I was on the other side, doing something in the surgical ward, and heard all this noise. Fortunately one of the MOs was around so I shouted for him and we ran across … it was terrifying … Very next morning, they were off and we never saw them again.

Jessie Higgins especially remembers working with surgeon Peter Greening, who was not much older than her but a wonderful surgeon. The Far East didn't offer much for a surgeon beyond very basic work, but one particular patient presented an unusual challenge. Flight Lieutenant Mike Bush, a South African pilot with the RAF, had been out on a mission to the jungle in one of the little aircraft which, says Higgie, could land on a sixpence. Having brought back a patient for the hospital, he went to hand in his revolver, but somehow the gun went off and shot him in the stomach:

> He had twenty-two holes in his intestines! And we couldn't find the bullet! All night! It was dreadful. This dreadful theatre and this silly light, and … Finally, we closed him up, tied up all the holes in the intestines – Peter did, and me giving him the anaesthetic – and of course we didn't dare move him, because we didn't know where the bullet was. We never did find out, until he was finally flown to Calcutta – we had no proper X-ray or anything – and there it was, lodged in between his vertebrae. Another quarter of an inch and he'd have been paralysed.
>
> Anyway … he was flown home to England, went to the spinal and head injuries place at Wheatley … they couldn't operate. He had that bullet inside him to the day he died – he died last January [1998].

She always wrote to the mothers or wives of patients who couldn't write for themselves and she struck up a friendship with Mike Bush's mother, staying in touch for over fifty years.

Higgie also remembers being permanently wet – either from sweat or from monsoon rains. 'The rain was unbelievable! It would rain for five days at a time and it never stopped POURING down!' Hospital staff were drenched going from basha hut to basha hut:

> and of course we had those latrines, all in a row, with palm-woven walls between … boys from the dysentery ward always out there. I remember going out one day and … a terrific blow of wind, and both the walls … and there were all these lads … I just walked past, thinking, Oh God, Higgins, don't go purple.

A visiting senior matron:

> was astounded at the conditions under which we were working … Snakes of all types and sizes, bed-bugs galore, cockroaches, ants … rats and snakes in the roofs of the huts, and iguanas very active … At the monsoon time everywhere was soaking wet, roads and paths all mud, and snakes very obvious … [since] we only had lamps – and electric light if the generator worked – the dark wards were not very welcoming to a sick man … We had no pillows and patients had to use their kit-bags … Most patients lay in a blanket (no mattress) and possibly a blanket and sheet in the cooler weather in December and January. Linen was a nightmare as we did not have the facilities for laundering. Lack of so many comforts was heartbreaking.

She need not have worried – her patients found the hospital a haven of comfort. C.E. Beale, of the RAF Regiment, fondly remembers the PMs he met at Chittagong. 'I shall never forget their kindness to me and many others. It was wonderful to find oneself in a very comfortable bed with sparkling white sheets after months of no bed, a groundsheet and a rough blanket.'

An unexpected reunion took place one day as Jessie Higgins 'was walking across the grounds of the hospital when a voice behind me said, "Miss Higgins, I presume?" – and it was my brother!' Her brother was in the army, stationed then in Burma. Her sister Joan was in the navy, seconded to Lord Mountbatten's personal staff. When Mountbatten became C-in-C Far East, the three Higgins siblings managed to meet:

> for one single day! I managed to get across to Calcutta, my brother had just come back from the jungle, and Joan … don't whether she got a flight up, but we all met in Calcutta – so broke, we had about five shillings between us! It was lovely to see them … And my mother had no idea where any of us were!

A visit from the Viceroy

When Lord Wavell visited Chittagong in his role as Viceroy of India, Senior Sister Higgins attended a dinner party in his honour, held at the local United Services Officers' Club. 'It was an experience,' she says drily:

> That so-called 'Club' had been one of the tea-planters clubs – it just had a bar! Every CO of every unit within miles was invited. The matron from the Indian Medical Service hospital and I were the only two women, other than Lady Wavell and a lady-in-waiting of some sort. We had to turn up in our khaki trousers, khaki kerchief round our neck, khaki bush shirts, and she walks in with a tiara, a beautiful grey chiffon dress, with a train, and diamonds … talk about feeling like Barnardo's girls!
>
> It was all so official! They had a hundred staff. They came on the train. All these waiters … It was unbelievable, because we had nothing, no knives and forks, and they brought everything – and all the staff with their white gloves on! We were presented to them when they arrived, and then after dinner they had these four little tables with chairs round … and everybody that was an official guest was taken round and sat for five minutes at each table and chatted … and there's us feeling like nothing, our khakis all perspiration … And then, of course, they got on the train and disappeared, went back to Calcutta.
>
> That was the beginning of '44. Lord Mountbatten wasn't in charge then. What a difference when he came. It was like turning a page! Things began to arrive – things we'd been waiting forever for. People came alive. That was when the fun really began, because Mountbatten decided there was no coming out of the jungle in the monsoon.

Until then, when the monsoon came the troops had been withdrawn and fighting virtually ceased until the rains cleared.

62 MFH

After a while, Rona Black and her colleague Jay Gardner rejoined their own unit and moved to a place named Cox's Bazaar, nearer to Calcutta. Rona reported to her mother:

> Life here is primitive. We're blessed with electric light but … bare wires sticking out of the bamboo, with no sockets and no bulbs … We have no furniture at present except our camp kit which we brought from England, and a carpet each … Tonight we have a turned-up packing case to write on – in the basha – an oil hurricane lamp each, and a glass of rum. We are quite happy, thank you.
>
> The hospital is getting ship-shape at last under our auspices. We think we are a little more appreciated by the orderlies as they see we are here to help, not only to order. We're taking mepacrine now, to try and suppress malaria. We're getting a great number [of malaria cases] in already, so I hate to think of what we shall have when the season is in full swing …
>
> The camp is in two small valleys, one taking the medical unit and tents for convalescents, the other the surgical unit and officers. The bamboo huts we live in are most intriguing. The bamboo is split down in narrow strips, opened out quite flat and interwoven with hundreds of others … so there's plenty of daylight between the cracks. The door is the same material with the odd bamboo pole to strengthen it

and a piece of bamboo strip bound round to make it fast at one side. The windows are the strips of bamboo put criss-cross. There's no glass anywhere for about 300 miles, so the air just blows in and we're thankful for it. The roof is just bamboo criss-crossed with rushes laid on top like thatch, and more bamboo to keep them on.

Sanitary arrangement is very pukka. We have a very deep pit about thirty feet deep and two feet wide, surmounted by a round petrol tin and a pukka wooden seat with lid. The bath is the inevitable canvas square type, just big enough for me to sit cross-legged in, cold water, and a slant in the mud floor to the trench …

We are about a quarter of a mile from the 'road', which is a good thing as the dust is frightful. Women and children are employed along a stretch of about 130 miles of road, to throw water … to keep the dust down. Our little 'lane' doesn't get watered under this scheme, as we built it, so clouds of dust come sweeping up the valley daily and into the wards … All day aircraft buzz overhead. It's very cheering because we feel the Japs are really getting what they deserve. The lads down here are grand, they are doing a wonderful job.

Imphal

In February 1943 a guerrilla force of British, Gurkha and Burmese soldiers – the 'Chindits' – marched into the Japanese-occupied jungles of northern Burma, supported by elephants, mules and bullocks, with a few supplies dropped by air. Their successes alarmed and mystified the Japanese, and galvanised morale among the dispirited Allied armies in India, but the main value of the expedition was the lessons learned for the later airborne expedition, which began in late December 1943. It coincided with a fierce Japanese offensive and, by the time it ended, the myth of Japanese invincibility had been dispelled.

For three months during this long engagement, British and Indian forces were besieged in Imphal, the chief town of the remote Indian border district of Manipur. Steep jungle-clad hillsides surrounding the town saw some of the most desperate fighting of the war. For both sides, defeat was unthinkable. The RAF made the difference – along with the USAF they flew a continuous shuttle service, bringing in supplies and reinforcements and taking out casualties and civilians. For the Japanese besiegers, at the end of an over-extended supply chain, reserves slowly ran out.

Later that year, after the siege was lifted, a New Zealand pilot, hero of eighty-eight dog-fights and with 500 flying hours to his credit, crashed near Imphal and became seriously ill with tetanus. Squadron Leader Doran, the RAF doctor attending him, decided he might benefit from expert nursing, so radioed for nurses and special drugs. As an *Evening Standard* correspondent reported:

Two Royal Air Force nurses have been flown to Imphal in an old bomber, to help save the life of a New Zealand airman … They are Sister Barbara McDonald, of Calne, Wiltshire, and Sister Patricia Dawson, of Leigh-on-Sea, Essex … The girls are the first European women to re-enter Manipur since the fighting of five months ago … When [they] arrived, Sqn Ldr Doran took them to the patient and said, 'Look what I've brought you.' The airman opened his eyes and said one word: 'Popsies!'

Jungle conditions

An idea of the dangers faced by troops in the Far East may be gleaned from the contents of 'jungle packs', which contained tubes of aspirin (to alleviate pain and fever) and quinine or mepacrine (against malaria); tablets for sterilising water; a snake-bite outfit; needles and thread, safety pins and a fishing line with hook and float.

For everyone, supplies were scarce. Rona Black told her mother:

We have room for about 100 patients and are equipped for fifty … you can put up a bed here and there but the equipment doesn't arrive. The linen problem is quite acute – no sheets or pyjamas. We have mostly malaria, dysentery and jaundice. We haven't had many very ill patients, but we are thankful as the staff is inadequate … I long for a comfortable chair, a good film, a decent table to do my writing, a cool refreshing wood of primroses, and our home. We wear khaki, no caps, no stockings, and heavy shoes. I have a pair of native sandals …

March 1944: I had a lad in with malaria. He had been out fourteen days trying to escape from the Japs. He was in a bad state when he came in here. We tried every kind of treatment, but he died about six days later. It really upset me and that evening I had a quiet weep to myself. Yesterday we had another busy day, admitted fifteen new cases of malaria, so we now have topped the 100 mark … Half my staff have malaria. The sun is so hot I have to wear a hat now, and sunglasses. We work hard in the morning, sweat in the afternoon, and work in the evening …

In the early hours of the morning we admitted a cerebral haemorrhage, another serious case. Tonight I went over at 8.30 p.m. to see how the lad was and the whole way was lit by fireflies darting about – really lovely. The orderlies are wonderful, and would do anything for me. I had more volunteers than I wanted for duty tonight with that sick lad. I give them a great deal of freedom, smoking on duty, etc., and they thoroughly appreciate it …

My underclothes have been wrecked by the washerwoman, so I'm living in rags, but no one cares as we are both the same. We just wash them ourselves now, and wear them rough-dried … Jay and I are wearing our oldest clothes and my pants at the moment are the flowery voile ones we bought years ago, with a little vest to match, remember? at Dickens and J. They are, needless to say, falling to pieces … I'm wearing my 'Dick' at the moment but we have put in for 'Terri' hats – rather like a girl guide's hat, khaki with a stiff brim and RAF ribbon on one side, very snappy. It's RAF issue.

Three of the four MOs are off sick with malaria, that leaves the CO, the Dental Officer, the other sister and myself to cope. We've had about half the orderlies off

> with malaria, too, so it's great fun! … You are lucky to have fish as we live on hammerhead shark. It's usually done up in batter. It's very tough and tastes bloody awful, putting it mildly … We are expecting to move when the monsoon comes, so we shall get away from the malarious area.

Before this could happen, the unit's surgeon, suffering from a third bout of malaria in three months, killed himself with a bullet through the head; then Sister Jay Gardner also went down with malaria and had to be flown to Chittagong:

> I flew up with her, in a Moth … We were transported by ambulance to the other hospital. I stayed there two days and lazed about. I really was nearly passing out with exhaustion as I had had Jay to nurse and cook for, and the whole hospital to supervise. However, at the end of two days I contacted a Wg Cdr down here who flew up to Calcutta and took me back to the 'drome in the Gp Capt's Chrysler, and so home in his private plane and jeep. We flew along the shore and round the islands, then made inland, circled over the hospital and landed in a paddy field. I felt a little sick going, but the return was superb. I've been on my own for ten days now.

Relief in the hills

Because of these troubles, 62 MFH moved to the hill depot at Shillong, a much cooler spot which offered a better social life, with lots of dances and parties at various local units. Occasionally the medical team swapped places with staff from 61 and 63 MFHs so that the others might also have some relief from the heat.

From Shillong in May 1944, Rona writes:

> It's cool, even cold, at night especially. I've had four blankets and a hot water bottle. We have been so energetic, it has been a treat. The orderlies have bucked up their ideas. The first few days they were awful but it nearly always takes a week for them to settle down and get into running order. They called us the 'binding sisters' and so we were, but now they reap the benefit and it's so much easier to be organised. We've had nearly all malaria and dysentery … very little nursing except routine. So we have plenty of time for making the hospital interesting, and the diet appetizing.
>
> It's the most lovely country around here – hills, pines, lakes. A lot of rain, but it's so marvellously cool it doesn't really matter. There are also some very good shops – though not as you would imagine them. It's different from Cox's Bazaar, which was very much in the jungle.

On 7 June 1944, she reports: 'I was feeling ropey last night – rather sick, but with the news of the second front and a few sherries I changed and went to the dance!'

News of the Normandy landings, D-Day, 6 June, took only a few hours to reach this far corner of the Empire.

10

Towards a Second Front

At the Casablanca conference of January 1943, the Allied war lords had agreed that after they pushed the enemy out of North Africa the next step must be an invasion of mainland Europe. Such an enormous undertaking needed long and careful planning: they anticipated it would take around eighteen months.

Over the next year, England witnessed a great gathering of troops and materials. American servicemen poured in to charm the female populace, and the accents and uniforms of many other friendly nations became familiar in the streets and pubs. Whole swathes of southern downland sprouted a thick coating of armour – tanks, aircraft, lorries, armoured cars, field guns … People joked that the only thing keeping the laden island from sinking was the support of hundreds of tethered barrage balloons. An elaborate deception was taking place, designed to make the enemy think that the coming invasion would strike near Calais. In fact, the objective was Normandy.

Since Operation Overlord could not succeed without great human cost, the authorities made plans to cope with casualties. RAFH Wroughton was designated the main casualty clearing station (CCS) for wounded troops flown home from Europe. Its available beds would expand to over 1,000, with eighteen extra nursing sisters ready to serve as required. Other sisters were posted to airfields at Down Ampney, Blakehill Farm and Broadhill, all within easy reach of Wroughton and all preparing to act as reception centres for the incoming wounded. Most fortunate of all, in their own estimation, were four PMs who received orders to join the new mobile field hospitals which would follow the troops into occupied Europe.

Under starter's orders …

Monica Railton Jones (Mrs Chandler) had the impression that the male staff of 55 MFH felt 'very dubious' when she and her colleague Pam Renton arrived to join them at a large house in Weybridge, Surrey. The transport sergeant immediately put Monica behind the wheel of a truck and gave her a lesson in driving, through the busy streets of the town. 'The following evening I had to drive a 3-tonner on a night convoy using only reflectors for light – a gruelling experience.' She slowly worked her way through every vehicle that travelled with the MFH – every member of the team had to be versatile.

Early in January 1944 the unit moved to Fontwell race course, near Bognor Regis, where they erected their tented hospital for the first time and began to practise: pack the equipment, load up the twenty-eight trucks, travel in convoy to a new site, unload, unpack and set up the tents; then pack again, load, convoy …

Fluffy Ogilvie, who had, as we have seen, survived the bombing of hospitals at both St Athan and Torquay, was working at the RAF Medical Rehabilitation Unit at Loughborough. She was now a war-widow – Squadron Leader Donald Ogilvie's bomber had been shot down over Holland, with no survivors, a few months after their wedding. In response, feeling that she 'wanted desperately to make some contribution', Fluffy had asked for permission to serve with one of the mobile field hospitals. She joined 50 MFH, whose winter quarters, like those of 55, were at Fontwell race course.

She too found her welcome less than ecstatic. 'We don't want any bloody women in this outfit!' was the general opinion among the medical orderlies. But the sunny Sister Fluffy soon won them round. 'We lived in fields, woods, sunshine and mud, but the wonderful spirit of comradeship … made everything worthwhile.'

While based at Fontwell, the MFH teams went on practising mobility. They travelled with their own generators, field telephones, water supplies, kitchens, signals unit, operating theatre, X-ray equipment, dental unit and, of course, all available medical supplies. They knew they were to be part of the coming invasion. The question was, when would it be? While they waited, they enjoyed some fun and laughter – one particular incident left Sister Ogilvie blushing to the roots of her fluffy blonde curls:

> Our unit was visited … by some VIPs, including the Air Marshal, Director General of the RAF Medical Service. I was walking towards my tent when I saw them all standing stiffly to attention, saluting my 'smalls' hanging on a line. One of them turned to me and said, 'I'm certain they will bring us luck!'

D-minus 30 and counting …

At RAFH Halton one bright spring day, twenty-two-year-old WAAF clerk Con Smith (Mrs Gilbert) was summoned to Ward 10 to take dictation from an officer who had been admitted with a minor skin complaint. She was amazed to find herself sitting beside Group Captain Frank Whittle, famous as the inventor of the jet engine. She still has his autograph, dated 3 May 1944, to prove it. But she often wishes she had kept the shorthand notes, too. They concerned 'something mysterious called Operation Overlord'. That enigmatic title became far more meaningful a month later, on 6 June 1944.

As spring turned to summer, the RAF and the USAF combined to prepare the way. Attacks on German oil installations virtually stopped production of enemy armaments; in France, to interrupt transport and communications systems, the Allied air forces knocked out such places as marshalling yards and big railway junctions; and finally on the night of 5 June they concentrated on German batteries guarding the Channel coast.

Through the 'sausage machine'

In her war memoir, Fluffy Ogilvie wrote:

> I sat in silence in my battle dress and tin hat, with a Red Cross armband prominently on my left arm. Straight ahead, jeeps, trucks and ambulances could be seen mounting the hill in the distance. In spite of the familiar sound of the convoy making its progress, it seemed incredibly still, almost unreal. The memorable day was the fifth of June 1944 and I was setting out on what was to be the greatest adventure of my life.

She and colleague Mollie Giles were the only women in the massive host that day. (No 55 MFH, with Sisters Railton Jones and Renton, was to follow some ten days later.) They were heading into the 'sausage machine', whose funnel lay at Old Sarum, Wiltshire, and whose nozzle lay at the south coast, pointing towards France. The vast concentration area had hard standing for 1,650 lorries, and enough tents to accommodate 8,500 personnel at any one time. The rows of canvas seemed to stretch for miles. Once they reached the area, troops were sealed off from the world, behind barbed wire and armed guards. The success of 'Overlord' depended on total secrecy and surprise.

Just after midnight on 6 June, a fleet of landing craft laden with men, guns, tanks, transport and armoured cars, all protected by navy warships, set out to cross the gale-tossed Channel. During the hours of darkness advance troops flying by glider and parachute opened the way, and as daylight came fighter aircraft of the RAF and the USAF went in to protect the first sea-landings. Within hours, though at terrible cost of life and hardware, the Allies established several beachheads, and on the first evening the advance party of four doctors from 50 MFH arrived on the Normandy beaches. One of them, Squadron Leader Grant, was killed during the landing. It was to be some days before his colleagues back at Old Sarum heard the news.

The MFH remained at the concentration area for a few days, during which time Fluffy Ogilvie and Mollie Giles stayed in the WAAF officers' mess, where it was assumed their purpose was to tend the sick among the encamped troops. This caused some puzzlement: 'Do you find much work to do? The chaps must all be pretty fit.' Until the last moment none of the WAAFs knew that the two PMs were actually 'going over' with the troops.

At the MFH one day they were handed emergency packs whose contents included concentrated porridge, some chocolate, a piece of chewing gum and a tiny box containing a collar stud with a compass at one end. Fluffy thought that if she had to depend on that she would probably end up in Germany! Aware that the 'off' was not far away, that night in her quarters she made sure her backpack contained everything she might need – tin plate and 'eating irons', with a tin mug dangling from a strap, and 'very important as far as I was concerned, a little waterproof bag with my Elizabeth

Arden make-up … I wasn't going to land in Normandy looking a sight! Bright red lipstick did wonders to pull one's face together.'

She and Mollie lay on their beds waiting, in full battle dress, with Red Cross arm bands on their left arms. It was just before midnight that the dispatch rider came to call them, much to the astonishment of one of the WAAF officers who saw them leave.

In pitch darkness, with only reflectors for lights, Fluffy clambered to her familiar seat beside the driver of one of the trucks and they were off, making for the marshalling area at Fareham. Years later, one of the officers told her that he owed her a debt of gratitude: 'I used to say to myself, if she can go, I can go!'

After two days at Fareham, on 11 June they travelled the final few miles towards the 'hards' at Gosport – the beach where they would embark. Just after dawn they paused in the town and housewives brought the troops tea, and hot water for a refreshing shave. Some of the men accepted invitations to breakfast in homely kitchens. A woman gave Fluffy a tin of peaches, 'such a treasured possession in the war. I sat on the pavement and ate the contents of the tin with relish. Morale was tremendous … the generosity and kindness of the people did so much …'

Finally, as the seaborne convoy continued to move slowly out into the Solent, they boarded their landing craft. 'In addition to all the tanks and vehicles, it carried hundreds of troops … It seemed enormous to me …' What struck Fluffy most was the silence maintained by nearly everyone: the enormity of the undertaking held them in thrall. But she doesn't remember being afraid. 'A couple of men started counting the vessels aloud, they reached two hundred … I felt strangely elated as there came a roar of aircraft …'

All day Allied aircraft came and went overhead. The landing craft's commander offered the two women use of his cabin, but mostly they remained with the men. Then night, and silence, descended:

> There was an eerie darkness filled with differing sounds from nearby vessels. Troops sat on the deck, in every available space … In the comfort of the cabin I slept soundly for a few hours – I remember crawling into the bunk in full battle dress, thinking, I'm going to sleep if it kills me.

Somehow she did manage to sleep.

Next morning they were near the Normandy coast, with the sky full of Allied aircraft, fighters taking off from a strip near the shore, and navy warships firing their guns to answer enemy shore batteries. The landing craft with the two nursing sisters on board waited for hours for the tide to allow them in close enough to land; but the first lorry down the ramp tipped into a vast mine-hole in the shingle, blocking the way. They had to wait again, while more hours passed, and darkness came. And still the guns kept firing:

> At some stage we became aware that disembarkation had started again. I remember standing next to Mollie in the dark, on the left side of the lower deck, facing the ramp. The inside towered above us. I felt as though I was inside a monstrous whale. I couldn't see what was happening in the darkness but I was very aware of the noisy vehicles and personnel dashing about. I felt No emotion, nothing at all, just standing there with my pack on my back looking down towards the ramp … We didn't speak a word. Suddenly we were told to go. We scrambled down the ramp and the next thing I remember was feeling sand under my feet. I had landed on Juno/Red Beach, in pitch darkness, on June 12th 1944.

They stepped into history, being the first women to land with 'Overlord', several days ahead of any others.

Into battle

Fluffy and Mollie spent a short while in an underground bunker with some appreciative troops. The men had prided themselves on being among the first to enter France; now to their amazement they found two slender RAF nursing sisters along with them! One of the men joked, 'Watch out, Adolf, you've had it now!' Amid confusion, under night skies filled with the boom and glare of gunfire and the glow of red-hot shells that the men called 'flaming onions', the two PMs accepted a lift in a lorry going to the assembly area, where they rejoined their colleagues.

The area was so closely packed with men, vehicles, ammunition dumps and anti-aircraft guns that attacking enemy planes could hardly fail to hit something. The waiting 'slit trenches' – short ditches dug into the ground and covered by a tent – looked very inviting to Fluffy and Mollie, who took off their packs and occupied a trench each. Exhaustion did the rest: 'I put my tin hat over my face and fell fast asleep.'

Next day the MFH in convoy moved slowly amid active tanks and firing guns, past signs bearing a skull and crossbones with the words '*Achtung Minen*' (beware mines). The battle went on, guns booming both in front and behind, shells whistling overhead. But a cleared track, denoted by white markers, led them to their allocated site, in a field where they erected their hospital tents in tidy lines, dug slit trenches beneath the canvas, and laid out a huge flag, with its red cross on white ground. As the first of the wounded came in the nurses sprang into action, saddened by the need but relieved that at last they could do the work for which they had been training for so long. 'Ambulances arrived in a long convoy. There were just over two hundred surgical cases to be evacuated, and many in poor shape. Some had to remain for immediate surgery …' Fluffy found herself changing field dressings, preparing intravenous infusions and giving injections of morphine and precious penicillin. She and Mollie distributed gallons of hot tea, fed those who could eat, handed out urinals and bed-pans and lit cigarettes for men too wounded to do it themselves. Most of all they talked to the men, trying to keep up their spirits, rewarded by smiles on bloodied faces and warmth in weary eyes.

More ambulances took the men on, some to return home by sea, more urgent cases to fly from the improvised airstrip nearby. The two PMs took it in turns to accompany casualties to where, amid clouds of white dust, trusty Dakotas came and went on a runway that was no more than a stretch of ground flattened by the Royal Engineers and covered with wire meshing. In the nearby woods, tank battles continued, while Allied warships fired from the shore and German guns answered from inland.

When she reached the first Dakota, Fluffy was surprised to see WAAF nursing orderlies on board, the first WAAF to take part in the air evacuation. Nursing of casualties in transit was a risky business: the airstrips came under fire on occasion; the transport aircraft wore no guardian red cross; and, as WAAF Corporal Biddy Spencer (Mrs Wilson) recalls, the air ambulance nursing orderlies went into service 'without 'chutes because their stretcher patients couldn't have 'chutes; and there were casualties. The ones I knew were Leading Aircraftwomen, probably being paid around 24*s* 6*d* per week.'

Within six days of their arrival in Normandy, the staff of 50 MFH had seen 1,023 casualties safely aboard flights for home. One of the Dakotas was struck by flak as it flew out and Fluffy Ogilvie later heard that it had seventy holes in its fuselage, but by some miracle no one had been hurt.

A vicious storm blew up on 18 June and lasted for five days, delaying the Allied build-up and destroying or stranding 800 ships. Torrential rain poured down, along with shrapnel, churning the ground into mud and preventing aircraft from flying close-support missions – including air ambulance evacuation. The weather also allowed the Germans time to redeploy. All the time casualties kept arriving to await the return of the Dakotas. 'Some of the injured were in a poor state,' Fluffy Ogilvie noted worriedly:

> One night was particularly noisy, due to the gunfire and shelling and we were all busy … I stopped by one of the lads, who was very poorly, lapsing into periods of unconsciousness … This time he had his eyes wide open and said in a perfectly clear voice, 'Where's your tin hat? Who do you think you are, a blinking fairy?' … I went to find my hat and hurriedly put it on. I returned to reassure him, to find he had just died. It was an incident that shook me greatly and that I could never forget.

They were followed into Europe by 52 MFH, staffed by the Royal Canadian Air Force, which erected its tents near Caen. Then, in early July, 55 MFH also went through the 'sausage machine' and set up in what Monica Railton Jones describes as:

> an orchard two miles inland at a small place called Banville next to the airfield … We received casualties immediately from the forward Field Dressing Stations … Air Evacuation was very successful … We also had quite a number of German PoWs … many of them were young arrogant Nazi youth, and although badly wounded were very aggressive.

A more grateful patient that July was Lieutenant Eric Brown of the Royal Artillery:

> Having been burned and wounded as a result of a direct hit on my Mobile A/Tk Gun (Tank Destroyer), I had been rescued from the battlefield and taken in by the Canadian Field Hospital near Caen. Swathed in bandages and plaster from head to foot, I was taken to Mulberry Harbour by an RAF ambulance. For hours and hours we waited to be embarked and during all that time the two RAF nurses took the greatest care of me … the courage they gave me to soldier on was absolutely vital … PMRAFNS were a really VITAL LINK in my preservation. Thank God.

Casevac procedure

As soon as a new landing strip opened, transport aircraft brought in urgent stores or extra troops and went out laden with casualties. Fighter planes gave them cover. As the fighting front moved away, the airstrip would be extended to an airfield, with a casualty evacuation (casevac) unit capable of tending up to 200 patients as they waited for the next air ambulances. Wounded men from any nearby medical unit, whether RAF, army or civilian, would be examined, fed, treated and operated on if necessary, or, if not considered well enough to be flown out, would be sent back to a field hospital.

The forward air shuttle service removed thousands of casualties from under the noses of the enemy, taking them straight to Britain and later on to temporary base hospitals in France, Holland and Belgium. The same aircraft returned again to the front bringing stores, equipment, and medical supplies, including around 162lb of blood and 700lb of drugs, every day.

Back in Britain, RAF Down Ampney was one of three airfields which served as 'feeders' to the Casualty Clearing Station at Wroughton. The other two chosen airfields closed down before the end of 1944 after problems with flooding, leaving Down Ampney to cope. More of the ubiquitous and endlessly useful wooden huts, erected near the airfield, formed emergency sick quarters manned by RAF doctors, PMs and members of the medical service.

A dozen or so WAAF drivers worked at Down Ampney. Among them, Kay Chamant (Mrs Watts) drove 'one of the fleet of small standard ambulances, all of which were fitted up inside with supports and rails to receive four stretchers, two on either side'. As the laden Dakotas came winging in, she and the other drivers revved up their engines, forgot missed meals and headed for the aerodrome.

'About three-quarters of all patients were stretcher cases. They would be transferred from aircraft to ambulance by trainee aircrew and Italian prisoners of war drafted in as bearers.' Kay Chamant drove her wounded passengers slowly and carefully back to the emergency medical huts, where:

> seeing the Princess Mary's Sisters always looking so neat and fresh in their blue and white uniforms I often wondered how they managed this, working as they did

> among battle-soiled boots and uniforms and the bodies of men on stretchers in confined spaces of little huts as they arrived off planes, before they had been examined, washed, shaved and fed.

Some patients came fresh from battle, with only field dressings on their wounds; some arrived with the letters 'M' or 'T' written on their foreheads to indicate that morphine had been given or a tourniquet applied. Medical staff graded them as: A (immediate emergency treatment), B (less urgent) or C (suitable for transfer straight to other units). Most of them went first to Wroughton RAF hospital, which took patients in every other night. They stayed two nights before being transferred to other hospitals, freeing the beds for a fresh intake.

As Winifred Gardner (Mrs Penman) recalls, a prisoner of war camp was situated 'at the far end of the hospital's vast grounds, occupied originally by Germans, then by Italians. They made a valuable contribution to the work force. Some made efficient ward orderlies, others cleaners and gardeners.'

For Joan White (Mrs Cool), her 'first patient after D-Day was a Canadian soldier from the Regina Regiment, still in his uniform with field dressings …' After Arnhem (17 September 1944), patients down one side of the ward all had fans playing over their legs 'to see how far their circulation was reaching down their limbs in order to decide how extensive an amputation was necessary'.

The flow of casualties through Down Ampney and Wroughton steadily reduced as the Allied armies moved on into Germany and in their wake more permanent hospitals, RAF and army, opened across Western Europe.

Following the Front

That summer, Matron Helen W. Cargill, in charge of nurses at the Convalescent Hospital at Matlock, Derbyshire, was summoned to London where she learned that France was to be her next posting. Just as she was leaving the Air Ministry, a flying bomb exploded nearby. Though shaken, she was unharmed and, after a few moments, continued her journey to Austin Reed of Oxford Street, to order more uniform dresses. Only as she bent over to write her cheque did she realise how narrow an escape she had had – showers of splintered glass fell from the 'Dick Turpin' hat which had acted as her shield.

Her new unit, No 8 RAFGH, formed at RAF Aston Down in Gloucestershire. Its convoy of trucks and equipment, with some staff, went through the 'sausage machine' and opened temporarily in Bayeux, France, on 30 August 1944. Its contingent of twenty-two PMs went by air, in an RAF Dakota, flying from Northolt. Helen Cargill comments, 'Never before had so many "Dick Turpins" been seen on any airfield and we caused quite a stir … The sun was shining and it was a perfect day for our flight, which took two hours.'

Christina Watson (Mrs Hunter), one of the sisters travelling to join No 8 RAF General Hospital, remembers wearing battledress and sitting on her camp kit on the floor of the Dakota. She too writes of the sunlight, which showed up 'many wrecked ships and plenty of debris floating' in the Channel below. When they reached the airstrip near Bayeux, she heard a sergeant exclaim, 'Heavens, they've sent women!'

No 8 RAFGH, despite its impressive title, turned out to be six marquees in an orchard, with sisters accommodated in smaller tents in an adjoining field. Christina Watson found that, 'Water was in short supply, a tanker came twice a day and filled our buckets. Food was mainly white bread (so white it looked bleached – and was supplied by the Americans) – and corned beef just as it came from the tin, or fried.'

The hospital had ten wards, each with twenty beds. All of them were soon filled by patients 'pleased to have proper beds and sheets. We had started to use penicillin – what a wonder drug that was!'

As the nurses soon discovered, some of their sleeping tents were less than waterproof – the occupants came to breakfast looking as if they'd just washed their hair. They remedied the problem by sleeping with towels for turbans. They also resorted to wellington boots to combat the mud. They did their own washing, while a mobile laundry dealt with hospital linen and patients' clothing.

Helen Cargill felt the people of Normandy were 'not at first amicably disposed towards the British'. This was partly because of the heavy bombing they had endured, and partly because the Germans had treated them well, had plenty of money to spend and gave sweets to children – largesse which the impecunious, sweet-rationed Brits could not match.

One night Helen woke to hear peculiar noises which turned out to be a horse sniffing round her tent – farm animals shared the orchard. Apples and mushrooms grew there too, a welcome addition to the dreary diet of bread and bully beef, and farmers' wives sometimes gave flowers to brighten the hospital. Though social life was minimal, off-duty one could walk in fields and country lanes, and another small blessing was a generator which powered both lights and steriliser – and an iron! It did not, however, supply heat and when the nights grew cold paraffin stoves warmed the marquee wards. A bucket of water placed on top of each stove by night sisters as they came on duty allowed a mug of hot water for each patient's shave next morning.

The cold prevented Christina Watson from sleeping, but 'my "great treat" came when the theatre instruments were unwrapped – they came in large sacks, padded with shavings and straw. I thought this the best bed I ever had, and so warm!'

No 8 RAFGH had been near Bayeux for six weeks when came the exciting news of the liberation of Brussels and the unit prepared for a move to a proper hospital in Belgium. Matron Cargill and her nurses travelled to Brussels by air, at first sharing hospital facilities with an MFH and an Army general hospital. However, the number of army casualties far exceeded those of the RAF, so in October the PMs 'quite cheerfully packed up their wards for the second time' and moved to L'Hôpital St Gilles on the outskirts of the city – the same hospital where the British heroine Nurse Edith Cavell hid prisoners during the Great War. Earlier in the Second World War it had been used by the Luftwaffe and some of the beds still displayed the names of captured British pilots. The Germans' haste to evacuate had caused them to abandon much of their equipment – the operating theatre still bore evidence of the last operation to be performed, and bottles of three-star French brandy displayed labels stamped 'German Army Stores. Commercial sale forbidden.' Sister Eve Loxston (Mrs Hall) took one of these bottles home with her when she flew back for some Christmas leave. She adds:,

> One of the sisters always called out 'Hello darlings' when she came on duty. When an air raid was on and the flying bombs started coming over, the patients would say, 'We can't have these darlings frightened by the doodlebugs!' They would then break into song so that the sisters, busy with the dressings, would not hear the sound of the bombing outside.

Whenever she hears the voice of Edith Piaff singing 'La Vie en Rose', it still reminds her of those times.

Living under the path of the V1 and, later, the V2 rockets could be nerve-wracking. The sisters knew very well that the missiles were heading for their homeland, and every now and then one of the rockets failed and came down over Belgium or Holland. The night of 21 December 1944 was one of those 'noisy nights' when a flying bomb landed on a tenement block not far from St Gilles and No 8 RAFGH took in many of the casualties. They themselves escaped with only slight injury to two sisters, plus the shattering of several windows – a nuisance in mid-winter, with glass hard to come by in war-torn Europe.

Meanwhile, No 50 MFH, with Fluffy Ogilvie and Mollie Giles on its staff, had been augmented by the arrival of PMs Ellen Robison and Mary Griffiths. During the long and terrible battle for Caen they had been at Camilly, close enough to hear the noise of guns, rockets and aircraft, and at night the skies seemed on fire. Many severe burns cases came in, as Fluffy recalled:

> Part of the treatment was to cover the affected areas, after initial cleansing, with a very thick application of Tulle Gras, impregnated with an antibiotic, then the limbs and body, if necessary, encased in a loose plaster. This was more efficient than anything else in our field conditions for their subsequent journey by air.

When thunderstorms kept air ambulances away, burns patients encased in plaster lay waiting in the tents for days. One day, to their horror, the nurses saw maggots crawling from the plaster on a man's leg. They decided to remove the plaster and reapply the dressings, but to their surprise the healing process was well begun. It continued so after the patient returned to hospital in Britain.

At the end of August, 50 MFH moved through the 'liberated' city of Caen, where bulldozers had cleared a route through the rubble left by the bombing. Whole streets lay in shattered mounds littered with the charred remains of German equipment and dead pets. Human casualties had been removed by burial squads before the convoys went through, but the stench of death was still heavy in the air. Further on, in Paris, three days after General de Gaulle led in the Allied forces, liberation celebrations were still in full swing. The nurses all enjoyed being greeted, kissed and fêted by so many friendly, happy people, laughing through tears of joy and relief.

They pushed on, heading north in stages, opening up their hospital to deal with casualties, speeding them on their way and then packing up to move again. At Eindhoven, in Holland, the MFH housed itself for the first time in a proper building – St Joseph's Hospital, one of the most modern civilian hospitals in Europe, where they were joined by the Canadian-staffed 52 MFH. The two units had been leap-frogging each other across France and now, to their mutual pleasure, they were to work in close harmony. The building had been untouched by the bombing and street-fighting, and the MFH remained there over the winter.

Before long, local nurses and VADs swelled the strength. One of the Dutch nurses spoke fluent German, which was a great help in dealing with the fifty-five German patients who had become prisoners of war and were kept under guard. Fluffy Ogilvie enjoyed being back in a proper hospital, walking along solid corridors and tending patients in clean, well-equipped wards – and sleeping in a real bed again. They made friends with the Dutch people and at times they took in Dutch patients, including two boys peppered with burns that glowed in the dark – they had been playing near a sulphur bomb when it exploded.

One of the Dutch helpers, an attractive young person who spoke perfect English, told of escaping through the German lines with only the clothes she stood up in. She made many friends among the Allied personnel – until the day she was uncovered as a German spy. A complete PMRAFNS uniform had gone missing and when the girl was arrested the military police found a quantity of money in different currencies, hidden in her mattress.

Over that winter, while the battle front advanced ever deeper into Germany, nursing staff had time to relax at the RAF Club. Celebrities paid morale-boosting visits. There was even skating on a frozen lake. And at Christmas the two MFHs threw a party for 200 Dutch children, saving rations for weeks to supply them all with sacks bulging with toys, chocolate, wooden clogs and rosy apples. St Nicholas and his traditional assistant 'Black Peter' gave out the gifts; then the young guests enjoyed a Mickey Mouse film show before going down to the dining room for a feast.

Last salute from the Luftwaffe

On New Year's Day 1945, horror returned to both Brussels and Eindhoven when the Luftwaffe staged their last revengeful raids on nearby airfields.

In Brussels many of the PMs from No 8 RAFGH had attended a New Year's party at the Regent's Palace, Headquarters of 2nd Tactical Air Force. To Christina Watson it seemed 'a very splendid place – and food likewise, and plenty of champagne – Air Marshal Cunningham made a speech where he likened it to the grand ball given on the eve of Waterloo.' The likeness deepened when the Luftwaffe struck before dawn next morning.

By that time Monica Railton Jones was working with No 1 Casualty Air Evacuation Unit, sited near the airfield at Evere, in Brussels. 'On New Year's morning we had a surprise raid by German Junkers 88, who strafed the airfield just as we were entering the mess for breakfast. We had no breakfast that day but all got rapidly into the vehicles and went to the airfield …'

At the hospital in the city, Christina Watson and her colleagues 'worked all day and into the night in both theatres [while] minor injuries were treated in the corridor, like a casualty department … The Luftwaffe did not return again.'

Similarly, the airborne attack on Eindhoven caused an influx of casualties at St Joseph's Hospital – eighty-two of them within the first hour; the chapel which was used to receive them soon filled with stretchers and Fluffy Ogilvie walked with the surgeon as he made quick decisions on who to treat first, who could wait, and who, sadly, had to be passed by. 'Everyone gave a hand. The aircraftmen who were not medical orderlies were a tremendous help … One of my most vivid memories was seeing them continuously mopping up blood …'

To their amazement, on 2 January Fluffy Ogilvie and Mollie Giles learned that their names had appeared in the New Year's Honours List. Both of them had been awarded the MBE for their work in Normandy. Soon afterwards, VIPs including Air Marshal Sir Harold Whittingham, Director General of RAF Medical Services, with Matron-in-Chief PMRAFNS Miss Gladys Taylor, arrived at the hospital. Fluffy was not impressed: 'We didn't take too kindly to officialdom after all we had been through. Red tape in our lives had gone by the board. However, we were determined to put on a dignified performance.' After months in battle-dress while under canvas, they dressed up in their smartest white uniforms with their blue capes and flowing white head-dress with RAF wings at the back. The visit went well but, as the VIPs were leaving, a huge truck went by carrying some Canadian aircrew who called out, 'Hiya, Fluffy!' Matron-in-chief was not amused!

Endgame in Europe

Inexorably, the Allies marched on towards the Rhine and beyond, while from the east the Russians advanced, both forces closing in on Berlin and the bunker where Hitler lurked. Following the troops, 50 MFH convoyed deeper and deeper into Germany. Fluffy Ogilvie enjoyed being under canvas again: 'We began to see columns of civilians, mostly just walking with their belongings, but some had various forms of transport. This time there were no waves or smiles …' At the Rhine their means of crossing was a pontoon bridge, but they had to wait as a long column of German PoWs trudged over the river, making towards them. 'We stood by the ambulance in complete silence. I seemed to be witnessing inevitable despair. We waited until the last prisoners and their guards were over [then] our convoy started moving … it was quite an historic moment, crossing this famous river …' On they drove, past burnt-out German vehicles and gutted buildings. They reached their next intended site numbed by so much devastation, and once again set up their unit. They found their workload lighter than expected – by that time the Allies were making good headway and, with victory near, the human toll had lessened.

The next advance took the MFH to Celle, 20 miles north of Hanover and near to Belsen. The PMs themselves didn't visit the detention camp, but the medical officers did. Just four days after liberation the scene was horrendous: 'The dead were still being buried and hundreds of emaciated victims were near death. Dirt and excreta everywhere … stench overpowering …' Accustomed as they were to witnessing horror, the MOs came back physically sickened.

The strongest of Belsen's former prisoners were to be flown to hospital in Belgium. They arrived at the airstrip in ambulances and medical orderlies carefully set the stretchers on the grass near the runway. That was when Fluffy became aware of the overpowering stench and remembered how pilots had said the stink of Belsen sometimes got into their planes if they flew low over the camp. She felt stunned. These tragic people looked like old men. Their eyes haunted her, staring and almost lifeless, without emotion. She wasn't even sure whether they knew what was happening. She did give them the odd drink and saw to their comfort, but what she afterwards remembered with great sadness was that she didn't smile at any of them. Perhaps she was, this time, just too shocked to react in her usual cheery way. When the last of them had been loaded, she and the others simply stood and watched until the plane took off. They were deeply affected, feeling helpless.

While they stayed in Celle, the war ended. A corporal rushed past the tent, shouting, 'It's all over!' and everyone became very emotional. But after all they had seen and experienced it was hard to take in the reality of peace at last.

Number 50 MFH moved on again to Luneberg Heath, to Kreussen, near Fassberg. While working there, Fluffy was able to return by air to Holland and visit Flushing, where her husband Donald had died. The area had been deliberately flooded as a defence against the German takeover and they were taken in a little motor-boat along drowned streets to the hill where the cemetery lay like an island. She placed 'some flowers on the grave we had come to find'.

After only two weeks at Fassberg they moved to Schleswig, on the Baltic. The date was 1 June 1945, just less than a year since they landed in Normandy.

The MFH finally disbanded in April 1946 and Fluffy Ogilvie flew home to her next posting, at RAF Cosford. Weeks later she was off to Palestine, then Egypt and Aden. It was in Egypt that she met Major Bower, the man who was to become her second husband and the cause of her leaving the PMRAFNS in 1949.

Matron Helen Cargill returned to Ely from Brussels in May 1945 and her career continued. In 1948 she became the Service's fifth matron-in-chief.

As for No 8 RAFGH, it left Brussels in September 1945 and settled to care for post-war RAF personnel from a base in Rinteln, in the valley of the River Weser, not far from the Pied Piper town of Hamelin (which, happily, was untouched by bombs).

In the eleven months between D-Day, 6 June 1944, and VE Day, 8 May 1945, the RAF evacuated 77,348 patients to the UK from the Continent. Figures for 1944, the busiest casevac year, show that across all the theatres of war almost 300,000 patients were evacuated by the RAF, all without a single flying accident.

The war with Germany was over. In the Far East, however, the war against Japan had still some months to go.

11

Dressing Down

In January 1945 the Nursing Advisory Board proposed a new beret-type hat instead of the unpopular 'storm-cap', and on the wards button-through coat-dresses should replace the old, gathered-waist style. However, PMs in the Far East had already made their own, unauthorised, adjustments.

In 1944, the new Chief Principal Matron (the first to hold that post) had arrived at Chittagong to be shown around by Senior Sister Jessie Higgins: 'We'd all got into khaki trousers and kerchiefs and what have you, and she was appalled to see nursing officers dressed like that.' The visitor particularly wanted to know why no sister was wearing mosquito boots. Higgie had tried them and:

> they left you red raw – they came right up your thighs! … So I said, 'Well, ma'am, I'd like you to try those boots.' (Cheeky, really; other girls were saying, 'Don't you say a word!') But of course she couldn't even wear them for one night, so that was forgotten.

Rona Black had had a visitor, too. Writing again to her mother, she enclosed copies of some photos, saying, 'If you are half as amused as I am about this, you'll be sure to have a good laugh.' It seems that a certain Wing Commander Webb, of the Inter-service Research and Development Section (Clothing and Equipment), had been tasked with accoutring some Canadian military nurses for the Far East. In order to observe conditions and to ascertain what the well-dressed nursing sister should wear while in India, he visited 62 MFH and took three pictures as examples: Rona holding up 1) a scuffed mosquito boot, 2) a pair of khaki slacks and 3) a crumpled khaki dress. She herself wears an unironed khaki drill dress, with huge black buttons and four bulging patch pockets, fetchingly accessorised with puttees and black lace-up shoes!

Calcutta

A signal dated December 1944 ordered Jessie Higgins to report to the Principal Medical Officer (PMO) at Calcutta. She flew down to the city, where the RAF had taken over:

> this huge old Indian school. Huge ceilings, went up for ever … there wasn't a bed, wasn't a chair, wasn't a sheet … The PMO said to me, 'It's all yours. If you go to the

> accounts department, they'll give you the money and you just go down to the souk, the market, and buy all the things you want.' I had to employ all the domestic staff; I had to get the nursing officers' mess ready … I don't know how I did it.

No 9 RAFGH Calcutta, as it became, took over from an army transit hospital sited in La Martinière School. This one-time palace, inevitably filthy and impossible to clean, had wards opening off one another and some lavatories accessible only via the tiny kitchen. A single sphygmomanometer (for measuring blood pressure) and one inaccurate weighing machine totalled its clinical equipment, while laboratory facilities comprised one small room with a sink, a water tap and a partitioned shelter containing bucket latrines. The carefully locked 'cholera cabinet' held nothing but button-cleaning materials. And this hospital was due to take all RAF patients from nearby units on New Year's Day! Undaunted, Jessie Higgins set about the task.

In the midst of her labours, still in her working khaki, she had to hurry to the station to meet a contingent of eighty sisters arriving from Bombay. They had been cooped up on a train for four days, wearing their heavy white tricoline. Higgie:

> knew exactly what they'd all been through. But no matron with them. And no letter from Air Ministry saying, 'You're to take over and do the best you can, Miss Higgins,' not a word … I gave them the first day off, but said, 'The next day it's sleeves up and just see what you've got to do.' But they were marvellous! Every one of them. There they were up to their eyebrows in soap-suds, and making up beds, and there was every Tom, Dick and Harry from the market bringing in all the stuff …
>
> Meantime … the doctors and ancillary staff, quartermaster … they all came out in a bunch. Fortunately I knew the physician very well, I'd been his ward sister for a couple of years, and the other chap – a VD man!

With Christmas only a few days away and the hospital due to open at New Year, members of the Aircrew Club in Calcutta asked permission to invite all the sisters to a dance on Boxing Night. Senior Sister Higgins replied:

> 'If they can get the hospital ready they can come.' Well, they worked like Trojans, so that by Christmas Day we could have taken people in, all the beds were made … mind you, they only had sheets on them, no blankets or anything … Must have been over three hundred patients we actually took in on New Year's Day, from all the different army hospitals – there was the Indian Army Service, and the Army Nursing Service, and a lot of ratings, Naval people …. they came from all these odd hospitals all round Calcutta … by five o'clock that night there they all were. The doctors had never nursed anyone with dysentery in their lives … And of course the sisters, most of them, had never been out of England before, let alone the Far East. All went down with snips and snows and tummy ache.

RAF hospitals, South East Asia Command

As the Allies pushed the enemy back through Burma, new casualties demanded attention and longer-term cases needed beds. Apart from Calcutta, three more RAF General Hospitals opened in 1945. Of these, No 11 settled in Allahabad, No 12 in Cawnpore and No 10 at Karachi, surrounded by the Sind Desert. As the only European hospital for some 100 miles, No 10 RAFGH boasted a female wing, including a maternity ward, for servicewomen and families.

More nursing sisters came to augment the staffs of all three units. Among a large party who arrived aboard *Orontes* was Maureen Lumley: 'We had three Matrons with us. One went with about forty-five sisters to Karachi; another took a similar number to Cawnpore; the rest of us went to Calcutta, by train.'

Jessie Higgins was still acting matron in Calcutta. She never did discover what had delayed the new matron and sisters:

> whether they'd been held up, or torpedoed … The hospital had been open about five weeks before they arrived … and [the incoming matron] gave me hell because she had been told that *she* was going to open No 9 RAF Hospital. She really was unkind to all of us – all the girls that were there then. Then she brought this whole bunch more out with her. All the girls that were there with me were intended for all the field hospitals, not for the general hospital … PMO was furious about it all. He asked me if I'd be happier going back to Chittagong and I said, 'Oh, yes, please, let me go back to the jungle!' So he said, 'I think we'll just inform matron that you're being posted.' The joke was … news got back to Air Ministry that the hospital had been opened by a very junior sister … Nothing to do with me, I'd been posted there to do it.

Good news from Europe

In a letter dated May 1945, Rona Black told her mother of reaction to the victory in Europe:

> Everyone went quite mad. But the war out here means so much more we couldn't be over-enthusiastic – and we don't see an early settlement, either … What relieves us most is the fact that all those who are left are safe. It must be grand to be at home at this time.

Another MFH, No 67, had settled just off the west coast of Burma at a place named Kyaukpyu, situated on Ramree Island. One of the sisters who served with it (now Mrs Joy Knowles, of New Zealand) remembers they were miles away from the fighting but 'close enough to feel the earth rumble and see the explosion into the sky of flaming mud'.

RAF Corporal Denis Winstone, a patient stricken with a tropical wasting disease, took away more lyrical memories:

> One of the nursing sisters arranged for a dozen or so stretcher cases to be taken down to the nearby beach and placed in a circle on the sand. On that warm moonlit tropical night we lay beneath the stars with land crabs scurrying around us and fireflies and other insects flitting round the hurricane lamp. In the centre of the circle the nursing sister sat with her portable gramophone, winding the handle … I can only remember one of the 78rpm records she played. It was 'The Dance of the Sugar Plum Fairy'.

Meanwhile, 61 MFH, still in Chittagong, now had the benefit of eight PMs on its staff. Jessie Higgins was relieved to be back with them, though the food was awful: 'Corned beef came squelching out of tins … I lived on mangoes.' Her friend 'Tommy' Thomas (Mrs McGregor) remembers a night when 'the makeshift cook-house went up in flames, after which the cook managed with two sheets of corrugated iron over the stove – he really did wonders with bully beef every day, no fresh vegetables and very little fresh fruit'. She has never forgotten the wonderful boys whom she met and nursed, especially those who were never to return to their distant homes. 'We did have some very ill boys,' Jessie Higgins agrees. 'Jaundice was one of the main things. And typhoid. We even had smallpox. I don't know how many times I was vaccinated in those two years.'

Into Burma …

With the war front moving ever southward, clearing Burma of its occupying enemy, the MFH expected to be moved any day. The signal came in July 1945, summoning Jessie Higgins and surgeon Peter Greening to Rangoon:

> That was the first time we realised the war was nearly over, because Rangoon had been absolutely saturated with Japs. Off we went, in an old Dakota, sitting on the floor of the aircraft, sliding about. It took about three hours, and we had to land on Mingaladon, which we had been bombing for months. Poor aircraft came down, in and out of pot-holes …
>
> We arrived and, of course, nobody expected us – everywhere you went, nobody expected you. Peter and I didn't know one end of Rangoon from another, but we were told just go out and find a building, suitable for a hospital. We finally settled for a building without a roof, but it had water and electricity.

When the rest of the unit arrived, they needed accommodation:

> We found four beautiful houses out on Lake Victoria, which had belonged to the Directors and local Chairman of the Burmese Oil Company, but they'd all been stripped. No bolts, no locks, no taps, no toilet seats … Hadn't been there more than a month than a new Commander-in-Chief was posted out and he liked our house,

> so we had to go into horrible little places, like cheap four-roomed bungalows, nothing in them. Just snakes.

How she detested snakes!

> Oh, snakes until they came out of your ears … so bad in Rangoon, mainly because of the monsoon drains … So it was decided we'd have to have a crew of coolies to come and catch them. They had to chop their heads off, lay out the rest of the body and at night the sergeant or whoever would go round and count them all and pay them whatever it was – about 1*s* 3*d* [about 6p] a head.
>
> And then we had the trouble with the dacoits [robbers] … looting was terrible. There was never any glass anywhere, just iron bars across the windows. You'd lie in your bed at night, four or five to a room … and all these mosquito nets and wretched camp beds and things … you'd lie in bed and you'd see these poles coming through the window, with a knife, and a hook, and they'd pinch anything they could pick up. We never attempted to move. It really was not funny.

War's end

In the closing stages of the war, two new MFHs formed part of the Allied 'Tiger Force', which was preparing to invade Japan. However, as their convoy reached the Admiralty Islands, news came of the atom bomb strikes on Hiroshima and Nagasaki. Japan's subsequent capitulation ended the need for invasion and Tiger Force separated back into its individual units. The two MFHs, Nos 80 and 81, were diverted, one to Hong Kong, the other to Singapore, to give medical aid to released prisoners of war and to the forces who were mopping up the last of the Japanese stragglers.

No 81 MFH was the first RAF hospital in Singapore, the embryo for the later station sick quarters at RAF Seletar. No 80, with two nursing sisters on its ration strength, took over the Central British School in Hong Kong. The school building was relatively clean (with 'only slight insect infestation'), but stripped of all but its basic fabric – looters had removed all fixtures, including floor tiles – they had even taken the plaster off the walls. Apart from that, writes Squadron Leader (Rtd) Cedric Rosenvinge, who was Deputy CO of 5358 Wing, RAF Airfield Construction Branch, the place was in 'a fairly clean condition'. Somehow, No 80 MFH swiftly opened adequate wards for all ranks of air personnel, but the senior of the two sisters:

> was not entirely satisfied with the feat and asked the Chief Executive Officer for some white sheets, only to be curtly informed that there weren't any, but she could have as many service-issue blankets as she wished. That was not good enough for the lady and her powers of persuasion prevailed! … The Senior Administration officer somehow or another produced, within twenty-four hours, enough lily white sheets to complete bedding arrangements to the Senior Nursing Officer's satisfaction!

Troops in Burma rejoiced at the announcement of Victory in Japan, as Jessie Higgins remembers well: with thousands of drunken men out celebrating, she and the other PMs in Rangoon thought it prudent to lock themselves in! Later, though, they experienced the other side of the coin:

> the joy and heartbreak of nursing returned Prisoners of War. They were flown in from all camps and were examined to decide if they were fit to travel on to Calcutta … I hope never to see such a thing again as one could never forget such wickedness and cruelty to human beings.

For some ex-prisoners the long sea voyage home proved curative; for others it added torment. Fran Keech (Mrs Judson), who was stationed in Aden on VJ Day, went aboard:

> the first hospital ship bringing home the very sick servicemen, many of whom had suffered so cruelly under the Japanese … These men were too ill to be flown home and needed time to readjust to normal living again. The mental strain [they] had endured was plainly evident and quite a number had to be warded in our hospital … Normal diet was impossible after so many months of near starvation.

When the MFH in Rangoon disbanded in the closing months of 1945, Jessie Higgins was posted to Karachi. Care of RAF patients in Burma devolved upon a new unit, RAFH Mingaladon, where Matron Collie Knox and eight sisters led a nursing team which included Japanese prisoners-of-war acting as orderlies. Posted in from Calcutta in January 1946, Maureen Lumley found the Japanese orderlies strange, especially one named 'Son of Heaven': 'It was odd to call, "Son of Heaven, come here!"' She asked him to wash a patient and returned to find Son of Heaven washing the floor. When she tried gestures, he started to wash the bedstead – he couldn't seem to understand that a human being might need cleaning!

With little or no electricity, the PMs often worked by the feeble light of hurricane lamps. In the monsoon their rain capes came in handy as drapes across window openings and they went 'improperly dressed' – in all the humidity starched white caps ended up drooping comically round one's ears, so they were discarded except during panic moments when a senior matron loomed. In a quiet period, Maureen and her friend Elsie Lay planned a treat for the patients:

> Elsie made peppermint creams with sugar and peppermint oil, dipped into melted ration chocolate. These were moderately edible, but when I attempted to make toffee it set hard on the plate … in trying to break it, the plate smashed before the toffee!

However, a large mango tree grew outside their mess, bearing fruit 'so lush and juicy that the only way to enjoy eating them with decorum was in the bath! … We were really very happy there,' Maureen adds. 'I wrote glowing letters home, apparently. It was all quite an adventure. When you think back on it, we were very lucky.'

Early the following year, the two confectionery-makers went to Singapore, where they helped to open a sick quarters beside Changi jail, the notorious former prison camp. Together with 63 MFH they formed the nucleus of what became the well-known RAF Hospital Changi. The arrival of a matron and a team of sisters allowed Maureen Lumley and Elsie Lay to return to England.

In Burma today, the Second World War cemetery at Chittagong contains the graves of over 700 soldiers from Commonwealth countries and Japan, while near Kohima, north of Imphal, stands the monument which reads, 'When you go home, tell them of us and say: For your tomorrow, we gave our today.'

Land of the rising sun

Immediately the war ended, British Commonwealth forces arrived in Japan to oversee demilitarisation and to repatriate prisoners of war. Air force personnel from Britain, Australia, India and New Zealand formed BCAir – British Commonwealth (Air) – with squadrons stationed at Miho, Bofu and Iwakuni. The main BCAir hospital, at Iwakuni on Honshu Island (only a few miles from Hiroshima), was staffed by all ranks of the RAF Medical Service, including a strong contingent of PMs. A Royal Australian Air Force (RAAF) base at American-controlled Okinawa provided a stopping point for medical teams flying ex-prisoners of war to Changi hospital, where they would be assessed and, wherever possible, put on hospital ships.

The BCAir hospital dealt with accident victims, too. On a Saturday in June 1946, a military jeep crashed on the north-western side of Honshu Island, badly injuring an army officer. He was taken to the SSQ at RAF Miho and signals went out for an aircraft and medical escort to convey him to the BCAir hospital. The aircrew assigned to this duty had just completed a long flying day. Instead of enjoying a good meal, they had to make do with a few sandwiches rushed to them when they briefly landed at Iwakuni to pick up Sister L.M. 'Sally' Blaen and an RAAF surgeon. During the flight to Miho, Sally Blaen was invited to take the co-pilot's seat, where she became acquainted with the pilot, Flight Lieutenant Bill Drinkell. He takes up the story: 'I don't think she was much impressed by the dishevelled appearance of the crew, nor by the answer to her enquiry as to when we would arrive – "The sandwiches are finished, so we must be almost there."' He, however, admired her aplomb as they landed in the dark on a poorly equipped airfield, and also the calm, efficient way she handled her patient. Their friendship developed from that beginning and on Easter Sunday 1947 Sally Blaen became Mrs Drinkell.

Matron 'Tilly' Tillbrook and Sisters Pat O'Kelly, Beryl Irving and Doris Stanford (Mrs Kent) were in the China seas aboard the troopship *Dilwara* when a typhoon struck. The storm hurled the PMs out of their bunks but fortunately caused few casualties. At Iwakuni they discovered that the sisters' mess had not been completed; so they stayed in the officers' mess, with Japanese 'room girls' to tend them. Doris Stanford was particularly impressed by the baths – 'miniature swimming pools … we were rinsed clean by the room girls, with additional uncontaminated water'. She found the devastated Hiroshima an awe-inspiring sight, but elsewhere Japan remained a tourist paradise. Off duty the PMs went skiing, toured beauty spots and temples, enjoyed a Sukiyaki party and marvelled at Mount Fuji's 'glistening white snow cap on a spring morning with a profusion of cherry blossom surrounding the lake … unbelievably beautiful'. These highlights are still vivid, though 'the more mundane routine of night duty and hard work on the wards is a fading memory'.

In May 1947, eight more PMs bound for Japan shared a cabin aboard the *Empress of Scotland*. Mary Williams (Mrs Hancock) recounts how she and Angela O'Brien were later detached from Iwakuni to RAF Miho, where the young pilots christened her 'Mary the Matron of Miho'. Male orderlies did the routine work while the sisters:

> gave injections, did dressings and other advanced treatments, plus all the administrative work … The busiest time was when we had an outbreak of Japanese encephalitis, caused by a special type of mosquito. The patients were very ill and needed a great deal of nursing, though thankfully most of them survived.

During a party to mark the departure of one of the squadrons, the Indian officers' mess caught fire and the PMs 'had to return to sick quarters to deal with very merry smoke-inhalers'.

Hundreds of Japanese worked on the station as personal servants and if Mary Williams rested on her bed in an afternoon she would wake to find her own little Japanese maid fanning her very gently. This treasure also 'invisibly mended everything within sight'.

The BCAir hospital at Iwakuni closed in March 1948, but during the Korean War both the hospital and the RAF base reactivated from October 1951 to March 1955.

Loose ends

The letters that have flowed in as contributions to this history bear witness that, fifty years on, many patients still gratefully remember the care and kindness they received in RAF hospitals during the war years. One of those patients, John P. Soltau, tells of a lengthy stay in Halton after he was shot down over the Channel in August 1943. One of his enduring memories is of being taken out in an oversized wicker 'pram': 'These vehicles enabled relations, friends and staff to take out bed-ridden patients for "walks" in the fresh air. The destination was either a cafe in Wendover or the nearby woods, depending who was taking the patient out!'

Later, Mr Saltau spent some while at the RAF Rehabilitation Unit at Hoylake:

> In the spring of 1944 some wounded exchange prisoners of war came back to the UK through a scheme arranged by the Red Cross. Most were amputees and it was amazing to note the quality of some home-made artificial limbs … made by DIY enthusiasts in the prisoner of war camps, using bits of scrap metal, beds, bedsprings, Red Cross parcel cases, odd nails, etc. … They included intricate knee-locking and other devices … some of the patients were not too happy when they received the Roehampton standard issue limbs!

The RAF considered rehabilitation one of the most important factors in effecting a patient's swift return to health and duty. A rehab centre at Blackpool dealt with airmen; Hoylake looked after airmen aircrew; Cosford took in technicians and, after Torquay was bombed in 1942, the officers' medical rehabilitation unit (MRU) transferred to Loughborough College. WAAF nursing orderly Corporal Louisa 'Pat' Hill, who worked with physiotherapists in the early mobilisation room, remembers that this former PT centre had excellent facilities. She recalls some famous sportsmen who acted as instructors: 'Raich Carter, the footballer, took groups of "leg patients" for walking and leg movements and Dan Maskell, the tennis coach, was in charge of arms and shoulders when the patients were ready to progress on to more advanced movement.'

When Loughborough reverted to civilian use in 1947 another MRU, at Collaton Cross, took over its work; then in 1949 Headley Court opened. In its early days, it too boasted tennis ace Dan Maskell on its staff. (Many readers will remember Dan Maskell as a much-loved tennis commentator for the BBC.)

The RAF's skill in treating burns had borne fine fruit, thanks largely to the skill and insight of its chief consultant plastic surgeon (Sir) Archibald McIndoe. At the end of the war a network of specialised units existed across the UK, to which RAF specialists flew from Halton airfield to teach others the new skills and techniques. In his 'Short History' of PMRAFH Halton, Squadron Leader Richard Laurence retells some of the stories of those days:

> Patients were flown into Halton from all over the world … one DC3, laden with cargo, crashed in the woods behind the hospital. Staff rushed out to see the pilot, unharmed, dangling from a tree. What really drew their attention, however, was the cargo – several tons of then-rare oranges scattered around. Clear-up was achieved in record time! … When stores of olive oil (used in the treatment of scars) ran dry, fresh supplies were flown in by Mosquito bombers over the Atlantic Ocean from Canada … One extraordinary story is told, of a young USAF airman who was admitted with a live anti-aircraft cannon-shell embedded in his chest. The bomb disposal squad, duly called, could only offer soon-to-be-dispensed-with lead shielding. The patient survived and the defused cannon-shell became a memento for the brave surgeon.

The war hastened and improved diagnostic techniques for many diseases and conditions, especially the use of mass X-ray which, in the closing stages of the war, vastly increased the detection-rate for tuberculosis (TB). The disease proved rife among returning PoWs and in May 1945 RAFH St Athan made available sixty beds for TB cases, beginning a new specialism which lasted long after the war ended. When demand exceeded bed-space, further TB wards briefly opened at RAFH Church Village in Glamorgan. Such advances, accelerated by the demands the war had made on doctors, nurses and scientists, continued to bring benefits to humankind long after the peace was signed.

But not all wartime memories were of sickness, sadness and horror. Many nurses write of happier times – singing Christmas carols by lamplight, amid falling snow, magical even in wartime; others tell of tennis parties in the jungle, dances in the desert, and romance flourishing everywhere. Another theme is clothing – the difficulties of remaining starched and ladylike (as matron required) while scrubbing filthy rooms, coming under fire or facing freak weather conditions; and let us not forget the problematical hats – the storm caps, the bush hats, the fur-trimmed hoods for Iceland, the broad-brimmed white tropical felt with the RAF ribbon and, always, the cherished four-cornered 'Dick'.

Following a party, Beryl Chadney was forced to order a new quatrecorne as a matter of urgency because her own had been 'confiscated by air crew to drop over Germany'! Fran Keech's friend Jean heartily hated her 'Dick Turpin' and 'instead of wearing it square with the badge to view over the forehead, she had cut at least one inch off … to enable her to wear it on the back of her head'. As Fran and Jean sat on the train which would take them back to Yatesbury after leave, they were joined in the carriage by Matron-in-Chief Gladys Taylor, who was horrified by the sight of this mutilated and non-King's Regulation headgear. She leaned forward and adjusted it to sit on Jean's head 'in the correct manner, resulting in the two side corns resembling wings'. Poor Jean was confined to the mess until she had bought a new hat. 'You can well imagine the embarrassment she suffered,' says Fran, 'but the hilarity amongst the rest of us lasted for days.'

Jessie Higgins finally returned to England in January 1946, accompanying 'a very ill soldier with a cerebral tumour … Everyone looked grey, everything drab. And there was me, yellow as a guinea, having been on mepacrine for two and a half years!'

Left behind at Karachi, Rona Black heard that she had been awarded the ARRC – the equivalent of the DSO. She wrote home:

> Phew! I've been sitting up in bed thinking, this a.m., wondering if it's really me … The award has been given to all of us who came out and stood the test … Higgie and Lawford got theirs last time … I hadn't dared tell you that Higgie flew home ten days ago … I pictured you making your way to Air Ministry to ask why your daughter hadn't been included … Anyway, I'm off tomorrow. All my love. Rona.

Jessie Higgins and Rona Black both joined the PMRAFNS as regulars: 'Higgie' made the service her lifelong career, but Rona chose to leave after the war 'because there are so many other things which interest me'. As for the wartime reserve sisters, they were gradually demobbed and allowed to resume their interrupted lives. In 1947 Beryl Chadney took away a gratuity of £39, being £1 for each month of her war service as a sister with PMRAFNS(R).

For those who like statistics, the official history of the RAF Medical Service during the Second World War records that, at home in the UK, seven general hospitals and seventeen station hospitals offered over 6,000 beds. Most patients belonged to the RAF, next came the WAAF, but RAF hospitals also treated personnel from the Dominions and Allied nations, as well as those from the British Army and the Royal Navy. To take only one year and one hospital, Halton's records for 1945 reveal a total of 11,311 admissions, all but eight of them being air force personnel – the exceptions were a VAD and seven civilians.

For their wartime service, 145 members of the PMRAFNS won official honours and awards:

> No human praise can do justice to the debt we all owe to the nurses … Their skill, their care and their compassion for the sick and wounded, often under fire from the enemy and in conditions of great danger and hardship, were a real inspiration to the men and women they tended and worked with.

So wrote Britain's great war leader, Winston S. Churchill.

12

Empire's End

The war had brought a pause in the rising desire for independence among colonial countries, but when hostilities ended nationalist feelings began to resurface, sometimes with violent results. On a few days' leave from RAFGH Allahabad, Joyce Kellow (Mrs Wyatt) and Dot Ashley flew to Calcutta, where they visited the bazaar and had lunch at the then-famous Firpo's Hotel. As they left, they were confronted by the sight of thousands of angry Hindus:

> all shouting 'Jai Hind!' (Quit India!) and waving sticks … I said to Dot, 'Come on, we must fight our way through this mob.' We stepped out from Firpo's and walked through the moving wall of natives, waving our arms in a breast-stroke motion to force our way back to the YWCA … we were through before they had time to realise what was happening.

Having seen the appalling slums of the city, where people riddled with disease starved in hovels, the two PMs understood the anger they had witnessed.

That same mood caused native workers to strike, closing the airfield at Dumdum, so Joyce and Dot decided to take the train back to Allahabad – an eighteen-hour journey. That evening, in uniform, they went to the station in an open taxi:

> We were surrounded by a violent mob of rioting Hindus. Shouting 'Jai Hind', they stood on the running board of our taxi and spat on us … we were hit by stones … we lay face down on the floor of the taxi and thought we would be killed. I screamed at the driver of our taxi 'Jeldi Jao, Jeldi Jao!' which means 'Go quickly'. When the car moved, the rioting mob stepped back for fear of being run over. The taxi drove through the seething mass …
>
> The train for Allahabad was due to leave at 10 p.m., so we went to the ticket office – and found only enough money between us for one ticket! This was a minor problem I felt, having escaped with our lives. All night we travelled in the train, dozing fitfully. Next day, with no food or drink, we were silent and apprehensive. At midday a ticket collector approached our carriage. Dot locked herself in the latrine and I showed our one and only ticket! He nodded and departed. Later, when he returned, I hid in the latrine and Dot showed the same ticket! Thus we had yet another escape.

They arrived in Allahabad at 4 p.m., twenty-four hours absent without leave. Joyce envisaged being sent home in disgrace, or court-martialled. Instead, 'we saw Matron, Miss Minchin, running towards us … she hugged us with tears streaming down her face … they had heard about the riots in Calcutta and were certain that we were amongst those British who were murdered.'

Demobilisation called home all nursing sisters of the reserve, necessitating their replacement with members of the regular PMRAFNS. Thus, when on 12 August 1946 the MV *Georgic*, of the Cunard White Star line, departed Liverpool, it carried around 2,000 troops, officers, civilian workers and families, plus twenty PM sisters. One of them was Winifred Gardner (Mrs Penman), whose first impression was of the food aboard ship: 'luxury to have white bread rolls after years of eating wholesome (no doubt) but monotonous "utility" bread'.

They reached Bombay on 29 August and spent a night at Worli transit camp before setting off on the four-day rail journey to Karachi, four sisters and two armed escorts to each compartment, self-contained with toilet and washing facilities. They stopped at stations for most meals – fried eggs, bacon, chips and tea seemed to be the staple fare, be it breakfast, lunch or dinner – and they slept in bed-rolls while the train chugged on through the night. Winifred Gardner was fascinated by the changing scenery and the local fauna: 'water buffalo, kingfishers, peacocks, many strange and brightly coloured birds, but always the sweet cheeky sparrows … cows, goats and camels … primitive wells, waterwheels turned by yoked oxen, ancient wooden ploughs, washerwomen at the water's edge …' At the Braganza Hotel in Lahore they enjoyed 'the longest, most welcome shandy ever, followed by a BATH (pure joy!) and a good meal. 2nd Sept: Woke early to the sound of bells from passing bullock carts …'

Entraining once again that evening, with two armed sergeants for escort, they found the compartment filthy, so:

> we 'Dettol-ed' it from top to bottom before sitting down … Woke to find ourselves surrounded by grey sand, inside as well as outside! Everything was covered with a thin layer of it, and when we looked at one another we dissolved into hysterics! The sand had stuck to our moist faces and little rivers of sweat ran down … This was the Sind desert, which is always crossed in daylight, never at night for fear of raiding tribesmen.

Winifred thought the sisters' mess at No 10 RAFGH Karachi delightful. The PMs lived in eight-room bungalows, each room having a bed with mosquito net and its own bathroom – stone floor, cold tap, tin bath, basin and wash-stand, plus 'thunder-box'. Bearers, dhobi-wallahs and sweepers looked after the practicalities, and armed guards patrolled at night. The hospital spread over a wide, sandy area, each ward fringed by a veranda; the families' ward and maternity unit stood a few hundred yards away, near the main road. Patients came from nearby RAF units, the Black Watch (the garrison regiment at the time), and the Indian Army, with some Royal Navy officers, plus service families and British, French and Dutch civilians.

RAF men John Barrow and Reg Wheeler, six months apart, underwent serious mastoid operations in RAFGH Karachi. Both write with high praise for the care they received. 'Sisters and nurses did a wonderful job in the conditions, always cheerful and always had time for a chat,' says Reg Wheeler, while John Barrow remembers an occasion when two intrepid sisters accepted a dare and 'took a bike ride to a small village called Mango-Pir. There a pit of sacred crocodiles existed and each day a goat was killed, skinned, and thrown to the crocodiles.' He adds warm thanks for the 'dedication, high standard and professionalism which made it possible for me to be writing this letter today', though in fact his wife wrote the letter for him, since Mr Barrow is now registered blind.

In those days, says Evelyn Addison (Mrs Glen), despite:

> the awful disease, lack of hygiene, flies and incessant heat, we sisters were really able to nurse the patients, 'spongeing' to get high temperatures down ... there was very little air conditioning and few antibiotics, and so many snakes in the grass at night that on night duty we had to be escorted across the gardens with a torch light. We wore long white stockings, a white overall and big RAF cap.

While at Karachi, Evelyn met and fell in love with a pilot who had earlier flown many missions over Germany. 'I had barely finished my first year in India and had to ask the Matron for permission to marry ... She said, "Do you realise you are going to marry a man who has the highest bar bill in the Officers' Mess?!" However, the marriage lasted fifty-one years ...'

One by one, the RAF hospitals in India closed. MFHs dispersed as soon as their last patients were transferred to one of the general hospitals. In turn, the hospitals in Allahabad, Calcutta and Cawnpore gradually emptied their beds, posted their RAF staffs elsewhere, and handed over to Indian control during 1946. That left only No 10 RAFGH, Karachi. But Pakistan Independence Day came on 15 August 1947 and by the end of the year British withdrawal was well under way. 'We were privileged to see history in the making – the end of the British Raj and the birth of a new nation – Pakistan,' says Winifred Gardner (Mrs Penman). She and fellow PMs Mary Coffey and 'Greg' Gregory, left Karachi on 5 January 1948 and sailed for home aboard the *El Nil* (a yacht once owned by King Fuad of Egypt).

This was not the end of the RAF in India, however. The sick quarters at RAF Mauripur, near Karachi, became an invaluable staging post on the long-haul aeromedical flights which were soon to send PMs winging round the world.

The promised land

For half a century Palestine had been troubled by unrest between resident Arabs and the Jews who wished to be allowed to return to their historic homeland. While the country remained under British mandate, strenuous efforts to reconcile the two sides all ended in failure. From 1945 the revelation of the horrors of the German death camps caused fresh demands for the creation of a Jewish homeland, and when the area erupted once again into violence Britain asked the United Nations to find a solution.

The original RAF hospital in Palestine had closed in 1940, but a new unit, transferring from Tripoli, opened at Tel Litwinsky, near Jaffa (Tel Aviv), in February 1944. One of its wartime patients, Geoffrey Hobbs, had been taken to the army hospital at Nicosia, in Cyprus, after his 'two-fan, two-place harasser ship' crashed in flames. He was badly burned while rescuing his pilot and, after a couple of weeks in an army hospital at Nicosia, was scheduled to be transferred to Tel Litwinsky, which had a special burns unit complete with saline baths. 'Came the day and I was put on a Dakota accompanied by an elderly [army] nurse who, shaking, asked me if I was all right whilst four soldiers held my stretcher down as we took off …' Travelling via Beirut, he eventually reached No 3 RAFGH Tel Litwinsky, where he was transferred to a stretcher trolley:

> Running along the path between Nissen hut wards, one of the front wheels left the path, the trolley tipped over and shot me off into the bushes. The orderlies were very concerned … but despite my initial groan I took it in good humour. Why not? In a few minutes I was to be at the Burns Centre with its soothing facilities … [but] pinned to the door was a notice 'Closed for re-decoration'.

Despite this bad start, Mr Hobbs evinces his life-long admiration for the treatment he received from 'those angels of mercy' of the PMRAFNS.

Airman L.A. Murray was still in his teens when, stationed in Palestine in 1946, he became dangerously ill with jaundice. During his five-month stay in Tel Litwinsky he came to know several members of the PMRAFNS, including a 'lovely matron who sat by my bed and wrote a letter to my parents and girlfriend (now my wife) telling them that I was "making it". Because I tried to grow a moustache she referred to me as "Murray – you shocker" – but what a lady.' There was also 'Sister Flowers, face of an angel and everyone's favourite,' and 'a nurse called "Dot" … so attentive to me, doing things I couldn't do for myself … Although I said thank you at the time, if any of them could know how valuable their efforts were, wouldn't it be grand?'

Those days are still vivid to Sister Dulcie Flower (Mrs Wright):

> we could not leave the camp without an armed escort, but the hospital was on the same camp as the 6th Parachute Division, so there was no problem there! I can well remember climbing into an armoured car in cocktail frocks to attend a cocktail party at HQ in Jerusalem!

Susan Armistead (Mrs Sutcliffe) had started with the Service in 1943, at RAFH Weeton where after D-Day she helped to nurse many very sick ex-prisoners of war. In 1945 she was posted to No 5 RAFGH at Cairo, in time for a typhoid epidemic, and the following year saw her at Tel Litwinsky, where she nursed the first British officer to be shot by terrorists – 'he was desperately ill, but I am pleased to say that he recovered'.

A brief glimpse of Tel Litwinsky awaited Doreen Francis. Posted to Cairo, she and her friend Mary Spink joined other sisters waiting at a transit camp at Burtonwood, from where, 'after five wet days trekking backwards and forwards to the ablutions hut across the strategically placed paving stones, about sixteen of us embarked at Liverpool on SS *Britannic*'. Arriving at Cairo, Doreen and colleague Eileen King discovered they were posted on yet again, to Habbaniya, in Iraq. They were taken to Heliopolis airport and rushed by jeep to an aircraft waiting on the runway. Too late, they discovered it was the wrong plane – though bound eventually for Habbaniya, it was at the disposal of a Group Captain on an inspection tour. 'He did not speak to us,' says Doreen. 'He thought we were cadging a lift.' She recalls that Eileen King's tin trunk 'hand luggage' came in useful as a passenger seat.

The Group Captain decided to spend the night at Lydda, which had no accommodation for women and so, because of the terrorist troubles in Palestine, 'one of the officers collected a pistol and ammunition and escorted us to the RAF hospital at Tel Litwinsky, where Miss Williamson was the Matron, and we were given beds for the night. The following morning we were taken back to Lydda early, before the roads were checked, to resume our journey.'

Their Anson was overloaded and the pilot:

> had to nose between the mountains to get to Iraq. We also needed to refuel and landed at H3, an oil station on the pipe-line. The personnel there were intrigued to see 'skirts' and drove over to investigate. As a result, we were all treated to an excellent lunch.

When they finally arrived in Habbaniya they were greeted with relief by colleagues who had thought them lost. It was February, but Doreen Francis thought she had arrived in Eden: 'The mess was surrounded by Parma violets – the scent glorious – [and] between the sleeping blocks, where we had bedroom, bathroom and box-room, were apricot trees in full blossom.'

RAFH Tel Litwinsky closed on 1 January 1948, anticipating the end of the British mandate and the creation of the Jewish state of Israel.

Casevac to aeromed

Although the Second World War had ended, equally bloody conflicts – in Malaya and then Korea – soon called for air evacuation of yet more casualties. Much had been learned during the wider war, and as early as January 1945 plans had been laid for an extended service, to be known in peacetime as aeromedical evacuation. These flights would bring patients back from the Far East in five or six days, flying eight or nine hours each day and resting overnight at RAF staging posts. Nursing orderlies would accompany the patients in flight, but nursing sisters were to be posted to each of the stops en route, to care for in-transit patients in station sick quarters overnight. (In practice, from around 1950, PMs did accompany patients aboard air ambulances, much to the delight of the ladies involved.)

Pioneering the Far East aeromed

Anne Caird (Mrs Austin) borrowed her flying gear from WAAF supplies when she and an orderly boarded one of the Dakotas doing the 'casevac run' during the Korean war. The Australian air force brought the patients from Korea to the BCAir hospital in Japan, from where the RAF ferried them back to Changi. They flew out from their base at RAF Kai Tak, Hong Kong, to the USAF base at Okinawa, where they refuelled, then on to BCAir hospital Iwakuni. The patients they collected were a mix of British, Turkish, Greek, Australian and New Zealanders, some on stretchers, some able to use passenger seats. One group, whom Anne Caird remembers with affection, were:

> Turks who spoke no English, so we communicated by using a board containing basic English–Turkish phrases, primitive but effective ... Onboard conditions were very cramped ... moving about was an exercise in agility! No one had a clue how the stretcher harness fitted to the fuselage, but fit it we did – and prayed it would not collapse.

Returning by the same long, slow route, they stayed overnight in RAF sick quarters in Hong Kong before reloading the Dakota for the onward flight, first to Saigon for refuelling and then on to Singapore. Anne Caird usually spent two days at Changi before returning to Hong Kong to begin again. It was 'a tiring schedule, but a real challenge and the most gratifying experience of my nursing career'.

Monica Railton Jones (Mrs Chandler) says the sturdy Dakotas they used 'had been swiftly adapted to carry casualties, having recently been taking part in the Berlin airlift, carrying coal!'

Joy Harris did only one trip, but:

> it took quite a long time. We did it in a Valetta, which meant we came down in Borneo for refuelling, spent the night in the Philippines, came down in Okinawa ... that was where the chaps had to pee into the hydraulics to get the wheels down! ... The Australians were so welcoming ... I felt I'd gone home when I landed there. We got up at 4 a.m. every morning, to take off, and every morning the aircraft was still u/s [unserviceable], so they did something with me for the day. I was sent off round the sacred islands in a boat. I was sent on a train to Hiroshima ... there I was, not long after the war, walking round in uniform. No one thought anything about

> it, there was a great acceptance … I even managed to spend the day in a Sunderland [flying boat], which I certainly shouldn't have done … They took me up for the day and we did sweeps round the islands.

Eventually the Valetta was ready for take-off. 'I think there were only about ten patients. One was on a "striker frame". He'd injured his spine, so he was on something like a stretcher and you could screw another stretcher on to him, so you could tip him over – we just had one orderly with us.' They returned as they had come, stopping at American bases in Okinawa, then in the Philippines, then on to Borneo for refuelling:

> They off-loaded the boys each time – they used to be off-loaded for refuelling in those days. And they'd all get back on again, or be carried on, with cartons of cigarettes and gum. But they never did anything in these medical centres about their dressings – changing them, or making them comfortable … Anyway, when we stopped at Borneo, the boys were all out on the rough grass near the airfield and the planters' wives came along and sat down with them, and they'd brought a tin of boiled sweets with them, and they handed these round … and when we got back on the aircraft the chaps thought this was wonderful … people who had spoken to them, interested in them, human beings again, not just being passed through. They were terribly impressed with these planters' wives and their boiled sweets – and hadn't thought very much of the Americans.

An unusual air evacuation took place in April 1953 when an aeromed team, including PM Jean Weir, went to Moscow to bring home seven civilian ex-prisoners of war who had reached the Russian capital by the trans-Siberian railway. The RAF team flew via Berlin, where a Russian navigator and signaller boarded their plane to escort them through Soviet airspace. Their patients included a former British Minister from the Embassy in Seoul, and an Irish missionary who turned out to be related to one of the seven flight sisters waiting on standby at Wroughton!

The Korean War armistice was signed at Panmunjon in July 1953. Soon afterwards, to her delight, PM Tessa Lawless, stationed at Changi, was chosen as a last minute-replacement for a casevac from Japan. The rush to prepare included having two pairs of khaki trousers made (in two hours flat!) by a tailor in Changi village. Trousers were still non-regulation, but 'necessary for climbing steep and narrow steps into the aircraft, and when nursing patients at floor level in cramped conditions'.

The old, unpressurised aircraft lumbered along at low altitude, on piston engines, for stretches of seven or eight hours at a time, taking its usual overnight stop in the Philippines. Next morning as they waited on the tarmac some technical trouble with the aircraft became apparent. The crew asked Tessa if she had a hair-clip: 'I didn't use hair-clips, but by some miracle I had one in my make-up case – just in case!' The clip helped the pilot to effect repairs and off they went.

At the Australian air force base at Iwakuni, Tessa Lawless learned that, rather than returning to Changi next day, she was to wait two weeks for the first batch of PoWs released from Korea. In the meantime she had a house to herself and a car with a driver who showed her the sights. These included Hiroshima, rebuilt into the most modern city in Japan. But the legacy of the atom bomb remained in the burned and limbless casualties Tessa met, and in the stories told: '22,000 bodies had floated down the river and the whole place was gutted except for one skeleton of a dome-shaped building.' Elsewhere she found shops full of the latest technological gadgets, and she loved the scenery of tiered mountains with every inch of land under cultivation, and 'pagodas, bridges and small streams, sacred gateways and cherry blossom …' The fortnight of waiting flew by.

She brought back thirty-three patients, including eight stretcher cases, loaded in tiers, all needing feeding and close nursing. Some of the sick men had beriberi, and two of these cases, mentally affected by the disease, were placed at the front of the aircraft, where the crew and some of the fitter patients could keep an eye on them. 'My lasting impression,' says Tessa, 'is of total commitment … the crew and the walking patients were co-operative and helpful, to me and to each other …'

The final leg to Singapore ended with a landing in monsoon rain. Tessa had a glimpse of a crowd of VIPs – including Matron! – waiting under umbrellas to greet these very first returning prisoners of the Korean war. A team of RAF men swiftly took the patients to waiting ambulances and transported them away while Tessa, very aware of her non-regulation trousers, 'went down the stairway feeling very scruffy, only to be greeted by flashing cameras … within seconds I found myself facing Matron amidst this crowd of people, and the crew, with the Press bombarding me for my name … Rather than upset RAF protocol, I declined …'

The return of the PoWs made world headlines, on TV, radio, in the papers and even on Pathé News in cinemas. The Korean War was over. Perhaps an era of real peace had arrived at last.

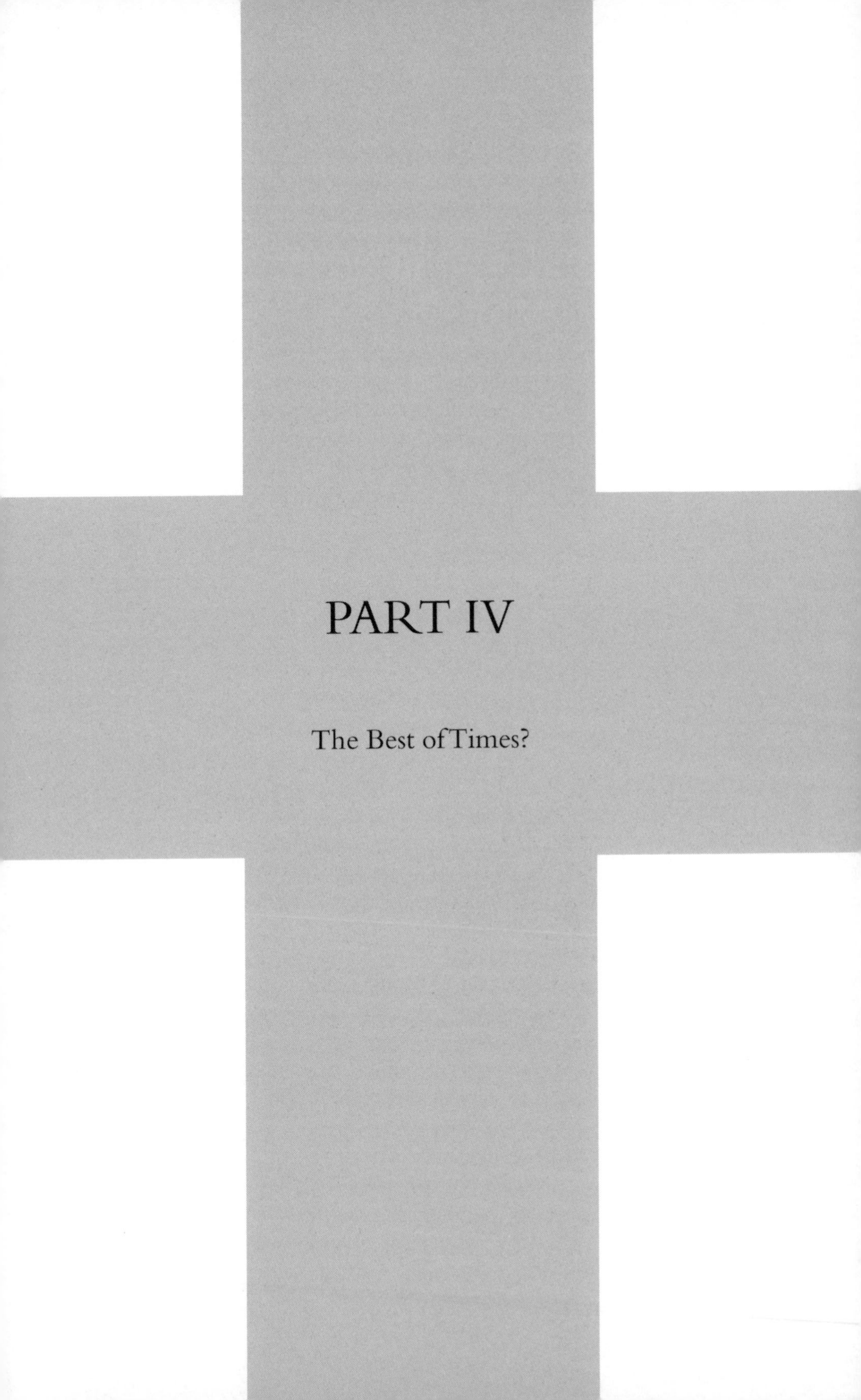

PART IV

The Best of Times?

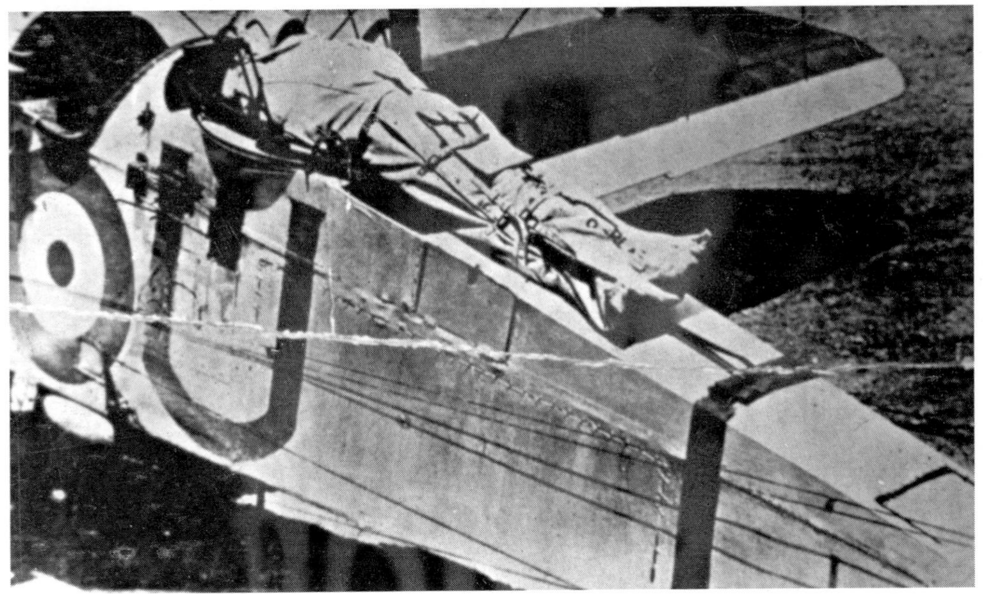

Precarious position for patient during early aeromed. (Ministry of Defence © Crown copyright)

Front-loading a patient into a DH9 in the desert, 1919. (Ministry of Defence © Crown copyright)

First sisters posted overseas, bound for Iraq aboard the troopship *Braemar Castle*, 1922. (Ministry of Defence © Crown copyright)

Early casualty evacuation flight by helicopter. (Ministry of Defence © Crown copyright)

Walking out uniform (note varying styles), with original black 'Dicks', 1930. (Ministry of Defence © Crown copyright)

Patients recuperating at an RAF Officers' Hospital 'somewhere in England', 1940s. (Ministry of Defence © Crown copyright)

Sister Rona Black shows off the glamorous style for PMs in India, 1944. (Photos courtesy of Mrs Rona McAlpine)

Medical staff with local patients, No 81 MFH, RAF Seletar, Singapore, 1946. (Ministry of Defence © Crown copyright)

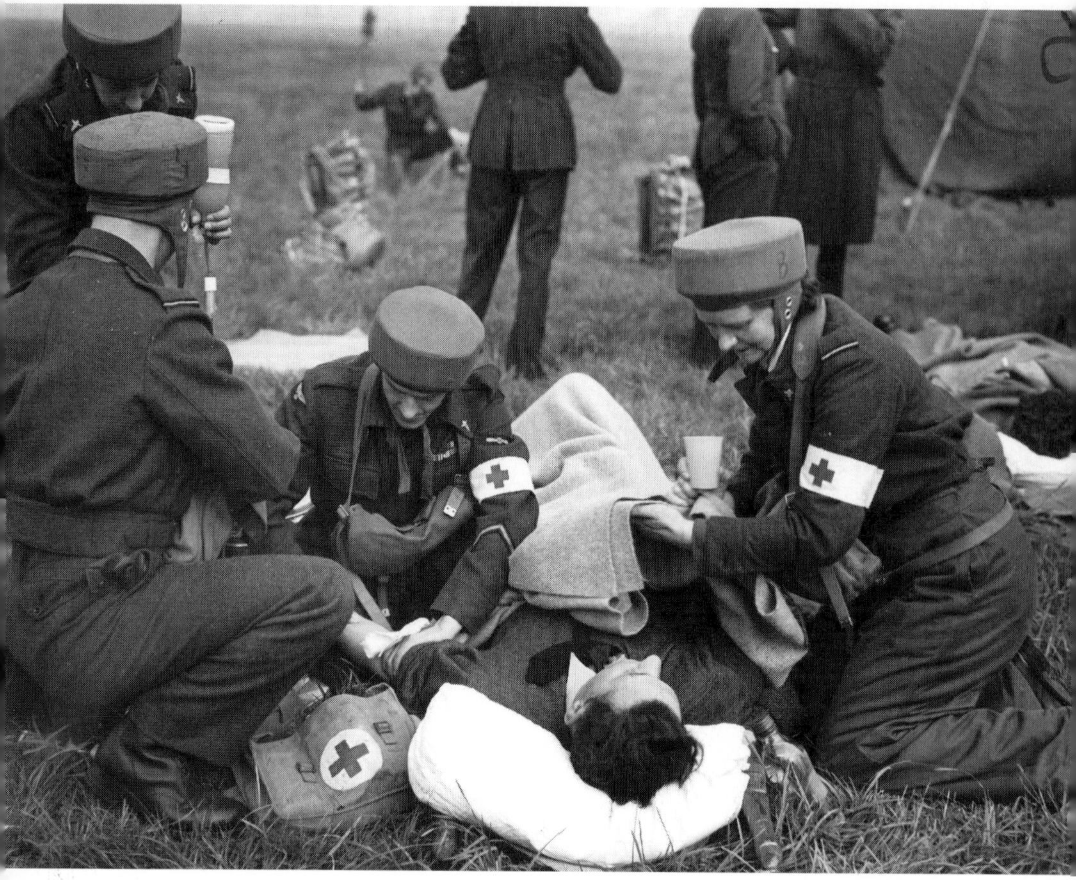

First PM Sisters to be parachute trained, with RAF medic (centre), 1948. (Ministry of Defence © Crown copyright)

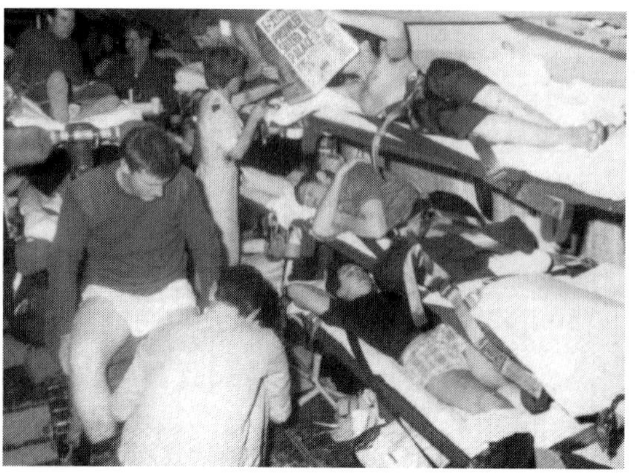

Caring for the wounded, 30,000ft over the Atlantic, Falklands War, 1982. (Photo courtesy of PMRAFNS archive)

Fork-lift loads patients into a Hastings. (Ministry of Defence © Crown copyright)

Two PMs are a regular part of the Medical Team aboard HMT Devonshire, 1950s. (Ministry of Defence © Crown copyright)

Aircraft familiarisation for new PMs, 1960s. (Ministry of Defence © Crown copyright)

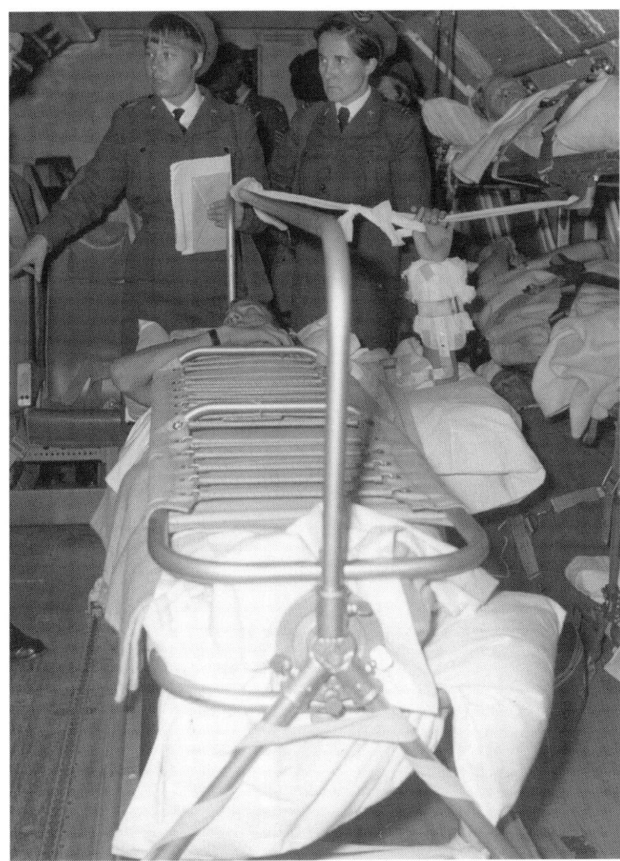

A Stryker frame in use. (Photo courtesy of PMRAFNS archive)

Unofficial shield of Halton's Renal Unit, motto *Per Ardua Ad Urinam*. (Photo Sqn Ldr Tony Cox)

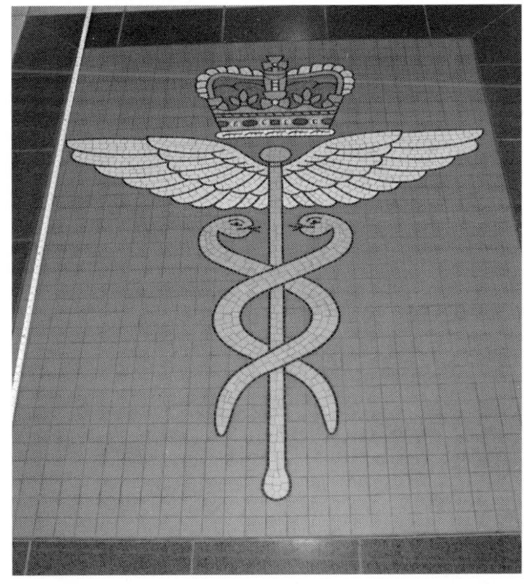

Mosaic of the RAF medical caduceus at RAFH Wegberg, western Germany, 1990s. (Photo Wg Cdr Kev Mackie)

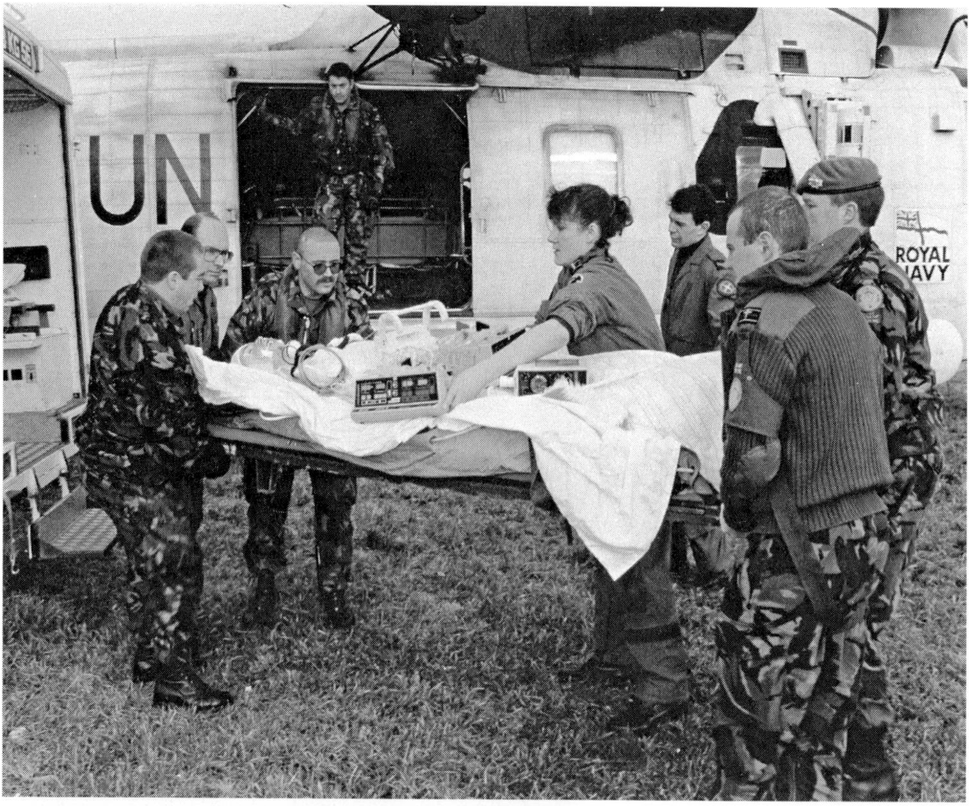

A busy time during Operation Grapple, Bosnia, 1992. (Photo courtesy of PMRAFNS archive)

Air Commodore R.H. Williams, RRC QHNS, Director of Defence Nursing Services and Matron-in-Chief of the PMRAFNS 1995–2001. (Photo courtesy of PMRAFNS archive)

Patient and escort on the helipad at Kisiljak, Former Republic of Yugoslavia, during the Balkan War. (Photo courtesy of PMRAFNS archive)

PMs at Kosovo, 1992. (Photo courtesy of PMRAFNS archive)

PM students and tutors march past the reviewing officer on closure of RDMC, Gosport, 2002. (Photo courtesy of PMRAFNS archive)

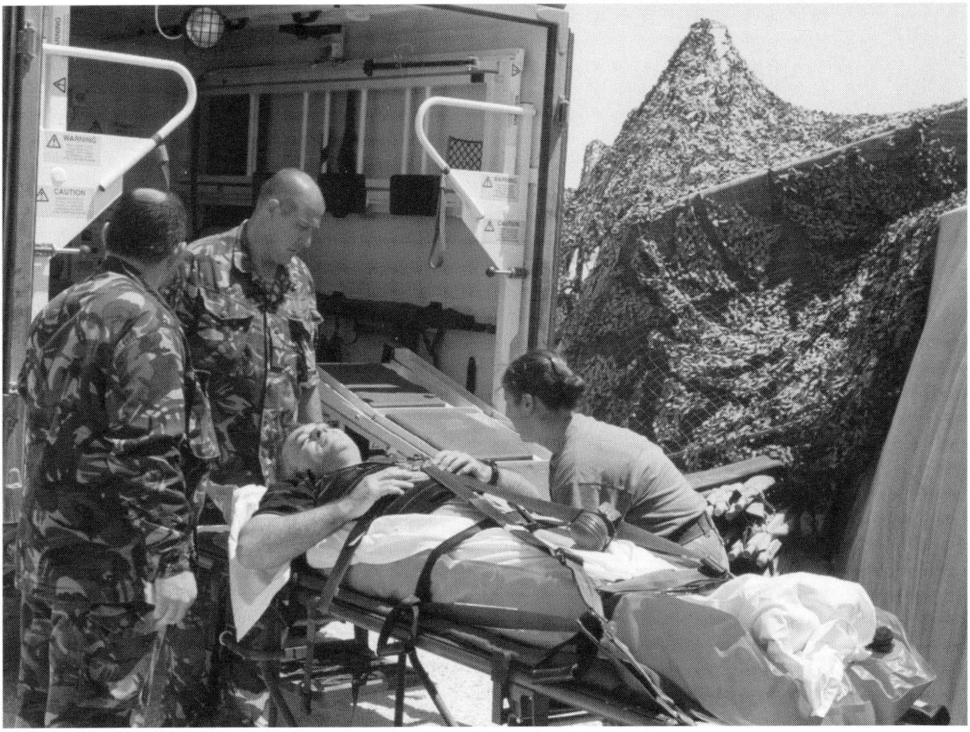

Operation Veritas, Oman, 2001–02. (Photo courtesy of PMRAFNS archive)

Beautiful setting for the Royal Hospital Haslar, Portsmouth. (Photo courtesy of PMRAFNS archive)

Gp Capt R. Annie Reid, OBE, Matron-in-Chief PMRAFNS, plants a commemorative tree at the National Memorial Arboretum, Staffs, 2003. (Photo Wg Cdr Kev Mackie)

PMRAFNS Memorial at the National Arboretum, Staffs. (Photo Wg Cdr Kev Mackie)

Critical Care Team with patients aboard a Hercules, 2003. (Photo courtesy of PMRAFNS archive)

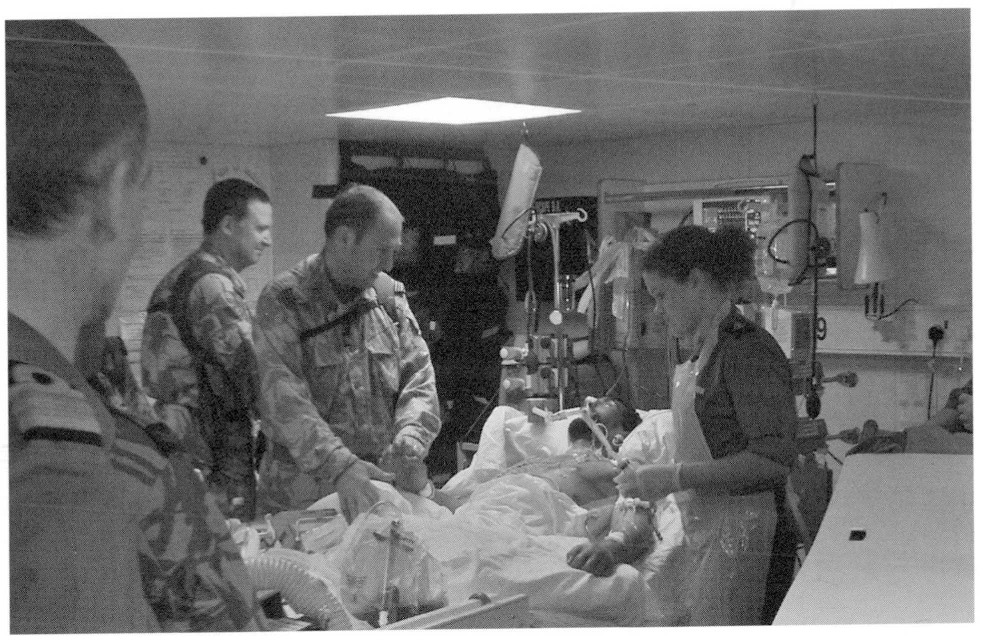

Intensive Care Transfer, 2003. (Photo courtesy of PMRAFNS archive)

Staff of War Hospital Muharraq, during Operation Telic, 2008. (Photo courtesy of PMRAFNS archive)

NATO Command HQ, Kandahar Airfield (KAF), Afghanistan. (Photo Wg Cdr Kev Mackie)

Medical Emergency Response Team work to stabilise an injured Afghani boy, 2009. (Photo courtesy of PMRAFNS archive)

Home-made leisure facilities at KAF, Afghanistan, 2009. (Photo Wg Cdr Kev Mackie)

Wg Cdr Kev Mackie (PMRAFNS), and Major Eléna Kereun, a French flight surgeon, prepare to take medical aid to the Afghani village of Lundey Kalay, October 2008. (Photo Wg Cdr Kev Mackie)

Hand-painted sign at KAF, Afghanistan, 2009. (Photo Wg Cdr Kev Mackie)

A warm welcome for the medics and their escort from the children of Lundey Kalay, Kandahar province. (Photo Wg Cdr Kev Mackie)

Tribute to RAF Hospital Halton, unveiled 2011. (Photo Cpl Anthony Beynon)

PMs attend the dedication of the RAFH Halton memorial, 2011. (Photo courtesy of Cpl Anthony Beynon, seen far right)

PM Flt Lt Alison Beresford, OC MERT, Camp Bastion, July 2010. (Photo Wg Cdr Kev Mackie)

PM Sgt Jas Robertson, Aeromed Liaison, Camp Bastion, July 2010. (Photo Wg Cdr Kev Mackie)

Sign which becomes obsolete on British troops' withdrawal from Afghanistan 2014. (Photo Wg Cdr Kev Mackie)

Closing ceremony for The Princess Mary Hospital, Akrotiri, Cyprus, November 2012. (Photo courtesy of Colonel D.J. Vassallo RAMC)

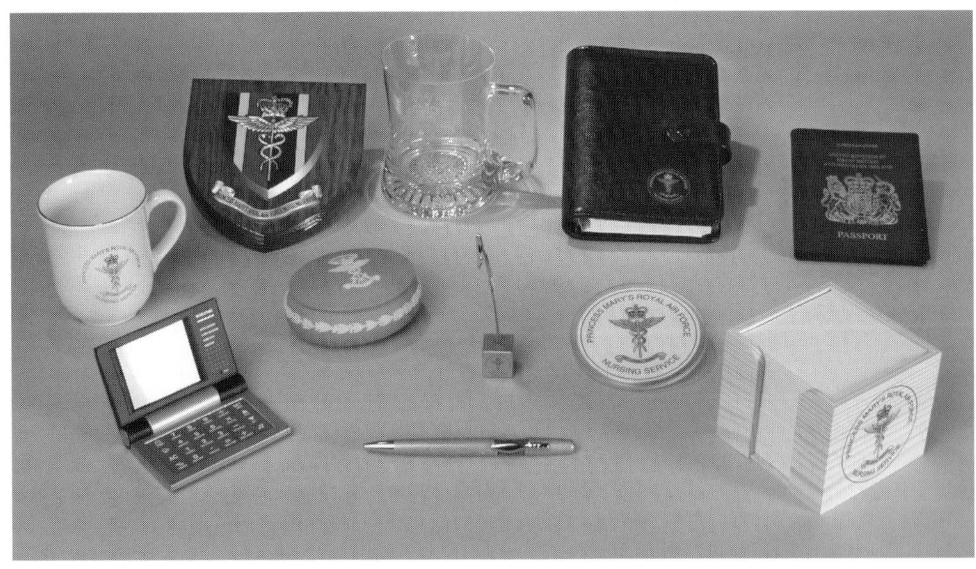

Items of PMRAFNS memorabilia. (Photo courtesy of PMRAFNS archive)

13

Peaceful Days

The bombs that fell on Hiroshima and Nagasaki starkly announced the opening of the nuclear age. But devastated cities rose again, transformed into utopias of modernity, and as production lines restarted, bringing more employment and better wages, so new consumer goods began to reach the shops – refrigerators, washing machines, Coca Cola … At the same time, with the doctrine of Communism spreading, the Great Powers braced themselves for the stand-off that became known as the Cold War. In the field of medicine a more subtle enemy, called infantile paralysis (poliomyelitis), posed a fresh challenge for doctors and nurses.

The RAF's temporary war-time hospitals, at home and overseas, had closed. In Britain, the remaining five general hospitals (Cosford, Ely, Halton, Nocton Hall, Wroughton) and another five station hospitals (Padgate, St Athan, Weeton, West Kirby, Wilmslow) adjusted themselves to meet the needs of a peacetime air force. Abroad, RAF hospitals in Aden, Egypt and Iraq were joined by new ones in West Germany and Singapore, and staging posts on the transport and aeromed route from the Far East to the UK all opened sick quarters or small hospitals. These new units offered exciting postings for PMs such as young Joy Harris, who was on leave when a telegram came to inform her she had been posted – to Greece! She was thrilled! Then she reread the telegram. Not 'Athens' in golden Greece but 'St Athan' in wet Wales. Even so, for Joy it was 'the furthest I'd been from home in those days!'

Olympic event

When crowds of athletes arrived in London to take part in the 1948 Olympic Games, Sister Pam Love (Mrs Batchelar) was stationed at Uxbridge. The small hospital lay in the grounds of the RAF station, whose CO 'did the weekly round with matron, which caused a lot of tension; hospitals with sick people are, after all, most unlike barrack blocks'. That summer, the Uxbridge barrack blocks served as billets for teams of Olympic athletes. At the hospital, Pam Love recalls:

> duties varied from giving enemas to overweight boxers to dressing injuries, and even comforting some athletes who were panicking and overstressed.
>
> On one notable occasion a dinner was held at the Mess for VIP Olympic people as well as many RAF VIPs. Curried chicken was on the menu, but sadly the day

> was hot and the chicken was off. There was no mean panic when our beds quickly filled up with very sick men suffering from food poisoning. I was the only sister on night duty then and my big problem was to keep the story from the press; reporters phoned in all manner of guises … The Daily Express somehow got hold of it and splashed it on their front page the next day.

One of the men badly affected by the bug was the station CO, with whom Pam Love 'had crossed swords over a ward inspection. It may sound callous but … when I literally caught him with his trousers down I felt somehow that justice had been done'.

Parachuting PMs

A different kind of athletic challenge occurred when seven PMs became the first British nurses to undertake a parachute-jumping course identical to that used in training paratroopers. This training was intended to cover any future emergency in some remote and inaccessible area where medical teams might literally have to leap to the rescue. At Wroughton, in the spring of 1948, a notice in the sisters' mess called for volunteers to undertake a 'parachute medic' course (not to be confused with 'paramedic' as we now understand it). When no names appeared on the form, it became a case of 'You, you and you'.

Vi Craig (Mrs Gibbons), one of the chosen few, accepted the challenge with wry humour: 'Life had seemed a little dull after two and a half years in India, the weather was lovely and Upper Heyford was in a nice part of the country …' She went along to No 1 Parachute and Glider Training School, at RAF Upper Heyford in Oxfordshire, where she joined the rest of the experimental group: Senior Sister Joan Maffey; Sisters Margery Bradley and Molly Savage; four male nursing orderlies and a doctor, all of the RAFMS; and Audrey Penfold, OC WAAF of Upper Heyford. They spent their first day in a hangar, 'swinging around, learning to roll', under the eye of RAF instructors and other interested observers.

One of those instructors, Mr T. Wilson, remembers being 'surprised to receive these ladies'. A few women had parachuted into France during the war, as wireless operators or resistance leaders, but nurses were an innovation. What was more, safety rules decreed that no one over thirty-five should parachute onto land, and 'these Sisters were obviously over this age, so we looked after them with care'.

The standard course involved eight jumps, three from a balloon and five from a Dakota, including one jump by night, using parachutes of the old 'X' type, with no reserve 'chutes. Trainees wore overalls, heavy military boots and rather fetching protective 'helmets' filled with Sorbo rubber. They also avoided late nights in the bar.

Before they could jump down they had to climb up – 'first a perpendicular ladder attached to a wall … to reach a platform 30ft from the ground … next a 90ft tower'. Vi Craig found the next stage, from a barrage balloon tethered 800 feet up, 'a bit of an ordeal', but when they finally came to jump out of a real aircraft 'there was so much engine noise and hustle and bustle … you jumped on your number, with no hesitation'.

A former CO of Halton, J.G. Kingan, recalls that on a later course, as the plane took off for their first real drop, tension reigned among the group of male and female embryo parachutists. Then one of the PMs took out a mirror and nonchalantly checked her make-up. Tension evaporated – if she was so relaxed, what was worrying all those husky males?

In 1950 the PMRAFNS Advisory Board commented that nursing sisters had done excellent work in 'demonstrating the capacity of women to undertake arduous and unique duties'. However, after a year or two when no need for emergency medical teams arose, parachuting disappeared from the PMs' curriculum.

Ranking officers – at last

On 1 February 1949, long-awaited changes confirmed the vital role performed by all women in the modern air force. The WAAF ceased being a mere auxiliary service and regained its original 1918 title of the Women's Royal Air Force; its members, along with members of the PMRAFNS, achieved full integration into the RAF. At last PMs became recognised holders of the King's Commission: where before they had held only 'emergency' wartime commissions, they could now apply for permanent or short service commissions, on salaries commensurate with other service scales of pay, and, although on the wards they would continue to be known as 'Sister' and 'Matron', officially they held officer rank titles equivalent to the WRAF:

PMRAFNS	**WRAF**	**RAF**
Matron in Chief	Air Commandant	Air Commodore
Principal Matron	Group Officer	Group Captain
Senior Matron	Wing Officer	Wing Commander
Matron	Squadron Officer	Squadron Leader
Senior Sister	Flight Officer	Flight Lieutenant
Sister	Flying Officer	Flying Officer

King George V later approved the appointment of the Princess Royal as Air Chief Commandant of PMRAFNS.

A changing role

To proclaim the advantages of a career in the PMRAFNS, Matron-in-Chief Helen Cargill instigated a new recruiting drive. She had observed that, while many nurses enquired about joining the PMs, few returned their application forms, partly because of false rumours that no acute nursing was done in service hospitals. In fact, recent changes meant that the work of RAF hospitals was as vital and varied as that of any civilian hospital.

After the foundation of the National Health Service, on 5 July 1948, the ten RAF hospitals accepted patients from local civilian communities and also offered extended care for service families. Midwifery was becoming a speciality: until 1948 only one RAF maternity unit had existed, at St Athan, but two years later both Halton and Cosford had opened 'midder' wards, and other hospitals followed suit. The PMRAFNS established a first-class midwifery organisation and, since babies rapidly grow, soon introduced children's wards too.

Wherever possible, PMs were appointed to work in their field of preference, be it theatre nursing, midwifery, orthopaedics, paediatrics, oncology or plastic surgery. Such a comprehensive choice – allied with postings across the world, the chance to work aboard troopships and on aeromed flights, good prospects for promotion, plus decent pay and an attractive uniform – ensured that a career as a nursing officer in the peacetime PMRAFNS offered an excellent future for any SRN. New recruiting literature was to spread this message far and wide.

Five PMs stationed at Uxbridge, including Pam Love (Mrs Batchelar), were summoned to matron's office, where:

> we were inspected by an arty gent in a velvet cap. He looked at us from every angle and announced that there was only one possible choice, though she was far from ideal – that possible one was me. I had to spend a day in a dusty studio having my photo taken, with the deputy matron-in-chief as chaperone. This arty chap produced tea in jam jars for his refreshment and mine, but nothing for the deputy matron, which was most embarrassing.

The new posters and booklet encouraged a steady stream of trained nurses to apply for membership of the PMRAFNS.

New girls

Pam Love had joined the service in 1947. She arrived for her first day at Wroughton:

> feeling very odd in my uniform with its wretched tricorn hat which slipped over the eyes when one stood to attention. I had no square-bashing training, nor did I know how to salute, so panic set in when I passed the guard room. I vaguely raised my right hand and hoped for the best.

(NB: Many PMs refer to the hat as a tricorn, though it has always had four corners to its brim, not three).

'Our tricorn-shaped hat,' says Margaret Crombie (Mrs Price), 'had a badge at the front. We used to wear it on the back of our heads, at which Matron observed that the badge "had to be seen by pedestrians, not by oncoming aircraft!"' This witticism has been borrowed by so many matrons down the years that no one is sure who first uttered it.

A few years later, new member April Reed bought her uniform from Boyd Cooper's, as instructed, but forgot to include white shoes. For her first day on the ward another nurse lent her some shoes, but they were half a size too small and by coffee break next morning April's feet were 'ghastly'. She changed into black shoes with her ward whites, much to ward sister's horror: 'Matron's about to come round! You'd better hide in the sluice!' Being a junior sister was never easy.

What was more, as full ranking officers in the 'big air force', PMs had to do more than know their jobs – they had to learn service procedures, how to fill in official forms, how (and whom) to salute correctly and, of all things, how to march!

After joining in 1951, Margaret Kingston went on the first-ever Nursing Officers' Course, held at RAF Hawkinge, near Folkestone:

> I'd only been in the Service six weeks and I hadn't a clue what they were talking about – all this F Med 12s and 50s and all these numbers and things – so one of the girls on the same course every evening used to translate it into English for me.

The ladies also learned:

> square bashing on the cliff-tops at Folkestone … We had to take it in turns, seven of us, taking the squad, marching, and Flight Sergeant Pomeroy – I can see him now with his pacing stick, you could see your face in his boots … It was my turn to command this little gathering of PMs. And he stopped them and he came up to me and he said, ''Scuse me, ma'am. Permission to touch?' and with that he put his hand on my tummy and he said, 'From there, ma'am!'

The drill instructor doubled as a vocal coach, too!

Another course of six trainees went on parade in their new best blues. It was raining and one of the innocents turned up holding a red umbrella – she didn't want to get her nice new uniform wet!

Most PMs were not called upon to march very often, but a few proudly remember taking part in one of the annual Festivals of Remembrance at the Albert Hall. Olive Kirkham and eleven other PMs gathered at RAF Uxbridge and:

> each morning we were taken to the Hall where we met Ralph Reader, who was the organiser … As part of the large muster we practised marching up and down these wretched stairs and across the arena for hours on end … When the great day dawned, we dressed in the whitest of our uniforms, starched sleeves and caps and shining white shoes … I shall never forget waiting at the top of those dreaded stairs.

But, she adds, the most poignant moment, then as now, was the floating down of the millions of poppy petals.

Another year, at a similar event, Margaret Kingston represented the PMs:

> When we went up on the stage, Chelsea pensioners were next to me, and this old boy sat next to me – must have been well in his eighties – and he nudged me and said, 'Duckie, would you mind if I took my teeth out?' So he took his teeth out and put them under the chair. Well, the whole service, I was terrified that he'd go off without his teeth!

In due time, prospective PMs undertook courses at the female Officer Cadet Training Unit (OCTU) at Henlow, and later they joined the men at the OCTU at Cranwell. But in the interim, in the late 1950s and early 1960s, training in RAF ways became an integral part of the first few weeks of a PM's service – usually at the 'home base' hospital, PMRAFH Halton, Bucks.

Doreen Smedley recalls that when she first went to Halton in 1955, every morning new sisters had half an hour's training with a deputy matron. Doreen still has her notebook, in which she wrote copies of the various formal letters she might need:

> you had to write a letter if you wanted leave; when you came back from overseas you had to write to MOD and go for an interview; if you wanted to get married, of course, you had to write a letter … there was even one if you had to write on behalf of the mess to thank Princess Mary for her annual Christmas card!

A little later, Liz Sandison spent her introductory month at Halton, 'before OCTU at Henlow or Cranwell and all those goodly things'. She learned to march behind Halton's garages, where 'on the last day there was this great cheering and hullabaloo and here were the kitchen staff, holding up score cards as if it were "Come Dancing".'

Therese Saunders (Mrs Ayres) also had a memorable introduction to the Service. On her first night at Halton – a winter night, with ice and snow on the ground outside – she stood on a chair in order to draw the curtains in her allocated room. The chair collapsed. She clutched the curtains to save herself but the curtain rail came away from the wall. Rail and curtains landed in a heap on top of her. Wondering if it was worth even unpacking after such a disastrous start, she decided to go across to dinner. Stepping outside the main door, she slipped on some ice, fell flat on her back and gashed her head open. 'I arrived at the Sisters' Mess with blood everywhere … I shall never forget the look on their faces! I'm sure they thought me a very weird addition to their number!'

The 1950s

For those PMs who experienced them, the two decades following the war were the best. It was the heyday of sea-trooping and of the long-haul aeromed flights which suddenly became much faster with the introduction of jet engines. Those halcyon days offered the widest range of postings, while national servicemen added their own sly humour to the wards. Though everyone worked hard, they also had time for fun. Sisters wafted down the polished lino in high starched headdress, white dress and short blue cape (with officers' rank markings proudly displayed on epaulettes), looking like 'graceful and compassionate commissioned angels' – at least, that's how they appeared to eighteen-year-old bronchitis-stricken J.M. Pettigrew. The only item that seemed to detract from the overall effect was 'rather clompy white ward shoes – which nevertheless served to warn our illicit smokers of the approach of authority'.

Kathleen Hird (Mrs Bion) sums up the feelings of many PMs who served during those post-war days:

> How very lucky we were. We had trained during the war, when life really didn't consist of anything else but hospital – no social life or excitement. Suddenly there I was in beautiful Buckinghamshire being treated as an officer and all the perks, and then overseas … In the days when holidays or travel didn't exist for the average public, we were spoilt, and I'll always be grateful for the memories.

By the end of the 1950s, however, several of the RAF's overseas hospitals would be defunct.

South of Suez

In Cairo, the wartime No 5 RAFGH had closed in 1947 and was due to be replaced by a new unit on the shores of the Great Bitter Lake, south of the Suez Canal, an area where several RAF stations then existed. An officers' club by the lake provided a base where personnel could swim, sunbathe and socialise.

Dulcie Flower (Mrs Wright) had been at RAFH Tel Litwinsky in Palestine, but remembers how:

> in 1947 a couple of us were posted with four other PMs to open a hospital in the Canal Zone. As nothing was known about us or the hospital, we did not know what to do, so we took ourselves down to the Great Bitter Lake most afternoons. Then more officers arrived who got on with building the hospital and the sisters' quarters (up until then we had been housed in appalling conditions in a disused NAAFI hut). In the meantime, the wives of the troops serving in the Canal Zone were arriving from the UK, so it was decided to open a Families Hospital at Abyad, just up the road.

While this hospital was being prepared, the two midwives and the obstetrician all went on leave to Cyprus, confident that no babies were expected before they returned. However, Dulcie Flower was on duty one night when the ward-master rang to warn her of the imminent arrival of a maternity patient. 'Having only Part

One Midwifery Certificate, I was not allowed to do a delivery without a doctor in attendance, so I dragged a sleepy Duty MO out of his bed …' The patient arrived, in advanced labour – she had been at a cocktail party at the officers' mess in Ismailia and what with the gin and the heat … Happily, she produced her baby without problems, but the puzzled MO asked, 'Was there any question of you having twins, Mrs Evans?' She replied, 'No, that was the other Mrs Evans.' X-rays had got muddled! Just as doctor and sister were relaxing and congratulating themselves, another expectant mother turned up, also well into labour. She too had been drinking gin cocktails at that party in Ismailia!

With both mothers and babies comfortably settled, Dulcie set off across the desert taking the linen to the sluice room:

> I knew that the electric light had not been fixed yet, but it never occurred to me that the rest of the building would be unfinished because the water was laid on. When I started the sluicing, I found to my horror that my feet were getting wet. With typical Egyptian (in)efficiency, the pipes had not been connected!

The Fayid/Abyad hospital opened officially on 1 January 1948, when it was joined by all staff from the defunct hospital at Tel Litwinsky, which was now in the new state of Israel. Later that year, Doris Stanford (Mrs Kent) was sent to Fayid from Habbaniya to help nurse an epidemic of typhoid which affected two hundred RAF and army patients. With the temperature outside up to 100°F, no air conditioning and few, if any, antibiotics, the sisters relied on good nursing and tepid sponging. It was back-aching work with patients on low iron bedsteads, but it paid off – they didn't lose a patient.

Margaret Kingston and her friend Meg Goulbourne had:

> only been in the service about six months when, to our amazement, we were told we were going overseas. 1951, November – you can imagine, trying to get summer clothing in November … We were called by the Wing Officer matron to say goodbye … [Her] last words to us were, 'I do hope you enjoy Germany.' We were off to Egypt!
>
> We eventually got to Fayid … and were met by the Wing Officer, Margaret Ashworth, with an enormous Alsatian dog – we felt very honoured to be met by the Wing Officer. We learned afterwards she'd come to the plane to see if they'd brought the dog food for her Alsatian! And another sister, a very beautiful Irish girl, Kay, had come to meet us, which was very sweet, but, when she turned round, the back seam of her white dress – with all the washing, the cotton had given. A belt held the top, the hem held the bottom, and there was her backside with these white panties … Tropical kit!

A military coup in 1952 overthrew Egypt's King Farouk and launched a strongly pro-Arab republic, providing a focus for anti-Israeli feeling. Britain held on to control of the Canal

Zone, but, as political tensions grew, at RAF Fayid dissidents blew up some ammunition dumps. For security reasons most local mess servants were barred from camp.

To Margaret Kingston, however:

> Egypt was a nice posting, although we were confined to camp because of the Suez trouble, and the mess servants had gone … Off-duty in the afternoon we could go swimming, in the Bitter Lake, but we had to have an armed escort. There was an open garry [truck], and four airmen with guns at each corner, and the sisters on deck-chairs – you can imagine, bumping over the open desert.

Two of the bearers, who had been security-vetted and allowed to stay, decorated the mess for Christmas while off-duty staff went to church:

> When we got back … all our bras and pants, and any old cotton dresses we'd thrown out during the year, were chopped up in bits and all on strings … We had to be very tactful, but the CO was coming over for coffee and we had to do a very quick removal!

Theatre sister Eileen Adams (Mrs Knapper) remembers Christmas fun when she and the surgeon swapped uniforms and did a full ward round – 'It went down well with the patients!' She had specifically asked to be posted to Fayid, so that she might visit the grave of her brother, an airman who died with two others in a road accident while serving in Egypt. This she was able to do. She recalls having plenty of work: during a severe outbreak of dysentery, tents had to be erected to take extra beds; a flying officer was brought in from the desert, having had to bail out of his aircraft; and a surgical team remained 'on standby, with equipment packed and ready. Early in the morning we were called to a sick airman at RAF El Adem, a staging post inland from Tobruk.' Having nursed the airman for two days, they flew him back to Fayid for an operation.

The desert outpost of El Adem (described by one PM as 'two camels and a sand-dune') found itself short of women in 1953, so 'an aircraft known as the Sisters' Special was laid on to take some of us over for their Summer Ball,' says Eileen. She also met her future husband while stationed at Fayid: 'When I informed Matron Miller that I was getting engaged to Flt Lt Knapper, within forty-eight hours I was sent to the RAF Hospital Aden. Then on marriage I had to resign my commission – what a waste!'

In July 1956, when Egyptian President Nasser nationalised the Suez Canal, Britain withdrew all her personnel from the area. Joan Metcalfe was aboard the troopship *Devonshire* on a historic moment at Port Said when 'we brought out the last troops of the Grenadier Guards, who had been the first troops into Egypt after Napoleon had left'. When RAFH Fayid, the last RAF hospital in Egypt, closed, its staff moved to the newly opened hospital at Akrotiri, Cyprus.

Sea trooping

In those days of slow aeroplanes with limited passenger space, British troops and their families moved around the world by sea. Nursing and medical officers, with a full sick quarters staff, went with them to look after their health on the long voyages.

Jessie Higgins also sailed aboard the famous troopship *Devonshire*:

> backwards and forwards to Singapore and it used to take thirty or thirty-one days. Went through the Med, down the Canal and through the Red Sea, to Aden, then straight across to Colombo, in Ceylon … *Devonshire* had 120 hospital beds on it. We had all the families, umpteen wives and children … Coming back, we used to bring all the sick … It was before the days when antibiotics were being used properly, and a lot of people being given penicillin couldn't take it. People with prickly-heat, penicillin made it ten times worse … We had to put them up the top where it was airy. We got to the stage where we'd say, right, we're going up the Canal tomorrow, turn left into the Med, and they'll all be better in a day – and they were!

The ill-advised Anglo-French invasion of the Canal Zone early in November 1956 ended in humiliation, mostly because of pressure from the United States, but Nasser retaliated by sinking forty-nine ships to block the canal. The seaway remained closed for five months.

During the closure of the Suez Canal, troopships faced extra-long voyages. When the civilian-run *Orwell* called in at Singapore, on the way home from Japan, Joy Harris was one of the medical team who were asked to bring home:

> a tremendous number of psychiatric patients. In those days, the aeromeds only ever carried one, or two, psychiatric patients – they weren't very happy about having a lot, because they were slow aircraft … Both the doctor and myself were worried about this, neither of us had any psychiatric training at all. So, the psychiatrist at Singapore came on board and said, 'They'll be all right. Just humour them. Let them do more or less what they want.' The ship's captain wasn't too pleased about that [but] we all got on very well until we came into port, when one of the sergeants on board, being evacuated home because he had ideas of grandeur and went around selling everything – he tried to sell the Raffles Hotel in Singapore – he kept going ashore and we thought he might try to sell the ship while he was gone! … They didn't come to any harm, they all got home safely. It was a marvellous trip … when we got to Cape Town the South Africans were so hospitable. They all turned up on the quayside and every passenger on board, being trooped home, was taken off for the day, and we were 'sung out' [by] the 'lady in white'. She used to sing as the troopships went round in the war. She had a beautiful voice.

On the doughty *Devonshire* again, in summer 1957 Joan Metcalfe and Christine Bramley (Mrs Bull) sailed, with men of all three services, out to Christmas Island for Operation Grapple – the first British hydrogen bomb tests. Calling in at Singapore, they picked up the Fijian Regiment, who had been serving in Malaya, and took them home, anchoring in Suva harbour for three days while welcoming ceremonies took place. Then they sailed to Christmas Island, where most of the British troops disembarked to prepare for the coming tests.

'With an almost empty ship,' says Christine:

> we sailed on to Honolulu, where a small army team was to set up a staging post for troops flying out to Christmas Island via the States. Before any of us could go ashore we had to be interviewed by US immigration officers, who were amazed to find females on a troopship. Not only that but the ship was not 'dry' like the US troopships!

Because of currency restrictions they went ashore with an allowance of $3 a day so, 'being short of ready cash, we took our packets of Devonshire sandwiches and bottles of Merseyside lemonade and went off to Waikiki beach to surf and swim'.

The three-week voyage back to Singapore, on an 'empty' ship, seemed like a leisure cruise, with interesting fish swimming by and spectacular sunsets blazing across ocean and sky. 'I kept saying, "This is the best Pacific tour",' recalls Joan Metcalfe, 'just lounging around – we had nothing to do.'

They made up for it later, coming home from Singapore with a full complement of men, wives and families, via Colombo in Ceylon, Mombasa in Kenya, Cape Town, Dakar, and finally north through the Atlantic. Hitting rough weather in the Bay of Biscay reminded Christine Bramley of the story of another PM encountering terrible weather, which had *Devonshire*'s treatment room 'awash with gentian violet and liquid paraffin … she hadn't been able to decide which to save if they were told to abandon ship – her fur coat or her jewels!'

HMT *Devonshire* made many voyages with PMs on duty in her sick bay. Doreen Smedley was aboard when they took Irish Fusiliers out to Tripoli and brought the King's Royal Rifles back. EOKA terrorists were active in Cyprus at the time, so the ship stayed in the harbour and everything was brought out to them, including the station band, on a float, to play for them. On another trip they had 200 children aboard: 'The first measle appeared as we sailed down Southampton Water …' But generally, says Doreen, for the wives and families it was like taking a six-week holiday.

However, Kathy Mogg (Mrs Ostler), sailing with a shipload of soldiers and their families, recalls ill-feeling because of:

> insufficient cabin space for corporals and below to share with families … [and despite] talks on living in a hot climate, health advice and lists of necessary clothing, many of the young wives were out of their depth. Young children were dressed in

> non-absorbent materials, resulting in skin problems. The general overcrowding … for the third class passengers added to the misery.

And of course there was sea-sickness:

> I had it! I remember attempting to give a bed-bath to a patient in sickbay when I was feeling terrible. After two days I was told to pull myself together and get on with it … I was given some special ground-up powder to take, which cured me! … Meanwhile one was expected to enter into the social whirl … bingo, dancing, talent night, a raffle, and film shows. Later, when the weather improved, we had a fancy dress ball.

But sea trooping was coming to an end. *Devonshire*'s last trooping voyage was in December 1961, when on leaving Malta the ship received a rousing send-off – she had been a favourite visitor at Mediterranean bases. But all the troopships are fondly remembered by the many PMs who served aboard them. They provided a means by which single girls could get away from home and see the world – an opportunity not to be missed in those pre-Women's Lib days.

Long-haul aeromeds

Two-year postings to overseas hospitals provided a more in-depth method of sampling foreign climes for some PMs. Others saw the world in fleeting glimpses, as they escorted patients on the aeromedical evacuation flights which, more and more, became a vital part of a nursing sister's career.

The object of post-war aeromeds was to bring back to England any ill or injured service personnel, members of their families, and other British government employees (such as teachers and diplomats) who, while working abroad, might require specialist or urgent treatment not available locally. Other patients might benefit from the service if circumstance warranted. At first, any nursing officer might be plucked from her ward and sent to escort an aeromed patient halfway across the world. She learned, perforce, by doing the job.

For a while Dakotas and Valettas continued in use for medium-length flights, but from 1948 the Handley Page Hastings became the RAF's standard long-range transport aircraft. It could be fitted out to carry between twenty-eight and thirty-two patients, with stretchers fitted in tiers down each side of the central aisle. However, flying aeromed aboard a Hastings was not ideal: being unpressurised and unable to fly above 10,000 feet, the aircraft encountered a good deal of turbulence. Respiratory distress among patients, allied with cramped working conditions, and the need to shout to be heard (while sometimes wearing ear-protectors against the deafening noise of those slow old piston engines) caused added problems for nurses, especially on those long, long flights to and from the Far East. The minimum time for a flight to

Singapore was five days, including stops for refuelling and overnight rest breaks when patients would be unloaded and taken to the hospital or sick quarters attached to each staging post. In practice, journeys often took longer than scheduled. Many stories of early aeromeds include the words 'the aircraft went u/s [unserviceable] and we were delayed'. The delays could last hours or days.

Some flights were one-off specials, others more routine – for instance, once a month, in the early 1950s, flight sisters based at Wroughton packed their medical panniers and flew from RAF Lyneham to Wildenrath in Germany, bringing back mainly TB patients. While airborne, the nursing sister would not be sitting, like a tourist, with her feet up, snoozing, reading a book and/or enjoying 'duty-frees'; she had too much to do keeping her patients comfortable, seeing they were fed and watered, supplying them with bottles and bedpans, ensuring comfortable respiration at altitude, etc.; the list varied with the needs of each particular patient.

Many sisters spent the night prior to take-off at the 'rather bleak spot' known as Clyffe Pypard, a village near RAF Lyneham. Joy Harris remembers it well:

> I flew out to Singapore in 1951, on my first posting, in my first aeroplane, from Clyffe Pypard … I remember going into this room, with a coke stove … red-hot! I got into bed, next thing I knew was a chap who was driving the coach down to the aircraft was saying, 'You've been called, ma'am, you should be on the coach now!' I hadn't been called at all, although somebody produced a thing that I'd 'signed' – it was only a squiggle. I think I got dressed and was on the coach in two minutes – and when you consider those were the days of suspender belts, full uniform, collar with studs in it, tie, and greatcoat – I don't know how I did it … Nobody told you that the stuff you wanted on your trip had to be in a small bag. So all my tropical uniform, to change into halfway out, was going in the hold … One of the fellows who'd met me the night before helped me out – he must have been the Movements Officer, because he took me up to where all the stuff was and got my case out … He took a liking to me, probably had his eye on the main chance – you learn these things very quickly – he'd got me a bacon and egg sandwich … well, I was surprised to have my breakfast in a sandwich, but I'd have been even more astounded not to have had breakfast. You always had a cooked breakfast.

Doreen Smedley was posted to Wroughton to do aeromed though, unusually, she had not volunteered for it. At some stops, she recalls, there was no relief sister, as there was later; you did the whole trip on your own and the saying was that 'you walked all the way back from the Far East'. She was not too enamoured of aeromed duty, but adds, 'I will never forget the sight of the night sky at Idris. It was blue-black, and studded with diamonds – a wonderful sight!'

Ann Tickle (Mrs Waters) spent three and a half incident-filled years on aeromed duty at Wroughton. She specialised in nursing polio victims and escorted one lady back from Egypt in an iron lung. In Cyprus during the EOKA terrorist troubles, she and her colleagues drove with an armed guard in their car, escorted by an ambulance with a gun pointing out of the window.

Any flight might run into unexpected situations, as Julia Inkpen (Mrs Jenkins) found out. Her aircraft, with twenty French typists as passengers, made a forced landing at Sharjah, where the men hadn't seen a woman for five months. The CO spirited his female visitors to a fort on the base complete with double locks and armed guards! 'Despite the security, we had a great time in the twenty-four hours we were there,' says Julia:

> Men appeared from all directions. One doctor insisted that we visit his hospital and two locust-control officers took us off over the desert to Dubai where we met other European officials who laid on a party. We were quite embarrassed by the flimsy state of our cotton dresses as the local women were in deepest purdah with only their eyes showing.

Joy Harris tells of a stop-over at Car Nicobar, in the Nicobar Islands, Indian Ocean, which provided a staging post before the island of Gan came into RAF use:

> They had one very young officer – it was just a refuelling base, no doctor – they didn't wear any clothes at all unless there was an aircraft with some women on, and then they'd put shorts on ... When I got there the cook had the most terrible rash – he'd cut himself and the local 'witch-doctor' had shoved some paste on it.
>
> They'd seen on the manifest that there would be a nursing officer on board, so they thought they'd wait until we got there and ask our opinions. I asked if they'd got any medical supplies – 'Oh, in the safe' – so they opened the safe, and all they'd got was some codeine, some morphia, and a pistol! I think we told them to get on to Singapore to ask the next aircraft to bring them some anti-histamines.

14

Aeromeds Increase

As PMs flew more and more aeromeds, sisters assigned to this duty underwent special flight-nursing courses at RAF Lyneham. At first the course was fairly basic, consisting of lectures and demonstrations, with a session in what Sally Donovan (Mrs Pullan) calls 'the dreaded decompression chamber'. In this test, because of euphoria caused by lack of oxygen:

> we were quite sure we could survive everything, and then you looked at the paper afterwards – you'd written awful rubbish. And the most cocky amongst us was the one who passed out, of course ... You did all the bits of airworthiness ... when you were chucked around everywhere in those awful old Hastings – lovely old Hastings – to see whether you could cope.

Adult patients, whether mobile or strapped in stretchers, presented problems enough: for younger patients, ingenuity helped. 'You had a little crèche made up of four boxes – huge wooden crates with a red cross. You used to put three in a row and a rug on the floor, and the children all sat in there – obviously they weren't going to be pinned in a seat.'

As an illustration of the kind of workload experienced by flight sisters, Elizabeth Chalton (Mrs Walker) kept a detailed record of one of her missions, flown in a Hastings in August 1956. On 2 August they left Lyneham and flew to Idris, North Africa, journey time 6 hours 20 minutes; next day they flew from Idris to Habbaniya, Iraq, taking 8 hours 5 minutes. Habbaniya to Mauripur, Pakistan, occupied 7 hours 10 minutes of the following day; on 5 August from Mauripur to Negombo, Ceylon (Sri Lanka), took 6 hours 35 minutes and next day to Changi Singapore was 8 hours 35 minutes flying time. She enjoyed a free day on 7 August before flying from Changi back to Negombo in 8 hours 35 minutes; then on to Mauripur again in 7 hours 30 minutes. After another free day she was flying back via Habbaniya, to Luqa, and finally home to Lyneham over another three days, each flight taking roughly 7½ hours. Since in practice a 'free day' en route was often spent helping out at the local RAF hospital, these journeys were no rest cure.

Staging posts at El Adem, Idris, Mauripur and Luqa all had large sick quarters, most of which eventually claimed PMs on their staff; at the others, non-commissioned male SRNs of the RAFMS supervised the orderlies. These experienced male nurses also worked side by side with female nursing officers of the PMRAFNS at hospitals at Habbaniya in Iraq, Negombo in Ceylon and Changi in Singapore. But in Iraq and Ceylon the flags of the RAF were soon to be hauled down for the last time.

'Lido of the East'

By the late 1940s, RAF Habbaniya had grown into a huge sprawl, 'the second largest town in Iraq, after Baghdad', say those who knew it. Its airfield had an extra runway on the plateau above to take the huge new transport planes. The camp included quarters for families, churches of several denominations, shopping centres, well-tended gardens with trees and flowers, sports facilities (including grassed football pitches), clubs of all kinds, various messes, a riding school, a civil cantonment, a race track and even a taxi service to get people around the enormous 28 square miles of the camp. It was the 'Lido of the East', an oasis with permanent stone buildings and an elusive perfume of Arabia – gardens and football pitches stayed green by nightly flooding from irrigation ditches fed by the pungent waters of the Euphrates!

Doris Stanford (Mrs Kent) arrived in Habbaniya by air, in a York aircraft: 'I'll never forget that, because we were flying low and we hit a dust storm. We were all frightfully sick and we arrived feeling and looking like nothing on earth.' A team of twenty sisters, led by Matron Tisdale, staffed the large hospital. Sisters' rooms lay apart from the mess, beyond gardens full of oleander bushes and eucalyptus trees where 'coming back from a dance or from a club at night with our escorts, we might linger a little bit. Suddenly out of the bushes these men would appear – 'Halt, who goes there?!' They knew who we were but they would always jump out …' On occasion the guards were less vigilant. One sister was alone in her room when two men burst in and threatened her with knives while they stole all her possessions.

Most of the local people appreciated the work brought by the RAF station. Iraqi women helped in the hospital and Iraqi men did labouring work, or acted as personal bearers. But cultural differences caused misunderstandings, as Margaret Kingston points out:

> My bearer knew that I loved Marmite and Bovril – in the mess I often used to ask for it at tea-time. So, every morning, when he brought my cup of tea, I had a jar of Marmite and a cup of tea! What he thought I was going to do with a whole jar I don't know! Every day!

On the occasion of the coronation of Queen Elizabeth II, Habbaniya staged a military tattoo. Margaret Kingston says:

> We had to go in our mess kit, which in those days was like a white nightie. We had our rankings up on our shoulders, and brass buttons, and sleeves with pointed

> bits over our hands, and then a big white hat turned up at the side, with the RAF cockade at the side – we used to call it our bowling team outfit! And white court shoes, from Moss Bros. Well, we got to the arena and everything stopped – they didn't know what had arrived – the matron with her ten ducklings parading behind … It was a very good spectacle they put on, but like a fool I took my shoes off and, of course, come time to leave, I could not get them on. My escort very nobly put one in each pocket and I had to walk back in my stocking feet … They had solid toes, these shoes. We used to fill them with water and bang them on the handle of a broom, to soften them – they were really impossible.

The rest and leave centre at Ser Amadia, up in the Kurdistan hills, still required sisters to stay on short attachments. During her sojourn, Joan Metcalfe 'used to go out into the villages; you'd get a message somebody was ill, out you went on mules … In Kurdistan they were all so nice, so friendly – but so primitive – they had swinging electric light bulbs down the main street, with hovels either side.' Margaret Kingston also rode out on a mule to treat the tribespeople, some of whom still had stocks of old-style powdered penicillin, long past its sell-by date. 'You had to put sterile water in it and shake it … So, diplomatically, we used to take some fresh penicillin and treat their children …'

An adventurous incident recalled by Doreen Elston (Mrs Curston) began at Habbaniya when a signal came from Ser Amadia requesting urgent medical assistance for a member of the WRAF who was dangerously ill with a fractured dislocation of the neck. A team consisting of Sister Elston, a surgeon and a theatre technician, flew to the nearest Iraqi airfield, at Mosul. They were still forty-five mountainous, roadless miles from Ser Amadia. They spied a helicopter 'but we were told it was just for the use of King Faisal II'. However, by pulling a few diplomatic strings they obtained permission to borrow the helicopter and its pilot. 'We were sitting in luxuriously upholstered seats when the pilot informed us it was not safe for him to fly at more than 6,000 feet. The only compensation … was that we flew over some of the most beautiful mountain ranges and gorges we had ever seen …' Ser Amadia lay too high in the mountains for the helicopter to reach and, seeing the terrain ahead, they began to wonder how on earth they would bring the girl safely down the mountain. Landing at a local levies' camp, they had tea while the Iraqi soldiers saddled mules for the final leg:

> It was at this point that we learnt that the injury to our patient had occurred due to her falling from a mule …
>
> We set off on the final lap, the mules insisting on walking at the very edge of each precipice, with thousands of feet drop below, only stopping for the call of nature, after which they would take off at enormous speed to catch up with the others.

At Ser Amadia they found the patient in reasonable condition:

> She had a fracture dislocation of the cervical spine with, fortunately, no cord involvement, and a fractured humerus. We immediately set to work reducing the dislocation by traction and immobilising her in plaster … Next morning we enclosed her in a Neil Robertson stretcher and general service stretcher for transportation, and again with the help of the levy troops, we transported her down the mountain. The descent was a more gentle slope … but still very hazardous.

At the bottom of the mountain a pickup waited to transfer them along 'an unbelievably bad road full of pot-holes' to an airstrip where an Anson waited, piloted by the senior Wing Commander from Habbaniya. They managed 'to squeeze the patient into the plane and strapped her in firmly … Mountain sides flashed perilously close … as we banked and climbed steeply … our last view of the airfield was the adjutant of Ser Amadia down on his knees praying for us …'

The RAF's position in Iraq was, however, no longer secure. In July 1956 the status of Habbaniya hospital was reduced, with a sister-in-charge instead of a matron. Two years later, the assassination of King Faisal II ushered in a pro-USSR Republic with a determinedly neutral foreign policy. At this point, all British forces withdrew from Iraq.

Ceylon

Another exotic staging-point provided a posting for PMs from 1950 to 1960. This was Ceylon (now Sri Lanka), island of shady palms and coconut groves, warm western beaches and jungles where elephant and crimson butterfly roam free. From biblical times, merchants and invaders came here seeking spices and gems: Solomon sent for Singhalese jewels to impress the Queen of Sheba; later the Romans, the Moors, the Portuguese and the Dutch came, wanting cinnamon, rubies, topaz and moonstones; and planters settled to grow coffee and tap rubber. From 1815, Britain controlled the island. Plantations of coffee, which brought a seasonal influx of Indian pickers, were replaced by tea, which required picking year-round by Indian incomers – the Tamils.

During the Second World War the island acted as a springboard for Allied operations. Naval and army bases grew up, with the RAF at Katunayake and an MFH nearby. The airfield, some 4 miles south of Negombo, would eventually become Colombo International Airport.

On Ceylon's assumption of independence in 1948, the British Military Hospital at Colombo closed, but the flight staging post at RAF Katunayake remained in operation. In order to provide medical cover both for RAF personnel on the island and for patients brought through on air evacuation flights, Flight Officer Kathleen Hird (Mrs Bion) and Squadron Officer (Matron) Gwen Jones trooped out on the *Orduna* in 1950 to help open a new RAFH at Negombo.

What Kathleen Hird considered 'a lovely single storey hospital in the middle of the vast coconut plantation' was still in the building process when the nursing officers sailed in that February. They accepted their first patients in March, when Sisters

Robertson and Boutland arrived – as did the first baby, born before the paint was dry! The PMs lived in the officers' mess, which made for pleasant off-duty hours, with:

> long nights on the veranda with the chaps and visiting Hastings crews doing the supply routes, and many G&Ts. No swimming pool for us but a wonderful lagoon a couple of miles away with superb empty beaches and curry in the Rest House … Quite a few cases of poliomyelitis – someone found an old iron lung in Colombo and brought it back to us.

Over the ten years of the hospital's existence, Ceylon left different impressions on all the PMs who saw it. On leave from Aden, Margaret Kingston enjoyed a holiday there. She had visited the island before, staging through while on casevacs, but never for long enough to get used to the frogs: 'They never stop all night. This awful croak-croak-croak-croak-croak-croak … it goes on and on.'

Tessa Lawless recalls the beauty of the harbour lights at night as she arrived by ship, the dancing elephants at a zoo, and the brilliant colours of sunset fading to the paler glory of moonrise.

On the last Comet to stage through Negombo, Rosie Partington and a friend arrived from RAFH Changi to spend ten days' leave in Ceylon. They toured the island by taxi, the cheapest way, and the driver, asking if they were interested in 'stones', took them to the back of a wood, to a little shed where they saw all manner of gems in screw-top jars: opals, aquamarines, garnets. 'Afterwards,' says Rosie, 'we wished we'd known more about them.' The little man left them to pick out what stones they wanted and later he came back to fix a very reasonable price. Rosie only wished she'd bought more while she was about it!

Jessie Higgins (who had hated the bugs and snakes in Burma) spent six months in Ceylon. She remembers:

> a horrible little hospital. Absolutely open. No windows, just balconies. We were about 25 miles from Colombo and, with casevac, they were in and out twice a week, very hard work when they'd come in … I was terrified there, because … I'm one who sees snakes – or so I was told by an old boy in Ceylon: 'Missie see snake, Missie see snake.' We had maternity there, and we had a 'caesar' one night … I went over, being a midwife, and was bringing the baby back when suddenly I realised something was going across my legs – I had the baby in my arms, so I couldn't see down – I looked round and there was about ten feet of snake … How I didn't drop that baby, I'll never know. I could not move! I just stood and let the snake go. It was terrifying.
>
> The joke was, when I reported it in the morning they all said, 'Oh, go on, Higgie – you see snakes everywhere,' and I said, 'I saw [a] snake!' Then about two days later … we had those great big iron lungs in those days and I went and pulled the lid back

> – and there's a snake in the iron lung! I worried about them getting into babies' cots. I would have died if any baby had been hurt … I must say, I hated Ceylon.

Jean King (Mrs Flower) writes of 'the heat which hit us as we left the aircraft. Having left England in mid-winter wearing our blues, we changed into KDs [khaki drill] in Karachi, but even in lighter uniform we still wore stockings and regulation black shoes'. RAF Katunayake had a capacious officers' mess designed to accommodate crew and passengers on unexpected stopovers, from aircraft needing repair or otherwise delayed:

> I remember coming off night duty one morning and walking into our large mess dining room to find it full of American soldiers grounded from their u/s troop carrier – unfortunately repaired very quickly.
>
> The situation with the Tamils was in its very early stages but there was an incident during 1958 which resulted in us being confined to camp for six weeks … The station cinema was our salvation … the programme was changed every night!

Jean was one of six nursing officers stationed in Ceylon in 1958, of whom four were midwives; the 'midder' unit was kept very busy. It and the families' ward had Singhalese women as orderlies, but the airmen's ward had national servicemen. 'There were many long-haul flights in the '50s and the same crews dropped in … Casevac sisters came through quite often, and the girls coming to Ceylon on leave from Changi often spent a night with us on the way.' PMs and pilots shared balmy evenings on the veranda under the palms 'with a long cool gin and fresh lime in my hand [or] in the ante room listening to music … Records were few and precious, easily broken, so that the oft-repeated music from those days does stick around in my memory …'

The darker side

The happy, social side of casualty evacuation lingers in many memories. But there were dangers, too. In March 1953 an aeromed flight with Julia Inkpen (Mrs Jenkins) as flight sister approached Lyneham in thick fog. 'A dreadful crash and rending sound convinced us that our last moment had come, but then, with a roar, we climbed into the blue sky again.' They had hit the tops of trees and were told to divert to RAF Tangmere, near Chichester, flying no higher than 1,000 feet. After a safe landing:

> we were horrified to see that the wings were ripped to pieces, propellers bent, and the tail almost severed. Everyone at Tangmere was on the runway. I heard one officer remark, 'If I hadn't seen it with my own eyes I wouldn't have believed that an aircraft could fly in such a condition.' Getting the stretchers off was quite a problem (Lyneham had ambulances with opening roofs). It was achieved by backing three-tonners up to the door of the aircraft, unloading the stretchers onto the

> roofs, thence lowering them into other vehicles. I think we all suffered from delayed shock. The pilot's last comment was 'We must have had angels on the wingtips'.

In 1956 Kay Burrows (Mrs Bennett) was:

> escorting a small party of patients from Kai Tak [Hong Kong] to the RAF hospital at Changi, in a Valetta. We had just left Saigon when we lost one engine, then lost height. The pilot decided to put down in a paddy field, which was also a Chinese cemetery, so we hit a grave! We evacuated quickly for fear of fire. Nobody was injured except the pilot, whom we feared might have broken his spine (not the case, in the event). We put him on an aircraft door and tied him firmly. A crowd of curious Vietnamese arrived and brought up a car. We put the poor pilot in the back – at an angle with his feet sticking out – and I went in the front with the driver, and a marvellous Scots lad, a patient, ran as long as he could supporting the pilot's head.

On the main road an open truck met them and they loaded the pilot into the back of it:

> By then he was complaining of his eyes, which he feared had glass in them. The friendly villagers were still round us [so] I asked for water and one produced a bottle of lemonade – I washed his eyes out with that. We eventually reached the French hospital in Saigon.

Kay found accommodation with an American family, who drove her round to visit and distribute sedatives to her various patients, scattered among host families, but 'most particularly I was able to thank that marvellous Scottish boy who ran beside the pilot … The pilot made a full recovery.'

She adds modestly, 'This small incident was, I fear, exaggerated, but it brought a small measure of recognition of the PMs. I am very proud to have been a member.' For her part in this 'small incident', Kay was awarded the Royal Humane Society Bronze medal – the first award of its kind to be made in a peacetime incident.

An even more terrible accident occurred on 4 March 1956, when an Anson aircraft on a casualty evacuation flight over Germany lost oil pressure at 4,000 feet, obliging the pilot to feather the engine. Unable to maintain height and with the ground below obscured by cloud, he decided to make a forced landing, but on breaking through the cloud he found himself low over a heavily wooded area. He tried to turn to avoid the trees, but caught his starboard wing. The plane crashed. Flight Officer Daphne Jane Budgen of the PMRAFNS and SAC R. Flint of the RAFMS were both killed; the pilot and another nurse, Sergeant J.P. Moynan, suffered serious injuries.

Steamer Point, Aden

Aden's RAF hospital, set high on its hill above the busy port, took in all service personnel, their wives and families, merchant seamen of all races, and personnel from the BP oil refinery which, in the 1950s, was still under construction. Everyone who worked at Steamer Point mentions the heat and the impossibility of staying crisply starched. Matron and her twelve ward sisters had to change clothes at least twice a day to stay comfortable.

Margaret Kingston remembers the problems caused by having a families' ward on two floors, 'children down below where it was impossible to see them without going up and down outside steps'. However, one blessedly air-conditioned room provided a respite for certain very ill patients. One patient was resting there under Margaret Kingston's supervision when the air-conditioning machine, 'a large noisy tractor-like affair outside on the veranda', stopped working. Unable to persuade anyone from 'Works and Bricks' to come to her aid, Margaret:

> rang the CO, Group Captain 'Kiwi' Corbett. He immediately gathered up his tool bag and in his baggy KD shorts appeared on the scene. He had the thing in bits on the veranda when matron came to do her round. Kiwi kept his head down and continued banging. 'Sister!' says matron, 'Stop that man making such a noise when I'm doing my round!' With that, Kiwi looked up and laughed. Blushes all round.

Later, on a morning when a staff photograph was to be taken, nursing sisters and MOs, dressed in immaculate whites, stood around waiting for Kiwi Corbett to arrive. They heard his old banger chugging up the hill, and, 'at that very moment, a vulture flew overhead, having gathered a sheep's entrails from the village slaughter below the rocks … it dropped the mess bang onto the head of one of the sisters … she had to retreat for a quick shower and change of uniform.'

A genuine life-or-death emergency called Barbara Millar (Mrs Wight) into action when, in 1952, Flight Lieutenant Percy Henry Mason was accidentally shot – by a bullet in the heart – while shooting baboons out in the 'bundu'.

On theatre night call, Barbara Millar was woken at 1 a.m. with orders to be ready to fly at first light from RAF Khormaksar to Dhala, a primitive state 65 miles away in the Aden Protectorate. With the help of the corporal theatre technician and an Arab orderly she had to prepare and pack the necessary equipment which, with no pre-packed trays in those days, meant that:

> instruments had to be selected, rinsed, arranged in the trays wrapped in dressing towels and autoclaved [steam-sterilised]. This included all drums with dressing gowns, towels, etc. – sutures, needles, lotions … I prepared a general set, and specialised instruments such as bone cutters, large retractors, etc, and the corporal prepared the anaesthetic trolley.

Time was of the essence. They only hoped they had remembered everything.

Two Ansons waited for them at Khormaksar. The first flew with surgeon Squadron Leader Dickie Prior and his anaesthetist brother Derek; the second carried Sister Millar, the Corporal Tech and the equipment. After an hour's flight they landed at the airstrip in remote and mountainous Dhala. Local Arabs had gathered to watch proceedings and the Emir's young son arrived on a donkey, with his bodyguard alongside. Having assessed the situation, the surgeon decided it was too risky to perform heart surgery out in the rocky desert; they must fly the patient back to Aden. Barbara says, 'Dickie, Derek and myself … took it in turns to hold up the drip with the left hand and give slight pressure with swabs on his chest with the right hand, to stop the oozing.'

From the airfield at Khormaksar an ambulance took them the 10 miles back to the RAF hospital at Steamer Point, where the theatre team waited. Twenty-two donors from the RAF and WRAF each gave a pint of blood. Using a technique practised only once before by a British doctor (patients with perforated hearts did not usually survive long enough to reach the operating table) the team transfused blood via the patient's artery instead of a vein. Almost instantly his pulse revived and his blood pressure rose. Barbara Millar adds, 'Nursing care was excellent, bearing in mind that we did not have the facilities of an Intensive Care Ward … Flt Lt Mason recovered, with a slight enlargement of the liver.'

Changi, Singapore

Much further east, Singapore Island lies at the southern tip of the Malay peninsula, a cosmopolitan whirl of different tongues, religions, rituals and customs. At the eastern tip of the island, Changi village looks northward across the Straits of Johore, a vista of flowering trees and blue seas, with two or three miles away the deep green forests of the Malayan peninsula. The RAF hospital, opened in 1947, stood on a hill and was originally two large blocks of buildings separated by a famous flight of ninety steps.

Joy Harris arrived in Changi in 1951:

> On your first day there, you were sent down to the village to buy a packet of starch and some washing powder for the amah – oh, and an umbrella, because it poured with rain every day. And the amah starched everything. You had cotton dresses in those days – they'd stand up without you in them. And you had to wear stockings, and she'd starch those too, and your knickers and everything – awfully uncomfortable.

For Olive Kirkham, a visit to a leper colony at nearby Seletar proved thought-provoking. 'How sad it was to see these poor disfigured patients sitting cross-legged on their beds, which were so close together … some of them were suffering also from dementia … They had living quarters for families, so they could all live together …' A happier memory for Olive and her friend Meg McPherson is of being guests at the first day of a Malay wedding – a three-day feast at which one of the ward boys was married. Olive and Meg were the only Christians to join in the procession to the bride's house, where they saw the bridal couple 'beautifully dressed and surrounded by flowers'.

As always, romance was never far away. Joy Harris found herself 'having a difficult time ending a friendship, and he persuaded me to have one last evening out'. They ended up, inevitably, at a local beauty spot named Paradise Beach, where:

> a discreet survey of the scene revealed friends with their own chaps … I was upset, and finally reduced to tears … He never knew the tears were not due to him but to a rare moment of home sickness – I could hear the Grand National commentary on a car radio parked nearby!

The busy maternity unit at Changi Hospital, as remembered by Jan Smith (Mrs Campbell), had a main ward with fourteen or so beds; a side ward and a first-stage room, both with two beds; plus a delivery room just large enough for 'a bed, a delivery trolley, a sink, a stool and a bucket with a lid. It was half-tiled for easy cleaning and, biggest bonus of all, it was air conditioned.' In the nursery a table for changing nappies stood against one wall, with cots packed round two other walls, and against the fourth a steriliser and a trolley for making up feeds – a duty accomplished by passing kettles of boiling water through a hatch from the kitchen. Baby baths, too, were filled each morning in the kitchen before being carted through to the delivery room 'which, in the heat and hurry, was no mean task … One sister bathed and a nurse dried and applied a nappy. It was like piece work on a production line …'

Shelagh Glenn (Mrs Barber) worked in theatre, which was in the upper building, connected with the lower hospital and the wards by the famous steps. Many days, when on call, Shelagh would be left alone in theatre when everybody else had gone. 'I used to think, This is a bit silly, sitting here doing nothing, so I'd finish what I had to do and nip down, fifty or sixty steps, to the back entrance of the mess. I'd been doing this for ages.' One day, she was halfway down when she saw Matron Jessie Higgins on her way up. 'So, well, fair cop, I'd been doing it for ages and hadn't been caught … as she walked past me she looked at her watch said, 'Oh, you're late today, Glenn, it's usually about ten past when you come down' – she'd been watching me all the time!'

Shelagh remembers a new operating theatre being built, which made life easier because:

> when people came up to theatre they went into a ward, stayed there for twenty-four hours, and were carted down by ambulance, to the place at the bottom – three-quarters of a mile round by road! – from there they were carried by porters up the stairs, into the various wards … It was quite hysterical when they were building. A chap came into the surgical ward and said, 'We're having problems, can I bring my cement mixer through the corridor in the ward?' so the sister said, 'I suppose so, if it

> helps.' She thought he meant literally a cement mixer, but of course it wasn't – it was little men running through with yokes, carrying things.

Over drinks in the mess, tales of tigers swimming the Straits of Johore, straight from the deep jungles of Malaya, tempted Marjorie Eavis (Mrs McCandlish) to explore. She had joined the PMs in 1943, during the Blitz, and had been in India during partition and in Aden when the Arabs were fighting the Jews. Following quieter sojourns at hospitals in England and Germany, she came to Changi in 1956. Marjorie had won her parachutist wings in the late 1940s, and this qualification persuaded authority to allow her to go into the jungle, where Malay troops commanded by British or Commonwealth officers were still hunting Communist bandits.

The vibrant, flower-bright jungle, filled with monkeys and birds, swept by below as the small 'pioneer plane' flew to land in a tiny clearing. Marjorie was 'immediately surrounded by half-clad Kemar belles who had never seen a [white] woman before. I was in great danger of having my jungle kit of shirt, trousers, and tightly laced boots removed so that they could have a better look at me!' The plane had gone on to take supplies to other jungle outposts, but Marjorie was allowed to join the ground patrol, slithering silently through dank gloom, over lichen-covered tree trunks poised high above jungle streams, with deadly phosphorescent plants glimmering and on every leaf leeches that were 'well aware of my AB Rhesus negative blood … I did not realise until the patrol returned what a ghastly mess I looked – not the neat white dressed and veiled hospital Sister, but a creature crawling with ants after the blood seeping through my jungle gear.' Leeches festooned her arms, and the backs of her legs resembled bunches of bloated grapes. She was ordered to undress and don a towel and, 'protected by a circle of Malays, was passed lighted cigarettes to burn them off … Suddenly I felt hot breath on my back. It was the Sakai headman removing some in inaccessible places with his "Baccy-spittle"!'

Afterwards she heard that the headman had requested her as his sixth wife – 'the greatest honour he could bestow. However, with humility I replied that PMs were not allowed husbands … Madam regrets, but thank you just the same!'

West Germany

In the aftermath of war, British army and air force bases which opened in north-west Germany included two RAF hospitals, at Rostrup and Rinteln.

RAFH Rostrup, in the Bremen area, was built soon after the war, amid a landscape of bomb craters. Nearly a decade later, Doreen Hunt (Mrs Tomlin) found that time and nature had worked their spell: the hospital now enjoyed beautiful views across Lake Zwischenahn. PMs' quarters lay a short distance away, in a spacious, single-storey block flanked by tennis courts.

Rostrup provided medical cover for three nearby RAF flying stations. As more and more personnel acquired cars, it handled a good many road accident cases too. But the most demanding period Doreen Hunt experienced was during an epidemic of Asian flu, when 'the English school of Prince Rupert Wilhelmshaven was admitted en masse … We ran out of steam – everything that made steam was used, but it was not enough.' The RAF flew in with oxygen tents and other equipment, but despite all efforts a small boy and a young pilot died. 'Even the young National Service orderlies who would be counting the days to demob were magnificent. Their usual moans would be, "I didn't ask to work in a hospital, or join up." That was all forgotten and at last they became 'one of us'.'

In 1958, when many British troops left Germany, Rostrup gradually discharged its patients and staff went home. Joy Harris and two other sisters were posted a few miles north, to RAF Jever, where they opened a small maternity unit, and found themselves the only females in the officers' mess. Meanwhile Doreen Hunt and three other PMs attended Rostrup's final parade. Since they had not been certain of their final leaving date, they had not been able to send luggage ahead; the four sisters travelled with twenty-eight pieces of luggage, which did not amuse the customs officer who, at Parkeston Quay, asked what they had to declare. When Doreen said 'a wire bust' his face fell and 'he insisted on my opening the container. He looked quite bemused – it was my dressmaker's wire bust frame. They didn't ask us to open anything else …'

The RAF hospital at Rinteln, near Hanover, had an even shorter history. Once an SS barracks, it was taken over by the wartime No 8 RAFH in 1945, staffed mainly by the RAF with some army personnel. The sisters' mess, built as part of the war reparations and intended to become a hotel at some later date, was suitably spacious and well appointed, with a terrace where PMs could sit and chat while admiring the surrounding countryside. They did so until 1953, when the RAF handed over to the army and Rinteln became a British military hospital. It functioned in this capacity until 1996.

In its brief few RAF years, Rinteln provided a busy posting for PMs such as Susan Armistead (Mrs Sutcliffe). She enjoyed a lively MFH exercise dubbed Operation Pinnacle, and when the Commander-in-Chief's wife fell ill with an ulcer Susan escorted her home on casevac – and was rewarded by an invitation to lunch with the C-in-C himself.

Two tanks of the 11th Armoured Division collided and burst into flames at the end of an exercise. Alan Rosser was one of the survivors of the crash and the fire: 'After what seemed an interminable passage of time waiting for, and then travelling in, the ambulance, we arrived at Rinteln. By this time my burns had swollen and I was unable to see.' He remembers only 'a firm but caring voice which assured me I was all right now and that I would be "cleaned up" and given something to help me sleep.' He later discovered that the voice belonged to Sister Grace Haydock. But, blind as he was for several weeks, he couldn't see her. He came to know:

> her voice, her step … I knew the instant she arrived at the entrance to the ward. The hum of activity was hushed when she set foot in her domain. She was the personi-

> fication of the benign despot … her rule was absolute [but] she inspired confidence and calm … I believe I owe her my life.

He concludes: 'I was flown back to hospital in Aldershot in due course, but by this time Sister had taken her leave. So … I never did see Sister Haydock.'

When the RAF handed over the premises at Rinteln to the army, the sisters made sure they removed all mess property, including the red entrance carpet – 'I remember the looks of horror on the QAs' faces,' writes Muriel Dunn, who was about to leave with the Rinteln matron, Wing Officer 'Gertie' Grierson, in her red MG. They were moving on to a new, purpose-built RAF hospital, at Wegberg.

Early Wegberg

Wegberg lies just inside West Germany, close to the borders of Holland and Belgium. Its RAF hospital was designed and built within ten months: designed in January 1953, it admitted its first patients on 1 November that same year. It was of unique design, the main buildings forming two D-shapes, the smaller inside the larger, with very wide main corridors; subsidiary linking corridors connected the two Ds like spokes of a wheel.

Squadron Officer Doris Trick helped to equip the place and prepare for the opening and, when the day came, Margaret 'Jane' Clews and nine other sisters were posted out from the UK. Others came from Rinteln and they, as Jane Clews recalls, 'were not overjoyed with the move. We newcomers never failed to hear about that marvellous place up north!'

Coming from that 'marvellous place', Muriel Dunn's first impression of Wegberg was of a dark and unwelcoming hospital set in flat, unattractive countryside. The wide corridors, designed to hold huge numbers of casualties if needed (the Cold War was deepening and nuclear war a constant peril):

> seemed endless and it was said to be a quarter mile to the maternity ward where I worked. I delivered the first baby to be born there … Not all the wards were open immediately and the general night sister had a good step in between them. At one time she used a cycle to make her rounds!

That bitter winter, which froze the Wegberg lake and even saw huge blocks of ice floating down the Rhine, the lack of lagging on water pipes made itself evident. 'The water came down the metal rods which held the electric lights and light bowls, breaking them and scattering water and glass … One burst over an off-duty sister sitting on her bed …' They had ample hot water but no cold, so if someone wanted a bath she had to run the water and wait for it to cool (and hope that no one else nipped in first). Even the loos had to be flushed with hot water!

For Therese Saunders (Mrs Ayres), a memory that haunts is 'a dreadful outbreak of gastro-enteritis amongst children and babies in Wegberg, and so many died despite our desperate efforts to save them. All leave was cancelled and we worked flat out for what seemed a very long time.'

Princess Marina (late Duchess of Kent, mother of Princess Alexandra) paid a royal visit to Wegberg while Doris Stanford (Mrs Kent) was running the children's ward. 'I had to spruce them all up – you know what children are like.' It was all terribly formal, everyone at attention, no sitting on beds, counterpanes wrinkleless and so on. Tension reigned as the royal entourage appeared. Then one of the small patients, who had the habit of removing his clothes, suddenly started throwing off his pyjamas and 'made everybody laugh – it was rather nice'.

When a convoy of patients, including a baby with a serious chest condition, had to be rushed back to London's Brompton Hospital, Doris Stanford went with them. They flew in a Dakota, 'it flew very low, and I was so ill. I was quite ashamed – I was supposed to be looking after the patients …' After her earlier bad experience flying to Habbaniya, and now the Dakota trip, she realised she probably wasn't suited to aerial nursing.

National servicemen

Before conscription ended in 1960, many young men of eighteen or so were called up to serve their country for two years. Some came willingly, some less so. David Snell had imagined being aircrew, but, 'despite any amount of kicking and screaming on our part, a large proportion of us found that we were going to spend two years in the Medical Branch'.

Sisters hold fond memories of these 'National Service boys', who in civilian life might be apprentice engineers, carpenters, coalmen, clerks or ballet dancers; a few were trained laboratory technicians – at least they understood the rudiments of hospital life.

Joy Harris remembers how the boys pitched in when inspections were due:

> [We had] this awful brown oil-cloth you had to see your face in. You'd bumper it with these heavy great bumpers, and then everybody had to walk around with bits of old blanket on their feet. We had an AOC's inspection coming up at Ely and … We got on duty at quarter to eight in the morning, to get the place ready for the AOC's inspection, and it was spotless! – the boys on night duty had got it up to inspection standard.

As might be expected, the 'boys' had their favourites, among both PMs and patients. Nursing orderly M.J. Joy recalls that his job varied from taking temperatures and pulses to giving out bedpans. 'It has been known that some orderlies, dealing with an awkward patient who demanded a bedpan immediately, gave them a stainless steel one which had been under the hot tap for a couple of minutes …'

Tony Bowdler started his regular air force career as a nursing attendant at Wegberg. He was nineteen years old and most of his peers were National Service conscripts. They thought of the sisters as:

> ancient (all of ten years older than us), very efficient and wise. Most of the orderlies, for we were still called that at the time, detested the PMs as we appeared to do the work and they appeared to get the fun and money … The resentment was short-lived for me, but I do remember some of the old sweats being less than complimentary about the PMs.

From another posting, at Halton, Tony Bowdler recalls 'the dearest, most lovable PM … Sqn Off. Irene Turner … she had been in the service for ever.' She was in her early forties at the time, while he was a mere stripling of twenty-one. He most remembers her for the note pinned to her desk, which said, 'Orderlies are instructed not to rummage in sister's drawers at any time'! Tony doesn't think she saw the double-entendre. Oh no?

Both sides could play that game. Sylvia Emery (Mrs Pounds) says that she and her contemporaries worked on the wards in pairs, or sometimes alone, assisted only by National Servicemen 'in varying stages of training'. In order to help the boys widen their experience and perhaps gain promotion, sisters allowed them to do some of the extra routine tasks such as writing up reports. One chap noted that a patient 'took a little custard, and vomited a trifle'! He didn't know what he'd written, so Sister Emery believed.

Who was kidding whom?

Early dialysis

RAF interest in the renal dialysis field began during the Second World War, when doctors realised that many casualties died not from injuries but from kidney failure, a common factor in acute injury. As a result, the Renal Unit at PMRAFH Halton came into being, officially founded in 1956 by Air Vice Marshal Sir Ralph Jackson. It possessed one of the original Kolff Twin Coil Dialysis machines – of which only two existed in the world at the time. Initially the machine offered only temporary relief to kidney patients, but it led to developments which eventually allowed for long-term treatment of chronic renal failure.

Jessie Higgins, by then a senior matron (Wing Officer), arrived at Halton just as they were beginning to perfect the machine. 'It was like a huge great boiler! I was terrified of it!' Interest in the new machine grew swiftly, especially after Guy's Hospital became involved in the research work, and groups of doctors and nursing sisters were sent to Halton for training:

> We used to have them for two weeks – six working days each week. They hated it: 'Trained by the RAF?' … They thought we did just in-growing toe-nails and things. Didn't realise we delivered a thousand babies a year, apart from anything else. I put them straight, I said, 'Now … you came here to learn about something. There isn't another place in the world.'

One renal patient, Flying Officer (later Wing Commander) Clifford Blunt, says he developed an allergy and lost large patches of skin from the 'sweaty areas' of his body. Treatment consisted of frequent medicated baths, painting the affected areas with gentian violet and exposing them to the air – which in practice left him lying on his bed under a cage, with the sheet folded back and his nether regions in full view. 'When visitors came, screens were placed around my bed to hide the blue-bottomed baboon from sight!' The screens went up during a visit by Princess Marina, Commandant-in-Chief of the Red Cross. Matron endeavoured to distract Her Royal Highness, but the princess determined to see the mysterious patient. 'She stood at the foot of my bed and took a great interest in my treatment,' Clifford Blunt writes. 'Whether I was more violet or red I will never know – but I was certainly in glorious Technicolor.'

Bull

Official visits of all kinds caused a good deal of angst. On one occasion at Ely, when Mary Page (Mrs Payne) nervously escorted Princess Mary round the ward, in order to avoid embarrassment she 'changed the diagnosis' of patients recovering from circumcision.

Shelagh Glenn (Mrs Barber) recalls:

> I arrived at Halton the day before the Princess Royal was making a visit ... Sister said, 'Now, we're not having flowers in all the rooms, we're having potted plants in wards 1 and 2, and when ward 1 has been visited those plants will go to ward 3 and when ward 2 has been visited, they'll go to ward 4 ...' I could just imagine me, in the PMs for one day, coming down the corridor with a couple of potted plants and bumping straight into the royal party. Sister added, 'And if I introduce you to the Princess and call you Miss Smith, then you are Miss Smith.'

And then there was all the pre-visit 'bull' – scrubbing and Brassoing and whitewashing ... Matron Jessie Higgins heartily disapproved of the bumpering of floors of hospital wards and corridors to a high and dangerously slippery shine. At Halton she had many an argument with the CO on this subject – he liked to see every inch of space gleaming; she kept her floors scrupulously clean but not polished – even when a visit from the Air Chief Commandant of the PMRAFNS was imminent.

Her Royal Highness duly arrived and was officially greeted by Miss Higgins and others before being conducted round the wards. During the tour, the Princess Royal remarked what a relief it was to have unpolished floors on which she could walk naturally – usually on such visits she had to teeter around trying not to slip over, and in consequence spent the following day in agony with stiff and painful muscles. 'Ma'am,' said Higgie, 'would you mind repeating that to the CO?' Her Royal Highness obliged. One up to Matron Higgins!

St Clement Danes

As the 1950s drew to a close, an historic and moving ceremony took place, attended by the Queen and other members of the royal family. On 24 October 1958, the restored building of St Clement Danes, in the Strand, which had been badly damaged during the Blitz, was reconsecrated by the Bishop of London. It became the church of the RAF. Matron-in-Chief Dame Alice Mary Williamson represented the PMRAFNS, along with retired matron Miss M.B. Charlesworth and Miss G.M.I. Jenkins for the reserve. The Roll of Honour included the names of three PMs.

15

On a Jet Plane

Much of the aeromed work was, and still is, what one PM called 'hard slog' – long hours, difficult conditions and sheer drag of routine, with little of glamour about it. However, conditions vastly improved with the introduction of jet engines. Suddenly the Far East could be reached inside twenty-four hours, the Antipodes within two days. The first turbojet Comets joined Transport Command at RAF Lyneham in July 1956. In 1959 came the turboprop Britannia, and in the mid-1960s both the workhorse Hercules and the sleek, speedy VC10 joined the aerial fleet. These last two aircraft could take up to seventy stretchers at a time and – much to the relief of patients involved, not to mention the personnel who had the job of loading and unloading – stretcher cases could remain on board during the brief refuelling stops the new planes required.

April Reed experienced what she called 'this incredible change. After I'd done about a year at Wroughton, on the aeromeds on the Hastings, I went to Germany for a few years, and when I came back there was the Comet, and the VC10. Absolute luxury in comparison.'

Dinghy drill

The arrival of jet aircraft synchronised with a programme of more intensive aeromed training, which would culminate in a professional qualification. This began in 1959 when the RAF introduced an aeromedical course for both nursing officers of the PMRAFNS and non-commissioned personnel of the RAFMS. State registered nurses emerged from the course as qualified flight sisters or flight nurses while state enrolled nurses, medical assistants and administrators, became air ambulance attendants.

Once she had been in the Service for a year, a PM could volunteer to take this course, which took place initially at RAF Lyneham and later at RAF Brize Norton. At first, ground-training lasted for three days (later it expanded to eight days), small groups of trainees working with skilled instructors. They began in the swimming pool where, wearing black gabardine flying suits, students learned survival techniques – emergency escape from crashed aircraft, decompression in pressure chamber, use of life-jackets, and how to handle a huge and unwieldy rubber dinghy – righting it, if necessary, climbing into it from the water, and then hauling an injured patient after them. Back on dry land they studied the effects of altitude on both patients and equipment, became familiar with the various aircraft they might be using, and learned how to load patients correctly, fix stretcher harnesses and pack medical panniers; they studied the relation of GMT to other time zones, so that drugs could be given at correct periods, and they were taught how to handle a polio patient in and out of an aircraft while they were in a Monaghan cuirass – the RAF's portable version of an iron lung.

After initial instruction, students flew three aeromed missions assisting an experienced nurse, then one flight when they were in charge but under supervision; after that, fully qualified, they were on their own. Changing needs, improved equipment and more modern techniques were incorporated into the training as time went by, and eventually all PMs – including some rather senior ladies – were required to pass the aeromed course.

Joy Harris was one of those later students:

> I had done aeromeds in the days before you had to be trained, out in the Far East … but we found ourselves on a course with two nurse tutors and two matrons, I think it was … we got into great trouble doing the dinghy drill, because the only way you can really get into a dinghy when you're in the water – when you've got your Mae West [lifejacket] on – is to be dunked down, then you'll shoot up and they can grab you and pull you over. We couldn't get in, we kept saying, 'For heaven's sake, push us under!'

However comprehensive, no course can hope to cover every eventuality: each aeromed flight produces its own unique problems and PMs have learned always to expect the unexpected.

Sidelights

White ward dresses buttoned to the waist until 1960, when a Defence Council Instruction ordered somewhat daringly that 'In future, Nursing Officers will wear dresses unbuttoned all the way down the front.' Most PMs, highly amused, took the words 'which are capable of being' as implicit between 'dresses' and 'unbuttoned'.

As a junior sister in the early 1960s, April Reed found tights a headache: 'you had to have three colours: white to go with white uniform on the wards; black to go with the blue outdoor uniform; browns for mufti.' As for undies, at Ely one matron:

> … had this thing that we all had to wear white underwear under our ward uniform. It was a time when underwear was all bright colours. When you did a round with her, she'd be looking at you … trying to catch you against the light, to see, and – she always called you by your surname, of course – she'd say, 'Reed, you've got a blue petticoat on!'

A new member from 1961, Zena Cheel, says:

> When I first came into the PMs, any serviceman, on admission to hospital, had to come in in uniform … those that were up and about wore uniform until lunchtime and then they could change into mufti, but mufti had to be collar and tie and flannels, or cords or something.

In order to join the PMRAFNS, one had to face a selection board. Elizabeth Sandison travelled to hers by train, overnight from Aberdeen to London, in 1964. Next morning, after a medical, she went for her interview and came out wondering if she really wanted to join this 'club' where all they seemed to want was tennis-playing midwives – she didn't play tennis and she'd only done part one midwifery.

Valerie Hand, too, was asked if she played tennis. Yes, she did. 'But are you any good at it?' came the demand – they obviously had the Dame Joanna Cruickshank Tennis Tournament in mind! As for Sheila Power (Mrs Bellamy-Knights), she had been in the army nursing service for four years; when she attended her interview with the PMRAFNS they asked her how long she planned to give to the air force before she joined the navy!

Memorable aeromeds

In September 1963 an aeromed team including Squadron Officer Molly McNair set off on another trail-blazing flight. The signal which scrambled them is unclassified but still reads like gobbledegook to the untrained eye: UNCLAS H166/MED 20 SEP HQ PACAF AND HQ AAC … three lines later, it gets a little more comprehensible with SUBJECT IS AEROMEDICAL EVACUATION OF SERIOUSLY ILL PATIENT CMM FLYING OFFICER NORTHMORE RAF CMM AT PRESENT IN TRIPLER ARMY GENERAL HOSPITAL … To put it plainly, Flying Officer Anthony Northmore, a Transport Command pilot based at RAF Changi, had been employed in ferrying equipment between Honolulu and Christmas Island. While off-duty, swimming in Honolulu in July 1963, he broke his neck when he dived into shallow water. The USAF Hospital at Tripler looked after him but in September his doctors decided he was well enough, though permanently tetraplegic, to be flown home.

The team from Lyneham made news because of the route they took – it was the first time such a mercy flight had crossed the North Pole, via Greenland and Alaska. They returned the same way, bringing their patient back to Lyneham, from where a Whirlwind helicopter whisked him away to Stoke Mandeville Hospital.

Another well-experienced flight sister, R.A. 'Penny' Penrose, recalls that by the early 1960s regular aeromed flights served Germany, the Middle East and the Far East. In between these scheduled, routine flights, specials trips were often needed, 'for patients with poliomyelitis, fractured spines, burns, gunshot wounds of chest, sick babies and once six Aylesbury ducks to be taken to the Governor of Hong Kong to adorn his lake.' But her own most memorable patients were both world-famous.

In 1962, Sir Winston Churchill, aged eighty-seven, was holidaying in Monaco when he slipped and fell in his hotel room, fracturing his left thigh. Monaco surgeons performed an emergency operation but, as Penny Penrose explains, it was decided that the great man should be returned to England:

> for if his injury should prove fatal his demise should not be on foreign soil … Flying Officer Tilley and I were having tea prior to returning to duty at 1700 hrs at RAFH Wroughton. By 1900 hrs we were flying from Lyneham … an MO plus two SNCOs completing the medical team. We arrived at Nice at 2100 hrs. Everyone knew who we were and we were treated like heroes and thoroughly spoilt.

Next morning the two PMs waited at the airfield while the doctor and medics collected the stretcher-bound Sir Winston and took him on board the Comet:

> courtesy of a forklift. Fortunately I had the foresight whilst waiting to purchase all the English newspapers which were available. Sir Winston avidly read all the news about himself and discussed the tennis at Wimbledon and horse racing with his secretary, who was travelling with us. We arrived at the Middlesex Hospital in London, being escorted from the airport by six police outriders … we carved our way through the London traffic as a knife through butter. A second operation was then performed, the patient making very satisfactory progress, much to the relief of the world.

Her next VIP aeromed happened in 1965 when, 'I was posted to RAF Hospital Changi and in October I flew in an RAF Argosy with an MO and SNCO to Tonga, to escort Queen Salote, aged sixty-five years, on her journey for medical treatment in New Zealand.' The Tongan Queen had become a great favourite with English crowds when, during the Coronation parade, she rode through the streets of London in an open carriage, waving and smiling despite the rain. Now, when she was ill, Queen Elizabeth herself had asked that the RAF should provide transport and medical care:

> Being a small island, Tonga could only accommodate certain aircraft on its small airport. It was therefore decided that the Argosy with additional crew could be the most appropriate aircraft to take Queen Salote from Tonga and transfer her to an RAF Comet with a second medical team to fly her from Fiji to New Zealand … Queen Salote was very frail and a bed was loaded on board should she find it more comfortable for travelling.

From RAF Changi, it took the Argosy six days to reach Tonga, with overnight stays, refuelling stops and a rest day, flying via the Cocos Island, Australia (three days to cross Australia), New Caledonia, Fiji and finally to Tonga. 'Although the flying time had made for long days, together with the noise of the engine, when one saw the runway at Nakualofe the choice of aircraft was all too apparent.' Penny Penrose stayed with the hospital matron, a remarkable New Zealander:

> Not only did she supervise the nursing of patients, she administered the hospital, trained and lectured her staff ... The financial budget was limited and at times illness of many babies caused acute anxiety with lack of antibiotics, penicillin, etc. Fortunately, not quite knowing what to expect, we had included a considerable amount of medication to our routine supply, which we readily offloaded ...
>
> We were entertained to a sumptuous Tongan feast seated on cushions on the floor, a long strip of coconut matting in front of us laden with chickens, sucking pigs, fish, fruit, yams, etc., whilst we were served by staff from the Royal Household. We were also invited to tea served on the most delicate of porcelain ... seated on the veranda of the Royal Household and entertained by singing and dancing.
>
> The route to the airport was a mass of people watching their Queen depart. She was very frail but very upright and we remembered how she had endeared herself to everyone at the Queen's Coronation. Our flight to Fiji was uneventful. The Queen was then transferred to the RAF Comet for the remainder of her flight to New Zealand. Sadly, she died in hospital a few days later.

Penny Penrose concludes, 'My years as an aeromed sister were the most superb experience one could ever wish for ... Happy days indeed. Memorable years.'

PM 'Ronnie' Oxborough also relished aeromed duties, which for her began in 1970. They were 'a very exciting part of my career in the PMs ... some trips enjoyable, some frightening, some tragic ...' Recalling one particular trip to Washington DC, Ronnie Oxborough recounts how 'a big fellow in the Irish Guards' had broken his neck by jumping off the side of a boat and hitting his head on a coral reef. Paralysed from the neck down, on a respirator and strapped in a turning frame, he was being cared for in the Walter Reed Hospital in Washington when the aeromed team went out to collect him. They worked with him to wean him off the American respirator and onto theirs for the flight home, but the treatment involved frequent turning of the frame so that for some periods he hung face down – not a pleasant position for anyone. In order to reassure him, Ronnie Oxborough:

> sat on the floor under the frame, talking to him. One morning into the room walked a huge coloured gent built like Tower Bridge. He took one look at me, lifted me clean off the floor, put me on a bed and was about to send for the doctor – he thought I had fallen and couldn't get up! No harm done. Our patient had a good journey home.

Some of the most rewarding of aeromed duties, according to those who were privileged to be selected for them, were the two-yearly flights which brought holders of the Victoria Cross and the George Cross back to the UK to meet the Queen. Anne Taylor felt very lucky to be chosen to accompany these men and their wives. 'They were lovely people, with amazing stories to tell.' Liz Sandison agrees that meeting the war heroes was 'an amazing experience, never to be repeated or equalled'.

Gan

Just 2 miles long by 1 mile wide, the staging post of RAF Gan lay in the southernmost part of the Maldive Islands, in the Indian Ocean. The runway drew a broad line down the length of the island and in the lagoon lay remnants of broken concrete moorings, an air sea rescue launch and a rusting old ship, not to mention sharks, manta rays, turtles and Moray eels lurking among razor-sharp coral – plimsolls while paddling were a must.

When, in December 1961, Princess Alexandra had to make a night stop at Gan, Jane Stott was sent from RAFH Changi to look after Her Royal Highness, the only other woman on the island being a WVS welfare officer. Later, Jane was attached to the sick quarters at Gan for three months, to assess whether the presence of a nursing sister might be beneficial. She found it an unusual posting:

> The Maldivians came to work every day in their flotilla of single sail canoe type vessels from islands in the atoll, and left every evening at sundown. Sick Maldivians came to be treated, but only with permission from their headman … Any terminally ill person was removed from Sick Quarters as, if dead, they would not be accepted back to their island.

Since it was found impractical to have a female nursing officer permanently on the tiny island, Gan's sick quarters were left in capable male hands.

Cyprus

When British forces withdrew from Egypt they ensured a base in the Middle East by enlarging their presence in Cyprus. By the late 1950s about 30,000 British servicemen were stationed on the island, many with their families. The RAF Hospital at Akrotiri opened in 1956, some of its first PMs being transferred from the closing Canal Zone hospital at Fayid.

The island offers abundant pleasures, from skiing in the snow-clad mountains to basking on golden beaches or swimming in the blue-green Mediterranean. But strife between the resident Greek and Turkish communities has made Cyprus, on occasion, an uneasy place to be. The strong RAF presence has kept the hospital busy, and over forty years its non-service patients have included both Greek-Cypriot EOKA terrorists and their Turkish-Cypriot opposition.

Owing to its barren, rocky location, the first hospital was fondly known as 'Alcatraz'. It was situated on the southern tip of Cyprus (near salt flats where pink flamingos mass at migration time) and it comprised five single-storey, prefabricated buildings (intended as married quarters) set either side of a road. Its early days were not auspicious. When the first PMs arrived, the nearby airfield was still under construction and, what with heavy rains and lack of proper roads, hospital staff clumped through the mud in permanent gumboots. Orderlies bringing the first surgical patient, unconscious on a stretcher, found the trolley too wide to go through the door of the converted sitting room which served as the surgical ward; they had to manhandle the stretcher through a window (and send for Works and Bricks to widen the door). What was more, with a road running between, trolley-bound patients being wheeled from ward to theatre and back often had to wait for a gap in the traffic!

It was said that EOKA terrorists had tried to raid the hospital to obtain insulin for their leader, George Grivas, so the 'bundu' (the surrounding scrubland) was strung with trip-wires that occasionally set off rockets and startled everyone – especially at three o'clock in the morning. Security appeared to have forgotten that herds of wild donkeys roamed free around the camp.

By 1959, however, improvements had been made – several caravans acted as changing rooms, sluice and Red Cross library. But the PMs had discovered the delights of being so close to a warm blue sea and social life was excellent, with RAF Akrotiri becoming the largest flying station in the RAF at that time – it held 2,000 personnel, with squadrons of bombers and fighters. When the growth of new trees, shrubs and flowers began to soften the environs, the peninsula turned into a very pleasant place to be. Except for the bed bugs – and the terrorists.

During the hostilities of 1957–9, RAF casualties were few but bloody, mostly caused by snipers' bullets – often in the back – and by bombs. David Snell, a national service medic, recalls two particular incidents, the first with a Greek motorcyclist carrying a bomb:

> There was no need for any medical assistance … they were finding bits of motorcycle and Greek for some weeks. The second was far more serious in that they destroyed a hangar and over £3m worth of aircraft. Fortunately casualties were limited to three station firemen with minor to moderate burns.

There were, besides, many traffic accidents, and numerous cases of serious sunburn among newcomers who ignored all the warnings; the maternity unit was busy, too, with so many wives accompanying their husbands; but the hospital's main enemy was dysentery – one of the medical wards was kept filled by such cases and, given that climate, it was impossible to prevent infection from spreading. There was an outbreak in 1958 so bad that sick quarters, the NAAFI and empty billets had to be used as wards and operating theatres closed for all except emergency cases.

One of the inevitable flying accidents made Ethnea Hancock think twice about accepting an invitation:

> I worked chiefly as a midwife there, although I had done some theatre work before I joined the service. One weekend I was asked to stand in for the theatre sister. She said, 'Nothing ever happens, you'll be fine. Maybe an appendix, but you'll be fine …' And at two o'clock on the Saturday afternoon a glider pilot crashed and put the steering column through his chest. So we were doing chest surgery that afternoon. It wasn't something the surgeon was doing all the time, either … these small places were not that well geared up for that sort of thing. It put me off taking up the offer to go gliding!

Having no proper mess of their own, nursing sisters at Akrotiri had to travel some distance to the officers' mess for meals and social occasions, including film shows. Ann Golding can never see the film *Psycho* without remembering the first time she saw it, in Cyprus, when just at the most gripping moment the tannoy announced, 'Sisters' transport!' and they had to leave to catch the coach back to their living quarters.

Princess Mary's Royal Air Force Hospital, Akrotiri

Building began on a new hospital, at Cape Zevgari, 3 miles from the main RAF camp, in June 1961. The Princess Royal visited during the final stages and she came again in November 1963, when the hospital was completely operational, to open it officially and grant it the use of her name. Ethnea Hancock was:

> amazed by her stamina. The flight would have been eight or more hours at that time … She went up to Air House [home of the Commander-in-Chief] first, but then plunged into a really daunting programme – a fifteen/sixteen hour day, exhausting … She must have been quite elderly then, I remember she seemed terribly old.

The Princess was in her mid-60s at the time.

When Cyprus gained independence in 1960, exiled Greek-Cypriot Archbishop Makarios returned as President, and three years later the Greeks tried to seize total control. The Turks resisted. Britain tried to remain neutral. Margaret Kingston tells how a friend of hers invited a Cypriot Bishop to dinner and nearly got court-martialled for it – the Bishop was *persona non grata* owing to the troubles.

However, remaining aloof was difficult when battle casualties needed help. Over Christmas 1963, Iris Rawlings (Mrs Kerse) was at Akrotiri when:

> Greek-Cypriots were attacking their neighbouring Turks, burning villages and destroying property. On Boxing morning, Matron came up to my room to ask if I would go up to Nicosia, and to be ready within an hour. Three of us were to go – a midwife, theatre sister and myself as aeromedical sister …
>
> A Hastings came down from Nicosia to collect us … the landscape seemed to be ablaze as we overflew the burning Turkish villages. Fighting was intense in Nicosia, the walled city being held by the Turks and constantly bombarded by the Greeks.

Within the walls was a Turkish hospital where their wounded were being treated. Our first task was to go into the walled city and take them to the airport, from where they would be flown to Turkey.

A time was chosen when there was a lapse in hostilities while the Greeks were burying one of their martyrs. We went in, in uniform, in ambulances, and coming up to the walls was very dramatic … Above the sandbags, armed men were aiming their weapons at us. The ambulance driver asked if I was frightened and I said, 'No, I'm wearing this,' pointing to my veil. How naive can you get! He thought I was terribly brave! … We managed to evacuate our patients before hostilities recommenced. It was a great feeling seeing them off on the aircraft.

El Adem

During tours of duty at Akrotiri, a succession of PMs went on short attachment to the tiny staging post of El Adem, 500 miles away in the Libyan desert. Captured from the Italians during the desert campaigns of the Second World War, Libya was administered first under British control and then as an independent monarchy under King Idris. El Adem served initially as a refuelling base for short-range aircraft. From the time of the Suez crisis, El Adem's role as a staging post increased. Aeromed and transport flights paused overnight to rest and refuel; Comet crews arrived to practise 'circuits and bumps'; and a resident RAF Regiment squadron, living in tents, helped to clear the mines that still lurked among the sand dunes.

Most PMs stayed on the base for about six months; some stayed a year; Jane Stott reckoned her thirteen-and-a-half-month attachment to be the record. She and two colleagues named Jess and Joan arrived in January 1957, in the rainy season – they were glad of their Cyprus wellingtons, and of the break from terrorists and restricted travel. Along with Joan Parsons, of the WVS, plus her dachshund, the three PMs, 'lived in an Italian-built block of rooms round an open-centre square … Salt-water soap was most useful as all water came from Tobruk by pipeline and was extremely hard and impure … laundry "whites" turned out grey.' Tobruk, where the RAF families lived, was 16 miles away, still in ruins but beginning to be rebuilt.

The sick quarters at El Adem demanded special organisation: when surgical operations became necessary, the MO had to call in army doctors to make up the team; and when a woman went into labour two airmen of the same blood group would stand by in case she needed a transfusion. 'In hot weather an air cooling unit was transferred from the servicing flight, and the cool air was pumped into the theatre through a Dettol-soaked sheet …'

Two of the sisters owned a VW Beetle, so they were able to visit nearby towns, though they had to watch out for desert rats, baby tortoises and stray camels. In camp, the only source of milk was tins of Carnation, and scorpions presented a permanent hazard. But entertainers visited to put on shows for the troops and they even had dining-in nights, with snails and desert game birds on the menu.

Even so, Ethnea Hancock found her six months in El Adem:

> a bit of an endurance test. You were sent as a midwife … but not many deliveries so not much to do. You were 17 miles inland from Tobruk, fairly good road between but in all other direction nothing but bundu roads, pretty ropey, and only two vehicles on the station – SMO's and CO's jeeps. But we survived.

Tragedy in the desert

News of her own posting to El Adem left Jean Brown with mixed feelings, but fortunately two other Scots were to be with her: Isobel McDonald and Marie Morrison. During their tenure, in October 1961, a Maltese Regiment came to RAF El Adem on desert exercises. Training done, the soldiers set off home to Malta, but as their plane took off it crashed, engulfed by flame.

Jean, Marie and Isobel were relaxing in their sitting room when the call came. By the time they arrived at SSQ, casualties were being brought in, many of them screaming in pain. None of them spoke English, so the sisters had difficulty in calming them. But they had to cope until the two MOs could arrive – both had gone home to their married quarters in Tobruk. Fortunately, says Jean Brown, she had checked the crash ward only the previous day and had made sure of a good supply of intravenous fluids. She wonders if premonition prompted her.

Some of the men had 90 per cent burns. They died within a couple of hours. The English Padre Hodgson gave the last rites, while ambulance boys and orderlies helped to set up intravenous drips – not having enough drip-stands, they improvised with broom handles, which the orderlies had to hold. Meanwhile the sisters administered morphine supplied by the pharmacist. Within half an hour the MOs arrived and soon the team had everyone sedated and assessed. Jean says she will never forget the smell of burning flesh.

A couple of years later, on his way back to London after treating King Idris, the eminent London-based orthopaedic surgeon Sir Reginald Watson Jones accepted an invitation to dine with the CO and officers of El Adem. He sat next to a nursing sister to whom he 'recounted his horror at having to do an operation in the Palace, surrounded by the King's advisers and many flies! Even in 1963 this was not what he was used to.'

RAF El Adem closed in 1969 when King Idris was deposed and Colonel Mu'ammar al-Gaddafi came to power in Libya.

Khormaksar Beach, Aden

The Yemen, of which Aden is a part, was troubled by civil war after its ruler, the Imam, was overthrown in 1962. Britain declared a state of emergency and British forces became embroiled in the struggle for the hinterland territory of Radfan. The insurgency spread into Aden itself and continued until 1967, when British forces withdrew from Aden and the Marxists took over.

The RAF hospital at Steamer Point had been operating since 1928, with RAF Khormaksar Beach 10 miles to the north, on sandy flats on the shore of the old harbour. Also at Khormaksar, a camp for the Aden Protectorate Levies (APLs) had its own sick quarters, with male wards staffed by male SRNs of the RAFMS and a women's/families' ward supervised by four part-time British-trained civilian nurses. The hospital also employed local auxiliaries and 'ayahs'.

Barbara Millar (Mrs Wight) was one of the sisters from Steamer Point who visited the APL sick quarters 'once a week, to give treatment of various sorts to the Arab soldiers and their families'. Then in 1959 the Khormaksar Beach APL Hospital (known as KBH) became a regular posting for PMs. The first contingent of four nursing officers, including Shelagh Firth, went out from the UK; two more were posted from Steamer Point. They were supposed to live in a building converted from two flats not far from the hospital, but, says Shelagh Firth, 'As might be expected, the conversion was not completed, so [we] were accommodated in the Rock Hotel …' This lay in the main shopping area of Aden, 10 miles away at Steamer Point. When problems with distance and transport made life fraught, they 'were assigned to a room in the Commanding Officer's (Wing Commander Cooney's) house – rather cramped, and I dread to think how much we disrupted their life!'

A strike of the local auxiliaries exacerbated early difficulties but, despite problems of language, cultural differences and the auxiliaries' lack of medical knowledge, after a short time 'they became very reliable and supportive'. Shelagh Firth enjoyed the social life, too, exploring Aden, shopping in Steamer Point, visits up-country and leave spent in Kenya, picnics with the BP fraternity at Little Aden, camel racing, shark fishing, amongst other things.

Everyone who worked at Khormaksar Beach APL Hospital found it 'very different'. It consisted of huts with wide verandas, set about by trees and connected by black sandy paths. The huts offered 163 beds for local levies and their dependents, who could be numerous – a man might have several wives, each with children, plus his parents, his unmarried sisters and his juvenile brothers, and staff suspected that friends sneaked in under guise of 'relatives' too – who could tell? Consequently, beds were kept full, and nurses busy. As a general rule, men nursed men and women nursed women, with female and children's wards well away from the rest because of purdah rules. Common illnesses included all tropical diseases such as malaria, leprosy and TB; more unusual cases included mycetoma (also known as Madura foot, a severe fungal infection peculiar to Arabia, which often calls for surgery to excise the affected area).

For Zena Cheel, Aden provided a first overseas tour. She spent seven months at Steamer Point, then was posted to KBH: 'Khormaksar Beach sounds romantic, but it wasn't. Black sand, and very near Khormaksar airport. We used to have terrible trouble with aircraft flying over, especially if they were practising for an open day …' Having been brought up in India, Zena was unfazed by the local smells and noises, but some things did present:

… a bit of a culture shock. For instance, the first day I was there …

It got nearer and nearer to lunchtime and I thought, they don't seem to be doing anything, so I said to this other sister, 'What do we do about lunch, then?' and she said, 'Oh, you'll see in a minute!' and across the bundu came this little chap with two huge great buckets, one full of rice and one full of curry, and under each arm a loaf of bread, and two big ladles. The patients dived into their lockers and brought out these little things that looked as if they should be under the bed as opposed to eating out of them, and those that were up went out onto the veranda, and he went round and he dolloped a bit of rice, and a dollop of curry, hacked off a bit of bread – and that was lunch! In the evening, they invariably had chapatti with a hard-boiled egg – that was their supper. We used to have to go afterwards and hose down the veranda, where they'd been eating, because whatever they didn't want they just spat out, or threw out.

When Zena became sister-in-charge:

one evening I was sitting there writing my report and I thought, I can smell something cooking! … these ladies had got one of the dressing bowls and into it they'd put onions and tomatoes and all sorts, and they were boiling it all up in the steriliser!

But it was very interesting … I never thought in my life I'd look after lepers … and we had people with all these different diseases, like bilharzia, that you hear about … A lot of these people had never been out of their villages and quite often if they became ill the first person they would go to would be the witch doctor, or whatever they called him … We had a young boy about fifteen brought in, with meningitis, but he also had this terrific wound in his head, where they had put this red-hot needle, almost like a poker, into his head, to get rid of the evil spirit, so not only was he delirious from the meningitis but also from a high fever from the infection.

In time, Khormaksar Beach Hospital benefited from the permanent presence of twelve PM sisters and twelve male SRNs, plus local male orderlies and Somali ayahs. To Kate Crompton (Mrs Wilmot), her posting came as a shock: 'I had heard stories about KBH and was very apprehensive.' Nevertheless she, too, found it a fascinating experience:

Many of the female patients brought their babies into hospital with them whilst they received treatment. They made little hammocks under their beds for the babies. Mealtimes were an eye-opener … The toddlers, and all the babies old enough to eat solids, had minced liver and rice at lunchtime. They would sit down in a semicircle and an ayah would roll the rice in a little ball and pop one into each child's mouth. She repeated this using minced liver. All TB adults had chicken curry and everyone else had ordinary curry – I've no idea what was in that!

On night duty, one sister would be in charge of the whole hospital. Says Kate, 'It was very strange walking between the female and male sections with Arab male nurses asleep on their beds by the roadside.'

In Britain, a new Labour government, elected in October 1964, decided that its forces could no longer afford to act as policemen to the world. It began to close some overseas bases and over the next few years British troops withdrew from the Middle East. When Doreen Francis arrived in Aden to take up matron's duties at KBH, she was told that within two or three years the British would be leaving Aden; meantime, the new hospital being built for the local troops (who would become the Federal Regular Army) would be used for British patients. Over the next three years, the work of this 'European Wing' at KBH proved to be almost exclusively surgical, operating on casualties shot and injured by Arab terrorists.

Doreen Francis comments, 'We had a secure ward for Arab dissidents, and a helicopter pad where casualties were landed, particularly at dawn. And we had many army units posted in.' Some army lines lay just outside the fence which abutted the levies' TB ward; hand grenades would be lobbed over to explode in the British lines. Pilfering posed another problem – hospital equipment had to be watched closely and even pushchairs used to convey babies to X-ray were padlocked to the veranda, otherwise they walked. After eighteen years spent mostly in operating theatres, it was quite a change.

One of her nursing sisters, Alma Barnard (Mrs Tyack) enjoyed nursing the children: 'They were very trusting … They loved having injections – they thought that was something special, real medicine.' But their names raised difficulties: 'they were all called Ali or Mohammed, so they were numbered as by beds, surgical or medical – SB1/2/3 or MB1/2/3 – we had to make sure they stayed in the same beds so they didn't get muddled.'

Liz Lown (Mrs Armstrong) noted that:

> a very special relationship grew up between the 'Sistera' and the Arab, Indian and Somali women (the ayahs) who provided the basic nursing on the Arab families' ward. Ayahs always threw a tea-party for a departing Sister. They were being trained by the PMs to take over nursing care when the British finally withdrew.

Troubled finale at Aden

Terrorist activities began to affect Steamer Point hospital, on its hill above the main harbour. 'Once the fighting really got going in the Radfan,' says Monica Fern:

> we used to have the helicopters bringing casualties down to the hospital, a bit like 'M.A.S.H.'. If the telephone rang you automatically put your uniform on and went over to the hospital … I looked after a nineteen-year-old soldier who had both his hands blown off by a hand grenade which he held too long after pulling the pin …

> Another patient had the top of his skull sliced off by shrapnel – he was flown back to England and a plate put in, but you wonder what sort of life he had.

For security, all buildings had to be searched once the Arab orderlies and bearers had gone home and on two separate nights midwives found something that made them call the bomb disposal squad. New mothers dressed in nighties and housecoats, with babes in arms, trooped from their ward to wait nervously outside while the lads disposed of, first, a wrapped loaf of bread and, second, a tobacco pouch inadvertently left by one of the proud new fathers. On another evening, Monica Fern heard a commotion in the labour ward – one of the Arab guards had fallen through the ceiling while checking the roof space.

The hospital itself remained secure, but outside the walls terror reigned. Sisters were on the patio of their mess enjoying an evening drink when a bomb went off at the Post Office just below. Monica Fern, 'craned to see, and somebody yelled, "Get down!"' As she ducked, machine-gun fire erupted.

Another lucky escape occurred at a dinner in the officers' mess at Tarshine. PMs present included a theatre sister named Diane, from Steamer Point. They had reached the soup course when a hand grenade landed on the long table. Diane pushed her chair back, flung up her hands to guard her face, threw herself sideways … The explosion peppered her with shrapnel. Monica Fern recounts the denouement:

> Diane was prepared to have the shrapnel removed from her arm and side, but drew the line at exposing her backside to the medics with whom she worked every day. So she got a mirror and a pair of tweezers and removed the bits herself!

Others were not so lucky. Following a Christmas dinner on 23 December, as Monica and her fellow PMs relaxed over drinks with their guests, 'the telephone rang to tell us a bomb had been thrown into a room where a teenage party was being held, children of senior rank officers – the C-in-C's son, the PMOs' daughter …' The girl was seventeen. A piece of shrapnel had sliced into her neck. 'Wing Commander Wynne-Griffiths was a few doors down and when he heard the explosion he charged down to the house and sent for an ambulance. He apparently sat astride her with his thumbs on her neck … but she was dead on arrival at the hospital.' The C-in-C's son had a piece of shrapnel in his leg, 'just underneath the femoral artery. It rather ruined everyone's Christmas.'

By May 1967 Steamer Point hospital was on the point of closing. All work transferred to Khormaksar Beach. Shelagh Glenn (Mrs Barber) was one of the last PMs to be posted in:

> We were very busy. Awful lot of casualties. One thing I remember, if we had a dissident in [for surgery], they had to have two soldiers in the theatre, guarding them with guns. One of the regiments was the Argyle and Sutherland Highlanders, and

> there'd be these great big huge brawny men, who'd come and say, 'Sister, I don't have to go into theatre, do I? Can we stand outside?' So we used to put theatre gowns on them and let them stand outside the door.

Aden itself became a war zone and RAF personnel were confined to base. 'They had one little shopping centre which was open for an hour every afternoon, when it was guarded,' Shelagh remembers:

> That was the only time we could go out, we were almost like prisoners in the mess. Some of the MOs used to go by car down to the BP place at Little Aden and I knew a couple of them, so they used to take me, but even they would carry guns ... When we were working in theatre they kept their guns in the dangerous drugs cupboard, and I had the dangerous drugs in my pocket. Bizarre, yes.
>
> And then Sue Quinn (Morgan now) and I were told that when the British went out of Aden, when the hospital closed down, we were going out to work on HMS *Albion* for about two months, to take casualties. We were kitted out in new uniforms, because we'd be on the mess deck, climbing on bunks, so we wore trousers and jackets. The week before we were due to go over, I went over by helicopter every day to get the mess deck sorted out and get the theatre ready – there was a small theatre attached to it, which was quite amusing because it was absolutely full – jam-packed! – with 2 mil. syringes.

All the other PMs left Aden, Liz Lown among them:

> The day we abandoned KBH to its fate will live in the memories of the sisters involved till the end of our lives. All European patients had been casevaced out. Numbers of Arab patients had been reduced to an absolute minimum – the rest, those too ill to leave the hospital, we simply had to abandon. To us, Western-trained nurses, it was a traumatic experience. To the locals ... a soldier summed it up: 'We managed before the British came, we'll manage when you've gone - Allah karim [Allah will provide].'

Shelagh Glenn and Sue Quinn were the only ones left in the sisters' mess. Sue decided she couldn't bear to be alone and so moved in with her friend; they put wardrobes against the windows. 'I don't know what we thought was going to happen,' says Shelagh:

> but we felt safer that way. We were just going to sleep when we heard these footsteps coming along the veranda, so she squeaked, 'Oh! It's happening! They're coming!' and this voice said, 'It's all right, sisters, it's corporal of the guard, we're just doing the rounds. I'll be coming round every hour to see you're all right.'

Next day, they moved to HMS *Albion*, at anchor in the bay, where they lodged with the Royal Navy:

> It was a bit difficult at first, being the only females on board with all that lot. But I must say they were very nice. We'd got a very nice suite – actually, it was the marine commandoes' Colonel's quarters … Luckily, we didn't have too many casualties. Most of the operating we did, the surgeon-commander, every day, used to go round the fleet and see what he could find – hernias, appendix, things like that, so if we weren't kept busy we were at least kept working.

The press went wild in their eagerness to record the startling presence of female officers aboard a marine commando carrier (back in 1967 it was very daring); Shelagh and Sue were subjected to:

> photo sessions – the TV cameras came, and while we were on deck having photographs taken all flying had to stop, so there were we walking up and down the deck and everyone staring, making rude comments … The whole session finished and one of the photographers – I think he was from the *Daily Mirror* – said, 'Oh, I haven't got a film in my camera!' so we did it all again.

Now that they were removed from it, the war seemed distant. By night, sometimes, they saw flashes as bombs and guns went off, but gradually the trouble died down and though a few casualties arrived by helicopter, the prepared 'casualty ward' on the commandos' mess desk was not needed:

> The idea was that if there'd been a lot of casualties we'd have gone on with the ship - round to Mogadishu, and everybody would have been flown off from there, but luckily that didn't happen. When we left the ship, we went on a Bristol freighter to Bahrain … and then we flew from Bahrain back to UK.

Hospital patients from Aden also travelled via Bahrain, where they were prepared for aeromed back to the UK. The last of them flew home from RAF Muharraq, cared for by a medical team which included Elizabeth Sandison. She recalls it as:

> quite an event, a full patient load on a Britannia, diverted into Gatwick – you can imagine all the panic at that in those days! One of the patients … Foreign and Commonwealth Office, stretcher case, not allowed to get off the plane … Customs came to see him on board and said to this lovely, jovial-looking gentleman, 'Have you anything to declare, sir?' He opened his briefcase and there were two revolvers with I don't know how many rounds of ammunition … They quietly took it away from him. He must have had the guns all the time, in the hospital, during transit.

Duty done, Liz Sandison returned to her base – the newly named Princess Alexandra's Royal Air Force Hospital, Wroughton.

A new royal patron

Following the death of the Princess Royal in 1965, the Service obtained the Queen's consent to the appointment of Princess Alexandra (the Hon Lady Ogilvie) to the role of Patron and Air Chief Commandant of the PMRAFNS. The appointment could not have been more appropriate: Princess Alexandra is not only a niece of the PMs' first Royal Patron, she is also the only daughter of George, Duke of Kent, who died in a flying accident in 1942 while serving with the RAF. She has two brothers – the present Duke of Kent and Prince Michael of Kent.

Like her aunt before her, after completing her education Princess Alexandra took a nursing course at Great Ormond Street Hospital before assuming her official duties. In April 1963 she married Angus Ogilvie (he became Sir Angus in 1989), second son of the Earl of Airdrie.

Since accepting the role of Air Chief Commandant of the PMRAFNS in 1966, Princess Alexandra has paid many visits to RAF Hospitals, welcomed as a well-loved presence by all members of the Service. In 1968 Her Royal Highness visited RAF Hospital Wegberg, West Germany. As part of the preparations for the occasion, Sandra Cranswick (Mrs Philpott) vividly remembers being selected to accompany the princess to the ladies' room:

> I had to practise shaking hands and curtsying, and was instructed in the exact words I had to say to her! However, she will never know of the concern shown beforehand to ensure her privacy. She was to use the bathroom in the flat of the matron, Wing Officer McNeill. This had a glazed door, but it was decided that a new curtain should be added for extra privacy. A maintenance man and I were tasked to decide how many layers of net were necessary for complete privacy – he held the net to the door and I stood at the end of the corridor to see if I could see him through the glazed door and net! We finally arrived at three layers of net being necessary to secure her complete privacy … However, on her arrival, she immediately put us at ease and my 'chore' became an enjoyable and memorable occasion.

16

Nurse-training, 1950s and 1960s

The story of nurse training within the RAF is complex. It started in 1951, when the General Nursing Council approved RAF hospitals Halton, Ely and Wroughton as training schools for recruits of the RAF Medical Service. Students both male and female might qualify as state registered, non-commissioned staff nurses, ready to work in hospital wards and station sick quarters. In some places they worked alongside nursing officers of the PMRAFNS.

However, from October 1962 the RAF also introduced nurse-training within the PMRAFNS, for 'intelligent young women with four O-levels or the equivalent', who wished to attain State Registered Nurse standard. Direct entrants from civilian life or transferees from the WRAF, entered what was officially designated the PMRAFNS NCE (Non-Commissioned Element). Their three-year training typically consisted of six weeks' basic instruction at Halton and the rest at Ely or Wroughton, from where secondments to Wegberg and Uxbridge provided, respectively, maternity and oncology experience. These students, like their colleagues of the RAFMS, graduated as staff nurse junior NCOs, with the chance to rise through senior NCO ranks to become Warrant Officers.

Six years on, in 1968, the Service also began training to State Enrolled level for the non-commissioned element; then in 1969 a new scheme enabled qualified SENs and pupil enrolled nurses to enlist on 'local service' engagements. That is, they lived at home but were employed at a nearby RAF station or hospital – Nocton Hall, Ely, Cosford, Halton or Wroughton. The first member of PMRAFNS to train as an SEN while living at home was also a married woman – Aircraftwoman Mrs Marian Potter, who did her training at Wroughton.

Already qualified SRNs and SENs continued to be recruited, though, as had always been the case, only female SRNs could apply for commissioned posts; state registered male nurses and state enrolled nurses of either sex were offered non-commissioned posts.

Student tales

These were the 1960s, the era of the Beatles and the Campaign for Nuclear Disarmament, and also the time when young people began to question the authority and wisdom of their elders. Stories told by student nurses reflect this change in mood.

Anne Sumner (Mrs Wynne-Jones) was in the WRAF, training at Wroughton for her SRN, when news came that student nurses could join the PMs:

> change uniform, have our own rooms, and our own cleaners, but not have quite the same pay structure … the thought of an end to 'bull nights' was amazing to me, so off I went … There was a bit of rivalry between us and those who elected to stay in the WRAF. They were right at the other end of camp, by the NAAFI, still in billets, while we were in the hospital itself, in our own rooms … but we were still training on the same course, and working side by side on the wards …
>
> We were the first PM student nurses at Wroughton. We had the white dress and the cape, and we had our cardigans taken off us, and hats – these were replaced by the standard 'bowlers'.

Only nursing officers wore the 'Dick Turpin' quatrecorne; nursing students' best-blue hats were standard WRAF-type, which at the time had high, rounded crowns:

> We went to have our heads measured for these bowlers … It was at the time of the fancy hairstyles, the French-pleat and back-combing, so mine was stuck up there – I'd been to a dance the night before and it was still back-combed up when we went into Stores to get measured. By the time the hat arrived the hairstyle had dropped, my head was about two sizes smaller! I ended up with this dubious-looking bowler hat that sort of rested round the top of my nose … I was very often sent back off parade. They'd look at me with my funny bowler, my skirt that seemed longer than anyone else's because my legs were so short, and they'd boot me off.
>
> We had some interesting little 'run-ins'. First of all, I mentioned they took the cardigans off us because we had the cloaks, but it was freezing cold in winter. We had a big dust-up about keeping our cardigans. Also, they gave us white canvas shoes – whereas Sisters had nice soft white kid shoes, we had these really, really hard white canvas shoes, they were terrible, they rubbed our heels … I led this mini revolution, I said, 'Right, nobody's listening to us, so we'll all go and report sick.' So after about the third person had reported sick with blisters on their heels, the MO came out, said, 'All right, how many are here for problems with your feet?' so we all stood up … It was agreed that they'd give us a chitty, or some money or something, to buy softer white shoes, but by the time we got that the damage had been done, the shoes were broken in.

On the question of cardigans, minutes of a matrons' meeting of 1969 may reflect this minor revolt in the ranks: 'When the weather is very cold, white cardigans may be worn by students and pupils, WHEN IN SCHOOL, but on no other occasion'.

From civilian life, in January 1964 Linda Kendall (Mrs McKenzie) joined Course 3, a mix of direct entries and girls transferring from the WRAF. She too writes of rivalry between the two elements, 'especially as we had done less basic training than the WRAFs'. But in many ways little had changed – students were still being asked to bend over to see whether their popliteal space (backs of knees) showed. If it did, they had to let down the hems of their ward dresses.

Course 4 began in June 1964, graced by the presence of Nadine Gay, along with six other girls who first met at Halton and still remain close friends. Nadine well remembers their transfer to Ely:

> a mass of girls in blue uniform, luggage everywhere … People stared in horror at the bevy of beauties, looking more like the cast of *St Trinians* than student nurses …
>
> The first time we were ordered to get ready in best blue uniform – to be interviewed by the matron, Wing Officer Higgins, a formidable character – had us all rushing about, pressing and polishing. I, too busy talking, accidentally poured Brasso all down the front of my jacket. Nothing we did could remove it! We went in one by one to see her [but] she barely lifted her gaze on me and my jacket.

Later, Miss Higgins mistook student nurse Nadine Gay for student nurse Gaynor Morris, and when Nadine pointed out the error, 'she snorted and said, "It doesn't matter, you're all as bad as one another"'.

In their second year, students gained paediatric and maternity experience during a twelve-week attachment to RAFH Wegberg, West Germany, and in their third year a sojourn at Uxbridge's Cade Unit provided sobering insights into the suffering wrought by cancer, as Nadine Gay reveals: 'The permanent staff had seen more death than any of us, but were mostly kind and optimistic, which these poor patients needed. We will never forget one lovely RAF doctor in the final stages of bladder carcinoma …' But one of the RAF medics at Uxbridge made the girls laugh: 'his life's ambition was to kill Matron's bad-tempered Pekinese, which had savaged his ankles more than once'.

Students dropped out of the course for a variety of reasons – 'failed exams, failed hopes, failed contraception …' However, Nadine adds, despite all those legends of free love and flower power, 'not all of us had wild sexual adventures in the swinging sixties'. One of her friends dared to invite a boyfriend to have coffee in her room and 'a particularly nasty WRAF NCO, who despised PMs and must have been tipped off, decided to do a spot check … Keith, hearing her coming, tried to hide in the wardrobe. This was always full of clutter, even a budgie cage, so unfortunately he was discovered.' The pair were ordered to report to the CO, who made an example of them: Louise went to Guildford in Surrey for two weeks' punishment; her boyfriend spent a month in Colchester Military Prison, where 'he rubbed shoulders with the likes of murderers and high-profile offenders. None of them believed he had been sent there for having a cup of coffee in a nurses' home!'

From Uxbridge days, Cynthia Mayfield (Mrs Brown) recalls 'the noise from other service activities near to our quarters … the Central Band of the RAF rehearsing, the Queen's Colour Squadron of the RAF Regiment likewise practising their drill, planes from Northolt flying overhead …' Sleeping during the day while doing a spell of night-duty was not easy! Neither was learning to give injections:

> oranges are one thing, real live people something else altogether. But gradually we built up our confidence, and our ability to be convincingly economical with the truth … 'Oh, yes,' we would say in response to the occasional nervous enquiry, 'I've done this HUNDREDS of times before!'

For student Pat Maslen (Mrs Perry), her association with the PMs began years before. Her father was in the RAFMS, stationed in Ceylon accompanied by his family, when his wife fell ill and had to be aeromeded home – husband and children, including Pat, all flew with her. Pat later joined the PMRAFNS NCE, Nursing Course 5. The very first injection she gave proved fateful – three years later she married the patient involved.

Diaries kept by 'Beth' Smith (Mrs Hamson) reveal how much of her off-duty time a student spent on uniforms: ward dresses, returned daily by the laundry service, had to be damp-ironed to make them presentable, and caps had to be starched. Her first ward at Ely was a 'dirty surgery' ward known as:

> 'bums and gums' – haemorrhoidectomies and dental surgery, plus infected wounds. I was very naive but keen to learn and visiting X-ray one day I asked what the small blue radiation machines pinned to the X-ray personnel's coats were. A lovely man whose name I've forgotten told me, 'They're virgin detectors'.

Beth remembers some eccentric PMs, too, especially the sister in the maternity ward at Wegberg, who 'decided that all baby boys under her care should be called Julian'.

The girls may be surprised to know that they were regarded by at least one of the young male nursing attendants as 'super confident bunches of goddesses … in their spotless white uniforms'. Enrolled nurse Geoff Holliday was still in his teens, at the stage of peeling slivers of yellow soap into a large jug bubbling on the stove, making the 'goo' to clean the floor before he swung a heavy bumper 'recklessly to and fro to achieve a superlative but non-slip shine'. Having survived the temptations of becoming top of the 'black list' of undesirables which deputy matron read to each new entry of female students – 'it always guaranteed an early assignation if you were in writing as "best to avoid" in the dating stakes' – Geoff before long developed 'aspirations, some would say delusions', to emulate the girl students, and set himself on the long road to passing the exams he needed to become a state registered nurse himself. (Did he succeed? See Part V.)

Because of general cut-backs and a reduced need for newly qualified staff nurses, SRN training ended in 1977. But not before a few changes had been made: minutes of matrons' meetings for 1975 report that 'Wroughton School of Nursing has been moved to a permanent site – in a Porta-Cabin.'

Nocton Hall

A hospital which provided a favourite posting for many PMs was Nocton Hall, secluded amid acres of rolling Lincolnshire farmland. It took over the work of RAFH Rauceby in June 1947. The Hall itself became the sisters' mess, while the wooden wards reposed in grounds noted for the scent of wild garlic and the dance of springtime daffodils. Starting with just four wards, by 1954 Nocton Hall offered most of the usual hospital facilities for service personnel from the many RAF stations in Lincolnshire and for local people from the Sleaford area. Further departments added over ensuing years widened its scope to include a maternity wing, twin operating theatres, a central sterile supply department and a neuro-psychiatric centre.

Margaret Kingston, who knew Nocton in the early sixties, loved it:

> The hospital was nothing, just hutted, but it had a happy atmosphere ... The first time I was posted there, I went for a walk in the woods and picked some white flowers, put them in a vase in my room. My bat-woman said, 'Sister, d'you know what you've picked there?' I said, 'No, but they don't smell very nice.' She said, 'It's wild garlic! ... I remember she was a bit late one morning. Eventually, in she comes with my cup of tea, saying, 'Sister, I've had such a fright! I was cycling up the drive and a BLACK MAN was walking towards me. He'd got white teeth, but ... he was black!' ... I explained he was one of our American patients and a lovely boy. But she was so frightened ... lived in that village all her life, and Lincoln so far away.

In those days of few cars, 8 miles could be a day's excursion.

Many PMs enjoyed joining in amateur dramatics, 'Particularly when National Servicemen brought their many varied talents,' says Marion Wood (Mrs Donaldson). Nocton Hall's Drama Group produced a plethora of plays and pantos and 1961 seems to have been especially prolific. That year Kathy Mogg (Mrs Ostler) took part in three productions. During rehearsals for *Waltz of the Toreadors* she was almost knocked unconscious when the chap playing her husband 'flung me down and tried to strangle me. There was an iron bedstead (Airmen for the use of) underneath the flounces and my head hit the bottom rail.' Later both she and Marion Wood had parts in *Babes in the Wood*, in which Kathy played Robin Hood:

> rigorously rehearsed in singing and dancing by a professional actor doing National Service who had written and directed the show. After the second performance all the PMs involved went to the officers' mess for a party and I'm afraid the shellfish got me – food poisoning. By the next afternoon I was admitted to Ward 9 and the search was on for a replacement.

Plucked from the obscurity of the chorus to save the day, Marion Wood was 'given the afternoon off to learn lines, refusing an offered phenobarb to calm my nerves – thought I'd better have my wits about me'. Visitors to Kathy Mogg's sick bed assured her that the show had gone on.

Uxbridge cancer unit

The Cade Unit at Uxbridge dealt with over 1,000 cancer patients a year; more than 800 of these received chemotherapy and others were referred to the Westminster (now Charing Cross) Hospital for radiotherapy. As a junior sister, having finished her initial six weeks service at Halton, April Reed came to work there. She remembers the patients as 'nearly all senior officers. We had Lord Trenchard, who died. They were practising his funeral long before he was dead.' But she was particularly moved by the bravery of younger patients dying of the disease. Everyone who worked on the unit felt the same. When the hospital closed in 1972, the Cade continued its invaluable work from premises at Halton.

Today, RAF Uxbridge still serves as a parade-training base for personnel chosen to represent branches of the RAF at commemorative events in London. Over the years these have included the Coronation parade of 1953 and many Festivals of Remembrance. In 1967 RAF Sergeant Kenneth 'Tug' Wilson was to lead the RAF contingent down the steps at the Royal Albert Hall:

> We trained at Uxbridge and on the Tuesday afternoon there was a roar from the Officer Commanding the Queen's Colour Squadron, 'Sergeant Wilson! Leave your squad and take these b— women, put 'em in proper shoes and teach 'em how to march up and down steps!' What a task for a drill sergeant! I was used to drilling male recruits, not nurses …
>
> I became very diplomatic, pointing out that high heels and court shoes were really not intended for marching in. Once they had changed into more suitable footwear, I very gentlemanly grabbed two sisters by their arms and with me in the middle marched them up and down the steps at the bottom of Uxbridge square … Talk about shift work – three pairs of sisters to take up and down steps all afternoon.

Marching might not have been a forte, but nursing sisters had their followers. Security-conscious RAF police wanted to put a ring of security lights around the sisters' mess at Uxbridge, but Matron Kennedy refused to allow it. Her reason? 'My girls should have privacy to bid goodnight to their friends.' What a treasure!

Halton House

For a long time, Princess Mary's Royal Air Force Hospital Halton remained dearest to the hearts of most PMs. Halton was where many of them spent their first few weeks in the service, where the pulse of the PMRAFNS seemed always to beat strongest.

They particularly enjoyed the ambience of Halton House, then as now the officers' mess of RAF Halton, which still hosts balls, reunions and other glamorous occasions, as it has done since the days when Edward VII was a regular visitor and when (allegedly) Lily Langtry bathed in the champagne-filled swimming pool.

'I particularly remember the balls at Halton House,' writes Kate Crompton (Mrs Wilmot):

> The setting was superb, with an imposing staircase sweeping down to the main entrance hall. There was a minstrels gallery and the north and south drawing rooms opened into the main hall. The bar was painted gold … I lived in the Sisters' Mess [but] when it was being enlarged and refurbished half the Sisters moved to Halton House. That was rather a quiet, sedate Mess with lots of senior officers [who] must have had quite a shock with the invasion of the PMs.

Isobel Hipkin (Mrs Bedford), who was part of that invasion, found Halton House 'very much a male domain, with just a few WRAF and Red Cross personnel … An influx of twenty Nursing Officers caused quite some disruption.' The PMs were assigned to shared rooms on the second floor, far from the bathrooms and poorly heated by coal stoves – which came hard on two sisters recently returned from steamy Aden. Because of varying duty hours, mealtimes in the officers' mess had to be adjusted. At breakfast the resident male officers 'normally had a quiet meal behind the daily paper. They took some time to get used to these female intruders who talked!'

But the glamour remained: 'A real highlight of our stay was the Summer Ball, with trumpeters on the main staircase,' says Isobel, while Judy Cooke (Mrs Owens) remembers 'being shown the big V-bombers while wearing a long, emerald-green evening dress'.

However, it was not all high-jinks and dancing. Kate Crompton worked long hours in the plastic surgery centre, whose senior surgeon had worked with the famous Archibald McIndoe during the war. Starting in 1963, Kate 'did night duty every five weeks … 8 p.m. until 8 a.m., we worked fourteen nights non-stop, with a sleeping day and two days off … Shortly before my time, the girls used to work three weeks non-stop!' The weather added its own inconveniences – Kate arrived at Halton in February, when the weather was so atrocious that 'the laundry van couldn't get through and nursing officers had to wash their own uniforms'.

Improvements at Changi

The building of a whole new unit to link the two separate hospital blocks made RAFH Changi, Singapore, an easier place in which to work. Margaret Kingston, who went out to open the new families' ward, found it a delightful posting, but some of the other girls became depressed, for which Margaret blames the climate:

> It was the same all the year, you didn't have seasons … we used to say, wouldn't it be lovely to wake up and see some clouds? … and orchids – I never wanted to see another orchid. Coming from this flower area [she is a native of Spalding in Lincolnshire] I used to say, 'I'd love to see a daffodil, or a tulip.'
>
> One Christmas, the whole place flooded. The monsoon drains couldn't cope with the water and it just poured everywhere. Nobody could visit the patients. Nobody could go anywhere. And the sisters on duty were crying and the sisters off-duty were crying, everybody was home-sick.

Judy Hopkins (Mrs Foote) and her colleagues dealt with the monsoon in a practical way; they went to work in flip-flops and changed into white shoes on the wards, leaving off stockings. The hospital became a refuge for residents of the local children's home, which regularly flooded with every monsoon. But the handicapped youngsters loved it – it was like having a party.

In the row of married quarters which acted as accommodation for Changi PMs, Margaret Kingston lived close to her friend Molly McNair, at a time when the Ministry of Defence (MOD) were:

> trying out new mess kit for PMs. We'd had all sorts, and somebody had the brainwave to use natural tussore [coarse brown silk], of all things, to make a mess dress. It was all tucks – most elaborate. Well … I used to look out from my balcony, most evenings, and there was Molly, in this new mess kit, gardening! I thought 'the heat has got her'.

After observing this performance for a few evenings, Margaret asked Molly why she was gardening in mess dress. '"Oh," she said, "MOD want it testing in all different climates, so that's what I'm doing." But it was hopeless, they didn't have it for long.' Margaret Kingston adds ruefully, 'It used to cost us a fortune every time they changed the mess kit. I think I had three different sorts.'

Poliomyelitis was still rampant in the early 1960s. April Reed nursed many very serious cases, 'with the iron lungs and things … A sister named Margaret Wood was specialist aeromed polio-trained.' And there were civilian patients, resident Singaporeans, such as 'a chap brought in one night who'd been carved up [literally] by the rest of his family'. Shelagh Glenn (Mrs Barber) was a theatre sister on the case. 'We worked for hours just suturing him up, then he went back into the ward and eventually, after a few days, was transferred to the civilian hospital in Singapore. As he walked out after being discharged they got at him again and finished the job!'

Marion Wood (Mrs Donaldson) says:

> Weddings, christenings and, sadly, deaths, were part of life in Changi. Four sisters married in my two years there. We had the Hospital CO in after a severe heart

> attack, and one of our physicians with a young family was killed in a road accident on his way home to lunch.

The CO of RAF Changi was also taken ill and casevaced home, but died soon afterwards. A memorial service was held for him at Changi and Marion and her friend Jane Bullen (Mrs Selway) attended. Marion says, 'It was a solemn service, but my abiding memory is of having to tiptoe on PSP – pierced steel planking used on many airfields – in heeled court shoes which were part of our best outdoor tropical uniform – black court shoes, travel dress and white Dick.'

On a lighter note, she reveals that, in order to feed the four night-duty sisters:

> a basket of food was provided by the Sisters' Mess, the meal prepared by the WRAF Nursing Orderly, and eaten in 3rd floor Sister's office. We sometimes requested a cake mix in the basket, and if no one was in labour as we went on duty it was easy to whip up a sponge and pop it in the ward oven.

Friends (and their boyfriends) often popped in to join the sisters at coffee break; they too enjoyed the cakes – until one evening when one of the sisters happened to mention that 'it had been mixed in a delivery bowl (sterilised, of course!)'.

After one of these convivial midnight feasts, as Judy Cooke (Mrs Owens) recalls, one of the naval officers sent a telegram saying, 'Thanks for the coffee and cakes and love to Ann Marie …' Unfortunately the matron, Wing Officer Dickson, saw the telegram and hauled the PMs up for a 'severe telling off'. But the navy laid on the charm and matron was 'invited to very many pukka cocktail parties on such ships as the *Ark Royal*, and after that called them "such dear boys".'

Romantic dallying on service premises was strictly forbidden, but some matrons could blink when it suited them. In once case, twenty-five-year-old Flying Officer David Dodds was 'seriously courting one of the girls,' and he relates how Wing Officer Jessie Higgins lent tacit approval – she addressed him as 'David, dear,' though the object of his affections, Flying Officer Eileen Smith, remained simply 'Smith'.

Deputy matrons also played Cupid at times, as Judy Cooke (Mrs Owens) explains:

> I think there were twelve midwives and thanks to our Squadron Officers we organised our working shifts according to which boyfriend's plane or ship was in … One of the midwives, Jane Bullen, had a notebook with all of the ship's numbers in. The maternity unit was right on the sea and the ships had to pass in front to go up to the Naval base so, busy as we were, if a ship passed we used to tip the louvered windows up and wave the nappies out of the window.

In the late 1960s, Clare Woolley (Mrs Fowler), ran the children's ward. Among hospital personnel she found a talented amateur artist, who 'kindly painted Walt Disney characters over the cots and beds. Unfortunately, one child took great exception to having the bed "belonging" to Dopey!'

Hong Kong

By this time the only other Far Eastern post for PMs was in Hong Kong, at the sick quarters of RAF Kai Tak, whose resident squadron was cared for by a small medical team: two doctors, a dentist and one PM, assisted by local orderlies. April Reed was the last PM there in 1960, after which the Medical Branch took over all Hong Kong duties.

Fifteen years later, however, the authorities decided that it might be useful to have a qualified aeromed sister on hand at Kai Tak. Following total withdrawal from Singapore, in 1975, they sent in Valerie Hand, who had already done a year's duty at Changi. She thought Hong Kong:

> an amazing place. The airstrip went out into the sea, and when you flew in, low over the sea, there was this strip of runway stuck out … you had to cross this six-lane highway and go up the hill to the officers' mess, which was on the side of the hill. From the balconies of the rooms, you overlooked this highway and RAF Kai Tak, and then the main Kai Tak airport beyond it. It was absolutely fantastic, the view …
>
> I used to do the local casevac flights with 84 Helicopter Squadron. They and the local Royal Hong Kong Auxiliary helicopters took it in turns to be on call, and the two doctors and I also had a call rota. We'd get called out to all sorts of things, like some Chinese woman in labour having a problem out on Cheung Chau island, and we'd fly to pick her up and transfer her to one of the local hospitals … [Or we] had to rescue somebody from the hillsides … depended whether you were in a Wessex or with the Hong Kong auxiliaries, who flew Alouettes. But it made a change from the daily grind. Hong Kong was an experience. I loved it.

Valerie Hand was followed at Kai Tak by Shelagh Utley, who stayed there for two years. In 1978, soon after Shelagh left, RAF Kai Tak itself closed down and the medical centre moved to Shek Kong (pr. Sek Kong), out in the New Territories. Other PMs were to be posted there in their turn.

With the 'Boat People' crisis at its height in 1979, refugees from Vietnam, fleeing the war with China, crowded into boats and sought safety in Hong Kong. The derelict sick quarters at RAF Kai Tak was opened again by the British Red Cross. One of the Red Cross workers who helped with the refugees until they could be resettled was Helen Cookson, a retired squadron officer of the PMRAFNS. For this work she was later awarded the Florence Nightingale Medal, the highest honour in nursing, regarded as the 'Nurses' VC'.

Decade of diversity – the 1970s

Change and unsettlement loomed with the advent of the 1970s. Reduction in the overall commitment of the RAF saw withdrawal of forces from the Middle East and the closure of some overseas hospitals. Cuts in manpower led to additional closures of smaller hospitals in the UK – Uxbridge, Padgate, Weeton and Cosford. However, for the PMs it was also a time of interest and diversity, including chances to work in unusual places and with nursing services of other nations.

As a prelude to the decade, a poignant occasion took place in 1970 when a service in the Nurses' Chapel at Westminster Abbey, attended by the Queen Mother, dedicated the gift of special seats and kneelers made by skilled needlewomen of all three nursing services. Wing Officer Jessie Higgins (who had retired in 1968), being an expert tapestry-maker and member of the Royal College of Embroidery, was asked to work a cushion with a design showing the PMRAFNS medical badge. Using the best materials supplied by the Royal College of Embroidery, she considered it a labour of love and was very proud to have been chosen. So she was somewhat upset when matron-in-chief, having been to see the work in an exhibition, remarked in amazement that there wasn't a mistake in it. 'As if there would be!' says Higgie.

Changing courses

The General Service Training Course, held at RAF Henlow, had by this time become a requirement for all nursing officers. It evolved into the Professionally Qualified and Re-Entrants (PQRE) course, which in turn later became the Specialist Entrant and Re-Entrants (SERE) course, and moved to the RAF College, Cranwell. The course is designed to turn ready-qualified professionals into physically fit and service-aware officers, ready to take up their first posts with the Royal Air Force.

Miche Shaw, practising midwifery at Nocton Hall and longing for a posting to the Far East, was summoned to matron's office and informed that she had been chosen to go to Henlow as flight commander on the very first PQRE course. Although she had no teaching experience and had never even seen a signal, much less considered how to teach the subject, she accepted the challenge and with a good deal of homework and application her initial six-month posting turned into two years in the job. A PM is nothing if not adaptable!

Journey to the past

The Gulf state of Muscat and Oman (now Oman) was an isolated Islamic society, riven by blood feuds and slavery and ruled by a despot who turned the revenues from his oil deposits into gold which he kept in his palace in the capital, Salalah. In 1970 the Sultan was deposed by his son Qabus, who determined to introduce a better way of life for his people.

Seeing medical aid as a priority, Sultan Qabus asked the British government for help and an RAF medical team went out – surgeon, anaesthetist, nursing officer, two male registered general nurses, two female state-enrolled nurses, a sergeant operating theatre technician and 'a Corporal Med Sec with 20 minutes Radiography training' – so writes Connie Bull, the nursing officer involved. The six men, fresh from UK, stayed at RAF Salalah, an all-male domain; the three women, from the RAFH at Muharraq, in Bahrain, had a flat in the Sultan's palace.

The former ruler had begun to build a hospital but abandoned the project. So the 'hospital' set up by the RAF medical team consisted mainly of two bungalows which had been intended as accommodation for the staff of the uncompleted hospital. The local populace dwelt mostly in palm frond huts, deprived of most modern benefits including running water and electricity. However, the bungalows – which served as wards, theatre and night duty quarters – obtained power from a generator and 'water was pumped up to tanks in the roof, from a bowser filled two or three times a day from the supply at RAF Salalah, by one of our RGNs (misemployed!)'.

In the air-conditioned bedroom (the operating theatre) patients were anaesthetised on the table – women had to be undressed while comatose because they wouldn't knowingly let men touch them. In the lounge (the ward) eight beds and several mattresses held patients – since they were accompanied and fed by relatives, the crush and scramble the nurses faced while trying to tend their patients may be imagined.

Modern sanitary facilities in the bungalows puzzled the local people – normal practice was to visit the beach, dig a hole, perform the necessary function, bury the evidence, and clean themselves with sea water and rocks. They tried to do something similar in the hospital toilets, with messy consequences which Connie Bull and the two SENs had to clean up several times a day. Writing to a friend about it, she added:

> To get my women and local girl nurses (under training from us) to know how to use the toilet, I decided the only way was by demonstration!! If you could have seen me surrounded by Arabs I think you'd have been in hysterics.

Connie was horrified to learn that her letter describing these events to matron in Muharraq (humorously intended) had been seen at Air Ministry by matron-in-chief et al.:

> Imagine my thoughts when anyone of higher rank years later said, 'I've heard of you'! I had also ended my letter (I was a Flight Officer at the time), 'yours sincerely, Connie Bull, Matron of Salalah, Consultant Obstetrician and Gynaecologist (true – Arab women would not let men touch them), Consultant Physician to Royalty (I attended the Sultan's mother and sister, and the harem of his father), Jack of all trades and glorified char!' I was convinced my career was definitely limited to sixteen years and no promotion.

She was wrong! She spent twenty-four years in the PMs and retired as a Wing Commander.

Despite inadequate facilities, equipment and drugs, plus the inconvenience of being separated from the doctors on camp by a mined 'no man's land', there being a war on locally, their work varied from delivering babies to treating TB, performing minor surgery and vaccinating the Salalah population against cholera. For this last, Connie set up her clinic 'on a tree stump, armed with two syringes and four metal needles (as in the old days) and a spirit lamp to "sterilise".' She vaccinated about 500 people in one day.

Major surgery was impossible without laboratory backup, but they began with hernias and cysts and eventually undertook:

> some rather drastic surgical action to relieve abhorrent medical conditions … We drained a hydrocele of 6.8 litres of fluid – he'd carried his testes in a wheelbarrow (Arabs don't wear trousers). We also removed a fungating breast cancer, which relieved the smell and made a husband very happy, [and] we borrowed the local carpenter's saw to amputate the leg of a twenty-eight-year-old. We then had to turn a broom upside down for a crutch … the 'boys' at RAF Salalah kindly made him a peg leg … I will not forget the faces of those – like the amputee – who although deformed by the surgery were so exhilarated by it, because of their freedom from pain.

Connie Bull was in Salalah from September to December 1970 and again during March and April the following year:

> We also 'trained' four local Arab girls – who were not even used to running water – to scrub up, lay up for a dressing, do it and remove sutures in a sterile manner. Achieved in six weeks mainly by sign language. I often wonder if they are working at the hospital, so modern today, and what status they hold … It was an experience not to be missed.

A PM in Texas

For Elizabeth Sandison, then a Flight Officer in the PMRAFNS, new challenges opened when she became the first PM to go on an exchange posting with the United States Air Force (USAF). Attached to their flight school, at Brooks Airfield, San Antonio, Texas, for six weeks, she went through a flight-nurse training course there before joining the 11th Aeromedical Airlift Squadron at Scott Air Force Base, Illinois:

> It was at the height of the Vietnam conflict, so the amount of internal transfer of patients was phenomenal. We criss-crossed Continental US and Alaska, and down as far as Puerto Rico. Thousands of patients were airlifted around San Francisco, then moved on to bases near their homes, or to more specialist facilities.

Liz was also involved with casualties after Hurricane Celia hit Texas and devastated 85 per cent of facilities, including the hospital, around Corpus Christi Naval Air

Station. Flying aboard a C-9 Nightingale, Liz and her American colleagues airlifted out twenty-one stretcher patients and fifteen walking wounded.

Her US detachment over, Liz Sandison returned to aeromed duties at what was now the Princess Alexandra Hospital, RAF Wroughton. She flew with an aeromedical team on one particularly harrowing mission when a civilian VC10 crashed on take-off from Addis Ababa, with huge loss of life. Among the passengers were 'numerous Embassy children going back to school, there'd been many fatalities and the survivors were desperately burned'. The aeromed team, flying in an RAF VC10 from Lyneham, evacuated sixteen severely burned patients. They staged through Cyprus, where the aircraft refuelled and where medical teams from TPMRAFH Akrotiri assisted at the airhead, providing much-needed equipment. Most of the patients recovered, but one woman died as the plane made its descent to England and later two little girls and a man died in the burns and plastic surgery unit at Halton.

Radical changes at Akrotiri

In 1973 another terrible air crash, in the Kyrenia mountains on Cyprus, killed thirty-eight people, including Helen Deery and Sheila Noble, two off-duty PMs from Akrotiri.

The hospital itself remained extremely busy, a lively place where social life was good and nursing officers enjoyed their postings. On one occasion, for a royal visit by Princess Alexandra, patients on Ward 6 were decked in made-to-measure pyjamas with matching cravats!

However, problems were soon mounting: first Whitehall ordered cut-backs which affected British forces on the island; then in 1974 Turkish forces invaded and once again civil war broke out between Greek and Turkish factions. In response, the Akrotiri hospital was put on a war footing: staff did not return to their homes but slept on the job, working an eight-hour rota. Most of the casualties coming in were British expatriates caught in crossfire, or shot while refusing to leave their homes, but before long a nasty strain of diarrhoea began to spread across the island. As civilian hospitals overflowed, Akrotiri treated both local Cypriot home guard and a crew of Turkish sailors from a sunken destroyer. Lying sick alongside one another on the wards, the rival factions got along amicably enough.

From Britain, PMs Helen Tyler and Margaret Luck arrived to help care for Turkish refugees at RAF Episkopi. Prepared for uncomfortable living, possibly in tents, they brought their uniforms, thick sweaters, wellington boots and sleeping bags – and were startled to be asked if they had evening dresses for the Christmas and New Year parties! Their main task was making up hundreds of four-hourly milk feeds for mothers and babies, a production-line that flourished as trust and friendship grew and older Turkish girls helped out. Eventually when the trouble abated and the island was partitioned, the Turkish families moved north, hopefully to enjoy a more settled and peaceful life.

The trouble subsided and curfews ceased, but travel for British nationals was restricted to Greek Cypriot areas in the south and parts of Nicosia. Owing to the reduction in numbers of service personnel on the island, only three wards remained open at Akrotiri. Enrolled nurses continued to live in their billets in the main WRAF block, but the sisters' mess closed and remaining nursing officers shared the No 1 Officers' Mess on the main base.

1976 saw Akrotiri reduced even further, to only two wards. Nevertheless, preparations began for a visit by Princess Margaret. The programme had to be rehearsed, with PM Ethnea Hancock chosen as stand-in for the royal visitor. She says it was:

> the strangest thing I have ever been asked to do. It started with standing at the top of aircraft steps with no aircraft behind me! I then had to walk slowly down the steps to inspect a guard of honour before being driven to Air House at Episkopi with the Air Officer Commanding. Being a relatively junior officer at the time, this was all rather daunting. Later I had to walk round the Sergeants' Mess being introduced as if I were Her Royal Highness and having to respond with appropriate small talk before going to the Officers' Mess for a similar reception followed by a rehearsal lunch!

Joy Harris, who was in Akrotiri in 1977 as senior matron, recalls being a passenger in a helicopter which disturbed the flamingos on the salt flats, causing them to rise in a cloud of pink wings – a magical sight.

But for the RAF the best days in Cyprus had ended. On closure of the British military hospital at Dhekelia, the RAF hospital at Akrotiri became bi-service under RAF command, having 60 per cent RAF and 40 per cent army personnel. In its new role, caring for the tri-service community on the island, it was known simply as The Princess Mary's Hospital (TPMH).

Philatelic flight

To celebrate the fiftieth anniversary of the royal charter which officially launched the Princess Mary's Royal Air Force Nursing Service, a philatelic first-day cover was issued. The stamp showed a tiny 1923 Vickers Vernon air ambulance, contrasted with a 1973 VC10. It was designed by Squadron Officer Dorothy Hutchins (who had shared the Belize aeromed adventure, post-Hurricane Hattie in 1961). She flew to Akrotiri on a VC10 aeromed flight, taking with her 11,250 special envelopes, and in Cyprus she stuck commemorative stamps on them all and had the covers date-stamped before flying home again. Proceeds from the sale of the covers went to the RAF Museum at Hendon.

Half a century on from its formal beginning, the PMRAFNS had over 1,000 members, including non-commissioned officers and trainee nurses – the trainees earned as much in a month as had been paid annually to a qualified sister in 1923.

Only seven RAF hospitals remained, but PMs on exchange duties could be found as far afield as Asia, Australia and the Americas.

Imperial Iran

For a brief but memorable period in the 1970s, PMs were stationed in Tehran, on loan to the Imperial Iranian Air Force, for whom they set up a school of nursing. Among the nursing officers involved was Liz Sandison. In a varied career she had just spent three enjoyable years with the Inspectorate of Recruiting, responsible for spreading the word of the PMRAFNS, via high schools and nursing courses, to 'young people who often had no idea what to do with their lives … I loved it, a wonderful job.' Now she found herself heading for Iran.

Dorothy Lane and Polly Perkins had already undertaken the daunting task of setting up a school of nursing, and Dorothy Reid (Mrs Westman) had joined them when the course was established. In 1977 Liz Sandison and Margaret Ross (Mrs Upfold) relieved that original team.

Liz recalls that the task of setting up British-style administration and introducing Nursing Council policies:

> was a most uphill job because of their attitudes and the way they conducted business … you'd spend two hours with 'the Generals', playing with a cup of coffee and a piece of sticky cake that you didn't really want, to get £50 to replace a suction pump or other equipment for the school, whereas they would spend £5,000 on a silly piece of ornate nothing … [but] I would never leave without getting exactly what I wanted!

Although most Iranians considered nursing a very inferior occupation, some of the students came from wealthy backgrounds. Liz and her colleagues took them up to an Iranian air force holiday camp on the Caspian Sea. The girls had never had so much freedom before and they went mad painting their nails and plastering on make-up. Remembering those fashion-conscious, elegant girls that she knew, Liz finds it odd to see Iranian women now, on television, swathed to the eyes in black robes and veils. 'We left just as the Shah was about to be thrown out – the last few months were pretty tricky.'

Moving with the times

PM Susan Pound (Mrs Gray) made minor history in 1976. Her husband-to-be was based at RAF Stafford, with Susan at the closest RAFH at Cosford. However, 'Matron of Cosford Hospital, a rather formidable lady, would not consider me getting married and travelling from Stafford to Cosford.' Much paperwork later, Flight Officer Susan Pound/Gray became the first PM to be granted a married quarter in her own name. It was her husband who had to do the travelling!

However, Cosford itself was to close on 31 December 1977 after nearly forty years of service. It had been built in 1939 with the expectation of a useful life of ten years but, thanks to careful repair and renovation, the same buildings were in use thirty-seven years later. Cosford's last matron, Doreen Smedley, recalls the sadness of 'standing in the cold drizzly rain, six PMs with a lone RAF nurse …' as the flag was hauled down for the last time.

Jubilees

As part of the celebrations for her Silver Jubilee, Her Majesty the Queen reviewed her Royal Air Force at Finningley on 29 July 1977 and, for the first time, a squadron of PMs was present on parade for the presentation of a new Colour. Squadron Officer Judy Hopkins (Mrs Foote), chosen as officer commanding the squadron, says, 'To express fully in words how I felt is very difficult, but I was, and still am, extremely proud.' However, before the great day many hurdles had to be leapt, not least mastering the marching: 'Those few half-hours by the garages at Halton eleven years previously did not seem much help!'

The selected PMs went first to Uxbridge, to the Queen's Colour Squadron, for four days' intensive training to help them 'bond' and set them in the right direction. 'Drill sergeants have a reputation for a colourful turn of expression,' Judy Hopkins recalls ruefully. 'We were no exception in stimulating some memorable phrases. For years I had been led to believe that ladies should never shout and suddenly I was expected to have the voice of an RSM …' When Judy revealed that she was going on holiday to Wales, the drill sergeant suggested a good way to develop her voice would be to shout at the sheep!

Glossing over the nightly 'bulling' of shoes and worries over the fainting attacks that seemed to hit at random and deplete the squadron, Judy mainly recalls 'the sheer horror of arriving for the first rehearsal: there were all the other squadrons busy falling in, forming two ranks, then three, then turning about … and all the orders at true parade ground volume. No way were we going to do THAT in front of THEM.' However, they did do it, with a little help from the more practised chaps (and trying to ignore the laughter in the ranks). At last the great day came:

> I shall never forget marching on to the parade ground, with the music, the stands a sea of spectators – our backs were straighter and we marched so proudly – 850 men and women with the six Colours of the Royal Air Force, and 68 Squadron Standards on parade. I know I speak for all the PMs when I say that being on that special parade in the presence of the Queen was a very moving experience.

The PMs' own diamond jubilee year of 1978 (sixty years since the original 'temporary' Service was formed) was celebrated with a thanksgiving service in the central church of the RAF, St Clement Danes, London, followed by a reception at

St James's Palace attended by HRH Princess Alexandra, Air Chief Commandant of the PMRAFNS.

This year also saw the very first issue of the *PMRAFNS Magazine*. Valerie Hand, who shared the editing with Sheila Joy, says it all began during a tri-service middle-management course at Aldershot, when she and Sheila, faced with having to do a 'project', chose to test the feasibility of starting a PMs' magazine. Questionnaires sent out to retired members elicited a favourable response and when Matron-in-Chief Barbara Ducat-Amos heard about it she told them to get on and do it! Valerie enjoyed the challenge of 'getting it off the ground, finding material to put in it, deciding the format, going round publishers … it started off with that nice blue cover, gold crest …' Twenty-two years on, the annual magazine is packed with news and fascinating articles, all written by members of the Service past and present.

In her Foreword to the first edition of 1978, Barbara Ducat-Amos told her members of cuts in the Defence Budget which, for the PMs, had meant closure of the hospitals at Changi, Cosford and Uxbridge. It had also caused Princess Alexandra's Hospital Wroughton and The Princess Mary's Hospital Akrotiri to drop the 'RAF' from their titles. Although still under air force command, at both locations RAF personnel now worked with army colleagues. Indeed, amalgamation of all three forces' nursing services was again under discussion – it had been a recurring background theme since 1918.

Halton's renal unit

The busy renal unit at PMRAFH Halton occupied two wards, comprising a renal investigation ward and acute renal ITU on Ward 14 and a chronic renal dialysis and care unit on Ward 15. In addition the staff provided two full mobile dialysis teams which could be deployed to anywhere in the world at very short notice.

Tony Cox worked on the renal unit for eight years, from 1980 to 1988. He writes:

> A small group of us were trained as Renal Technicians, performing all the acute and chronic haemodialysis, haemofiltration, peritoneal dialysis and filtrating poisons from patients suffering from conditions such as iatrogenic overdoses of drugs … Lithium, paracetamol, even Paraquat weed killer ingestion. Indeed, the unit depended on the RAF premise of being paid twenty-four hours a day, seven days per week!! If patients needed our specialist care we put in the hours to achieve, where possible, a positive outcome.
>
> I was officer in charge of Ward 15, my team were the renal techs and we covered all the acute, chronic renal care and dialysis. We trained new renal techs and renal nurses; we were extremely busy and often stretched! We also mounted and staffed all the mobile deployments, which could be to civilian hospitals in UK (usually ITUs), or military situations overseas. Most of the renal techs were Flight Nursing Officers

(FNOs) as well, enabling us to function alongside the aeromed teams. We normally did two weeks out on mobile and then changed over if possible. We would try to feedback updates to a duty nephrologist on a daily basis if possible. It was extremely demanding work with no margin for error!

Our patients were a mix of both military and civilians, sometimes including foreign patients who through proximity to our overseas activity came under our care. We worked [all] hours required and I must say the Dedication, the standard of care shown by the team was second to none!! I feel both privileged and humble to have been part of it.

Aeromedical advances

Although the closure of overseas stations had reduced the need for regular long-haul aeromed flights, short-haul flights, plus world-wide emergency missions, remained an important duty for members of the PMRAFNS. For longer journeys the VC10 was still in use; shorter aeromeds employed the more rugged Hercules aircraft and, increasingly, helicopters.

While Halton's renal unit continued to treat patients on its wards, the RAF's mobile dialysis teams – the only ones in the UK – were constantly on emergency call, often with two or three teams out at the same time on different missions. Advances in technology increasingly allowed their life-saving equipment to operate via aircraft power supplies.

In-flight nurse training is, of course, constantly up-dated, becoming ever more specialised. On long flights the change in time zones and the need to calculate the correct interval for giving drugs may entail wearing two watches; and, at altitude, changing air pressure may affect the drip rate of intravenous infusions. Particular injuries require patients to be placed in particular areas of the aircraft – those who need regular nursing attention must be easily accessible; others must lie where there's least vibration. And, if a patient's condition changes in mid-flight, with the nearest doctor perhaps hundreds of miles away, the nursing officer involved must know exactly how to phrase the questions which the aircraft captain will relay by radio. In such cases clarity is vital: even a small misunderstanding could be fatal.

MSU(?)

On the subject of misunderstandings …

Useful as they are for those in the know, jargon and acronyms, unwisely used, can cause confusion. An example comes from Valerie Hand, the first PM to do the Basic Staff Officer's Course at Bracknell. This was, she says, 'for those who wanted to get on in the "big Air Force"', and a somewhat reluctant Valerie was persuaded to try it. The course covered service writing, operations, orders, courts martial and public speaking, and included a variety of exercises and team projects. It was the exercise involving an

MSU that caused the problem – in that context MSU meant a major servicing unit, but when Valerie 'told the guys what it meant to me, they fell about laughing'. In nurse's jargon, an MSU is a 'mid-stream sample of urine'.

'Anyway,' says Valerie, 'I passed the course.' And she did indeed 'get on in the big Air Force'; she was appointed matron-in-chief in 1994 and went on to become Director of Defence Nursing Services, retiring as air commodore in 1997.

PART V

End of an Era

17

The Male Element

In the light of demands for equal opportunities, it was inevitable that a purely female service such as the PMRAFNS should succumb to the pressure for, in this case, 'Men's Lib', and allow professionally qualified male nurses to become PMs. Although state registered senior NCOs of the Medical Service had had opportunities for commissions since 1976, these appointments had been in the Medical Technician Branch and applicants had had to complete full initial officer training; female SRNs were required only to complete the shorter 'special entrant' course before being commissioned into the PMRAFNS. However, on 1 April 1980, the Air Ministry inaugurated a Unified Nursing Service, which made all suitably qualified SRNs, male or female, eligible for direct entry as commissioned officers of the PMRAFNS. Those with SEN qualifications became part of the non-commissioned element. On the same date, female nursing officers assumed the traditional male ranks of Flying Officer, Flight Lieutenant, Squadron Leader, Wing Commander, Group Captain, Air Commodore and so on.

The changes did not occur without a few ripples: sisters at Wroughton caught hold of some of the 'boys', decked them in quatrecorne hats, handbags and capes, and made them walk through the mess. Gary Parkinson warns that someone may still have photos!

By this time, Geoff Holliday (who in the mid-1960s had dreamed of becoming an SRN) had passed his exams and been on several postings, including one to Muharraq in the Gulf. He was now a sergeant charge nurse at Ely, finding it 'more difficult, each passing week, to accept the anomaly which made my female colleagues commissioned and the men not'. He had mourned the fact that, as the service contracted, many fine NCOs of proven ability and with years of experience had been lost; so when the chance came to achieve a commission for himself he took it. 'It was a very proud me who went to the RAF College Cranwell … I was the first to do the Special Entrant and Re-Entrant four weeks Initial Officer Training, as a Flight Lieutenant in November 1980.'

Joy Harris was matron at Halton 'when we started commissioning our NCOs. We had an establishment committee going on at the time, with a very old-school RAF officer – a Wing Commander – in charge of it, who wasn't keen on the idea at all: "You'll have a male Matron-in-Chief one of these days!"' Fifteen years later, his prediction came true.

'But we did have trouble commissioning our boys,' Joy adds:

> They used to put the male officers through Biggin Hill – and some of the most suitable chaps were getting turned down. Then one chap who we didn't think was suitable at all got through … When Matron-in-Chief of the time went into it, the thing they were failing them on was 'lack of aggression', and of course you don't want aggressive nurses!

In 1982, male and female PMs, marching side by side, represented the Service at the Royal Albert Hall Festival of Remembrance. Among them were a husband and wife, stationed at Nocton Hall.

Another aspect of this mingling of the genders is illustrated by a moment of revelation which came to Joy Harris later, while she was a resident of the officers' mess at Brampton. She had enjoyed the camaraderie of mess living for nearly thirty years but, with retirement looming, she realised she must soon think of finding a home of her own. 'The final push was, I think, the drying room on my floor of the mess. All the other members on that floor were men, so my undies hung to dry in the middle of their shreddies. Pride and vanity dictated that only my newest and best lingerie should be worn. It was time to seek another home!'

Before long, however, this skirmish of the sexes was put into its proper perspective when British forces prepared again for war.

The Falklands War

The Falkland Islands, remote amid the vastness of the South Atlantic Ocean, consist largely of bleak, treeless moorland exposed to rigorous sub-Arctic weather. Inhabited over the years by settlers from several European countries, they have been maintained as a British colony since 1833. The inhabitants consider themselves British, but being geographically close to Argentina they have also maintained links with that country. However, since the islands form part of the continental shelf of South America, Argentina considers 'Los Malvinas' an integral part of its territory – a claim more keenly pursued since rich deposits of oil were discovered off shore.

The first real signs of strife came in March 1982 when a party of Argentinians, arriving on the outlying island of South Georgia to dismantle a whaling station, raised the Argentine flag. On 2 April, Argentina invaded the main islands and in response the British gathered a force of ships which set sail to reclaim their sovereign territory. They recaptured South Georgia on 25 April, but the battle for the main islands continued through May and into June, when British forces proved superior. A ceasefire was declared on 14 June. Casualties continued to be flown home throughout the following two months.

Initially, planners had anticipated that casualties would be brought by sea from the South Atlantic to the nearest British base on Ascension Island (part of the British colony of St Helena), a voyage of ten to fourteen days aboard hospital ships before the men could be flown home. However, in the event, Uruguay kindly offered hospital facilities at Montevideo, much closer to the Falklands.

Towards the end of April, air force and army nurses at Princess Alexandra's Hospital, RAF Wroughton, prepared to receive casualties. They shut down two-thirds of their wards and admitted only the most urgent new cases, thus freeing both bed-spaces and staff for the task ahead. The RAF hospitals at Ely, Halton and Nocton Hall released aeromedically trained staff to join the Operation Corporate team; their remaining colleagues willingly undertook extra duties, despite serious undermanning imposed by a recruiting embargo. At first a trickle of patients with everyday medical problems and injuries came in from Ascension Island, but as May progressed to June and the fighting grew more intense, the flow of casualties increased.

Those of us who, through the media, witnessed the consequences of that war will not need reminding of the terrible effects wrought by Exocet missiles and other weaponry. Memorials on the Falkland Islands attest to the fact that many men, on both sides, gave their lives in the cause. Of those who survived, more than half suffered gunshot wounds; one-fifth had burns; some were disfigured for life, some lost limbs or were blinded; many suffered the appalling pain of trench foot; many succumbed to the effects of the bitter cold; a few were psychologically devastated. All of them had to be cared for.

Good medical management of the wounded depended on several links of a chain, each one relying on the rest. It began at the heart of the battle, wherever casualties occurred – in ships or in the field. This vitally important early work was followed by treatment in the surgical unit at Ajax Bay and then a stabilising phase aboard the 'hospital at sea', SS *Uganda*, where naval and army doctors and nurses tended the wounded in zero temperatures with decks lurching under them. From the *Uganda*, both British and Argentinian casualties were evacuated by sea from the war zone to Montevideo, a four-day voyage during which ambulance ships HMS *Hydra*, *Hecla* and *Herald* battled gallantly through 40-foot waves. Despite atrocious weather, casualties swiftly found themselves transferred to the British Hospital in Montevideo where, once assessed and stabilised, those well enough to withstand the eighteen-hour flight home were taken to the waiting VC10s. Men on stretchers with broken and shredded limbs; blinded soldiers leaning on ragged, bandaged comrades; bullet and shrapnel injuries, burns … It was the largest movement of casualties by air ever undertaken by British armed forces.

For the PMRAFNS, the major task was the air evacuation link of the chain. This entailed a flight of 7,000 miles, by VC10, from Montevideo to RAF Brize Norton, with a refuelling stop at Ascension or, occasionally, in West Africa. From Brize Norton, patients travelled by ambulance or coach to reception and assessment at Wroughton. Finally, they were transferred to appropriate specialist units, base hospitals or, for the more fortunate, to their homes.

In all, twenty-nine flight nursing officers and seventeen flight nursing attendants took part in the Falkland aeromeds, working in rotation. During major airlifts, each team comprised two medical officers, six flight nursing officers and eight flight nursing attendants. Their aircraft could carry up to sixty-six patients, of whom one-third might be stretcher cases, all needing different types of medical care. When the aircraft paused on Ascension to refuel, part of the flight nursing team would remain on the island while the others continued to Montevideo. This pause was intended to allow half of the team to rest, but in the event they usually helped out at the medical centre on Ascension. In turn, the other half of the team continued to work throughout the return flight from Ascension to UK, during the transfer to road vehicles at Brize Norton, and finally on the journey to Wroughton. By the time they handed over to their hospital colleagues at Wroughton, the team had often been on duty non-stop for twenty-three hours.

At the peak of activity, Wroughton personnel assessed and catered for 120 patients within two hours, a hectic time with many elements to be juggled and efficiently set in place: not only the all-important medical aspect, but paperwork, bed allocation, catering, stores, transport, the press, amongst other things. Another vital consideration was the comforting, both physical and emotional, of anxious relatives who waited in welfare rooms being fed and cared for by a squadron of Red Cross and St John Ambulance volunteers. These relatives were taken to meet the arriving patients amid tears – joy mingling with sorrow – and nurses stood by, their own eyes wet as they carried on with their work, matching lists of patients to available beds in wards. Within minutes, the patients were either tucked up in bed and being examined by doctors or, for the less seriously wounded, taken to places where they could rest and perhaps enjoy a beer and a cigarette. Cooks hurried to provide hot food; admin staff arranged onward movement to homes or hospitals; every spare member of staff turned to, bringing whatever comfort was needed – clothes, goodies or perhaps only a smile and a friendly word. The returning men had lost close comrades, watched their ships go down in flames, struggled through moor and mud, endured all the horrors for which every fighting man prepares but which he hopes he will never see. Frequently, night-duty staff spent their time sitting on the grass outside the hutted wards, simply listening to wounded men recount their stories.

Many of the casualties had nothing left but what they had with them – underwear and ruined uniform, if they were lucky; the rest had gone to the bottom of the South Atlantic, along with their ship. But stores and local people, often unasked, gave unstinting support.

For the staff of Wroughton hospital, and for their matron, Wing Commander Zena Cheel, it was a time they will never forget. Zena says:

> I didn't get home for six weeks during the Falklands War and, quite often, on a Sunday, one of the nurses would say, 'You're here again this weekend, matron,' and

I used to say, 'Yes, but so are you!' … And when they went off, they'd say, 'I live in block so-and-so, matron, at Wroughton' or 'This is my address and telephone number, if you want any help, please ring' … I remember the CO (Air Commodore Hurrell) taking a civilian surgeon round one weekend, and this chap said to the CO, 'You're very lucky to have so many staff, to be able to cope with all this,' and the CO said to him, 'You won't believe this, but half these people are off duty, and they don't get paid extra for it!' They'd be demanding overtime in the NHS, wouldn't they? So, it was simple – I tried to remember I was a nurse first and a matron second …

Let's face it, none of us thought that in our service time we'd be looking after war casualties. We thought there was never going to be another war – so the thing that really got to me was the stoicism of the nursing staff. These pupil nurses … young enough to be my grandchildren, some of them, but when we got the bad burns, and the amputations and all these things, they just got on as if they were looking after ordinary everyday patients …

We knew the Falklands War was on, we knew people were sailing out there … we knew there was going to come a time when our services would be called upon, but how we were going to be called upon we'd no idea … Apart from getting beds ready, we didn't even know what preparations to make … We had this Red Cross department that was part library, part occupational therapy, but also had things like toilet bags with a flannel, toothpaste, toothbrush and some soap, so on each bed table we put one of these bags, and some towels, pyjamas, and waited … In the meantime, the Royal Naval Association and the RAF somewhere nearby had heard that these people were coming to Wroughton, and we were inundated with cans of beer and we had to get extra fridges! …

All these men, when they arrived, looked as if they were in the Navy, all dressed in navy or bluish shirts, and navy trousers, all clutching these black plastic bags … the first few had trench foot and minor injuries. We welcomed them and then they were assessed by the medical officer … Depending on how well they were, they were given a can of beer … that was a very humble start really. What we didn't realise was that these bags that they had were their entire worldly possessions. As the weeks went by we learned …

After the first lot had gone, peeled off to their respective hospitals – the navy went to Haslar, the army went to Woolwich, and we kept the air force at Wroughton – the next day the nursing staff were making up the beds and Jo Boase [Squadron Leader i/c the aeromedical ward] said to me, 'Matron, we're having great trouble with the linen store.' Unbeknown to us, the chaps had gone off with their towels, toothbrush and bits and bobs.

Stores were being difficult, fearing great loss of their equipment if this went on. So Matron Cheel appealed to the CO for some money out of the patients' comfort fund:

> if people wanted to donate money it went into his fund, basically for buying water jugs and vases, and little trays to put on people's lockers, that sort of thing, but I asked if I could have some money because, I said, 'I want to go down to Marks and Spencer's, in Swindon.' I went in my lunch hour, in my uniform, and I asked if I could speak to the manager and I explained who I was and said we were beginning to receive casualties from the Falklands war and I'd like to buy a hundred bath towels and a hundred hand towels, and maybe the odd flannels and things. I said, 'I've got an open cheque here and if you let me know how much it is the CO has said I can sign it,' and he said, 'Matron … we're going to give you half of everything.' So we got all these things. Some we paid for and others people gave. The shops in Wroughton … the little supermarket used to send pork pies and Dundee cake … the paper shop used to send all the newspapers that hadn't been sold … it all helped to make their lives that little bit nicer when they arrived.

Hospital staff eagerly watched the television, for news and to anticipate the kind of casualties they might expect. Then manifests began to come in, signals giving details of the wounded:

> They tended quite often to come in in batches. We got a big batch of the burns after the *Galahad* went up … We knew we were going to have all these burns in and we knew there were very bad ones …
>
> Anyway, we were looking this particular night on the telly and they were showing these people being transferred onto the hospital ships from Ascension Island, and we noticed they all had their hands in plastic bags … I did my plastics training in the air force, but when people had hands burned we used to wrap every individual finger, to stop them getting what they call the webbing … but evidently they found that if people put their hands in these plastic bags and they were occluded (so that no infection can get in), they can move their fingers, but all the exudate, which drips off their fingers, just collects in the bottom of the bag, but they can still use their hands within these bags … keeps them supple you see. So, once again, I went down to the local supermarket and I bought all the plastic bags that they had on their shelves. As I say, we learned.

One of the PMs at Wroughton was Squadron Leader Ann Golding, who recalls: 'when all the injured came back to Wroughton, it was horrific. All the relatives were waiting in the Red Cross room. [The casualties] had to be seen by the doctors before they would release them to see their families. All the burns …'

Ann, too, remembers how kind people were in giving things:

> It was fantastic … pyjamas, towels, toiletries … and television sets. It was a nightmare, because after they'd gone we'd got all these television sets. Did they give them

to us, or loan them? And bowls … you see, everyone had a plastic bowl, to put their burned hands in, for treatment … Zena was overwhelmed by the number of fruit farmers in the area that were donating strawberries, really to go back out to the Falklands – all very well, but of course you haven't got space on the aircraft … I would ring up to get the numbers of things coming in, and all I could get was the number of these blooming strawberries, so I used to get really irate in the office – 'I don't want to know about the strawberries, I want to know about the patients!'

Matron-in-Chief Joy Harris happened to be on the airfield at Brize Norton as one of the VC10s brought home a plane-load of badly burned Welsh Guardsmen, including Simon Weston. Joy found it:

Horrifying. I'd just gone down to see an aeromed in and … I do believe it was Ishbel [McCabe/Mrs Bennet] who brought him back, and left him in the ambulance, and she came out of it and … she was in tears, which she hadn't been able to give way to before, and at that point we saw his mother going into the ambulance …

I went to the NATO Women's Services Conference, either while the Falklands was on or shortly after. I managed to get Helen Renton, who was (D)WRAF, in tears on that conference … Just before I went, the Ministry gave me some photos to throw up and I gave a small talk on the people coming back from the Falklands, and the last photo that went up was a lad sitting in a pair of navy shorts and a shirt, sitting there looking so disconsolate … we'd spoken of how cheerful all the lads were, coming back, because they were all with their mates, and this boy … he looked disconsolate – it came out in the photo – I said, 'His friends have all gone off to different hospitals, or units, and so is he about to, and … what you see him sitting in is all he owns in the world at this moment' – and poor old Helen was quite upset. Well, rightly so!

Once settled in Wroughton hospital, the patients reacted in different ways, as Zena Cheel tells:

Some of them were terribly chatty and pleased to be home, but some of them were withdrawn … It was June, July sort of time, nice long evenings and the weather good. Some of them would just go and sit out on the grass, didn't want to be with anybody, others would sit and devour the papers because it was the only time they had got any news. Some learned for the first time how many of their mates had gone, or been injured …

But we improved on the reception bit – we were able to get relatives down to greet them, and the people in Wroughton village were super because they put the relatives up. The CO's wife and the officers' and airmen's wives, used to come over to the hospital and make tea and sandwiches and things. And we used to be swim-

> ming in beer … We had this huge great parcel arrive one day from Salisbury's, the people who make the handbags – they sent this HUGE great box, almost to the roof, full of bags, holdalls, overnight bags – a gift …
>
> Once again, I went to Marks and Spencer's with the hospital Warrant Officer and we got 'on loan', for want of a better word, trousers of various sizes, shirts of various sizes, underwear, socks and sandals … in one of the empty wards they set up this little 'tailor's shop' and after they [the wounded] had had a rest and had their treatments, they were kitted out, so they left us nicely dressed, usually with their relatives, their little holdall with a few goodies in it …
>
> One week we had one flight in that was all amputees – some of them what they call 'hind-quarters' – really bad, hip and everything gone and I remember going round the ward one evening and chatting with them and saying I hoped they had a good night, etc., and I said to one of these chaps, 'What are you going to do tonight?' and he said, 'Matron, I'm going to get legless!' Lovely sense of humour. And when they went out to the shower, the legless helped the armless and the armless helped the legless … with the shampoos and everything. The comradeship was incredible.
>
> We continued to learn … I won't say we were perfect at the end of the war, but we did a bloody good job.
>
> Then we had Princess Alexandra come down, which was lovely.

Staff and patients alike took heart from the informal visit which Her Royal Highness paid to 'her' hospital at the end of the emergency. She particularly wished to meet and thank members of the RAF, army and civilian medical teams who had helped to care for more than 600 casualties flown home from the South Atlantic. During the visit she also met the few casualties who then remained.

Nor was this the only royal interest, as Zena Cheel recounts:

> one day I had a phone call to say the Duke of Edinburgh's chauffeur would be arriving and could I have somebody there to receive him … the Queen had sent these most beautiful flowers. There must have been at least a hundred boxes, all grown at Windsor Castle … So that was lovely, we spread them all around …
>
> It was very nice to be able to get the families down to greet their men, so that they could see them from the word go. I remember Simon Weston's mother – she was a nurse herself – and I could hear him saying to her, 'Mother, at least I'm alive,' and she said to me later, 'He doesn't realise what he'll have to go through.' They'd been through so much, were so emotionally drained in many ways.

Among Helen Kell's many vivid memories of those days at Wroughton is an occasion when Matron Zena Cheel 'went ballistic' on discovering an on-going problem caused by khaki trousers issued for the patients. The trousers had rubber buttons which, says Helen:

> caused no end of problems with us trying to help with bodily functions! When the Wing Commander did her rounds and discovered this, an immediate signal was sent instructing stores to update and amend the style of trousers! Which occurred forthwith …
>
> A lighter incident I recall, one Welsh Guardsman had a water-stained bottle of Chanel No 5 on his locker – to much teasing, he explained that he had purchased it, for his wife, outward bound on the QE2. When the *Sir Galahad* was hit he grabbed his perfume and reached safety. I said to him, 'If I was your wife, I'd never open it.' He replied, 'She b— better, after all my trouble in getting and keeping it for her!' The tenacity of the Welsh Guards … a super bunch of men, and for a PM a humbling experience.

Squadron Leader Josephine Boase, who organised the aeromed side of the operation, commented:

> The staff throughout the entire hospital and supporting units were superb. Many of the flight nursing officers had only done their minimal basic training, but with assistance and initiative they learned – fast! Even the Head of Nurse Education (one of the many willing volunteers) was seen to administer care in the unique aeromed manner – pain-killers in one pocket, Y-fronts in another, lists in both hands and a pen clenched firmly between the teeth.

The man who became perhaps the best-known of the survivors – Simon Weston – does not, of course, remember too much about his stay in Wroughton. He was much too badly burned, facing years of plastic surgery and physiotherapy. But his family will never forget. His sister Pauline Hatfield wrote a long letter to Wing Commander Cheel, particularly recalling:

> the trays of sandwiches brought around for the boys. Simon hadn't been eating since he was injured, due in part to shock, and his mouth being burned. My mother persuaded him to try a sandwich which she cut into pieces and fed to him. In all, he ate five half sandwiches, which he thought was the most wonderful food he had ever tasted.

The family are convinced that those few sandwiches started Simon on the long and painful road to recovery.

Liz Kidman was in charge of nursing on the first Chinook helicopter that 'went from Wroughton and flew them up to London – Woolwich, I think it would be, the burns unit. I shall never forget that as long as I live. Twenty stretchers of burns patients, these lads … so glad to be back …'

In her formal report on Operation Corporate, Matron-in-Chief Joy Harris added, 'The attitude and morale of the wounded was tremendous. Nursing staff felt privileged to be able to help.'

The role of the rehab units

As always, in the aftermath of war, rehabilitation played an enormous role for badly wounded servicemen from the Falklands. Some of the disabled men went to what had become the Joint Services Rehabilitation Unit at Chessington, where 'Ronnie' Oxborough was a senior nursing officer. Most of her usual patients:

> were head injuries, both service and civilian personnel [but] after the Falklands War, I had the Welsh Guards on the unit for rehabilitation and treatment … Simon Weston eventually arrived at Chessington after many skin grafts and major surgery. He was my biggest challenge. He still required saline baths and many dressings which I'm sure caused him great pain and discomfort, but throughout all his treatments he still maintained a sense of humour. It was with great joy and delight – and tears – that we saw him and the other boys go home for the first time.
>
> The businessmen in Kingston-on-Thames decided they would like to entertain the Falkland boys – and the Northern Ireland boys – in some way, so they put on a dinner at the Seven Hills Golf Club in the company of Jim Davidson and Ed Stewart. It was a very funny and happy night out … Another proud moment came when I took my boys to Buckingham Palace to collect their Falkland medal from HRH Prince Charles.

Some of the staff from Wroughton also attended this moving ceremony, among them Matron Zena Cheel. She recalls that the event took place in the palace gardens, with medals presented to members of the various regiments by their royal colonels-in-chief:

> Prince of Wales for the Welsh Guards, Duke of Edinburgh for the Blues and Royals, Duke of Kent … I was lucky enough to be in the front row with my nursing staff and they came along and there was dear old Simon, at this stage with his face still terribly, terribly scarred. And along came this hoary old Warrant Officer and said to them, 'Remember, you don't have to stand up when the Prince of Wales comes to see you,' and one chap said, 'I will,' he said, 'he's my boss!'
>
> So … Prince Charles, Duke of Edinburgh, Duke of Kent, came along – and these people following with these trays of medals – and they had their medals pinned on … those in the first rank then turned and pinned medals on colleagues standing behind them.

For Zena Cheel it was another emotion-charged moment, one of many among her memories of those terrible months.

Chessington had for years been a medical rehabilitation unit (MRU) for warrant officers, NCOs and other ranks, and latterly it cared for army personnel as well as RAF. However, in July 1985 Chessington closed and its work transferred to Headley Court, formerly the officers' MRU. A new remedial block was opened by the Duke of Edinburgh that November, since when the unit has provided rehab facilities not only for all ranks, serving and retired, of the armed forces, but for members of the auxiliary services, civil servants from the Ministry of Defence and, where appropriate, some civilians too. Men hurt by the 'troubles' in Northern Ireland continued to come in; others came from Cyprus, or from Germany, and road accidents added to the list, as did orthopaedic injuries sustained while training or playing sport. While some problems, such as polio, have been eliminated, others arise to take their place: today's young service personnel are increasingly diagnosed with ankylosing spondylitis – fusion of vertebrae in the spine.

Writing in 1987, Angela Scofield (who was to retire as a Wing Commander) explained that Headley Court's motto *Per Mutua* (by mutual effort):

> encapsulates the aim of medical rehabilitation … It is the collective action of the team, each member making a unique contribution, that makes rehabilitation effective … The patient's day begins with the 15 minute 'warm up' session, followed by ten 30 minute classes … this makes up a full working day … It also means that most of the wards are empty for most of the day. In total contrast to a hospital ward, ours is busiest between 1630 hours and 0830 hours. During the day the nurses are encouraged to visit the departments to observe and assist the therapists … so that they can carry techniques over into the ward situation … To watch a patient struggle can be very frustrating for both of you, but it is the only road to rehabilitation.

It has been argued that rehabilitation, including such skills as 'mothering' and counselling, has no place in a nurse's role and may even be a waste of specialist nursing skills. Liz Kidman would not agree:

> Headley Court was probably where I learned the most of all. It was a humbling place. I learned there was a lot more to illness than just getting people better. It had a knock-on effect, not only on the person who was suffering but the families … Simon Weston … some that were paraplegic … they didn't give up, they went on to achieve an awful lot of good things that they might not have done if they'd remained SAC Bloggs or Private So-and-so.

Snippets from the 1980s

Musing on the whole question of reaching the upper echelons of the Service, Air Commodore Valerie Hand chooses her period as matron of RAF Hospital Ely as the most enjoyable time of her whole career:

> That year at Ely was the best. Ely Hospital had such a special place in the city of Ely. It had been given the freedom of the city in '78 and all the citizens thought the RAF hospital was their hospital … There was this mutual friendship. It was lovely.

> As Matron, you really felt quite important, included in everything … From that point of view I always think of it as the best posting. Everything after that was a bit of an anti-climax, really. You went up to MOD as a Group Captain and had to make your own tea, down to earth again.

At the other end of the spectrum, new recruits are constantly being sought. The nursing service liaison officer has the job of spreading the word and helping to assure that the brightest and best candidates come forward. In the later 1980s, Helen Kell had this job: 'I loved it – it was the most enjoyable I have ever had – the demand and diversity, the ability to respond and work independently … I felt part of the "big RAF" and not just the Branch … I averaged 50,000 miles a year, self-driven …' She did recruiting drives in Ireland where 'security was tight and prevented me from taking the staff car as I wished'; in Scotland, wishing to appear immaculate for each presentation at schools or shows, or at the local careers information office, she changed clothes en route: 'the Highland cows had a PM "full Monty"', and one day she and the schools liaison officer 'got lost and found ourselves at Glamis Castle – despite its being closed, we were offered refreshments, and a personal tour, by a member of Her Majesty's staff'. In England, she was stopped by red traffic lights at Greenham Common, scene of the camp-in by women protesting about the American nuclear presence, and there her 'staff car was jostled and rocked by a small crowd of women. I escaped, as did the car, unscathed, but slightly shaken … the eighties were a time of much political and social change and being in uniform one was at the centre of repressed anger, on occasions.'

By that time, government cuts in defence spending were chewing away at every aspect of the PMRAFNS. They continued to bite even more deeply in ensuing years. For Matron-in-Chief Valerie Hand, 'it really was very dismal and a time that I would much rather forget'.

However, despite gloom at the top, PMs continued to work hard and play hard. Many good causes have benefited from their activities over the years. In 1983, Senior Aircraftman Martin Hadnett of the PMRAFNS, serving at Wegberg, was one of a seven-strong RAF team of runners who competed in the First Open International Spartathlon. Their challenge was to run from Athens to Sparta, following in the footprints of legendary Pheidippedes, a distance of over 250km and crossing no less than five mountain ranges. This continuous run had to be completed in under thirty-six hours. Martin himself didn't quite make it, but he raised 1,000 Deutschmarks for worthy causes.

In that same year, Flight Lieutenant Tim O'Leary, also of Wegberg, rode, on a small fold-up shopping bike, the 400 miles from Wegberg to Wellington in Shropshire, where his son was at a school for handicapped children which badly needed a hydrotherapy pool. Collecting more and more money along the way, by laughing people who admired the courage of this 'crazy Englishman', and pausing only to sleep (and catch a Channel ferry), he made it in four days and raised a magnificent total of

30,000 Deutschmarks. Not only did the school get its hydrotherapy pool but Wegberg Hospital had a TV and video cable system installed from the proceeds of what Tim calls 'Operation Saddle Sore'.

And there's music: PM Amanda Cross was hailed as the first lady bagpiper in the RAF when she joined the Halton Pipe Band. They led the VIP Parade at the Burma Star Reunion in 1983 and took part in the RAF Pipe Band Championship. Another high point was when the band flew by Chinook to RAF Odiham and Amanda piped the way off the helicopter.

On a more serious note, NATO's Exercise Lionheart in 1984 provided a test of Western Europe's readiness in case of a war fought with all the horrors of modern weaponry, conventional and chemical. PMs under the leadership of Wing Commander Maggie Pedder were involved in setting up a war hospital and performing aeromedical duties. Ethnea Hancock (later group captain and matron-in-chief) speaks for most of them when she says:

> I had never dreamed, when I first joined the PMRAFNS, that one day I would be going to wear a combat suit and NBC [nuclear, biological and chemical] protective clothing (noddy suit) for days on end! Getting ready was an exercise in itself. Most of the nursing staff were unused to coping with camouflage suits, webbing, boots and NBC clothing, none actually designed with women in mind. Puttees [long strips of cloth wound round leg and ankle] are still used … in time of war they could be used as bandages, but … they are not an aid to fast dressing.

After an introductory session of written briefs, slides and lectures, the medical team flew out to Gutersloh, West Germany, and took over most of a two-storey building which became their command post and hospital. They had expected to have three days of preparation but 'suddenly, less than forty-eight hours after our arrival, we were on GENERAL ALERT'. Combat suits, numerous pockets bulging with essentials, had become normal attire, but all at once personnel had to start carting around a bulky haversack containing their personal protective gear – suit, boots and helmet. In the six days of the exercise they 'treated' more than 1,000 simulated gun-shot wounds, blast injuries and burns, a stern test of their stamina and adaptability, but an experience they all felt was well worthwhile.

Elsewhere, aeromedical flights continued. Most of them were routine; others were far from it. In Beirut, terrorists booby-trapped a lorry and rolled it down a hill. The explosion destroyed a barrack block full of American soldiers. On 23 October 1983, a medical team from Akrotiri, including PM Fran Wooldridge, flew to Beirut by Hercules to bring out the injured US Marines. As they assessed and gave initial treatment to the casualties, under the tailgate of the Hercules, two helicopter gunships gave aerial cover and, bizarrely, citizens of Beirut continued to sailboard merrily in the harbour.

Twenty-one wounded men were brought back to TPMH Akrotiri, where Rosie Partington was senior matron. 'It was nasty,' she says sadly. 'They were very distressed.' One of the casualties died; nineteen were airlifted to the USAF base at Weisbaden, West Germany; the other remained in intensive care until he was flown home to the USA a week later.

The Harrods bomb

Terrorist activity closer to home called Halton's mobile dialysis team into action when, on Saturday, 17 December 1983, an IRA car-bomb exploded outside Harrods of Knightsbridge, in London. Six people, including three Metropolitan Police officers, were killed and around ninety people injured. Among the worst casualties, a thirty-year-old police dog-handler, John Gordon, sustained massive multiple injuries, losing both his legs and part of a hand. He was not expected to survive the day.

He was taken to the Westminster Hospital, where his kidneys began to malfunction, but he was too ill to be moved to a dialysis machine. From RAFH Halton, a team of two doctors and seven PMs (five nursing officers, including Flight Lieutenant Terry Smith, and two senior aircraftwomen) raced to Westminster Hospital escorted by police with screaming sirens and flashing blue lights. On arrival, they faced a battery of cameras and crowds of onlookers – no, not for them but for the Prince and Princess of Wales, who had arrived to visit the casualties of the bomb. Soon after the team had set up their equipment the royal visitors arrived in the intensive care unit and, as Terry Smith reports, 'it was evident that they felt great concern over the horrific incident which had occurred some forty-eight hours previously'.

The young constable was critically ill with injuries over every part of his limbs, head and body. One of his legs had been amputated at the upper thigh and a dozen other complications tested the skill of the doctors and nurses attending him. What was more, his wife was eight months pregnant with their second child.

Later that month, Tony Cox came from Halton and took over from Terry Smith in caring for the patient in Westminster ITU. He remembers:

> I spent the Christmas/New Year living in, giving daily dialysis and slowly pulling him back from death's door. He had lost his police dog in the blast, and while I was with him he received letters and pictures of police dogs from all over the world, including Australia. Many wishes of good will.

Over a period of six weeks, as the patient began to show signs of recovery, the renal team from Halton were made to feel at home among their NHS colleagues. In the fifth week the patient's wife gave birth to a second healthy son, another aid to the man's recovery. Though he still had a long way to go, by the end of January his kidneys were functioning properly and he no longer needed dialysis; the Halton team packed up at the end of what Terry Smith calls 'a very satisfactory tour of duty'.

A second renal team from Halton, detached on 23 December to the Central Middlesex Hospital to dialyse another victim of the bombing, had a less satisfactory outcome: their patient, a police inspector, died on Christmas Eve.

The 'Bubble'

Perhaps the most unusual and, for the team involved, the most complex of the aeromed flights undertaken in this period occurred in 1985 and involved PM Helen Ryan. Out in Sierra Leone, Jill Sanderson, a civilian midwife working with Voluntary Service Overseas (VSO), became seriously ill after contracting deadly, and highly infectious, Lassa fever. She was being cared for in Panjume Mission Hospital, 200 miles from the nearest airport at Freetown, but she urgently needed to be brought home to the UK.

For some years the RAF had had its own mobile isolation unit – basically a stretcher and trolley covered in a sealed plastic 'bubble' whose air supply and lighting can be run from an external source such as an aircraft or ambulance. When the call came, within two days the RAF assembled its specialist aeromed team – nineteen personnel, some of whom were to undergo a rare opportunity for training in a real emergency. Their lessons started on the first leg of the journey, out to Ascension Island. From there they flew to West Africa.

On arrival at Freetown, they learned that the patient's condition was far worse than they had expected. Her planned transfer to Freetown, by road, was impossible, so the Sierra Leone authorities made available their only helicopter. Helen Ryan explains, 'We had brought with us a smaller isolator for the transfer, but this would not fit into the helicopter, so the anaesthetist elected to travel with the patient using barrier nursing techniques of gown, gloves and mask.'

The heat was another problem for the team, who arrived at Freetown dressed in theatre blues, plastic suits, overshoes and gloves, and then spent an hour on the sun-baked runway while the patient was transferred from the helicopter to the isolator, which was then lifted back into the VC10. They drank gallons of squash to keep themselves hydrated while they tended the patient, sited an intravenous drip and decontaminated themselves before getting back aboard the plane. The isolator had become like a greenhouse, but ingenious medical technicians rigged up a connection with the plane's air conditioning system, so the patient at least was kept cool.

Hampered by their plastic suits, ill-fitting rubber gloves and slippery plastic boots – lethal on a metal floor sprinkled with talcum powder (from their gloves) – they took it in brief shifts to care for Jill Sanderson. She was confused, semi-conscious and, among other problems, had a tracheostomy which required frequent suction. All of this, says Helen, 'may have taxed us on a ward, let alone at 30,000 feet, in two layers of plastic, wearing someone else's gloves!' The flight lasted seven and a half hours and they fought all the time to keep their patient alive. Some five minutes before landing, the intravenous drip stopped working and the patient required sedation. 'In order to achieve this and relieve her distress, which was compounded by the necessity to secure her stretcher harness for the landing, most of the medical and nursing team were standing when we landed …'

Some of the team accompanied the patient on her final transfer, still in the isolator and aboard an RAF pantechnicon, to Ham Green Hospital's exotic diseases unit. Thanks to their efforts, she recovered fully.

And Helen Ryan moved on to Akrotiri.

Tragedy in Cyprus

Considering the hours they spend in the air, the safety record for aeromed flights is second to none. Nevertheless, rare accidents have occurred – all the more shocking and saddening when they involve people on mercy missions.

In 1986 about a dozen nursing officers at TPMH Akrotiri, Cyprus, shared an accommodation block which Helen Ryan says was:

> fondly referred to as Tenko [i.e. like a Japanese prison camp], but I don't think it had quite as many home comforts. As a small group we knew each other extremely well and being a long way from home relied on each other very much for friendship and entertainment.

Among the group was Fiona Johnstone, 'a lively nurse who was the life and soul of most occasions'. In the early hours of Wednesday, 5 November 1986, word came that an expectant mother on the army base at Dhekelia was having problems in labour. A Wessex Mk 5 helicopter from 84 Squadron RAF Akrotiri was scrambled to bring the woman back to The Princess Mary Hospital. Aboard the aircraft, along with the pilot and the loadmaster, were the nursing team of Flight Lieutenant Fiona Johnstone and Corporal Martin Cook, both of the PMRAFNS.

'This was a very routine hop,' Helen Ryan comments, 'one which had been done many thousands of times before.' However, this time something went wrong. Shortly after take-off the helicopter crashed in Limassol Bay and swiftly sank into the deep waters. A full search and rescue operation was launched. Searchers rescued the pilot but had to report the other three missing, presumed drowned. Their bodies were never recovered. 'Those of us who were there at the time,' says Helen, 'were devastated.'

A memorial service was held at RAF Akrotiri, where Martin Cook had worked at the station medical centre; his wife and two small daughters had joined him in Cyprus earlier that year. Another service at RAF Stafford brought together Fiona Johnstone's family and friends in the UK. Group Captain Miche Shaw, matron-in-chief of the PMRAFNS, read the lesson.

18

The Defence Medical Service

Having been pruned to a minimum as part of the overall reduction of the armed forces, on 2 January 1985 the medical branches of the navy, army and air force became a tri-service organisation named the Defence Medical Service (DMS). Nursing branches, while still retaining their single-service identities, became the Defence Nursing Services (DNS). It was anticipated that better liaison would lead to an easier exchange of ideas and, in some cases, a further exchange of posts. Already, air force and army personnel worked alongside each other at the hospitals at RAF Wroughton and RAF Akrotiri; the naval base at Gibraltar and the army hospital at Rinteln each had PMs on their staff; and a naval nursing officer was stationed at RAFH Wegberg. In her President's Address for the *PMs' Magazine* that year, Matron-in-Chief Air Commodore April Reed commented, 'It has been a difficult year for the Medical Services, with some fairly swingeing changes hanging over our heads like the Sword of Damocles. In the event, the actual recommendations were less sweeping than anticipated, with no changes to hospitals and other medical units ...' Well, not yet!

The long-established classification of nurses was also in the process of change: SRN (state registered nurse) became RGN (registered general nurse) and SEN (state enrolled nurse) was now EN(G) (enrolled nurse, general). However, the 1980s saw a move towards a single level of trained nurse – RGN – and, as a result, in 1988 the RAF ended its programme of training for SEN/EN(G). Already qualified enrolled nurses could, if they wished, convert to registered general nurses by completing fifty-four weeks further training and examinations – this 'conversion' training entered the PMRAFNS programme in March 1987. Nurses not wishing to convert to RGN could choose to continue as they were until the end of their engagement.

Digital (individual) posts

In a few places across the world, unusual postings called for the presence of one individual nursing officer. Such 'digital posts' arose at RAF College Cranwell; St John's Ophthalmic Hospital, Jerusalem; the Medical Centre in Hong Kong; and at the British embassies in Islamabad and Peking. In the 1980s, these posts were filled by PMs.

Flight Lieutenant Wendy Williams found herself 'adapting to the navy way of life' when she worked as a midwife in Gibraltar. The hospital overlooked the bay, with southern Spain beyond, and the mess had views across the Straits of Gibraltar to the

Atlas Mountains in Morocco. Wendy thoroughly enjoyed the social life, the sport and the chance to see Spain, despite some ribbing about being in the 'junior service':

> I had to learn the language to survive and within a few weeks I was calling my room my 'cabin', going to the 'galley' for food and going for 'runs offshore' most nights – not, I hasten to add, athletic runs! My off-duty was now 'the watch', my uniform 'rig', and all the abbreviations I had just learned regarding the RAF were no use to me at all.

In China, the digital post at the British embassy in Peking had, until 1973, been filled by an army nursing sister, on a one-year detachment from British Military Hospital Hong Kong. After the PMRAFNS took over, each sister was employed at the embassy for a full two years. She left her rank and uniform behind and became instead a Second Secretary of the Embassy.

Ishbel McCabe (Mrs Bennet) was the fourth PM to take this post, from March 1978: 'It seemed too interesting an experience to miss!' However, having seen her predecessor off on the train to Hong Kong, she returned to her flat 'feeling as if a gate had clanged behind me'. There was no going back, no way out of China without an exit visa – the Communist regime controlled its borders and its people with an iron fist. Though Ishbel met many interesting people of many nationalities, her acquaintances did not include any Chinese nationals.

Her first impression of Peking was 'intense cold, a drab and colourless city and people. The streets were very dimly lit and scruffy, but the most alarming part was to discover cars or bicycles did not use lights.' Ishbel herself used a bicycle to get around the embassy and the British compounds which she had to visit, and, while off-duty, 'cycling round the *hutungs* – little back streets – was a pleasant way to pass an afternoon'. Of course British personnel were monitored everywhere they went: 'it's very easy to pick out a "round eye" on a bicycle', phones were tapped and no foreigner went anywhere without his or her personal China Travel Service guide. However, during Ishbel's two years these restrictions did ease and she saw signs of changes: 'Mao's portraits and sayings no longer dominated the city … goods like suitcases, woollens, watches and make-up were advertised … young men were growing and styling their hair, young girls wearing brightly coloured clothing, including skirts and dresses, a thing unknown a year previously.'

In the clinic, however, old ways still obtained. Ishbel was particularly struck by the intravenous infusion apparatus, rubber tubing with the fluid in an open flask that could be topped up. 'Disposable equipment simply hadn't arrived in China [and] blood transfusions were almost always direct. I never saw them take one unit, they withdrew what they felt was needed!'

Pakistan has provided another stimulating post for a senior nursing officer at the British embassy in Islamabad. By means of morning clinics and afternoon visits, the nursing officer is responsible for the health of all the staff and their families. Pat Surridge, working there in 1985, also held weekly antenatal and family planning clinics for the Sweeper (Untouchable) people, who live in mud huts without sanitation. For their welfare, tetanus vaccination was a priority.

In the British clinic, staff undertook only minor surgery. More serious cases, requiring general anaesthetic, were sent back to the UK by aeromed flight or, in an emergency, treated at the local hospital; however, 'because of inadequate facilities and poor standards of hygiene' such cases would be transferred as soon as possible back to the two-bed ward in the British clinic. Pat Surridge dealt with about 200 patients a month and, in her experience, 'the most usual symptom seen is dehydration caused by food poisoning or some form of amoebic dysentery'. Nurses who served in the east during the Second World War would have found it all very familiar.

Return to Singapore

Forty years after the ending of the war, the government agreed to sponsor a pilgrimage to the major British war cemeteries in the Far East. In 1985, a party of 230 war widows, veterans and ex-prisoners-of-war – senior citizens all – were accompanied to the rim of the Pacific by a medical team which included four nursing sisters – one from the navy, one from the army and two from the air force.

Liz Kidman felt privileged to be chosen as one of the PMs on that trip. She says that many of the elderly passengers 'had never flown before, so embarking on a seventeen-and-a-half-hour flight, halfway round the world, was quite an adventure'.

At Bangkok the party split up into different groups to visit their own most relevant memorials. Liz and her group went to Rangoon, from where they visited the Krangi cemetery. 'Forty years had dulled some emotions but many painful memories were revived of loved ones and comrades lost so long ago but never forgotten.' Sightseeing tours included a visit to Changi prison, which evoked more harrowing memories; and on the Sunday a multi-national and inter-religious Remembrance Service took place in the presence of the Duke of Kent and other dignitaries:

> Some of the widows revisited Krangi. This time it was a private occasion, wreaths were laid and tears shed without the world's press looking on. Despite other marriages, children, all those years, some of those women had been unable to grieve because they hadn't seen a body or visited a grave. It was, for me, the most moving part of the pilgrimage.

In 1987, Squadron Leader Annie Reid escorted another party of war widows to the Tychaun cemetery, Bangkok:

> As you can imagine, this was a very emotional trip. We could only help the ladies find the correct grave, then we left them in quiet solitude. I cannot express in words

how I felt during those first few minutes in that cemetery: the graves were kept in such an immaculate state that I am not ashamed to confess that I could not hold back my own tears. The journey back to the hotel started subdued, but the ladies soon began to feel that they had, finally, laid their husbands to rest.

Fun and dramas at Wegberg

In West Germany in 1982, Senior Matron Miche Shaw had to find some way of entertaining her matron-in-chief, Joy Harris, on her annual three-day visit to Wegberg. Hearing that there was an exercise on:

> somewhere in the wilderness of Germany, I got permission to go out and visit them with my boss. First I had to kit Joy out in combat gear, much to her surprise. Our driver was given a map reference and we managed to get into the area, where a patrolling Land Rover came to our rescue and guided us to camp. We were met by a medical officer Joy knew, which was a good surprise. He gave us a drink – almost surely a G&T! – and we watched as the men crawled around on their stomachs in the undergrowth! It was a day Joy never forgot – she really revelled in the experience.

Five years later, freezing temperatures caused havoc when (yet again!) pipes burst in several departments of the Wegberg hospital and the shattering of a high pressure steam valve caused severe damage to test equipment in the laboratory. The following summer, staff might have wished the water back to quench the disastrous fire that broke out destroying the roof of No 2 Maternity Ward and causing damage estimated at a million Deutschmarks.

PM Richard Laurence was working in the operating theatre when fire broke out:

> it was frightening. I'd scrubbed up for an ENT case. The surgeon was very miffed that we had to stop the operation … I remember distinctly waking the patient up in the car park. And the very next week, to the day, we had a bomb scare, so I woke another patient up in the car park.

In the late 1980s IRA terrorist bombers turned their attention to British personnel and property in West Germany, where Richard Laurence lived in married quarters with his family:

> It was a stressful time. They could hide bombs better than I could find them. You got in your car, turned the ignition, gritting teeth, wondering … We lived next door to Joint Headquarters where they put a big bomb, which blew our French windows out. The curtains flew up and the doors flew open. All you could hear was breaking glass, and all the car alarms went off …

> The car with the bomb was a Volvo estate, it left a crater in the road about ten feet deep. Cars next to it were in bits .... It broke about three thousand windows, so the German glaziers were clapping their hands! No, it was nerve-wracking. My daughters can still remember it. Not the thing going off, but the next day – it took them about two hours to get to school. Very unpleasant ...
>
> A few RAF people got shot, apart from the army people, in a few of our favourite shopping places ... One survivor came into theatre – he was in ITU and still getting death-threats, Northern Ireland phone number, calling up, saying, 'We're going to finish the job'.

But most Wegberg personnel have very happy memories of their years in Germany. Off-duty they had opportunities to play sport, and to travel around Europe; they held fund-raising activities, and enjoyed social occasions. At one summer ball the officers set up a bucking bronco outside the mess. A certain (male) nursing officer, full of bravado, climbed astride it and 'clung on for grim death despite his No 5 trousers opening up from crotch to turn-up ... He just clung on, would not let go, his best mess dress flapping around like a pair of chaps ... It was very funny ...'

In September 1992, Wegberg became the first RAF hospital to welcome a male matron (i.e. Officer Commanding Nursing Wing), in the person of Wing Commander Bob Williams. But in that same year government economies decreed that the number of beds should be cut from 171 to 90; as a start, the paediatric and special baby care units closed in December 1992. The following year saw the combination of the medical and surgical wards, and then the closure of maternity, which had been one of the busiest of units.

Undaunted, in 1993 RAF Wegberg celebrated its 40th anniversary in fine style, with a station party, an annual fête which included a fancy-dress bed-push – followed by a sunset ceremony, with the evocative sound of a trumpet accompanying the lowering of the ensign. A poignant moment. At least, it was supposed to be.

PM Kevin Mackie, the chosen trumpet-player, explains:

> everybody was in high spirits after the féte and the bed-push. I'd been in the Vicars and Tarts team, and I was still in my vicar's garb because we'd gone straight from the fête to do the sunset ceremony and everybody there had done the same – they were still in their civvies, apart from the Air Vice Marshal [AVM], he was in uniform and so was Wing Commander Williams ... I stood behind this tree to do it because I didn't want anybody to get me confused with the real vicar – I'd actually borrowed garb from the padre, so I looked the part! And because I had to wait for the cue, and the only cue I was going to get was from the AVM, when he started to salute, I had to keep popping my head round ... Lots of people said all they could see was this vicar with the trumpet popping his head round this tree! People won't let me forget it.

'Skywards' – the PMs' march

On the subject of music, the first-ever performance of a new PMRAFNS march was rendered in 1989 at HQ Music Services, Uxbridge, by the Central Band of the Royal Air Force under the baton of composer David Barker, to a select audience which consisted of Group Captain Liz Sandison and her staff officer, Wing Commander Bob Williams. Squadron Leader Phil Bush, a medical secretarial officer and enthusiastic member of the RAF Voluntary Band Association, had been in on initial discussions about the project. He recalls that 'listening to this jolly and bouncy march played for the very first time was an emotional experience'. The march is now available on a CD recorded in 1994 by 'probably the finest military band in the world' (of course!), the Band of the RAF College, Cranwell.

'Devastating …'

As the 1980s drew to a close, only five hospitals remained to be staffed by RAF nurses: Ely, Wroughton and Halton at home in the UK, with Wegberg and Akrotiri overseas. Nocton Hall hospital had closed in 1983, though a remnant Forward Outpatients' Department, linked with Ely, held clinics there for personnel stationed in Lincolnshire. That too was to end in 1991, shortly before its foster-parent hospital became the latest victim of defence cuts.

On 4 October 1990, the city of Ely learned that its RAF hospital was to be axed. For fifty years RAFH Ely had cared for both service personnel and the surrounding community, who regarded it as 'their' hospital. Indeed, only three years previously, it had been renamed The Princess of Wales RAF Hospital, with celebrations attended in person by Princess Diana. The *Ely Standard* now commented:

> If Ely's RAF Hospital is closed, it will be a bitter blow, not only for the RAF, but also for local people … If one hospital has to go, years of experience tell us it should not be Ely. We don't believe there is a better one in the UK.

Despite all protests, The Princess of Wales RAF Hospital Ely closed in 1992.

Nor was it to be the last. In 1989 the National Audit Office had recommended that, with the threat of global warfare diminished, the requirement for separate naval, army and air force hospitals should be reviewed. It was decided that only three service hospitals should remain in the UK, all jointly staffed by tri-service personnel under the Defence Medical Service banner. Additional secondary care facilities, termed Ministry of Defence hospital units (MDHUs), would open in certain existing NHS hospitals under the newly formed Defence Secondary Care Agency. Finally, the new Defence Medical Training Organisation would inaugurate a tri-service medical college at HMS *Dolphin*, Portsmouth, and Keogh Barracks, Aldershot.

Surgeon General Vice-Admiral Tony Revell commented: 'This is pretty devastating … but, when the whole service is up and running, people [will] see the advantages.'

The planned closures of Wroughton, Halton and Wegberg brought a great outcry, not only from air force personnel of all ranks and trades but from the civilian communities to whom these hospitals had given such excellent care over many years.

Ironically, in the period before these fine hospitals discharged their last patients they were once again called to stand by to accept war casualties – from the Gulf and from the Balkans.

The First Gulf War

In 1990 the RAF found itself at war with the country which, seventy years earlier, had hosted its first overseas hospitals. That August, Iraqi forces invaded the small independent Gulf state of Kuwait. The Kuwaiti ruler fled and Iraqi President Saddam Hussein, long a thorn in the side of Western democracies, declared Kuwait a province of Iraq. Peace moves began, but behind them the West gathered a coalition force, called Operation Desert Shield, designed to restore Kuwait and its rich oil fields to its legal rulers.

Once again members of the PMRAFNS found themselves on standby, at RAF Brize Norton and at Akrotiri. Nearly eighty personnel were detached from RAFH Wegberg alone and other specialists stood ready if needed; the RAF hospital at Muharraq in Bahrain, closed since 1971, was reopened and staffed by PMs; other nurses, attached to mobile field hospitals and No 1 Aeromedical Evacuation Squadron, went to prepare in Saudi Arabia and Bahrain. At home the three remaining RAF hospitals organised themselves to receive casualties, and many ex-PMs volunteered their services if needed.

In September, PMs Lesley Chew and Gillian Reid were part of a seven-strong tri-service team sent to work at the King Abdul Aziz Airbase Military Hospital in Dhahran, Saudi Arabia. As tension grew, politicians set a date by which Iraq must withdraw from Kuwaiti territory or risk the consequences; as a result, the two PMs redeployed to RAF War Hospital Muharraq, Bahrain, from where Lesley Chew reported:

> The RAF War Hospital is now a 100-bedded facility which can operate conventionally or as a chemically protected hospital … Hostilities broke out in the early hours of January 17 [but] few casualties are expected until the land battle commences. Meanwhile we continue to train all grades of staff ranging from musicians to GPs.

Squadron Leader Angela Scofield went out as nursing officer in charge at Muharraq. On her staff was Richard Laurence, who describes how the old RAF hospital lay waiting, as if caught in a time-warp:

> half of it was still used by the local population as a maternity hospital, the rest had just been left since 1971. One of the rooms was piled full of incubators and dressings trolleys that somebody had stuck in there. You could tell it was an air force hospital right away – all the corners, ceilings and floors were rounded off, for cleaning pur-

> poses … So we just washed it down and opened it up. Theatres, wards, that kind of area, triage … We set over a hundred beds in the COLPRO (Collective Protection Area, with nuclear, biological and chemical tents), a nightmare to work in, lots of zips, air-locks and things. The idea is that, inside, the air pressure's higher, so any contaminant gets blown out, away from the patients.
>
> We had no significant numbers of casualties, just the usual – army people, you know, shooting themselves in the foot, jumping off the side of tall buildings, as they do. We had the usual appendectomies and minor stuff. But that was the same for all the British hospitals. I know some of the army hospitals never even got unpacked, out in the desert.

No 1 Air Evacuation Squadron had flown out to Saudi Arabia in November 1990. One flight stayed in Al Jubail while the second split into two sections, some personnel going to Dhahran, others to 'glorious Bahrain' where, says Rachel Johnson, they spent ten 'very enjoyable weeks', with only the ground handling of one aeromed a week, plus 'endless NBC drills, to keep us away from swimming, eating out and shopping' (these drills were, in fact, designed to help them prepare for nuclear, biological and/or chemical attack). However, after Christmas they moved on, in convoy, to a spot 40 miles from the Kuwaiti border. 'Talk about a culture shock!' Rachel remembers:

> I think our lives changed 180 degrees in the 300 miles we travelled … It poured with rain and the road was like a quagmire, especially when following huge tank transporters … We were cold, hungry, tired, wet and miserable when we arrived at our destination about 2 a.m. [and] took shelter in the mud on the floor of 32 Field Hospital's newly erected evacuation tent.
>
> For days we worked like navvies, digging trenches, filling sandbags, putting up tents and cookhouses. We thought we would never finish in time for the fast approaching ground battle deadline … Nightly the Scuds flew over our heads and we had to don our NBC kit, just in case!

The air battle, tagged Operation Desert Storm, began on 17 January 1991. When Saddam remained defiant, the coalition's ground forces opened their offensive on 24 February. To Rachel Johnson, 'caring for our first group of war casualties felt very strange. It was difficult to believe that these young British soldiers had actually been under real battle-fire … Some were very frightened and some just relieved to be going home.' It also felt strange to be nursing British soldiers alongside Iraqi prisoners-of-war who were 'so pathetic and ill … poorly nourished, filthy dirty and dressed in rags. I felt such empathy for them …'

In Dhahran, Flight Lieutenant Colin McMillan was with Medical Support Troop Alpha (MST 'A'), sited at the vast King Abdul Aziz Airbase, which covers 20 square miles and has a runway 6 miles long. Colin and his team were sited:

> two miles from the flight-line, between the tempting targets of the base power station and the fuel dump! The Saudis were very protective of their sand and considered it holy … all the sand used for sand-bags at MST 'A' was imported! Neither would they allow non-Muslims to be buried in Saudi Arabia, therefore plans were made to repatriate all British dead.
>
> One remembers the heat, the sand, the smells and the sounds. The high temperatures of August days filling sand-bags merge with the freezing cold of the February nights on guard. I remember the 'buzz' I had, and the sense of freedom when I helped the Americans with some of their aeromed flights. The smells and sounds of the bazaars in Dhahran and Bahrain mix with memories of the Scuds coming in and the replying Patriots. The boredom of waiting being combated by learning German, developing computer skills or by learning to drive. I designed and made a unit flag which now lies in the RAMC museum at Keogh Barracks, Aldershot.

Aeromed teams in the UK waited to be called to action. Liz Kidman remembers the unbearable tension:

> an awful time, because nobody knew what to expect, or the scale to expect. We were all put in the Gateway Hotel, the accommodation at Brize Norton. There were three TriStar teams and about eight VC10 teams, all ready to go. I was i/c a TriStar team and what they said, basically, was, 'Prepare this TriStar to bring back two hundred walking wounded, but we don't know how they'll be wounded or …' Nobody knew what might happen or what we might have to do, or even where we'd be flying them back to, which Health Authority would take them. Thank God nothing happened!

The ground war ended after 100 hours; the air war lasted for six weeks. President Saddam withdrew his forces and most of the 'Desert Shield' troops, with their medical and nursing teams, packed up and went home, only too thankful that casualties had been so low. A few PMs remained deployed in the Gulf area as the devastation, including appalling fires and oil slicks, was cleared up.

Matron of the RAF War Hospital, Angela Scofield, remembers that the Sheikha of Bahrain invited 'all the "lady soldiers" on the Island to a Reception at her Palace, as a thank you. The Palace was magnificent, all marble, crystal and mirrors.' Each 'lady soldier' who attended the reception was presented with a leather box containing a solid gold commemorative coin.

Later, back at home, more expressions of gratitude were demonstrated when on 7 May 1991 members of both the PMRAFNS and QARNNS took tea at St James's Palace with Princess Alexandra, Royal Patron to both Services. And on 21 June the City of London hosted a Gulf War welcome home parade.

Angela Scofield (who was to retire with the rank of wing commander) was selected to lead the 'Female RAF Flight'. She also received an invitation from the Lord Mayor and the Corporation of London to attend the ensuing reception at the Guildhall. Guests of Honour were Their Royal Highnesses The Prince and Princess of Wales. 'I was put in charge of a group of airmen, none of whom I knew,' Anji recalls:

> and after being presented myself to the Princess of Wales I had to introduce my group. She was interested in my 'black Dick' and said they had been talking about it on the balcony. When I explained that I was a PM, Princess Diana said she would tell Charles when they got home!

Reflecting much later on the PMs' role in Operation Desert Storm, Squadron Leader Richard Laurence remarked rather sadly:

> Muharraq was probably the last ever RAF hospital to be set up. It probably won't happen again in the foreseeable future … Our role is aeromed now. We may provide staff for an army hospital, but … the other side of it we couldn't do, because we haven't got the medical staff anymore.

The new millennium would, sadly, prove this assessment to have been somewhat premature.

Akrotiri's role

During the Gulf War, The Princess Mary Hospital (TPMH) Akrotiri became a secure area for returning PoWs and RAF aircrew, among them Tornado flyers Flight Lieutenants John Nicol and John Peters, who had been shot down and held briefly captive by Saddam Hussein's forces. In their book *Tornado Down*, they remember a nurse who was 'all kindness, starch and cleanliness'. Bruised and dishevelled as they were, they tried to charm her into bringing them a beer, but she sternly reminded them of hospital rules. However, a few minutes later she reappeared with a smile and a six-pack of the local brew, saying, 'Just don't tell anybody that I gave it to you.'

Later that year other well-known heroes passed through Akrotiri, hostages released from long incarceration in Beirut. In turn, John McCarthy, Jackie Mann and Terry Waite received attention at TPMH before flying home to England escorted by PMs.

The Royal Yacht incident

At the conclusion of the Commonwealth Conference of October 1993, the Royal Yacht *Britannia* docked at Limassol, Cyprus. Her Majesty the Queen departed for home aboard a VC10, leaving the ship preparing to sail to Saudi Arabia to meet the Prince of Wales. However, that evening many junior ratings on the Royal Yacht went down with food poisoning, consequent to partaking of 'Tartan Cackleberries' (Scotch eggs). Happily for the more elevated of the ship's company, the dish had been served only in the junior ratings' mess.

At TPMH Akrotiri it was Sunday morning, just before lunch, when a phone call announced the imminent arrival of nineteen casualties from the *Britannia* with severe diarrhoea and vomiting. Squadron Leader Jan Oakman 'jumped into uniform' and got started organising Ward 5 to receive patients. Every available person turned to, helping in whatever way necessary, with bedpan washer and loos working overtime, a porter rushed about removing red bags of dirty linen and restocking the linen cupboard, and assorted ladies wheeled drinks trolleys, while the hospital kitchens 'did a roaring trade in sandwiches for everyone involved in the work'. Jan adds, 'the patients, needless to say, weren't at all peckish'.

Hospital staff later attended the first all-ranks cocktail party to be held aboard *Britannia*, while at the hospital the CO designated the men's toilet on Ward 5 'Britannia Ward', and a suitably inscribed sign was made and fixed. Despite fears of what his reaction might be, the Admiral of the Royal Yacht found the sign highly amusing and ordered a Royal Yacht plaque to be sent to hang alongside it. As a thank you to the CO and staff, he also sent a larger Royal Yacht plaque, which hung proudly in the hospital's reception area.

The PMRAFNS Association

One of the first editors of the *PMs' Magazine*, Valerie Hand, became also project officer for a proposed PMRAFNS Officers' Association. Open to all serving and retired officers of the Service, the Association was launched in 1992 and its membership continues to grow. Every member receives news of the annual reunion and other events, and those who cannot travel to gatherings may still remain in touch through the pages of the magazine, which includes personal stories of past adventures as well as features on current happenings. Its articles have provided a valuable source of additional information for this book.

Resuscitation training

Continuing, as ever, to move with the times, the PMRAFNS decided to move into the field of resuscitation training, to which end they appointed one of their members as resuscitation training officer for the RAF. Flight Lieutenant Kevin Mackie was the man involved:

> I was sent on an ALS [advanced life-saving course], and an instructor course and was posted to RAF Wroughton. There were very few RTOs [resuscitation training officers] in civvy street in those days. London, Manchester and Brighton were the main three areas … we were finding our feet. There's now an Association of Resus Training Officers and we've got people on the Resus Council of the UK. I still class myself as an RTO at heart, but at Wroughton, certainly, it was a new departure. I was

> responsible for the basic and advanced resuscitation training for all the staff, and as the role developed I was asked to teach at more and more places aboard. I ended up running an ALS course in Cyprus, went to Moscow …

The trip to Moscow, in February 1995, came about after former RAF medical officer Garth Manning, a retired wing commander working as a freelance consultant with the UN, was asked to assess the standard of in-flight care, within the former Soviet Union, for refugees under the aegis of the International Organization for Migration (IOM). He made thirty-six recommendations, possibly the most telling being the observation that during aeromedical flights the Russian doctors did not assess any of their patients but went to sleep in club class! When asked how the situation might be improved, he recommended that they should ask for help from the RAF Aeromedical Evacuation team, from whose personnel Cathy Henderson and Kev Mackie were selected to fly out to Moscow. As part of their equipment they took 'Resusci Annie', the doll used to demonstrate resuscitation techniques.

At Sheremetyevo Airport they underwent a lengthy arrivals procedure, 'and had all our luggage re-Xrayed, which caused quite a stir when my Resusci Annie torso appeared on the screen … two hours later we eventually cleared customs …'

They spent their first full day meeting IOM people and setting up their course, then enjoyed a weekend playing tourist around Moscow and even managed to get tickets for the Bolshoi Ballet. In the following four days they gave two training courses, each for an audience of twenty-five Russian doctors, covering aviation medicine, in-flight care, in-flight emergencies and the latest resuscitation techniques. Thirty years earlier, such a trip would have been unthinkable.

This project provided yet another breakthrough for the PMRAFNS. Membership numbers may be relatively low compared with those recorded during the Second World War, but the scope of experience for air force nursing officers continues to expand.

For Jackie Gross, one special experience was being part of the integration that took place in South Africa following the elections of April 1994, when apartheid ended and Nelson Mandela took up the reins of government. Jackie was attached to the British Military and Advisory Training Team which helped to recruit former guerrilla forces into the new National Defence Force. In this role she was:

> required to attend placement boards to see fair play, and to adjudicate on decisions made, if necessary. Almost without exception the recruits had been seriously disadvantaged by Apartheid. Some had returned from exile and others had been working 'underground' whilst carrying on with their normal jobs. It was a fascinating experience and one which I shall never forget.

Handover in Hong Kong

In the Far East, meanwhile, Britain prepared to hand Hong Kong back to Chinese rule.

Since RAF Kai Tak had closed in 1978, the British Military Hospital in Kowloon had looked after the health of British forces in Hong Kong, with satellite medical centres out in the New Territories where the Gurkhas were based. The largest of these medical centres, at Shek Kong, had provided a digital post for an air force nursing officer.

Says Liz Kidman, stationed at Shek Kong in the mid-1980s:

> … that also had its advantages and it was very good experience. There was one big Med Centre with seven little ones, all of which had Gurkha midwifery units … The actual Gurkha soldiers … anyone that needed to be in hospital within a couple of hours was flown by helicopter to BMH Hong Kong (Kowloon). Either one of the doctors or myself was permanently on aeromed call.
>
> One month in every two the RAF Squadron did Search and Rescue for the Hong Kong government. I was also on call for that … One night, there'd been an accident on a ship, 4.30 a.m. we flew out. The ship was just about on the flying limit of the helicopter … Because they couldn't understand me with the normal aircrew throat mike, I'd got a boom mike like the pilot used and, because it was windy and I was hanging out of the helicopter, they switched me off, so I couldn't hear what was going on. We didn't find anybody, and after a while I gathered that we had turned back. The crewmen were busy, getting things out, looking hassled, looking at me … They'd pointed to something outside but I couldn't see what it was and because they were busy I didn't ask. Anyway, we landed at Kai Tak, which was very unusual.
>
> Turned out that they had got lost. What they'd been pointing to was Chinese territory with gunships aiming at us because we were over Chinese water. And in fact we were out of fuel! All the comings and goings … the pilot had been preparing to ditch, getting ready to throw the lifeboat out, put us into it and then ditch the helicopter – and I'd missed it! Fortunately another crew went out and found the ship.

As the date for the hand-over to China approached, British forces elements in Hong Kong combined into one unit, called Shek Kong Station. Its medical centre's work had become more like that of a GP's surgery by the time PM Sharon Smith (later Squadron Leader Callcott) arrived there in July 1994. 'Never having worked in a Med Centre before, I was somewhat daunted by the prospect. I tried to reassure myself that I was a qualified nurse and that nursing was the same wherever it was performed. I was in for a big shock!' Fortunately she had on hand Miranda Wong, who had worked at the medical centre for twelve years as a general and children's nurse and midwife. Miranda helped to answer such questions as 'Is this a verruca?' Sharon had never seen a verruca, and as for 'Do you think these are monsoon blisters, sister?' …

HELP!! Chicken pox she was more prepared for, having found a copy of *The Woman's Weekly Guide to Spots and Rashes for Anxious Parents*, but she called on Miranda for a second opinion.

After six months in Hong Kong Sharon Smith felt more confident, but as draw-down to hand-over continued the unit contracted yet again when its Chinese medics departed; then when the army hospital in Kowloon closed, in June 1995, Shek Kong had to upgrade to medical receiving station level to take on the extra maternity work. But 48 Brigade of Gurkhas was being disbanded and RAF and army messes amalgamated. By the end of 1996 Shek Kong Station had closed and on 1 July 1997 the whole colony of Hong Kong returned to Chinese sovereignty.

19

Bosnia

The death of Marshal Tito of Yugoslavia, in 1987, provoked the outbreak of a bitter and bloody civil war among Bosnian, Serb and Croatian factions divided by religion, pride and the memory of ancient disputes. In order to protect the innocents caught in the middle, and to ensure the safe passage of aid, the United Nations decided it had to intervene. It gathered forces from many nations around the world, huge powers such as America and Europe joined by troops from small countries like Nepal and Bangladesh, all wearing the blue UN beret and designated UNPROFOR (United Nations Protected Forces). Among this force, members of the PMRAFNS formed part of the British Medical Squadron, based in an area known as Sector South-West. Regional aid posts offered immediate care for incidents in their locality while two medical support teams stood by to offer further help. And twice each week, from the small but vital Aeromedical Evacuation Cell based in Split, a VC10 or a Hercules lifted casualties to hospitals in Germany or the UK.

The very first aeromed involving medical personnel of all three services deployed to Split in Croatia. PM Debbie Meikle was on the team:

> I had about twenty-four hours' notice … It was the first tri-service medical support troop that had ever happened, and I was the only RAF, the aeromed nurse … I thought it was going to be awful, but I had done recruiting with one of the navy nurses a few years before and everybody was very friendly, you got on with it, worked as a team. That was a bit daunting, my first tour. Because I had so little notice, I didn't have time to do any of the training, but I look back now and think … well, you didn't have any of the build-up stress, just told you're going, and you get on with it. I had to go to RAF Innsworth to get kitted out and I wondered how I was going to get all that kit into one bag, but it went in.

The war in Bosnia dragged on. Dreadful atrocities were committed by all factions, with UNPROFOR forces obliged by political niceties to do little but pick up the pieces, bring food and blankets to refugees, and help the wounded, of whatever side. More and more PMs experienced the waste and futility of this war.

In 1995 it was Kevin Mackie, then based at Princess Alexandra's Royal Air Force Hospital (PARAFH) Wroughton, whose name:

came to the top of the pile for out-of-area operations.

We went as part of the Rapid Reaction Force and we sat in a place called Ploce [Plotchay], which was actually in Croatia. I had twelve medics who were assigned to me, who flew around on aircraft. Basically, if there was a helicopter in the air – an RAF helicopter, not a teeny-weeny army thing – it had a medic on board. We flew with crews at night, doing their night-training. We used the infra-red night-vision goggles, in the back of a kite with the lights off and doing tactical flying. We got shot at – as you do! Whenever anybody got into the helicopter, they'd ask me why I hadn't got a flak jacket on and I'd say, 'I'm sitting on two,' because if you're going to be shot from the ground it's going to be coming up through the bottom, so …

The site at Ploce was far from ideal, being on reclaimed land and below the water line:

One of the funniest things … well, it was funny at the time, but you've got to live with black humour … when we first went there we had very small 'dunnies' that were dug-out, and then we had these big effluent containers, chemical latrine tanks, sunk into the ground, and on top of them they just put a toilet seat – that's what field sanitation is like! But, because we were below sea-level, we had some severe flooding one night and these tanks just floated out of the ground and tipped up. So there was human effluent running past your tent … It was really quite challenging. What could you do but laugh? It turned into a health and safety nightmare, so we evacuated the site, and set up in some sheds in a nearby area that had concrete ground.

But the work side of it was great. I managed quite a few hours in both Pumas and Chinooks, and we did more than fifty aeromeds and casevacs in the time, so that kept us quite busy … We had a young Croatian lad, he was run over, nasty RTA [road traffic accident] and I actually took him to a local Croatian hospital, as a goodwill thing, in the back of a helicopter.

You don't expect in the field to look after children, that's a big thing the services have learned, from humanitarian aid, that midwives and paediatric nurses are as important as trauma people. You're not talking about bomb-blast victims, you're talking about people with barbed-wire lacerations, or dysentery … things which you and I present every day to the GP. We've got to be able to treat them all. Certainly the first casevacs from Bosnia were all Primary Care cases, troops who were just poorly, or dentally [sic] unfit.

Just before her retirement, Air Commodore Valerie Hand, in her role as Matron-in-Chief of the PMRAFNS and Director of Defence Nursing Services, paid a visit to Bosnia:

I spent a week there, flew out to Split, and toured the air force set-up there. I went on a merchant ship, Royal Fleet Auxiliary, absolutely incredible, the supplies they had in the hold, catering for months, stores for all the troops out in Bosnia, amazing, unbelievable!

I went up country to an army camp … They'd taken over what had been a large knitwear factory, just an empty shell of a building, and they had set up their field hospital – tents, emergency operating theatres, clinics and things, inside this shell of a building. And they were having a ball because this was what they'd been trained to do, what they'd joined the army for.

I was taken round into the village, the local town, and up to the village next door. We drove up in a land-rover, so we went through all this ravaged countryside … I've never seen anything like it. You see those pictures on TV, burnt out houses and things, shells, and it was like that all the way, village … after village … after village … after village … miles and miles and miles. I found it very moving. Couldn't even bring myself to take pictures of it. It was just awful. Awful! Imagine it being Northleach, or Bibury … It's absolutely horrendous. I was glad that I'd been. And the people were glad to see me. I think they are quite pleased when you go and see what they're doing in these remote places.

In the late 1990s, Nicola Duncan experienced a difficult aeromed when she was sent out to Kosovo from a post at the Peterborough MDHU:

That was a big learning experience. A big shock, really, coming from the NHS. I was based in Pristina, at the medical centre, which obviously is completed different from working in a hospital. We were organising the aeromeds from the air base there. In those Kosovo days we had just got e-mail, but we hadn't got internet access like we do now. We had 'bricks' – satellite phones that were huge.

The weather was absolutely horrendous. It was minus 20 at times. And the tents quite often fell down with the snow, and there was flooding … with all the stuff that was going on, the fighting and so on, it was quite scary. But the morale was fantastic. That's when you really know you've joined the air force. You go out there and you all work as a team, doing what you've been trained to do.

In Kosovo we had one particularly difficult flight, with the weather. It was bad. We had to move the patients from Kosovo across the border, travelling in the ambulance with them. We ended up staying on a French camp for two days – and none of us spoke French! Myself and the other nurse, we slept at either end of the tent, near the doors, to stop losing our patients, to keep them all together. Squaddies are not the best at waiting around, they did wander, they got bored. We had one [very] poorly patient, who was quite worrying. We had back-up from the French doctors if needed, but it was quite difficult, in an area we'd never been before, in a French camp, going back and forth to the air-head [to watch for our aircraft] while keeping everybody safe. [It was also difficult for] the people that were on that plane, trying to come in all the time. They had to keep going elsewhere, and the crew that eventually came in to pick the patients up were very tired. Not in the best of moods!

The last of the RAF hospitals

In 1995 members of the PMRAFNS welcomed the appointment of their first male matron-in-chief, Group Captain (later Air Commodore) Robert H. Williams. He had joined the air force as a boy entrant aged sixteen, starting his adult career in 1962 on the renal unit at Halton. He commenced his SRN training at Wegberg in 1965 and swiftly rose through the ranks to chief technician, gaining his Queen's Commission in the Medical Technical Branch in 1976 before transferring to the PMRAFNS in 1980. As we have seen, he was the first man to be appointed matron of an RAF hospital on posting to Wegberg in 1992. He was also the chief mover behind the implementation of this history of the PMRAFNS.

Sadly for him, one of Bob Williams' first tasks as matron-in-chief was to confirm, in the Foreword for the 1995 *Magazine*, the impending demise of the three remaining RAF hospitals: Wegberg in the reunited Germany, Wroughton in Wiltshire, and Halton in Buckinghamshire, all to be closed in 1996. As a result, PMRAFNS strength of 170 officers and 300 other ranks would be reduced to 102 officers and 178 other ranks, a total complement of 280.

News of the Ministry of Defence's latest cost-cutting plans brought a renewed clamour of protest. Service hospitals had a reputation as centres of medical excellence; they had provided care for thousands of civilians as well as members of the armed forces; and they had helped to pioneer many medical advances over the years. The remaining RAF hospitals were cherished, not only by all who had served on their staffs but also by the local communities who had come to rely on their presence.

RAFH Wegberg, for instance, had served personnel stationed in West Germany for forty-three years, caring for the sick and injured from a wide area and seeing the birth of thousands of babies. It was also well-known for its annual 'Bed-push Day', whose events over many years raised a considerable amount of money for charity, as well as providing fun for everyone.

The hospital at RAF Wroughton, near Swindon, had opened in 1941 to receive the wounded of the Second World War. In 1976 this large and busy hospital had become a combined service unit, staffed by RAF and army personnel. In 1992 it had proudly reverted to being Princess Alexandra's Royal Air Force Hospital, a renaming which came about with much ceremony, after five years of refurbishment, expansion and modernisation, at a cost of millions of pounds. Observers of all this work and expense could be forgiven for assuming that Wroughton's future must be secure. It was an invaluable asset to the local community.

One of its grateful civilian patients, Mrs Jan Gibson, says that her most memorable stay in a service hospital happened at Wroughton in June 1993, when she needed intense physiotherapy to alleviate her arthritis. 'Being blind and having a guide dog, I was rather apprehensive … I thought there was no way they would allow me to take my dog with me … How wrong can you be! A side ward was arranged for me to occupy, with my dog …' Guide-dog Yana became a focus of attention for off-duty staff, including the station CO, and nurses vied for the chance to take her for walks. Mrs Gibson says, 'that dog was pampered, even to being offered a nightcap of Horlicks and toast. I ended up borrowing one of the signs to hang on the radiator above her bed, to say "Nil by Mouth"!'

If it had ever been in doubt, the hospital's usefulness was further emphasised when, during the war in the former Yugoslavia, despite political turmoil and personal danger, an aeromed team from Wroughton flew out to Sarajevo to bring back twenty seriously ill Yugoslavian children who might well have died had they not been swiftly spirited to the specialist care available in UK hospitals. Nevertheless, closing their ears to the numerous voices that cried against it, the government ended the life of Princess Alexandra's Royal Air Force Hospital Wroughton.

Even Halton …

Not even the Princess Mary's Royal Air Force Hospital Halton could be spared, though for sixty-nine years it had been the home of Royal Air Force Medicine and much-loved 'cradle' of the PMRAFNS.

Nicola (Nikki) Duncan particularly enjoyed working in:

> a proper RAF hospital, part of a fully functioning RAF base. We reminisce about the 'good old days'. Which were absolutely wonderful! We had a nurses' social club and it was a big camp, so social life was good. It was a good grounding to start off with.

Lee Bond also started at RAF Halton, on the male surgical ward:

> It was a great hospital, an abundance of staff, the rich tapestry of social life, station life – hospital social club, variety of bars, and the camp itself. Even though the hospital was separate, you did feel a part of the camp. Good times. Actually, I was there during the closing of RAF Halton, so it was also sad times. That was the era we moved into MDHUs and you knew it was never going to be quite the same again. I was part of a working party to close the hospital down … mixed emotions.

Richard Laurence, writing the hospital's epitaph in a brief history, details some of its specialities: 'Medicine, General Surgery, Orthopaedic Surgery, Anaesthesiology, Nephrology, Urology, Gynaecology and Obstetrics, Burns and Plastic Surgery, ENT, Ophthalmology, Neurology, Psychiatry, Oral Surgery, Dermatology, Paediatrics, Maxillo-facial Surgery, Radiology, Oncology, Aviation Medicine, Tropical Medicine …' Halton had been the home of the Cade Cancer Unit, the Institute of Pathology and Tropical Medicine and the Renal Unit, including Britain's first mobile dialysis team.

These three great Royal Air Force Hospitals, last of the many that had existed over almost eighty years, all closed on the same black day, 31 March 1996.

The hospital at Akrotiri …

Akrotiri, too, was affected by the many swingeing closures and changes of that year. The hospital's RAF Ensign was laid up in the hospital chapel on 23 August, when The Princess Mary's Hospital, Cyprus, became part of the newly formed Defence Secondary Care Agency, which combined the medical and nursing branches of all three services into a single entity for purposes of secondary (i.e. hospital) care.

Ministry of Defence hospital units (MDHUs)

In the UK, following the closure of all other service hospitals, secondary health care continued to be provided at the Royal Hospital Haslar, Gosport (see below), while new MDHUs were established at Northallerton, North Yorkshire, Peterborough, Cambridgeshire, Frimley Park, Surrey and Derriford, Devon. Wounded patients needing longer-term care are sent to the Defence Services Medical Rehabilitation Centre Headley Court (Epsom). At all of these places, uniformed doctors, nurses and paramedics from the Royal Navy, the British Army and the Royal Air Force work alongside their colleagues in the NHS, running wards for both military and civilian patients.

It wasn't always quite so integrated.

The unit at Peterborough opened during the winter months of 1995, its RAF personnel being 'parented', as they still are, by nearby RAF Wittering. Lee Bond was one of them. He says:

> MDHU Peterborough was one of the first that came in. [I was] on ward 6X, which was staffed by purely military. It was at Peterborough District Hospital, the old hospital, up on the sixth floor, a poor partner of the rest of the hospital, pretty much the dumping ground for the patients that nobody else wanted … You could see the MDHU culture start to evolve.

Things improved a few months later when, in April 1996, the unit came on-line officially, with a more defined structure.

Also involved in those early days was Nicola Duncan:

> I came to Peterborough in 1996, [when] we had all military wards. This was near the start of the MDHU, so there were lots of teething problems. We did keep moving our wards around, started off with a medical ward up on the sixth floor, and ended up coming down to the third floor. Things were changing quite a lot, but it was good experience. Being at RAF Wittering, as well. At the time I lived in on the base.

Mental health care

Psychological illness among service personnel is recognised as a serious and often disabling condition. The Defence Mental Health Services focus their energies on recovery and rehabilitation for patients. Treatment is primarily delivered through fifteen departments of community mental health (DCMH) located in large military centres staffed by psychiatrists, mental health nurses, clinical psychologists and mental health social workers.

Since the amalgamation of all three services' medical branches, mental nurse Rob Morris of the PMRAFNS has found himself working in a wide variety of posts:

> When Wroughton closed I was posted to Catterick Garrison [DCMH, North Yorkshire], to the in-patient ward for eight and a half years – with the army! From there I went to the DCMH at Brize Norton for about four years; quite exciting to go from an army unit to an RAF unit, back with the air force after so much time working with the army. I went to Kinloss for a year [DCMH, Morayshire], really exciting! Nice air force unit [but] I looked after the Black Watch at Fort George! I looked after Hereford for a few months. Also SFSG [Special Forces Support Group] down at St Athan, I used to drive down there and spend two days a week in South Wales.

His current post is again with the army at DCMH Donnington, in Shropshire. In between whiles, just for a change, he has been deployed to look after patients in war-torn Iraq and Afghanistan.

As Lee Bond noted, when all of the big changes took place, for RAF nurses the world was a relatively peaceful place: 'deployments were few and far between, so you had a predictable work-force, you weren't having people sent on short-notice deployment, you didn't have the amount of pre-deployment training – the burden we have now in regard to that.'

We shall hear more of those overseas deployments as our story moves on. Meanwhile …

The Royal (Naval) Hospital Haslar

The Royal Naval Hospital at Haslar was one of the oldest of military hospitals, active since 1753. In the climacteric year of 1996, it became a tri-service unit of the Defence Medical Service and was renamed The Royal Hospital Haslar. From that time, PMs worked there alongside naval and army colleagues.

In a pleasing link with the past, Mrs Sybil Morgan writes of a time in June 1948 when, as ACW Unsted of the WRAF, she was stationed at RAF Bicester. On her way back to the station after taking leave, she was hit by a lorry and spent six weeks on the seriously ill list in RAFH Halton, with terrible injuries which almost resulted in her losing her right foot. For her eventual recovery she thanks 'the wonderful care and attention of all the nurses and doctors – they even came to see me when they were off duty.' She spent eight months in hospital, having several operations in that time, being taken for walks in one of the wicker 'prams', and even having the chance to meet Princess Mary when RAFH Halton celebrated its twenty-first birthday.

Fifty years on, in 1998, after suffering a heart attack she found herself again being tended by air force nurses, this time at the Royal Hospital Haslar. 'Several times I was under the care of the RAF and they were wonderful. I will always look upon RAF nurses as being special.'

In December 1998 the government announced its plan to close the Haslar Hospital. In 2001, the provision of acute healthcare within Royal Hospital Haslar was transferred from the Defence Secondary Care Agency to the NHS Trust. The Royal Hospital was the last MoD-owned acute hospital in the UK.

The decision to end the life of dedicated service hospitals, on grounds of cost, had been taken before the conflicts in Iraq and Afghanistan had been dreamed of. Nevertheless, despite considerable controversy, RH Haslar was destined to share the fate of all the other UK military hospitals, though it took a decade for the axe finally to fall. Several wards shut down in June 1999 as military personnel were detached to help in the aftermath of the Kosovo crisis and ten years later, in 2009, the hospital formally closed its doors. Its role has been assumed by the MDHU at Queen Alexandra Hospital, Portsmouth, Hants.

Aeromeds

In peacetime, aeromedical evacuations have taken PMs far and wide caring for patients while in-flight. They might find themselves in America, Australia or some tiny isolated island, wherever an 'entitled' person needs their help. Most of the patients are service personnel but they could also be civil servants, people working with the Royal Fleet Auxiliary or the BBC; they might be residents of the Falkland Islands or contractors working abroad for a company which has signed an agreement and which is prepared to pay for the service. It depends on the need.

Lee Bond enjoyed his years on the aeromed squadron, though:

> I wasn't looking forward to going to aeromed at all, because you don't have a social life – you don't have a life. It's all aeromed. You get one weekend off a month, the rest you're on call. I was married at the time, and I was also trying to do an MSc, so I had an interview with [a female squadron leader] who told me, 'There's two things I can guarantee, you won't get to do your MSc, and by the end of this tour you'll be divorced.' She was right!
>
> But I had a great time. I spent four and a half glorious years on the aeromed squadron and was fortunate enough to get involved with some of the more demanding aeromed moves. There were some great flights, saw the world, lot of business class … even flew to Australia and back business class! All that you surveyed was yours, there was a great social culture at TMW [Tactical Medical Wing, RAF Lyneham], a fantastic team, you worked hard, but you played hard. And it was blue, totally blue, and you felt an immense amount of pride, because it's our raison d'être and without that we might as well be in the army.

A rather unusual aeromed took place in May 2003. In the Saudi capital, Riyadh, a small party of British citizens, accused of illegal drinking, had been thrown into jail. This was in the middle of a sporadic campaign of car-bombs and, unfortunately, the dissidents had exploded a car bomb right outside the compound where the Brits were being held. It was a nasty incident, with thirty-six people killed and more than 160 wounded; so the British government ordered an aeromed team to go out and bring back the British citizens, whose medical condition was unknown.

'In aeromed there were lots of different experiences. Lots of quite trying times,' says Debbie Meikle:

> One of the most trying was the government tasking us to go out and pick up people who had been detained in Riyadh. I went out as a team leader; there was a doctor – a medical officer – a medic, and a media ops person, who kept the media away from us. We were told we had to bring those patients back from Riyadh no matter what state they were in.
>
> I never liked going into Riyadh because you lose your passport. You get checked in by the consulate office and you get your passport back as you leave. That never ever felt comfortable with me, but we had to go and assess these patients and it was all 'Quick, quick, quick …' and the hardest thing for me … I was female, and the doctor was female, and the Saudis don't speak to females really, and the media ops person wasn't a doctor, and I remember saying to him on the aircraft, 'You just need to keep us informed, if they tell you anything, you need to relay it to me and the doctor so that we can co-ordinate how we're assessing them before we get them on the aircraft' … but they were all fine to be emplaned. We got back to London quite swiftly, we were first off the aircraft, put in this mini bus that was waiting, with our seven patients, and whisked to this reception area which was full of media. It was a good job done and we'd got it done, really, before the media got wind of it, but the awful thing about that was … there was never closure, you never got to say goodbye to those people because obviously the families were there. It was lovely to look in the room and see them cuddling their families, we'd done our job, but … it would have been nice to say goodbye to them. That was probably the most challenging one, really.

However, Debbie also remembers:

> The most rewarding aeromed I ever did was taking a gentleman back down to the Falkland Islands. He was paralysed from the neck down. He'd been looking after reindeer and one of them had got a bit wild, so he'd jumped on its back to calm it down and it'd thrown him … one of the reindeer realised that he was on the floor injured and he'd gone up and tried to snuggle in to him … anyway he was paralysed from the neck down. Oh, bless him! This aeromed … we were leaving from Brize

Norton one night and the aircraft was u/s, so … I was doing the Ascension leg – Ascension [Island] to the Falklands, and a less experienced person who was doing the Brize Norton to Ascension leg, so we were going through as normal passengers at Brize and … over the tannoy: 'Can Flight Sergeant Meikle come to the desk?' so I went and it was the nurse doing the first leg, saying, 'I need your advice, the aircraft has gone u/s, so what do I do to look after this patient?'

So I said, 'We're not looking after him, he's too dependent, we need to function tomorrow night, with a twenty-four-hour delay, so he's got to go back to Stoke Mandeville.' So we had him and we had a young lady who was special needs, who had a reduced mental age, so one of my team was going to look after her in the Gateway House [the place where people can stay overnight at RAF Brize Norton]. So this poor man went back to Stoke Mandeville and we did it again the following night, and again the aircraft went u/s! So the next night we had to do the same, and the girl who was looking after the special needs lady had to stay again in the Gateway House, get all her clothes washed, so she [the flight medic] wasn't fit to fly with us, so we had to change the team around … we set off on the third night, got to Ascension, did the hand-over, and then we took off … About three hours out from the Falklands, the captain said, 'Can the aeromed team leader come to the flight deck?' so I went there thinking, We can't be diverting, no we can't! So the captain said, 'The winds in the Falklands are horrendous, we're probably going to have to divert,' and I just said, 'You have got to try everything you can to get us to the Falklands, because I have this gentleman who's unable to care for himself and this lady who would need me to care for her in hospital, and I really don't want to put them in hospital in Montevideo – that's in Uruguay – and I can't care for them in a hotel with the team we've got.' So he said, 'Well, I'll try my hardest, but if we go in to land and have to make a quick ascent, then we'll be going back to Uruguay.'

Anyway, he managed to land – and I have *never* been so grateful. Then handing the patient over to the hospital in the Falklands was lovely. It was a week before Christmas and he said, 'Thank you so much for getting me home.' It was lovely. This man had worked for the Falkland Island Government, and there was another gentleman on the island – with similar injuries I think – but he wasn't of the character to get things done for disabled people, so this patient said, 'Between the two of us we can now look at making things better in the Falkland Islands for disabled people.' What a fantastic way to look at things.

But they were long flights, sixteen-hour flights out there. The time used to go quite quickly, but it would be lovely when you landed in the Falklands because the wind would hit your face and … I used to love that feeling – the wind blowing through your hair … fresh air after sixteen hours in the aircraft … Lovely!

Part VI

New Challenges in a New Millennium

20

New Centre for Defence Medicine, Birmingham

While setting up the new military-staffed hospital units within existing NHS Trust hospitals, the Ministry of Defence (MoD) had also been considering the possibility of creating a large hospital complex which, in time of conflict, would offer comprehensive and up-to-date specialist care for injured service personnel and also provide training for service medical staff to prepare them for working in war zones. The chosen location was in central England: two hospitals in Birmingham, the old Queen Elizabeth Hospital and the Selly Oak Hospital. The Royal Defence Medical College moved from Gosport to Birmingham and became part of the University of Birmingham's Medical School, while the Defence School of Health Care Studies is based at Birmingham City University. This latter provides training for all military nurses and allied health professionals and it is here that many members of the PMRAFNS acquire their nurse training, often to degree standard.

By a happy coincidence, the original MoD report which urged the necessity for the new Centre for Defence Medicine was written by Captain Timothy Laurence RN, husband of the Princess Royal, who opened the new centre on 2 April 2001. A year later, on 1 April 2002, it obtained royal permission to use the prefix 'Royal', thus becoming the Royal Centre for Defence Medicine (RCDM).

Over the next ten years a magnificent new hospital building arose not far away. Transfer of services began in the summer of 2010 and the new Queen Elizabeth Hospital officially opened in 2012. Among its many specialities, the hospital has the largest organ transplant programme in the UK and the largest critical care unit in the world. It provides a whole range of services for civilian patients from across the West Midlands and beyond and it is also the main reception centre for all wounded servicemen and -women coming from areas of conflict. Many PMs have worked there since the RCDM opened in 2001.

One of the first RAF nurses posted to Birmingham was Lee Bond:

> [I had] an opportunity to go and work there, on the Selly Oak ITU, which was – still is – a big teaching centre. Totally different way of working to a district hospital, different patient groups, a lot more challenging … it was a regional trauma centre, regional burns centre. Phenomenal clinical experience.

> It was fortuitous that we got in there when we did, not due to good management, just good luck that we were put there, considering what happened in future years, in Iraq and Afghanistan. It was the right place to be. Certainly, from a trauma management perspective, it was superb.

In March 2007, some anxious relatives accused the hospital of not caring properly for wounded men coming back from the war in Iraq and national newspapers reported incidents of servicemen being verbally abused in the hospital by members of the public opposed to the war. Debbie Meikle was part of a small team sent to smooth troubled waters. She said:

> I worked at RCDM Birmingham from September 2006 to October 2009. Myself and about three orthopaedic and trauma nurses were moved up there quite swiftly in response to the negative media coverage on military patients – the care, or lack of care, that they were getting. I don't think it was so much a lack of care: the NHS were doing a good job looking after the people who were returning from Iraq and Afghanistan, but they didn't know the processes with regard to moving them on to rehabilitation, so it was delayed. That was why we were moved up there at short notice, to put processes and policies into place and to care for all the patients that were coming through.
>
> That was quite a challenging time in my career, and it was emotionally draining because, not only did you have the patients, you were dealing with the relatives, and the relatives wanted someone to blame, so a lot of the time they took it out on the staff. That was the hardest thing I had to deal with. But the experience was fantastic. The trauma injuries that you get up there are very good for learning. And with long-stay patients … it does test your nursing skills.

Aeromeds for the twenty-first century

As we saw earlier, the RAF's Tactical Medical Wing (TMW) was formed on 1 April 1996, initially based at RAF Lyneham, Wiltshire; when Lyneham closed in October 2012 the functions of TMW transferred to RAF Brize Norton, Oxon. Its role, as explained by Wing Commander Mike Priestley, current OC of the unit (2013), is to train, equip and deploy RAF Medical Services personnel in support of operations and exercises and to provide a quality worldwide aeromedical evacuation service. Its medical teams, always with a PM as the team leader, are made up of the permanent staff at TMW, sometimes augmented by, either, medical personnel from RAF Stations across the country or RAF staff from the MDHUs. TMW also has a deployable aeromedical response team capability (DARTS); one team of twelve medical personnel is always on call, with six hours' notice to move, to provide conventional first response medical capability and aeromedical evacuation to any crisis worldwide.

TWM provides training in several areas. Aeromedical evacuation (AE) prepares qualified clinicians for their roles as flight nursing officers, flight nurses and flight medics; it also prepares doctors and other allied health professionals and technicians for their role as part of the AE process on the ground or in the air. Operational training equips personnel with the field skills and knowledge to fulfil their operational role in often austere conditions. Training for critical care air support teams (CCAST) prepares specialist clinicians for their role in bringing home the most seriously wounded and critically ill patients, using the most highly technological electromedical life support patient transfer equipment. Already fully trained in AE, CCAST clinicians embark on a week of theory, followed by a week of actually undertaking the transfer of critically ill patients at the John Radcliffe Hospital in Oxford.

The forward AE teams who provide medical emergency response (MERT) are also trained and equipped by TMW. These teams project advanced accident and emergency care forward in the battlefield as close as possible to the point at which a service person is wounded or injured and deliver them directly back to the most appropriate deployed medical treatment facility, so that their definitive care can be continued. This team is again led by an emergency department-trained (ED) PM and includes an emergency anaesthetic consultant (who may be from any one of the three services) along with RAF ED nurses and RAF paramedics. Needless to say, CCAST teams have been especially busy during the first decade or so of the twenty-first century.

Lee Bond was one of the first to undertake CCAST training, around the turn of the millennium:

> At that time I was doing a lot of Priority One aeromeds and I could see the capabilities we didn't have, I could see where we were left wanting, and, if we continued with that, patients would die. The only way round it was to come kicking and screaming into the twenty-first century, not only to meet the ICS [Intensive Care Society] guidelines with regard to transfer of critically ill patients, but to exceed those guidelines, so that we could become world leaders in the aeromedical transfer – or transfer per se – of critically ill patients. That's where we are to this day, because of that.

He was delighted to be selected to attend the new CCAST equipment training, which took place in Oxford, at the John Radcliffe Hospital:

> I was a sergeant at the time, 2000/2001, somewhere around there, and it was a fantastic opportunity, scary, but a fantastic opportunity, with regard to what you were likely to get involved with. This was pioneering. New equipment, never been used before with real patients, potential issues with interacting with the airframe, how you managed such sick patients who need life support or High Dependency Care. It meant that, as soon as you had done that course, you were 'live' as far as being on call was concerned, because you had the skill sets to use the kit.

> We got Bosnia, we got Kosovo … suddenly the work-load started to increase, certainly from a CCAST perspective. I was on call quite a lot over that period … I'd just finished a fourteen-hour shift [at the hospital in Selly Oak], got back to my flat, just got into bed, eleven o'clock at night, and got this call. 'You've got two patients …' So I rang the unit and said, 'Look, I'm not going to be in tomorrow because I've just been mobilised.' They were very much aware that I had just done a fourteen-hour shift. They said, 'When are you going?' I said, 'Now,' because we were flying at two o'clock in the morning.
>
> The patients were out in Pristina [Kosovo] – two Guards, who had been on top of a train, on the carriages, on patrol. They'd seen something that had alerted them. Unbeknown to them, it was an electric train with the wires at the top. One of them touched it and they both got quite severe electrocution burns as a result. One was ventilated, one wasn't … they were both pretty sick and I started to prep the guy that was ventilated and … [my colleague] started to do a bit of concurrent activity, which you'd expect from your team when you're prepping a patient that's got so many needs. I've worked on wards and I know how busy it is, but you wouldn't believe that with just one patient, sometimes having one person is just not enough. You need more, because there's so much going on.

There were, of course, teething troubles with the new equipment, but Lee Bond believes that the innovations were invaluable, because:

> with regard to Iraq, and certainly Afghanistan, we would have been in trouble, there would have been some major issues, because a ground medical facility runs out of medical resources very quickly when dealing with critically ill patients. If you can't move those patients competently, safely, then you're either going to get a death on the ground or you'll get a death in the air. Both of which aren't particularly good.

Although the war in Kosovo officially ended in 1999, problems remained and British troops continued to be deployed there.

The Second Gulf War

The last decade of the old millennium had seen trouble erupt in Iraq, first with the Iraqi invasion of Kuwait, in 1990, countered in the following year by the aerial bombing of Iraq, known as Operation Desert Storm. This resulted in an uneasy ceasefire and brought Saddam Hussein to the fore as president of Iraq. In 1998 another bombing campaign, Operation Desert Fox, had as its aim the destruction of Iraq's theoretical weapons of mass destruction. As history revealed, these weapons did not exist. Nevertheless, tension grew, the bombing continued, and in the spring of 2003 the UN declared Iraq to be in breach of a series of resolutions. The scene was set for what became the Second Gulf War, known to the military as Operation Telic.

Nikki Duncan found herself doing aeromeds between two floating bases in the Red Sea. The primary casualty receiving facility was aboard the Royal Fleet Auxiliary (RFA) *Argus*, whose fully equipped 100-bed hospital includes a four-bay operating theatre, critical care unit and CT scanner. However, RFA *Argus* is not classified as a hospital ship and does not display the International Red Cross symbol because she is fitted with self-defence guns and may have operational units on board. Nikki says:

> We went to do the helicopter moves, from the ship to wherever we needed to go. That was quite scary, because you have to do the dunker drills to do the helicopter work, in a swimming pool in a simulated helicopter thing. I didn't enjoy that at all! I didn't mind being on a helicopter, but going over the sea in a helicopter worried me. So being on a ship and doing helicopter moves … it wouldn't have been my choice! We were out bobbing around in the water, not sure exactly where. We were completely blind, we had no television, weren't allowed mobile phones. We didn't have comms. Although we knew we'd gone to war, we didn't know what was going on. Just floating around in the sea somewhere, helicopters coming and going … Blackout conditions, doors all blacked out, curtains over … we weren't allowed out on the deck or anything. We had regular updates, but they were quite brief, so we were quite isolated. It felt very odd. The navy weren't particularly happy that we were there. They had, historically, done their own helicopter moves, but of course without specialist training, the aeromed course. They weren't happy, but they put up with us.
>
> The hospital ship [RFA *Argus*] was quite amazing, very impressive. Hundreds of people aboard. The hospital part was down below. They had one big ward, intensive care, radiology, labs … absolutely everything. There was a gym, different messes … yes, big. You would always get lost! We spent a lot of our time walking down corridors, because they all looked the same. When we weren't busy, we did the hospital laundry, we quite liked it, in the laundrette, putting in the quilts and the covers. I remember doing the laundry more than anything!
>
> It was mainly Iraqi patients that we were moving. Quite a lot of children, actually – the first time I came across children. But we weren't very busy. All the moves I did were just from that ship to the *Comfort*, the American hospital ship. But the American hospital ship is huge! It's like a normal hospital, loads of wards. The casualty part of the ship is bigger than our casualty department [at Peterborough City Hospital]. It had at least thirty bays. It was good to see it. The only thing that I remember from that is … because they'd had prisoners of war, or detainees, captured persons … in their intensive care, they would tie their arms up, with bandages, to the sides [the bedrails] … I'd seen prisoners, but I'd never seen anything like that … I just thought, They're asleep! They're in intensive care, sedated. How could you do that?
>
> But I was glad to be back on land. I didn't like sleeping on those little bunks, not being able to sit up. And they do a bizarre system. Their war-hours are six hours on, six hours off, which is not very long. You also have roll calls at seven in the morning

and seven in the evening to make sure nobody's gone overboard. You just slept on your time off. You also had gym time, there was a good gym on board. I got very fit.

In a long career, Lee Bond has experienced many different aspects of PMRAFNS life. In 2005 he was deployed to Iraq as OC IRT (Officer Commanding, Immediate Response Team), whose work he describes as:

Fly out to point of injury, collect the patient, resuscitate and bring back. We were based at three areas: in Basra, at Smitty and at Alamara, we rotated between the three. In Basra it was pretty much scoop and run – get the patient on to the helicopter as quickly as possible, get them to hospital … But Smitty and Alamara … Alamara, for instance, is at least fifty-five minutes away from Basra, so that's a long time to be with a patient that's dying in front of your eyes. The kit wasn't what it is today, the protective equipment wasn't what it is today … It was a difficult time but, fortunately, we learned from those experiences.

Debbie Meikle, another senior and well-experienced PM, had two tours flying in and out of Iraq:

doing the strategic aeromed back from Iraq to the UK. That was probably the hardest operational deployment I've done. You would fly overnight to pick the patients up, you'd have a night or two out there and then you'd be flying back, you were constantly back and forth. You might get a couple of nights at home in your own bed, which was nice, then you'd fly again. I never got settled. And the aeromed tent was right by the generators, near the kitchen – and you'd just get used to the generator noise and you'd be away again … I had four months where I hardly slept. I used to douse my pillow with lavender and had lavender behind my ears to try and make me sleep. Oh … that was quite challenging, purely because my body clock just couldn't adjust, not on that tour.

My second tour to Iraq was at Shaibah [near Basra] where I was in the hospital. Completely different. Yes, the surgical and orthopaedic ward was busy, with injuries and things, but it was quite a fun tour. Well, they all are … The good thing about being on ops is, you work hard and on your down time you play hard. You generally are quite well-staffed, in comparison to being back home. Those were both good tours.

Wing Commander Sonia Phythian was sent to Iraq after the main conflict ended:

but interestingly I was in Baghdad when the first elections were being held and so the region became very volatile. I deployed on [Operation] TELIC 2003–2004 and was based in Baghdad as the AELO and Practice Nurse for all UK military personnel, but with aeromedical evacuation responsibility for all UK civilians employed within the region. I worked out of the British Support Unit within both the UK and American Embassy; it was an isolated appointment away from the main UK medical facility at Basra. If my patient needed to be seen by a doctor I would take them to the American Combat Support Hospital. If my patient needed to be admitted I would stay with them and ensure they received the appropriate level of medical care and welfare support.

The experience was not particularly enjoyable and I found the whole environment very sinister. Perhaps I felt this way because I was operating on my own within the area … in hindsight it was a good experience, because you learn from it, but at the time I did feel quite vulnerable.

Operation Telic, the UK's military operations in Iraq, ended for most personnel at the end of April 2009, though a contingent of around 150, mainly from the Royal Navy, remained in Iraq until May 2011.

Meanwhile, yet another foreign war had called British forces into action some 1,300 miles to the east of Iraq. As always, the RAF and its nursing service answered the call, offering support and care to the injured of all sides.

Beginnings of the war in Afghanistan

Afghanistan is a landlocked country, much of it dry and arid, with temperatures soaring by day and plunging by night. The Hindu Kush Mountains tower north-east of the capital, Kabul, and there are wide areas of desert.

Because it lies in a strategic area where trade routes meet, and because its people belong to various tribes and persuasions, the country has long been torn apart by warring factions. In more recent history, military intervention has been tried by some outside powers, none of whom have been able to create a lasting peace. The Soviet army gave up trying in 1989. In their wake, civil war wracked the country; its government was taken over by the Taliban, a fundamentalist Muslim group, and the wild hills and dusty deserts became a hot-bed for terrorist training camps, from where insurgents went out across the world doing indiscriminate violence.

Then came the atrocity known to history as 9/11. On 11 September 2001, Al-Qaeda terrorists struck in the heart of America, bringing the twin towers of the World Trade Centre down in a shattering cloud of debris and dust, killing nearly 3,000 people. US President George Bush decided that the time had come to take action. He demanded that Afghanistan's Taliban government should give up the Al-Qaeda leader, Osama bin Laden, and close all the terrorist training camps. Predictably, the Taliban remained defiant and in October the USA and the UK began a bombing campaign aimed at destroying the Al-Qaeda camps. The Taliban were very soon in retreat.

That December, the United Nations Security Council agreed to the formation of an International Security Assistance Force (ISAF) which would move in and help to establish security in Afghanistan. All of the NATO nations and some of their partner states (such as Australia) sent troops in varying numbers. Their original mission was to secure Kabul and the surrounding area, but from October 2003 their objectives expanded and eventually encompassed the whole country.

The RAF was, of course, called in as a part of the British contribution to ISAF and, during the long years of conflict which have followed, many members of the PMRAFNS have been deployed to Afghanistan to care for the sick and wounded. In the early days they worked in or near the capital, Kabul, but when Helmand province became the main area protected by British troops their centre moved to Kandahar, from where a new camp was established out in the desert. Named Camp Bastion, it grew rapidly to a huge complex whose facilities included an airfield, a fully equipped hospital, accommodation areas, cafes, a gymnasium and sports facilities and, of course, up-to-date arrangements for the swift aeromedical evacuation of British casualties.

The PMs' Afghan experience began originally in the autumn of 2001 with Exercise Saif Sareea (or Operation Swift Sword). This was a major exercise involving military forces of the UK and Oman, creating the largest deployment of UK forces since the First Gulf War and using as an airhead the airfield at Thumrait, Oman. Following the attack on the World Trade Centre, Thumrait gave the Western allies a vital toe-hold in the area, from which to launch their war against the Taliban government in Afghanistan.

Among the PMs who found themselves caught up in the conflict was Lee Bond, who was in Oman with Exercise Saif Sareea when he and his team were deployed to Kabul, to help the troops fighting there. He took part in a variety of aeromeds involving injured soldiers, but he particularly remembers a less routine occasion:

> a chappie who wasn't related to combat, he was related purely to a parachuting incident. His parachute hadn't opened and he'd hit the ground pretty hard, and had been declared, pretty much, dead. His family were out there and … it was a very humbling experience. We went out and talked to the family, and brought them all back … We were bringing him back to die at Birmingham, basically. It's that element of not just offering life-saving care, but palliative care, that's beneficial for relatives. They helped care for him in flight, that was part of it, they were there and … an unusual situation, but quite heart-warming really. I should imagine that their closure of the situation was easier to deal with because they'd seen him through his journey.

After Exercise Saif Sareea ended, the airfield at Thumrait remained open as a convenience for the allies who were struggling to restore order in Afghanistan. There being no suitable Afghani airfields for the RAF to use in those early days of the war, larger aircraft would fly into and from Thumrait.

Nikki Duncan was with the aeromed teams working out of Kabul in the summer of 2002, though her work also involved holding clinics for Afghan civilians:

It was relatively safe at that point, because the Taliban had been pushed out. We were in Kabul, a city, so there weren't the IEDs that there are in the countryside.

We did lots of 'hearts and minds' out there. We were quite busy, lots of children. We would help out with the other nations and do a clinic. Every Thursday morning there was a clinic, meant to be to treat leishmaniasis [a parasitic disease transmitted through sand fly bites]. We would go and man a clinic and just do what we could, basically, because there were all sorts of people turning up, with all sorts of ailments. Mainly it was women and children, which was quite strange because previously they wouldn't have been allowed out. Under the Taliban you wouldn't have seen the women out at all. At the hospital later, in [Camp] Bastion in 2012, you never saw any women, but at that time, 2002, there were women everywhere, because the Taliban were no longer around. We worked in with the Americans, the Germans, the French … all the nations were there running these clinics. It was good experience in learning how to examine people, we got lots of advice from the doctors.

We also worked with the welfare people quite a lot – to do with compensation, where we had injured the children. We would go and visit them in the American hospital and we sometimes had patients that we would take back from there. We had to go into the villages to do liaison and drop bags of rice off for the families.

There was one little boy, who'd been run over by one of the army trucks. He'd lost an arm and a leg and he was in the American hospital. The Americans are very different … where we are 'hearts and minds', they want to get their hospitals emptied quickly. As soon as he was surgically 'better', they wanted to discharge him. But we had caused these injuries, so it was, 'You can't just send him home, he lives in a little wooden shack thing.' We actually managed to find, in Kabul, an Italian rehabilitation centre, run by the Red Cross – it's an Afghan facility, but run by an Italian doctor, and their self-sufficiency is absolutely amazing. All the workers there are amputees. They make their own artificial limbs. They have physios there and they have little assault courses, and a little factory part to it, where they make the limbs. And lots of rooms where people can stay. Anyway, we managed to get this little boy a room there, with his Dad. They took him on, to make his artificial limbs. We were very impressed with this facility, so we asked them about raising money for them; they didn't want money because the Red Cross were funding them, but they wanted shoes – decent shoes, because they just wear flip-flops over there most of the time. So we managed to get lots of shoes and boots sent out from the UK.

Working closely with our good friends from across the Atlantic has not always been 'a walk in the park', as some PMs have discovered.

Warrant Officer Debbie Meikle comments that 'The American way of doing things is quite different from ours. You'd have a British leader – boss – and you'd have an American boss, and it could be difficult on the wards if they didn't see eye to eye.'

Other differences struck Corporal Kirsty Scott:

All their nurses are officers, in the US army, but they have something like our SENs, enrolled nurses, and they're non-commissioned, but their way of working was completely different to the way we do things. We're very hands-on and will get a patient dressed and washed, whereas they leave it to someone else – they're a nurse, they just do medications. It took them a couple of months working with us to realise you can actually be looking after your patient, hands-on with them, and it's OK. They did start wanting to do things, but most of them would leave it to their non-commissioned nurses to do the hands-on nursing care.

Introducing MERT

The method of bringing casualties back from the front to the nearest and most appropriate medical facility is constantly being revised and improved. Historically, an immediate response team (IRT) generally consisted of a nurse and a medic, with a doctor if required, who would fly out in a helicopter to collect the wounded. In 2006 this metamorphosed into the medical emergency response team (MERT), which mostly uses a heavy-lifting Chinook helicopter, with a team of accident and emergency nurses, paramedics and a doctor. The numbers of the team vary, according to circumstances and aircraft availability, but the main difference is that the MERT has the capability of intubating patients, putting them to sleep, and keeping them as comfortable as possible during the transfer back to the hospital.

The MERT capability was introduced around the same time that UK forces moved out from Kabul into Helmand Province, one of the largest provinces of Afghanistan, lying in the south of the country. Here, medical personnel of the RAF worked alongside Americans, Canadians, Danish and French (to name only a few), their centre of operations located initially in the city of Kandahar. It was there that PM Stephen Doyle had his first experience of Afghanistan:

We were based originally in Kandahar, with 16 Close Support Regiment [RAMC], the airborne element. Bastion hadn't been built [though] the hard-standing for the hospital and the accommodation had been laid down. When it was partially ready they moved us down from Kandahar to Camp Bastion and … it was straight into picking up casualties.

Initially, when we were under tentage, it was all a bit stressful. Work was fine, we were busy, it was what people were trained to do. The attitude was really *can-do*, and it was good to show off the potential of the MERT asset, because no other country has that capability at the moment. The Americans were looking at doing something similar themselves. I think their problem is the possibility of putting nurses – and doctors – in harm's way. That's a big risk. The Americans have paramedics who they send out.

The hospital itself was a massive tent, and communications weren't the best – it was just getting off the ground. The food was … bearable! At least we weren't on rations. It was OK, considering the logistical problems, but everyone bonded together, it was a good show in the end. Morale was high.

The main problem was the heat, and the accommodation … They were supposed to have two air-conditioning units per tent, but some bean-counter had decided you only needed one, so they continually broke down and, if you were trying to sleep off night-duty during the day, you'd literally wake up in a pool of your own sweat. It was disgusting!

Because we were out in the middle of the desert, they didn't have any walls around the facility, they just had diggers building up massive banks of sand around the place. The idea of building out in the desert was that if anybody moved close they'd be spotted and taken out. But in fact there were so many people moving in and out of the place … that is a bit difficult, especially when, from day one, you're employing local people to empty bins, or do the toilets … you've got no idea who they might be.

It was very hot – extremely hot! And the amount of kit we had to carry, especially in the helicopter, was stifling, until some altitude, when it cooled down, which was quite nice, but then you had to worry about the patients getting cold. But then back to toasty warm when you came back down to the ground again. There were some roads, but most of it was just dusty, a lot of dust. The thing I remember was the accommodation tentage, which I think they're still in, after all these years.

Things had not improved much when Sonia Phythian arrived:

in 2006, I deployed on [Operation] Herrick, where I was based at the Role 3 at Camp Bastion. This was a completely different experience to Telic, much more positive, despite the fact that Camp Bastion had only been established that year – it had about one thousand UK military personnel, so it was very small and completely different from how it is now. I was responsible for co-ordinating the aeromedical evacuation of personnel from Helmand Province back to UK via the Aeromed Staging Unit at Kandahar. At Bastion we were remote and operated out of a tented hospital and tented accommodation (the same accommodation is used today); the runway was just a strip of gravel and there was no holding facility down on the flight line, there was no comms system or decent lighting but, it was a fantastic experience. Both the MERT and the CCAST operated out of the Role 3 where we would stabilise the patients prior to transferring them to Kandahar for evacuation to the UK.

During my deployment I had two different Deputy AELOs who were RAF Medics and they were both great. All the people I worked with were very professional …you make some really good friends because you share such significant experiences with them. It was a valuable experience to work in a tented hospital too, with all the problems the environment brings.

Military action in Afghanistan continued, as we shall see. Camp Bastion acquired its own airfield, the hospital grew and yet more PMs were deployed. As news of their work reached a wider audience, thanks to many news reports and documentaries, at home in Britain more and more young recruits signed on to join them.

Training today

At the turn of the millennium, members of the PMRAFNS fell into three categories: nursing officers, non-commissioned staff nurses and student staff nurses. Since 1997, when mental nurses and auxiliary air force nurses were incorporated, all RAF nurses have come under one banner, as members of the PMRAFNS. In addition, student staff nurses became tomorrow's nursing officers and NCOs. They are recruited to the RAF and remain members of that service, wearing appropriate uniform when on official duty, though nowadays, as we know, they work alongside nurses of the army, the navy and the NHS.

Squadron Leader (later Wing Commander) Pippa Ward, in charge of recruiting for the PMs in the late 1990s, observed, 'I spend a lot of time at careers fairs answering questions like "Do you have to wear uniform all the time?" or "Do you get leave?" and "Can you go home?" For anyone interested, the answers are No! Yes! and Of course! Before taking this job, I thought that recruiting would be a nice way of earning a living! In hindsight I can honestly say I have never worked so hard in my eleven years in the PMRAFNS.'

Following basic recruit and medical training, students in those days moved on to beautiful Hampshire, where beside the Solent they undertook their professional nurse training at the tri-service Health Studies Department of the Royal Defence Medical College (RDMC) at HMS *Dolphin* (aka Fort Blockhouse), in Gosport. Here, students and tutors from all three services worked amicably together. Initially the PMRAFNS took up only two places on a course of thirty students, but this number increased significantly over the years. All graduates became registered nurses with a Diploma in Higher Education (DipHE); PMRAFNS staff nurses graduate in the rank of acting corporal. Following two more years' service, all nurses have the opportunity to apply to be considered for a commission.

'Students always make you laugh, they do some strange things,' said Squadron Leader (later Wing Commander) Annie Warburton, who for much of the 1990s was head of nurse training:

> I've seen a pupil nurse collect up thermometers to clean, put them in a great big bowl and pour a kettle of boiling water over them. So we lost that lot! And I've actually witnessed a student nurse putting the one and only stainless steel bedpan in a papier mâché bedpan masher, which wrecked the machine and made a hell of a noise.

As for the tri-service environment, Annie found no real problems:

> in terms of nurse education, I think it was inevitable. The nurse-teachers were luckier than most because we, as groups of people, had worked together prior to this happening. We had RAF student nurses who were on the navy student nurse programme with the University of Portsmouth. I already had one teacher working on the Haslar site, even before the rest of us moved, so it wasn't as traumatic as, say, closing Wroughton and moving to Haslar was for clinical nurses, who were coming to work with people who they didn't know, perhaps had never seen before.

When Birmingham became the new location of the Centre for Defence Medicine, in 2001, nurse training moved to the midlands and a new degree course was written, enabling student nurses to emerge with a BSc (Hons), with the opportunity to go further and do a Master's degree, usually while working full-time. Although the PMRAFNS still welcomes nurses who have already completed their training within the NHS, by undertaking professional training within the service, under the guidance of some of the best nurse-tutors in the world, young men and women enjoy the advantages of imbibing military know-how along with their nursing skills.

Whatever career path they may follow, successful recruits and students all become fully fledged PMs, with the accompanying benefits and opportunities: good pay, with uniform and accommodation provided, the camaraderie of a service environment, a wide range of work experience, chances to specialise professionally, to gain further educational qualifications, to climb the promotion ladder, terrific opportunities for travel and social life, and more. With such prizes on offer, only the best of candidates win through.

The training path taken by Kim Wilson is fairly typical:

> I joined in 2007 and did my basic training; then I went to university, qualified October 2010 and came to Peterborough. I did the rotation programme. It has changed a bit now, but then you did a year and you went round three of the main areas which were going to help you on deployment. That's orthopaedics, surgical, and the assessment unit. I did that, then I did a six-week specialist placement, which was two weeks in A&E, two weeks in ITU and two weeks in theatres, just to give you a taster to see what you enjoy. I think, since then, they've added paediatrics and women's health.

In 2006, Kay Griffiths also attended the course at RAF Halton, where PMs are taught the military way of life, then did her nurse training at Birmingham. Kay says:

> When I was training at Birmingham I was quite lucky because, in most of our student placements, we managed to get anywhere where we get RAF nurses. I've been up to Catterick, the Friarage Hospital; Northallerton; MRS Dhekelia, Cyprus,

for primary health care experience; Derriford Hospital; Plymouth; Peterborough District Hospital and many more. I was also very lucky to have had an opportunity to undertake a student placement at the Royal Hospital of Neuro-Disability in London, and then a couple of placements around Birmingham, in Birmingham City hospital … and the neuro-disability hospital in London, which was very good. Going to all these different areas, you managed to get a military aspect on [the work], the extra things you'd be getting into.

Anthony Beynon was a fully qualified nurse when he joined the PMs in 2010, straight from Swansea University:

I did basic training at Halton, then I came straight into Wittering, so this [Peterborough MDHU] is my first posting. When you're newly qualified, you start off in a rotation programme – that was in the old hospital, PDH [Peterborough District Hospital]. I did four months on general surgery and orthopaedics wards, then I went down to the Acute Admissions unit, before we moved over here [to the new City Hospital], where I continued on my last placement on ESS [Emergency Short Stay]. They've just brought in a specialist rotation of two weeks in each speciality, so you can do two weeks in ITU, two weeks in A&E and two weeks in theatres.

Then I went down to Headley Court for a month, which was really good. Really interesting. It was so nice to actually get the full package, because … I'd done nursing outside the military, then here, just getting used to the military life, and then going down to Headley Court and getting full service access – patients are military, the whole environment is military. It set me in good stead because, later on, I was to go to Afghanistan, so I actually got the knowledge of what to tell troops, if they did get badly injured. I knew what the care package was like, back home.

Once nurses have qualified and completed their basic training in a hospital environment, many other opportunities open up. For Rachel Frearson, a PM since 2006, aeromed training was the most memorable (so far):

because you had the chance to go on the helicopters … lot of hairy, double fingers crossed moments. Flying between Lashkar Gah [capital of Helmand Province] and Bastion, they were the hairiest ones, and Kandahar and back … Living on KAF [Kandahar Airfield] was a bit frightening, they were sending the mortars in. When you get there it's frightening, but then you get a little bit complacent with it. Loved every minute of it, though I'm ready for the change, to work in the emergency department this time when I go.

Rachel was speaking in February 2013, just two months before her second deployment to Afghanistan:

> When you do the aeromed, the patient is packaged up in the nicest possible way, whereas this will be the front end of it, the raw side … but it's a challenge that I need, a little push into something I'm not quite comfortable with, so this will be the next step for me. There are awful sad moments, but that's what makes it good, in the way that people pull together, the camaraderie of it all, the team spirit, the dark humour … that's what pulls you through. When it looks as if the grass is greener [outside the service], I think, I'm lucky to have a job, lucky to have so many opportunities.

She explained a little about pre-deployment training, which prepares PMs for the things they will meet in the war zone:

> I'm just getting ready to do my pre-deployment. I'm going on the 8th of April, we go to Strensall Barracks, in York, and do HospEx [hospital exercise], the pretend hospital, but we meet the Danes and the Americans, so we're put into teams and practice together. There's a huge hangar [with] a big mock-up hospital. They have the ambulances coming straight in to the emergency department with the patients and then move on to stretcher theatres and then ITU, or the ward, or wherever, and then aeromedded out. You've got all of the teams there, and X-rays, CT and biochemistry, so you've got a little idea how it works – I'm lucky because I've seen it, so I can visualise it anyway … Then we go straight to Brize [RAF Brize Norton] from York, after a week there. And then out to Bastion.

From a more senior point of view, Flight Sergeant Rob Morris, who joined the Service in 1994, considers his own training to have had advantages over the modern kind:

> I trained under the old system, effectively an apprenticeship – three months on the ward, a week in school, three months on the ward, a week in school … as opposed to going to university, which is more academically driven training. A lot of people who do that go onto the wards very, very knowledgeable, but they haven't had as much day-to-day exposure to patients as we did. We spent a lot of time with patients, so by the end of your first year you knew whether that's for you or not. Today's students may be more academically knowledgeable, but they come out wanting to follow [a certain] course, to be managers, not patient-carers. I could work in management – I have the qualifications – but I prefer to spend my time with patients.

Military nursing in dangerous times

The more senior of today's PMs always knew that if armed strife did arise they would be deeply involved in caring for the wounded; some of them were involved in Bosnia and Kosovo. Younger PMs, signing on for service during the major conflicts in Iraq and Afghanistan, were even more acutely aware that they would very soon be asked to face danger and witness the horrors of war. None of them have flinched from the task; indeed, for some the prospect of being involved with the consequences of bloodshed and battle have been a positive bonus.

Squadron Leader Stephen Doyle joined QARANC (the army nursing service) in 1993, transferring to the PMRAFNS in 2000. He saw service in Northern Ireland during the Troubles, after which:

> Bosnia had flared up. I went to Sipovo, first as an ED nursing officer and then second time around I was nursing officer in charge. That was multi-national, as well, the second time, we had Belgians, Icelandics, Dutch, at the hospital. We were all fairly well cocooned, really. We saw some traumas but no great shakes. It was only in Afghanistan that we saw proper wounds.

When asked how he thought today's PMs nurses were coping with those traumas, he replied at once, 'Brilliantly!'

Warrant Officer Lee Bond: 'I joined in the Cold War era – obviously we went through Bosnia, Kosovo, etc., but I suppose that periods of conflict are partly what you sign up for.'

Flight Sergeant Nicola Duncan: 'It was always something that we knew might happen and, because we'd joined the service, we were all quite excited when we knew something might happen. You don't want war, but you want to go away – you joined to go away, to do your bit.'

Sergeant Sarah Perkins:

> I knew when I trained that I would be required to deploy to areas of conflict. I've deployed twice to Afghanistan. I was nervous, but I had spoken to people who had previously deployed and although I was aware it would be a challenge I was excited about the experiences it would provide.

Corporal Rachel Frearson:

> I don't think anybody joins up blind to the fact that we're in conflict. You'd stay in civvy street, otherwise. Although I've never been on the real front line, it's the danger element … adventure training and things, too. Pushing the boundaries, that's what I wanted from the beginning.

Corporal Anthony Beynon:

> I wanted the full service life and the going away was part of the experience, something I really wanted to do and looked forward to. I didn't actually find out until two days before Christmas Day that I was going away, and then I went in January, last year [2012]. I think that was harder on my Mum than it was on me. But I thoroughly enjoyed the experience. It really did develop me as a person.

Corporal Kim Wilson:

> I'm off to Afghan in September [2013], doing an aeromed role out there, so it will be completely different from ward work. I'm a bit nervous about it, but I am really excited. I shall be out there for four months. I didn't think I'd get the opportunity to go, because it's all winding down, and maybe it sounds a bit weird to say I'm looking forward to it, but I am. I was so excited that I rang my Mum up, and that was bittersweet because she doesn't really want me to go, but I really want to go, so it was a weird feeling, being so happy and telling her something that would upset her, but she knows that's what I want to do, so she won't stop me. It's easier being out there than being at home wondering … I don't think the civilian nurses can comprehend why we want to go out to a conflict. They think we're a bit odd.

Corporal Kay Griffiths:

> As I had joined the PMs when we were already deployed on operations, I had expected that it was likely that I'd deploy at some point. Because I had already expected to deploy, it wasn't a shock when I found out that I was nominated to go. It was more my family … my mum was worried. But my tour in Afghan was fine. I did four months out there – two months as an aeromed nurse and two months as a deployed aeromed evacuation liaison nurse (DAELO). For the two months as a flight nurse … it predominantly involved patient transfers on various aircraft to a number of locations and the difference that involves. The DAELO role involved the logistics side of a patient's aeromedical evacuation. It was tiring! [But] I wouldn't say it was frightening. You had a lot of good people around you. Obviously you had bad days, but …

Happily, the PMRAFNS has specialist psychiatric nurses who can help their colleagues endure those 'bad days'. Flight Sergeant Rob Morris, a long-serving mental nurse, has had much experience with troops traumatised by battle situations. He says:

> People may not imagine that mental health nurses are out there, but we are. Usually, when mental nurses deploy, we work very similarly to what we do in the UK, except when we run mental health clinics. It's very hard for patients out on the ground to keep coming back to us, so although we're based in Bastion we spend a third to a half of our time going out to forward operational bases, little patrol bases where there's a company … might be fifty guys.
>
> I flew into one patrol base and the helicopter that was due to come and pick me up got diverted on a priority tasking, so I was going to be stuck there for another week. The only way was to hitch a lift off a convoy, but the convoy couldn't get up to the base [which was in a village], it had to come as far as the street at the bottom,

> about 500 metres. So me and one of the medics had to patrol down through the village to the T-junction, to catch the convoy. It could have been hairy, but it wasn't.

On another occasion, Rob:

> went out to one unit, landed in the afternoon, and that morning one of their lads had died – tripped an IED, lost his legs, completely blown in half. Everybody on the patrol, when they came back, showered and changed and all that, came and spoke to me. I ended up sitting out on a little pile of sand, there was nowhere else, and one of the lads came and talked to me. The next had been standing in the shade in the gym, so when one had finished he'd go back to the little crew room – TV, video games – and the next would come out while another waited in the shade … I spoke to fifteen or twenty guys that day, all about that one incident, what happened and how they felt about it. They just wanted somebody, who hadn't been there, to hear their story. They don't need therapy, don't need treatment; they just want somebody to listen.

As the war ground on, many people were glad to have Rob and his colleagues around.

21

Preparing for War – BATUS, Canada

Combat training for today's soldiers is a vital precursor to their being sent to engage in the realities of warfare and armed strife. A feature of this training involves various battle groups in a trip to Canada, where, since 1972, the wide prairie land of Alberta has provided a base for the British Army to conduct large-scale training exercises. The territory available to them for their war games is seven times larger than the battle area on Salisbury Plain and it is known as BATUS – the British Army Training Unit Suffield, the hamlet of Suffield being the nearest residential area. BATUS is equipped with over 1,000 vehicles, including Challenger 2 tanks and Warrior Infantry Fighting Vehicles. Five battle groups, each comprising around 1,400 troops, train at BATUS each year, in exercises which last up to thirty days and which include realistic live firing training at all levels. One of the army regiments acts as the 'enemy'.

With so many people involved, medical cover is a necessity, providing primary care to cope with the inevitable occurrences of sickness and accidents. Today, in a tri-service world of military nursing, some PMs have been posted out to help man the BATUS medical centre during these exercises. Most of them have found it a wonderful career experience as well as a fine opportunity to enjoy the delights of western Canada.

Rachel Frearson spent four eventful months out at BATUS:

> That's where all of the infantry guys go to prepare before they go out to Afghanistan. They have a 1,000 kilometre-square training ground on the prairie bad lands – mosquitoes, coyotes, gophers – they take all their Challengers and their Warriors and do a four-week exercise where they battle against each other. I was there in the Med Centre, nine-to-five doing primary health care and anything else that comes in off the exercise, and after five o'clock you're up to your own devices and … anything that comes through the door. Plenty of fighting injuries … we had a couple of fractured jaws while I was there. Plenty of soft tissue injuries, people falling down gopher holes and ruining themselves that way! Just, all sorts. I got pushed out to do a medical briefing in front of 150-odd infantry Guards, which was absolutely frightening!

But I loved it. I got to go kayaking off the Broken Islands off the west coast of Vancouver, with the Gazelle flight – they have the Gazelle helicopters out there – and we went on a little expedition with the hump-back whales and the sea-lions, bald-headed eagles … We just travelled round from one island to the next, unpacked our kayaks and put up our tents, cooked our food, caught salmon, crabs … It was just beautiful. I never thought I'd ever be able to do that. The army have the opportunity to go outside of British Columbia, they get two weeks dedicated to training, so they can do that and all the activities like white-water rafting, quad-biking, mountain biking, horse-riding in the Rockies. So it was an interesting little place, in the middle of nowhere. I think when we set off to go to Vancouver, driving down the trans-Canadian highway, we put the satnav on and it was 1,700 kilometres to the next left turning!

I wasn't too sorry to leave because I wasn't really interested in being in the medical centre and dealing with minor injuries. At the time it's the 'twisted-sock' people, so not very interesting. I prefer A&E, that's the place for me.

Another time, it was Kim Wilson whose name came up:

I went to the British Army Unit Suffield (BATUS), in Canada and was there five months, August to December. My main position was to be the aeromed liaison officer, but I found when I got over there that it was all-hands-on-deck, so everyone just chipped in. Basically, they do a lot of the Exercises before Afghan. There's a Med Centre, and then a bedding-down facility, called an MRS [Medical Reception Station]. I was working in the MRS, looking after people that had come in with injuries off the ground, and we'd also help out in the Med Centre and do sick parade, which was really good – a different style of nursing, like basic first aid in some senses, like assessing, and although I'd worked on the assessment unit in Peterborough, this was completely different because it was fresh injuries, so it was like a triage. It was good, because you had the juniors to look after, which you don't always get the opportunity to do at the hospital; you had people to mentor, and then more experienced people that you could get help from. Also, it would be open 24/7, so people could come in whenever to get triaged, and [it could be] just you by yourself, because the medic would be asleep. I found it really challenging but I learned a lot from it.

The banter amongst the patients was fun as well – something you don't really get as much in the NHS! There was one day when I had over-worked in the gym and could hardly walk. When I went in for my shift, one of the patients, a sergeant, saw me and came running over and got me a chair and practically shoved me into it. He then started doing my blood pressure and other obs., mocking me as he did it – but all in good fun! He and the other patients looked after me that shift, getting me cups of tea and ice for my legs, lined up for me to take their observations. Don't suppose that would have happened in the NHS.

> I got to do some adventure training. I did a week's horse-riding. Like an expedition – we got the horse and trekked off for a week. I haven't ridden since I was little, so that was really good – being a cow-girl! I learned a lot, on the work side, clinically speaking, but it also gave me the opportunity to explore Canada. I did a trip to Vancouver, I went skiing quite a lot, I went to a rodeo … The people who were on Exercise didn't get that opportunity, they were there purely working for six weeks, then they had one five-day stint off, so when you saw that you felt lucky. That's what you hope for when you join the military, and because the opportunities aren't as many as they were, you've got to grab them when you've got them.

Afghanistan, 2012

In Afghanistan, the efforts of the International Security Assistance Force (ISAF) to quell the insurgency and restore some sort of order continued unabated. But in some respects the situation was growing worse: the insurgents grew bolder and more desperate; innocent Afghani civilians were threatened and blackmailed into helping them; seemingly friendly members of the Afghan police and army suddenly became suicide bombers. As casualties mounted so more and more questions were asked about the validity of the war, whether its mission could ever end in success.

Old and new members of the PMRAFNS were deployed for tours of duty at Camp Bastion, near Kandahar, some within a very short while after their training ended. In 2013, some of them spoke of their personal experiences, both good and bad.

For Kay Griffiths:

> My main memories are, probably, staying up late at night watching the aircraft leave, waiting for 'Wheels Up'. For me, that's one of the best points. You'd finished your job, waved the aircraft off [taking patients back to UK] and you knew that on that day you'd achieved quite a bit. Even on bad days, most of the time everyone laughed through it, though some of the humour might not be acceptable to a lot of other people, but there were always days when you'd end up joking about completely random things, just to get through it together. I was out there at Christmas. People who'd got children were finding it difficult, but you wouldn't see them upset that often because there were so many other things going off. Actually, Christmas was really nice out there, we had different services – carols and things – so even though you're there, away from your families, you still get through as a group.

Having done aeromeds in Kosovo in the 1990s, then from a hospital ship in the Iraq war, and having run clinics for Afghan children in Kabul, Nikki Duncan returned to Afghanistan in 2012, based at Camp Bastion:

> That was a completely different experience. I can't believe how busy we were. I started off doing aeromed, for the first month, just flying from Bastion into

Cyprus. I was quite enjoying doing the flying because I hadn't been away for quite a while, I'd had my children … and that's what we joined to do, to fly people back, it was a real pleasure because you're not just flying our UK guys you're flying all the locals, all around the country – they need to be moved out of the hospital. But actually flying our guys is what you get the buzz from, especially people who are quite poorly, they need to be back with their families, back in this country. And if you've got a big flight of squaddies they're just so much fun, they have a good sense of humour, just 'make the best of it', so you do have fun as well as looking after them.

'I worked on the wards, in Camp Bastion,' says Anthony Beynon:

It was all hard standing, a proper building, but only one storey. It had been like that for a couple of years, but they'd just built this new forty-bed ward. When you arrive, you really feel as if you're in a different place. It doesn't feel as if you are in the middle of nowhere, because where you are is so populated, so many people, so much stuff around you, it doesn't really feel as if you're in the middle of conflict, but you're on the edge, don't quite know what's going to happen next … You just get on with it, everyone's in the same boat. You make of it what you will. You can go out there and be really boring, or you can take every opportunity … go down to the flight line, the midnight Pedro run, which was fantastic.

PEDRO is basically the American Air Force version of MERT, but the PEDRO has a Black Hawk helicopter and they paint a moustache on it – hence 'Pedro'. The 'Pedro run' happens every full moon, where you run 5K down the flight line, in the middle of the night. It's really good. Everyone who's not working goes for this run. It's done for charity and you get a good T-shirt. The Dutch do a walk, as well, where you march in your kit. There's a lot of charity work goes on out there, it's a good way for everyone to get together and have fun.

During Anthony's sojourn in the hospital at Camp Bastion, the ward where he worked was half for military patients, including the Afghanistan National Army, the Afghanistan National Police and the ISAF, and half for Afghani civilians:

We almost always had at least five local patients, which was very interesting and also quite challenging because they had worse wounds than the patients you had on the other side. We do as much as we can do, but … sometimes it's a case of, just go home, though you know that when you transfer them on they're not getting the care that we might give.

[However] for badly wounded military patients, the transfer out is really quick. One came in one day and he left the next. It just depends if we've got the aircraft ready, but they do a really good job, getting them back.

More memories of that big forty-bed ward remain with Kirsty Scott, who says:

> It's a big learning curve. The clinical skills you learn out there are completely different to what you get at home. The ward that we were on, a forty-bedded ward, we had surgical HDU patients, coming straight from surgery. The Afghan patients that I had, triple amputations, bi-lateral amputees, they'd had major surgery and they came to us and … something I've never dealt with before. Here in the UK we use a scoring system called the MEW (Modified Early Warning) score: depending on a patient's observations, it can give us an indication how poorly they are, if they're getting better or deteriorating. Here we worry when it gets to four or more, whereas over there they'd come to us and were, like, twelve. And that would be their norm. It was a massive learning curve, and then chest-drains, and different dressings, and the language barrier … You couldn't find out if they were in pain, you couldn't find out what they wanted. We did have interpreters out there, but having to bleep for an interpreter every two minutes …
>
> We had a lot of the Afghan army. Very rarely had UK guys, but if we did … our guys would come in with back pain, or they'd hurt themselves, set something off and injured themselves, not massively injured. If they were involved in an IED incident, or something, they went straight to the ITU ward and then they were aeromedded back to Birmingham. So we got a lot of the Afghan soldiers, who were twelve years old and up. We had a couple of kiddies, as well, that had been involved in IED blasts, and the detainees, but mostly it was Afghan personnel that we had, Afghan army, Afghan police.
>
> With the kiddies … it was difficult. They're quite different to what our kids are. They don't know how to play. You give them a book, they're not interested, you give them a DVD player, they're not interested … They don't smile. If they've got pain and they're crying, their elder – whoever's looking after them – will say something and you never hear anything out of them again. It took a long time for them to come out of their shell and actually learn how to play and interact with us. They didn't want anything to do with us. It was obviously scary for them, and some of them came in without parents, because the parents had been killed in the incident, so they'd come in with an elder, could be just somebody who was in the village, not related to them, but classed as their next of kin because they didn't have anyone else.

Asked if she managed to hide her distress at such times, Kirsty said:

> I did, though I don't know how, because I'm the softest person there is. I think it was just, in the moment, you did what you were doing. When you got back to your room, thinking about it was a bit upsetting, but … there's a lot of support out there, from your colleagues, and your line managers.
>
> The really upsetting thing was, the Afghan army people, if they came in, the older guys, they never wanted to go back to the Afghan hospitals because they knew they

> wouldn't get the treatment that they were getting in our hospital. They would cry and say, 'Please don't send me, they'll kill me …' That was the worst thing. If they'd lost their leg, or something like that, especially a female, a little girl, who'd lost her leg, if she was going back to her family there'd be no use for her, she wouldn't be able to do anything, to earn a living, so she'd just be a burden to the family. So it would depend on how wealthy the family was, as to the outcome that little girl, or little boy, would have. But you tried not to think about that. You can't keep them in the hospital for ever.
>
> We put all this money, and time, into looking after these people, giving them the best care in the world, and then you send them back to a hospital that … within days they just go downhill. And the prosthetic limbs … whereas here they measure their stumps to fit the prosthetic limb, and get it remeasured, because obviously they shrink with time, in Afghanistan they just find any prosthetic leg, if there are any left, if they get one … of course there's no such thing as wheelchairs, they're very sparse …
>
> Despite all that, I did enjoy it. You might have a really crap day at work but you could go out and just get a coffee, sit with loads of people and have a laugh, a good time, good banter with people. Everybody's in the same situation.

Hearts and minds

While caring for the sick and wounded, British forces are also engaged in the battle to win hearts and minds among Afghani people. Mental nurse Rob Morris had a chance to interact with some of the locals who came to the medical facilities for care. He regarded it as part of:

> the hearts and minds effort. If we're around, wearing a big red cross, they'll come and speak to us. The average local Afghan is a very nice chap. You don't get to speak to the women, that's culturally sensitive, but the chaps are nice and the kids are lovely. The people causing the problems are not the locals, not the farmer down the street; it's insurgent activity, people coming in from other countries using Afghanistan as their own personal war zone.
>
> In the areas that have a heavy UK presence, like Helmand, the locals are reoccupying the villages where they weren't safe to live because of the planted explosives, the IEDs, or because of Taliban pressure. But the Taliban have moved out, we've gone in and cleared the IEDs, so they're coming back to their homes. It's really nice to see that positive side of it.

A chap who called himself 'Safety Steve' (being involved with health and safety issues) produced a series of 'Letters from the Front' which were regularly published back in the UK. In one of these, he described an outreach visit which involved senior PM Kev Mackie. This reads:

> The other day, the Chief UK nurse gave an excellent account of an outreach visit that he and a French medical team had carried out to a local village. The next time you read the appalling *Daily Mail* or hear someone moaning about our NHS, please poke them in the eye from me. Kev described the conditions that some of the sick were undergoing, often quite needlessly. Most were suffering from bacterial infections and lung conditions which were easily treated by simple antibiotics. The nearest medical facility 40km away is often unmanned and a trip to the nearest hospital unaffordable. The most poignant example he gave was of an 8-year-old girl who was losing her sight to a parasitical infestation. Without treatment she would have been blind in six months, [yet] two weeks on and she is almost completely cured. Kev and his team are making a real difference here and it's good to serve alongside him. He described their return to the village two weeks later as wonderful, they were greeted like returning messiahs.

'The Battle of Bastion'

While some of the local people may have been grateful for the help they received, others remained actively hostile. At frequent times the huge camp, its airfield and its hospital came under direct attack from rockets and shells fired from home-made mobile launching pads set up in the desert beyond the perimeter. Usually the insurgents would set off their weapons and swiftly vanish back among the dusty hills, but occasionally their assault was more prolonged, as the PMs involved remember all too well.

Kirsty Scott had joined the PMRAFNS because, as she said:

> I wanted to be part of the story. I was looking forward to doing my first tour in Afghanistan. In fact, I returned from there only a few months ago, in October last year [2012]. It was what I'd expected, if not better. But it was definitely an eventful tour. We were there when the Battle of Bastion happened, when it all kicked off … We did forty-hour shifts that week.
>
> I was coming off night-shift for a stand-down day and we got a call over the intercom saying that we had to report back to work and everybody had to be checked by numbers, to make sure everybody was there. When we got there, there were mixed stories about what was going on. We could see a fire in the distance as we were walking from our accommodation lines to the hospital about five minutes away, but we just thought something had happened on the airfield. Then one of the commanders told us that there'd been an attack near the airfield and about eighteen insurgents had got in. They'd used a suicide bomber to blow a hole in the wall. Some of them had already been on camp, apparently, infiltrated as civilian workers, some of them were wearing US Marine uniforms. This was what we were told. It was all hearsay at this point.
>
> We were told there were quite a lot of casualties – UK and US casualties – coming in, so we had to open one of the overflow wards, a second A&E, and we were going

> to triage them, but because I wasn't on shift my team was going to use Ward 2 to look after the guys that were coming off the ground.
>
> I think we had about eight guys come in with different injuries. Some came with blast injuries, or fragmentation wounds. One had been shot in the leg … It was quite scary, especially because you don't expect anything like that to happen, you feel quite safe when you're there in Bastion. Our guys were on the roof, obviously, making sure nobody was getting onto the hospital grounds, and we were told, if we heard gunfire, to get our weapons ready, be prepared to fire back. That was the bit … it reminded you it was all actually real!
>
> It took about two and a half days to get them all. Most of them were killed and they were brought back to the morgue at the hospital the next day, but we had one in the hospital with us, that was shot but not killed. He stayed in ITU for a while and then he came to the ward.

Kirsty had imagined it would be difficult to take care of men who had been attacking Camp Bastion, but in the event she says:

> I kind of distanced myself and didn't think about what they'd done. Quite a lot of them did what they did because either they were blackmailed, or their families were threatened. And some of them just didn't care, they could be quite rude. But you just did what you had to do, gave them the care they needed and then left. Most of them had guard on guard, one-to-one, for our protection, but most of them were well-behaved. Of course, they didn't like the fact that women were looking after them. They were a bit intimidated by us.

Sergeant Sarah Perkins recalls her time in Afghanistan as:

> a busy and challenging tour, one I will never forget. The night I arrived Camp Bastion was attacked; the 'Battle of Bastion' it was referred to afterwards. The attack started not long after I landed. It was such a bizarre and surreal experience, you could hear the firing and Apaches [helicopters] flying over; but we were unaware of what was happening fully until the next day. It continued to be busy for my first couple of weeks, as a result of the Battle of Bastion; I had to learn quickly and essentially hit the ground running.
>
> Another surreal experience was a female soldier being admitted with abdominal pain, only to go into labour and give birth to a baby boy. She had been unaware that she was pregnant and had been involved in frontline duties right up until she was bought into the hospital at Camp Bastion. My role was to organise her and the baby's safe transfer home to the UK. I never thought I would be organising something like that!

Life is never dull, or predictable, for an RAF nurse!

Stephen Doyle was heavily involved in training Afghan army medics who were billeted in the huge Afghan Army training camp just outside the gates of Camp Bastion and the adjoining Camp Leatherneck, a US Marine Corps base. Stephen said:

> [I] used to go there quite regularly for meetings and things. They had a small medical facility, with doctors – well, I think they were doctors, but in Afghanistan anyone with any real education, especially if they worked in the health service, would call themselves a doctor. So, the X-ray tech. was a doctor; the pharmacist was a doctor, the dentist was a doctor ... They had a medical facility – a small emergency room, a bedding down ward, but with hardly any patients ... what stopped them progressing was the fact that they had a Role 2 hospital across the street [in Camp Bastion], so at the drop of a hat they would just bring all their casualties to us. Practically sick parade stuff, at times.

Wing Commander Sonia Phythian had been OC Nursing at the MDHU Peterborough for just three months when, in 2011, she found herself:

> deployed back on Op Herrick, to the Role 3 at Camp Bastion. Four years on, the Camp had expanded and was much larger than when I left there in 2007. I couldn't believe it when I went back; it had grown from a few tents in the desert to hardened buildings and massive infrastructure.

Sonia's task was to establish a new role as OC Deployed Aeromed Squadron, designed to co-ordinate the three different teams who made up the aeromed element. These were the airfield staging unit, known as 'Tac and Strat' (Tactical and Strategic), the medical emergency response team (MERT) and the critical care air support team (CCAST) – twenty-seven people in all. Sonia was to draw them all together to work as a squadron. She was also employed full-time as aeromed liaison officer (ALO), so she was grateful to have some efficient deputies working alongside her. She found it a satisfying experience, despite the demanding work involved:

> I would get up at four-thirty in the morning, be in work by five and I would finish any time in the evening, depending on whether we had flights; sometimes it would be ten or eleven o'clock at night. Sometimes I'd work through into the morning if we had a CCAST transfer because I always wanted to be there to welcome the CCAST from the UK and make sure everything was in order for them to evacuate the patient. I did that every day for the four months so it was hard work, but I don't think I could have done it any other way. As the first person in the job I wanted to make sure I made a good foundation for the Squadron to build on. The introduction of the OC DAS was a trial initiated in response to assurance visits conducted

by HQ Air Med Ops and I am unsure whether the concept will be included in future doctrine.

But, again, the good aspects and results are all down to the people and their hard work. Some of the Squadron personnel were young and militarily inexperienced and could be side-lined, particularly if they had not deployed previously … but actually they are massively talented and completely professional. And that's what is needed, someone to spot their skills and give them the opportunity to flourish.

Working with NHS staff

Having completed their tour of duty, members of the PMRAFNS return to the UK and take up their everyday work in hospitals and other medical units. The transition can be trying since their civilian colleagues inside the NHS don't always understand exactly what the service nurses have been doing. Certainly in the early days of military nurses working within the NHS a fair amount of misunderstanding prevailed. However, thanks to some good coverage in the media – for instance, doctors and nurses figured prominently in the excellent Channel 4 series *The RAF in Afghanistan* – allied with presentations made inside hospitals to acquaint non-service colleagues with the facts, these difficulties are slowly being resolved.

Where problems do remain, the PMs take it all philosophically. With dry humour, Lee Bond observes:

> Nurses like to think they're the hardest workers in the world. They're not happy unless they've not had a lunch break, not slept for twenty-five hours … So, when SAC Smith comes back, as a medic, back [from deployment], they go, 'Oh, have a good holiday?' At times it was, 'You're just using it as excuse not to be at work' … But add a third dimension to it and bring that patient back, all of a sudden that's more credible. It's real. When they look at it and think, 'We couldn't transfer a patient like that, we haven't got the capability, or the skill-sets.' In a very short space of time, the relationship between us and Selly Oak unit was, I'd say, a lot more collaborative, a lot more open, because they understood what we were about. There's a lot more transparency now, for a lot of reasons. People are encouraged to talk about their experiences, [or maybe] it's a presentation. It gets that message across: this is what we do.

'They were probably a bit scared of us,' is Nikki Duncan's assessment of relationships in the early days:

> they didn't know what we were all about. Plus we had our own wards, so we weren't mixed in with them; although we had NHS patients, all our wards were staffed by pure military. So the other nurses didn't really speak to us. It was quite strange for everyone and it has taken years to integrate. But we've had the mixed wards, the NHS and the military working together, which has obviously helped things. People

> don't quite understand, when we go out on deployment, that we're not away on holiday for four months. They say, 'Well, you've been away for four months so now you can work weekends.' But we've done a lot of presentations to let them know what we're actually doing, and when they see it then it hits home and they understand better. Also over the last few years there've been a lot of programmes on TV which have helped.

Kay Griffiths agrees:

> Some of the civilians didn't always mix well with the military personnel. However, over time, as you got over the barriers, the fact that you wear uniform … when you explain everything to do with your job, people are a lot more accommodating. If there is any friction at any time, it's usually down to them not really knowing what you do … One of the big things is, 'Oh, you've been on holiday'! But the longer conflicts go on, and with a lot more publicity, I think the awareness has increased. The last place I worked, I didn't have any problems at all.

When Anthony Beynon returned from Afghanistan some of his civilian colleagues assumed he'd been having a nice break. 'I suppose it's hard for them to understand what you are doing over there, when they're at home doing the same thing over and over again.'

'We all work together very well,' says Rachel Frearson. 'They say things like, "How was your jolly?" but people get very easily jaded in the NHS, they're overworked, the paperwork … whereas we can get a break, go to a different environment, and come back with new eyes, refreshed.'

Sarah Perkins finds that:

> Sometimes it can be frustrating, when there is a lack of understanding regarding military training and courses and all they comprehend is that we're having time away from the ward. Most NHS staff comment that they like working with military staff – mainly due to our work ethic and efficiency. Although, I feel like the NHS managerial staff expect too much of us sometimes; allocating us the more demanding patients. This is a good challenge; however, it can be exhausting at times.

Perhaps it helps if the nurse involved began life in the NHS and only later came into the military; Kirsty Scott has certainly found this to be so:

> Being a civilian nurse from the beginning, I don't feel any different when I'm on the ward. I'm doing exactly the same as I would do as a civilian nurse. The only thing is, I wear a different uniform. But I'm exactly the same as them, we all work together as a team and you know you can rely on them, as they know they can rely on you. Some of them get a bit … well, not upset, but we do get some 'military

> time', for instance we'll do four days a week on the ward and then one of the days we'll go off and do some military time – leadership, team-building … On some wards there used to be some problems. The ward I'm on [at the moment], the emergency short stay ward (ESS), it's better than some wards I've heard about. Also, with us being near an RAF base, quite a lot of the civilian nurses have partners who are in the forces, or have been in the forces, so they know the situation.

It can be equally difficult for some PMs to return from the dramas of a combat zone to humdrum everyday concerns, as Stephen Doyle explains:

> The guys working in ED out there [emergency department at Bastion], they're getting by default more exposure, more interesting things to do; it's difficult for them to come back working in the NHS because … the *huge* problems that they think they have here pale into insignificance … It's taking a step back, really, back to working in a normal environment where it's the off-duty that's the main problem.

Stress management

As the general public learns more about the effects of combat on the men and women involved, questions arise about the resulting emotional stress. PM Lee Bond, with much aeromedical experience, is very much aware of the need for what he calls 'decompression' – that is, ways of combatting stress. After being in war-torn Iraq, he remembers sharing his concerns with a senior officer, that if something was not done to alleviate the emotional stress created by combat, then:

> You're going to have a lot of problems with people … It's different when you come back to a place like this [Peterborough hospital], because you're all like-minded individuals, on the whole, but when they [the patients] are going back to other MDHUs and Med Centres … a lot of them, fresh out of nappies …

He explained that emotional stress could be broken down into four stages:

> The first was pre-deployment, the second was deployment, the third was post-deployment, but the fourth one has been identified as a point post-post-deployment …. But how far down the line do you keep an eye on that person? Often it's the case that people will come back to the unit, spend a few days, put their leave in, have a chat with the line manager, do a post-tour interview …. [then] a gradual introduction back into work.
>
> Pre-deployment, they should have a recognised 'buddy', as it's classed, so that when they're out of area the buddy will have regular contact with the families. That's the way it should work. It's a formalised approach to looking after someone that's out in Afghanistan, or Iraq, or wherever … That didn't exist before.

In his role as a mental nurse, working frequently with the army, Rob Morris has also dealt with stress, though in his opinion military patients do not have as many emotional health problems as may be imagined:

> People often think we must be inundated with PTSD [post-traumatic stress disorder] because of the terrible things people see … and whilst we do get some, they are well trained, well looked after, very good stress management, specially over the last eight years in the military, and that is reflected in the type of referrals we get. I think, per head of the population, we are not much different from the NHS. It's very rare that we see anyone with an acute psychosis – maybe three cases in my nineteen years – although people who leave service may go on to develop PTSD, so that becomes more of a problem for veterans' agencies. It can take years. We still have people from the Falklands Islands conflict presenting for the first time – thirty years on.

Stress can affect doctors and nurses, too. While in Iraq, on aeromed duty one night, Lee Bond:

> was just taking my boots off and … you always used to listen, if ever there was a shout you'd hear them running out of the ops room going, 'Quick, quick! Gotta go!' Just got my boots off and I heard something going off. It was an improvised explosive device that hit a patrol. We went out in a Merlin, it was phenomenal, but it was a difficult landing – he had to get it as close to this motorway bridge as he possibly could and it took a lot of manoeuvring. We ran up onto the bridge and went to see the commander to begin with, because we were concerned that there might be secondary devices, and he was just shell-shocked – no response, no information forthcoming – the only thing to do was proceed and find out what had happened. There was me and there was a doc – a very junior doc – a junior medical officer, from primary health care, so … There were three casualties, two fatalities and one that was critically ill, needed to get back to hospital pretty quickly. Very difficult scenario, because … we're not there for the dead, we're there for the living, but their mates want to believe that they're salvageable, they're willing you to take them … I remember going down and there was this one guy … no signs of life, we checked him. Basically, he'd got no rib-cage, it had taken his chest away, but they'd covered him back up, so at first sight … and it's dark … and you get up off the floor and your trousers are wet, and it's blood … The other chap … The young doctor was panicking, she couldn't get a line in. I managed to get a line in, got him some fluids – he'd lost his leg below the knee. We took him back to Shibar and.. he did quite well, actually, he did OK, he survived, but …
>
> We got back, we delivered the patient, we came back to Basra and … I said to the guys, 'We've been on a shout, little bit hairy, I want to witness you unload your

> weapons,' and of course the doctor was so shook-up that she cocked her rifle, so I said, 'Just take it off, ma'am, just move away, I'll do your NSPs [normal safety procedures].' It just goes to show you how much it effects people. Big job, two fatalities, young lads, eighteen or nineteen … And all that was never briefed to people, because … to be fair, I don't suppose the system knew that that's what the case would be and just maybe they didn't anticipate the levels of trauma that we were going to be witnessing.

Lee firmly believes, however, that they are always learning new ways to save more lives, because of 'the equipment that we've got out there today, the combat application tourniquets and the various Haemostatic agents that are available – *and* the better training'.

Stephen Doyle adds:

> The way we look at casualties has turned on its head over the years. Whereas twenty, thirty years ago, an [operations] officer would give out his plans, 'Synchronise watches and … oh, oh, anything for the medics? No? Good, fine.' … nowadays, it's 'Medics, what can you provide, can you cover us?' And if the medics can't cover a troop insert, or an operation, then it takes a brave commander to give that go ahead without medical cover these days.

If warfare can be said to have a positive side, this could be it – the fact that under combat conditions medical teams are always learning, always striving to improve. Certain wounds can never be mended, but, as Kay Griffiths reveals:

> The one thing we have come across is the amount of research, the amount of advances in medicine as a result of conflict. You wouldn't ever want people to be injured, but if they are, then hopefully through research … we can't get people's limbs back for them, but we can aim to do the best for them … see someone walking, feel we've done the best possible we can for them, then that's good.
>
> Again, I was lucky in that I worked in the Royal Neuro-Disability Hospital in London, [which] cares for patients who have severe life-long conditions, neurological and disabling illness or injury. A few people had been admitted after attempting to end their own life – not military personnel – some of them could only communicate by blinking. You think, are we doing the right thing or are we not? But when I talked to them … Some of them said, 'I did want to end my life then, but now I can see my family grow up …' The hospital also used advances in research to help improve or return an individual's quality of life and at times to give a person back their independence. The experience I gained showed me how advances in healthcare could really make such an enormous impact in a person's life.

Kim Wilson experienced similar feelings during her posting to the Defence Medical Rehabilitation Centre (DMRC) Headley Court, in Surrey, where amputees and polytrauma patients are cared for. Kim went there very soon after completing her training. She says:

> When I'd finished my rotation programme I went straight to Headley Court on detachment. I wasn't sure how that would be, but I think it helped you improve in areas that you didn't have time to concentrate on in the NHS. Sometimes, even though you don't mean it to, communication can go out of the window a bit, but when you've got the time to talk you are gaining skills. People think, to be a nurse you've got to be running round like an idiot, but you don't. I found it really interesting, and an honour to work with people who have actually sacrificed part of themselves for the military. The majority of them were really quite positive, so it was humbling. Two patients I looked after had only one arm left – they'd lost their legs and one of their arms – and the way they dealt with it was really remarkable. Also, to see people who wanted to be independent, but found it hard, seeing their improvement, just in the couple of months I was there, was lovely.

22

Back in the UK

At home, a series of government reviews and rearrangements called for reduction in numbers of all three services. RAF stations which had operated for years were closed, much to the regret of both people living nearby and the many serving men and women who had fond memories of those bases. Among them was RAF Innsworth in Gloucestershire. Innsworth opened in 1940 as a training station for new recruits and later for members of the WAAF; it also became an administration centre, housing RAF Records, and from 1997 was home to Personnel and Training Command, including the head offices of the PMRAFNS, where matron-in-chief and the rest of headquarters staff sat when at work.

In 2005 the imminent closure of RAF Innsworth was announced. At the same time, Personnel and Training Command merged with Strike Command and a new facility named HQ Air Command came into being, based at RAF High Wycombe, Buckinghamshire. HQ Air officially opened on 1 April 2007.

90th anniversary of the PMRAFNS

The year 2008 saw the celebration of ninety years of the PMRAFNS. The main celebration was a cocktail party in the RAF Museum at Hendon, attended by Royal Patron HRH the Princess Alexandra, Matron-in-Chief Group Captain Jackie Gross, a cheery squadron of former matrons-in-chief, along with retired and serving PMs of all ranks. Princess Alexandra was presented with a bouquet and she took care to speak to everyone present, including the four musicians from the RAF Central Band, who provided suitable music. The evening included an introduction, by the author of this book, to a new video about the history and work of the PMRAFNS which may be seen on display in the museum. It was a happy occasion enjoyed by all. However … in an unfortunate juxtaposition of events, the following year saw the announcement of yet more cuts to the services.

2010 Strategic Defence and Security Review

The Strategic Defence and Security Review (SDSR), announced by the British government in May 2010, was published on 19 October that year. It decreed that, since the largest overseas deployment in the future was expected to number no more than 30,000 personnel in all – army, navy and air force units – all three services would take cuts in manpower. Considering that the invasion of Iraq involved 45,000 personnel, to many minds the new cuts seemed draconian.

For the RAF, the review planned the closure of yet more stations, though others would be upgraded to accommodate new aircraft and different operational methods. As this book goes to press it is still too soon to predict how these changes will affect people working in the services, though the headline figures give cause for concern. The RAF is to be reduced to 33,500 personnel by 2015 and 31,500 by 2020. A two-year pay freeze is in place and there may be changes to pension and tax allowances.

In his comments on the review, Chief of Staff Personnel and Air Secretary, Air Vice-Marshal Mike Lloyd, said:

> We have taken significant reductions in capability with the withdrawal of Nimrod and the Harrier Force, which is very sad because both forces have given outstanding service over many years and served their country well.
>
> A major concern is the compound effect that the outcome of SDSR has on our people. We are going through a period of uncertainty and change and part of the challenge is to look after our people whilst managing that change.

AVM Lloyd added:

> Fewer bases will help our intent for people to have longer tours in locations which will give families greater stability and so reduce some of the negative effects of the previous levels of mobility. In time, partners should be able to keep the same employment for longer and children should be able to enjoy greater educational stability. We are also seeking to support people's aspirations for home ownership. However, the long term goal is going to be greater stability in the future and therefore we are changing career management structures to be ready to enable this.

The SDSR of 2010 presaged, among many other cuts and closures, the demise of the only remaining UK military hospital overseas.

TPMH Cyprus closes

During its busiest period in the early 1970s, the Princess Mary Hospital at Akrotiri, Cyprus, was handling 20,000 outpatients and 5,000 in-patients every year. In the first decade of the twenty-first century, the facilities at the hospital reduced to only two wards – the maternity ward and a twenty-two-bed adult ward, though on average only a handful of patients at any one time required overnight stays. The time had come for the last permanent British military hospital to close its doors.

The announcement caused much sadness among those who had enjoyed working at the hospital over fifty years, but, despite being faced by the prospect of closure, the staff organised a year of celebrations to mark the fiftieth anniversary of TPMH. It had transferred from its original temporary site in 1963 and proudly taken the name of the first Royal Patron of the PMRAFNS. Its last full day of clinical activity was 31 October 2012, and the building formally ended its days as a hospital in April 2013.

The island still provides a home for British servicemen and their families, at RAF Akrotiri and at the army base in Dhekelia. Primary care is now provided for them by medical centres of British Forces Cyprus at RAF Akrotiri, Dhekelia, Episkopi or Nicosia Garrison and by the civilian hospitals of the republic of Cyprus. Secondary care, for those who require hospital treatment, takes place at the Ygia Polyclinic in Limassol.

The work goes on …

In the UK today, the MDHUs remain busy despite the fact that their nurses frequently vanish for several months at a time on deployment. Peterborough remains the city where the largest contingent of PMs are employed; their uniforms and smart appearance are much in evidence when patients and visitors pass through the magnificent atrium of the huge new City Hospital.

Peterborough MDHU moved to the newly built hospital in 2010 and began welcoming patients immediately. Its official opening came two years later when, on 28 November 2012, Prince William, Duke of Cambridge and his beautiful Duchess visited the city amid much excitement. Several PMs, as well as other members of the hospital's staff, were introduced to the royal couple and Wing Commander Kev Mackie, then CO of the MDHU, had the honour of escorting the Duchess on her tour of the hospital.

The MDHU employs more than 150 military consultants, junior doctors, nurses and registered health and care professionals. They are 'parented' by RAF Wittering, which gives them a base to live and relax in the 'blue' air force environment which they all enjoy.

Do military nurses regret the end of single-service hospitals?

The original version of this history, written in 2000, looked back on the then-recent closure of the big RAF hospitals with regret and misgiving. Have attitudes changed in the ensuing decade, with its terrible wars and consequences of wars?

Warrant Officer Debbie Meikle has been nursing long enough to remember the 'good old' days, but she was also there in the early days of the Royal Centre for Defence Medicine in Birmingham:

> We will never go back to our own military hospitals but, in the long run, I think it's a good thing. I've worked in the old hospitals and they were good, and often quite busy. The patients used to get fantastic nursing care, because generally we did have better staff-to-patient ratios, but we didn't have as much medical expertise. We only really did elective surgery, we didn't get so much trauma. Except during the Falklands War. Then we had Gulf War One, we were busy then.

But, having worked at Birmingham, and knowing the complex injuries that the ladies and gentlemen have, in the Forces ... some of them will be under seven or eight different consultants. I don't believe we would ever have been able to sustain that in our military hospitals.

Squadron Leader Stephen Doyle agrees, though he adds with nostalgia:

Don't get me wrong, I miss military hospitals. Looking back, that was a joy ... I originally worked in the Cambridge Military Hospital, for a little while, when I first joined, in Aldershot. That was interesting, a very old building with long 'Nightingale' wards. Which worked, I suppose – you could see all the patients. You were scared of Matron. The good old days when nurses looked very smart, still wore their tippets and head-dresses.

In retrospect, WO Lee Bond also believes that it is probably as well that the old service hospitals went out of commission, because:

we wouldn't have had the medical and clinical resources to deal with what's coming back from Afghanistan now. We hadn't got those facilities. Bed-capacity ... a well-oiled, multi-disciplinary routine that is pioneering in practice. That's what Birmingham offered. It was a good job we were there at the time, to receive that level of trauma. Of course, you never know whether you're going to cope with it until you're there doing the job in reality. You can simulate it as much as you like, but it's not until you're in the thick of it that you know whether you can possibly endure it.

Primary health care

Hospitals are not the only places where military nurses may be found. Wherever there is an RAF station or a military presence, there is access to medical care.

As we have noted, while many of the original RAF nursing sisters of 1918 had worked in hospitals, others had been posted to look after service personnel reporting on sick parades at station sick quarters. By 2000 these sisters had evolved into practice nurses. they offer primary care (doctor's-surgery style) at modern station medical centres across the UK and overseas, with the main focus on health education and preventive medicine. At present these medical centres remain under single-service control, army caring for soldiers, navy caring for sailors, so that those at RAF stations are staffed and run by air force personnel and cater mainly for air force patients – aircrew, ground-crew or other support staff, and, sometimes, families. The centres each employ a nursing officer or an NCO of the PMRAFNS (a few larger stations have both), and the work is both demanding and varied.

The first practice nurse at RAF Lossiemouth, in Scotland, was Debbie Gurney (Mrs Jones), who says, 'After many years of working in hospitals as part of a large team with numerous resources, I found myself working alone, at what appeared to be the "end of the world", with the nearest Nursing Officer working 300 miles away at RAF Leeming.' But Debbie soon had things organised, mornings taken up by routine appointments for blood tests, dressings and minor ailments:

> with the usual handful of accidents thrown in to keep me busy. I still find it amazing the number of people who 'walk' into aircraft. During the afternoons, as well as preparing patients for their medicals, I ran a 'Well Women's Clinic', immunisation clinics, and assisted the 'docs' with their minor op clinics.

In addition, Debbie found herself providing mobile emergency cover during flying operations, which at front-line Lossiemouth meant twenty-four hours a day. Two emergencies stick out in her mind: 'a Nimrod which, due to double engine fire, ditched into the Moray Firth; and a Jaguar which sustained double engine failure after a massive bird-strike and crashed into the sea. Luckily in both cases there were no fatalities, but plenty of 'tachycardias' in the Station Medical Centre.' She also spent some time training with Lossiemouth's Search and Rescue Squadron, assisting on one occasion in the rescue of a climber on Ben Nevis, and she spent a week in the sun while a Tornado squadron from 'Lossie' did armament practice at RAF Deccimommanu, on Sardinia. On leaving Lossiemouth she became the first practice nurse at another fast jet operational station, RAF Bruggen in West Germany.

Figures for 2000 show fifteen nursing officers and twenty-six NCOs in post at RAF station medical centres (SMCs), from Lyneham to Lossiemouth in the UK, and as diverse as Brunei and Ascension Island overseas. Squadron Leader Sharon Callcott, in charge of primary health care in the late 1990s, observes, 'With more posts becoming available on more stations, PMs are increasingly high-profile in the RAF – people no longer have to go to hospital to see one!'

By 2013 a few changes had, inevitably, been made. At SMCs now, the practice manager will be military and the practice nurses are usually PMs, but they might possibly be civilian nurses. However, as Wing Commander Sonia Phythian observes 'Some of the medical centres are small and run like satellite clinics from a nearby larger regional medical centre.' She adds that more changes may result from the move to Defence primary health care which took place on 1 April 2013; 'this has brought the delivery of primary health care under 2* command, but the delivery of patient care will remain cloth-on-cloth. The HQ is located at the Defence Medical Services (Whittington) and is currently headed by Air Vice Marshal Mozumder.'

Pride in being an RAF nurse

Whether in clinics, medical centres, huge modern hospitals at home or busy and bloody hospitals near a war front, all military nurses delight in their own uniform, their own service. Members of the PMRAFNS are, needless to say, immensely proud to wear the blue of the Royal Air Force and not afraid to express their pleasure:

'I've been lucky in that I've worked everywhere military patients have been,' says Kay Griffiths:

> so I've seen them from when they've come into hospital at Bastion to when they've been discharged. So, for me, being at Bastion sort of finished off the piece. Especially when they're coming up to being discharged and you know a little of what they've gone through … more often than not, they leave with a bit of a smile, at least.
>
> In fact, there's a lot more to being an air force nurse than I expected. When you talk to other people, especially people you've grown up with, or other nurses, when you compare the opportunities you've had, the PMs opens a lot more for you. Some of the experiences, the training courses … At the RAF Symposium, when we all get together, you realise all the things we're doing in the services. That's something both I and my family are quite proud of.

Sonia Phythian:

> saw the military as an opportunity to nurse in a variety of different areas, and I also liked the fact that the military recognise talent, irrelevant of your age, which, at the time, the NHS didn't really do – they expected you to be of a certain age before they deemed you capable of holding positions of leadership, whereas I wanted to develop and progress. I was drawn by the opportunities to nurse in more challenging environments and I do like the high standards of care, the working environment, the people … the desire to always do the best that you can. Because I felt that the NHS *at the time* – and I stress at the time because it may be different now – it always seemed to be a battle to maintain that high standard and be allowed to do the best for your patients, whereas the military engenders and promotes that way of working. That's what I liked about it.

Having begun his nursing career with QARANC, the army nursing service, Stephen Doyle transferred to the air force:

> Maybe because the PMs is a lot smaller branch than the QAs, there was straight away that management ethos of looking after you, seeing what you wanted, how they could make it happen, especially in my chosen specialism, which is Accident and Emergency. And it was the aeromed side of things which I was interested in.
>
> I've been lucky working in Peterborough. We do a lot of good training here, there's a lot of extended roles that emergency nurses are capable of. I work as a Nurse Practitioner here, as well, so I can see, diagnose, treat, send for X-rays, and discharge patients with minor injuries. I know other places where they're not as

> nurse-led, they're more doctor led, so doctors say,You can't do this, you can't do that … which is defeating the object of having military nurses in there – after all, they won't have a doctor hanging over them a lot of the time if they're out on operations. They have to crack on and use the skills they have.

It's the close, family-style relationships that Rob Morris selects for mention: 'The RAF is a big family and the PMs is a small family. I know so many people in the PMs, more intimately than my own family. Because we're a smaller branch than we were, that "family" feeling is getting stronger.'

Not only do the nurses enjoy being part of the military, their patients appreciate it too. Most nurses, when asked, were reluctant to give examples of praise, but Kim Wilson revealed:

> I think I've only had one military patient on [my current] ward, it's mostly civilians. They seem to enjoy being looked after by military nurses. Some of them say, 'Oh, you're much better than the civvies!' and you have to say, 'Shush, don't say things like that!' Especially the older generation. The younger generation just laugh – like when you have to call someone 'ma'am' or 'sir'. They look at you and start giggling.

Margaret Kingston, who retired as a squadron officer in 1971, saw it from a patient's viewpoint when, waiting in the outpatients' department at the old Peterborough hospital, she encountered a young PM:

> I was rather pleased … I went to this clinic and this girl came, and she looked so smart, and when she turned round I could see she was a sergeant PM. Got a nice little cap on and her dress was absolutely immaculate, and her sergeant's stripes up, so I called her over and I said, 'Excuse me, you're in the PMs, aren't you?' She looked at me, as much as to say, what's that old girl know about the PMs? So I told her I was a PM for twenty years. She was helping out at the Peterborough District Hospital – they've got a few wards there. And she looked so smart compared with the other girls.

The pride remains. Once a PM, always a PM!

Multi-skilled

In the twenty-first century, military nurses are far from the veiled and smiling 'angels' of fond memory, applying bandages and handing out pills. They're highly trained professionals both male and female, multi-skilled technicians in a tri-service environment where army, navy and air force work alongside each other as equal partners.

For instance, in the seventeen years since she joined the PMs, Sonia Phythian has fulfilled many roles, beginning at Haslar, Portsmouth:

> My first posting was to the Royal Hospital Haslar, which at the time was interesting because it was in 1996 and Defence had just closed all the single service hospitals in order to introduce new tri-service ways of working. Of course I didn't know any different so for me, working with both the Army and the Royal Navy as well as the RAF was great as I didn't have anything to compare it with. From here I moved into Primary Health Care, and worked as a Practice Nurse on a variety of stations both overseas and in the UK – some were flying stations, such as Wittering and Coltishall, and others were training stations, like Halton. The overseas medical centre I worked in was on Ascension Island, where I was the AELO [aeromedical evacuation liaison officer] as well as the Practice Nurse.
>
> During my time as a Practice Nurse I deployed to Saudi and Oman as part of a small medical team administering anthrax vaccinations to military personnel. The timing of this task was a little strange because the military operation within the region had reached stabilisation and then a medical team arrived in country to offer personnel a vaccination against anthrax. This was perceived as suspicious by the troops … normally people are pleased to see medics and nurses, but they weren't very welcoming because of our role. Administering the anthrax vaccination didn't match the political message for the Middle East … in that there was no threat and the situation within the region was stabilising … and then we arrived to offer the vaccination against anthrax? The messages were conflicting … They [the authorities] must have thought there was a real threat of anthrax being used as a biological weapon, but that didn't match with the political discussions going on at the time, so it was all a bit strange.

In 2000, Sonia undertook an out-of-branch posting to RAF College Cranwell, where for three years she commanded an initial officer training flight:

> My role was to train the officers of the future and it was brilliant! There had been only one PM who had previously completed this appointment – Gp Capt (Retd) Barry Wroe in 1993 – and so it was really good for the Branch to have a nurse involved again in training officer cadets through to their commission. It was great to work with the College staffs, who were from different branches of the RAF … this experience remains one of the best tours I have completed.

Some years later Sonia again found herself heading for Cranwell, as staff officer to the commandant:

> In addition to managing his workload I oversaw his outer office staff, including his aide-de-camp, driver, secretary and house staff. It was [a] two-year out of branch posting which I thoroughly enjoyed; to have a 1* as mentor, to guide and develop me was a privileged opportunity.

> I feel it is important that the wider RAF, and other services, are aware that nurses are massively capable and can do much more than deliver nursing care to their patients. We have a comprehensive skill-set, above our clinical and nursing knowledge that we can transfer and apply to other areas within the military. We have high standards, we are organised, we can communicate well, we can look at situations from other people's perspective, and all of those are useful skills to apply within a whole range of Defence activity.
>
> At the end of this two-year period I was awarded a place on the Advanced Command and Staff Course No 14 at the Defence Academy. There had been only one other nurse to previously attend Staff College and so this brought great kudos for the Branch. The course was an academic year in length and, although it was tough, it was an excellent experience and one where you learn as much about yourself as you do from achieving the Course objectives. In addition to the studying I had to complete, I took the option to also study for an MA and graduated with an MA in Defence Studies, majoring in political Islam.
>
> The Course was 300 people strong – made up of air force, army and navy from both the UK and overseas, with some senior MoD civil servants – and I finished in the top 20 per cent. It was mentally challenging but I left with a much better understanding of the international issues, from the perspective of the overseas students, who were from across the whole world. It was particularly interesting to hear their perspective on conflicts in which the PMs have been involved … both eye-opening and, at times, humbling.

At the time when she spoke of her career, Sonia Phythian was working within the Health Directorate at High Wycombe as SO1 Medical Personnel Capability, at HQ Air.

Flight Sergeant Nicola Duncan was working as a Practice Development nurse until July 2012 when she took over as Healthcare Governance lead at MDHU Peterborough. She found this:

> an interesting post. I investigate any incidents, any issues that we have happening in the hospital – patient safety, lessons learned, what we can do to improve things. I am surgically specialised. I've done high-dependency, but then for the last seven years I've been teaching, so I've done my teaching qualifications. So a bit of everything really. I'm a general nurse.

Nikki is rather more than that, evidently.

Most PMs with any length of service behind them have enjoyed a wide variety of roles within their field. Mental nurse Rob Morris went to Canada to represent the MoD at a 'Flying Phobia' conference to study ways 'to change how civilian air travel was done, how people are looked after in airports, to try and manage problems that people with a flying phobia are causing.' The latest scheme is to have a small specialist team at each major airport:

> though the main things you can do at an airport is either medicate or stop them flying. You can't do therapy and treat them at that late stage, so it's a case of calming them down, giving medication, and if it works then they can go, or if not they simply can't fly.
>
> We run a group-based course for a week and at the end of it take everybody flying. Usually 95 per cent come back saying, 'That was really good, I enjoyed it.' The one or two that don't go the first time come back and do another course and are absolute stars.

Rob added that:

> among RAF personnel the rate of aversion to flying is no different from among the general population. But of course we treat the army and navy too, and some of the young soldiers come along and say, 'I joined the army, not the RAF, now I've got this nineteen-hour flight out to the Falklands.'

Other unexpected skills involve compiling statistics, as Stephen Doyle and Debbie Meikle both found out. While working with the Americans in Afghanistan, Stephen found himself embroiled with Excel spreadsheets:

> Never done anything like it before, but I put together a package, trial and error, that looked at 9,000 missions, helicopters and casualties and locations, things like that, looking at monthly periods or six-monthly periods. It was all mainly round the Green Zone – that's where the bad guys are – but you also have areas where we have medical facilities, but with no real casualties nearby and no real casualties being sent to them by the helicopters. Strategically, it was good to have that sort of information, so I put it in and it went to the geographic people and they mapped it out, made a big map, put it on the wall and then had a meeting … It was a no-brainer: we can draw-down here, we can draw-down there, so it was good.

Having been happily running a ward in the Birmingham hospital, Debbie Meikle too found herself in unexpected areas on her promotion to Warrant Officer:

> I was moved down to what was then DMETA [Defence Medical Education Training Agency], which is now Joint Medical Command – based at Fort Blockhouse, Portsmouth – to be an RAF analyst, looking at statistics and things. I wasn't going to refuse my promotion, but it certainly wasn't my comfort zone, loading statistics onto an analyser. But I look back now and realise that I did gain a lot, and I met some invaluable people that I look to for advice now.
>
> It was a lovely part of the country. I was down there when Trafalgar 200 was on, so that was just the highlight of that time, down in Gosport. You had a bird's eye view of what was going on.

Debbie is also proud to be the first officially appointed warrant officer to the Director of Nursing Services (DNS, otherwise Matron-in-Chief):

> I don't work alongside him, but I am the interface between him and the other ranks, I feed back to him things that I think he needs to know. Likewise I take information from him out to the other ranks around the units. DNS has meetings twice a year with the leads of each units and I go and represent all the other ranks. One role within the DNS WO post is I'm a Trustee on the PMs' Trust board, the first non-commissioned person to do that. That's good because you get to see what's going on within the Trust and so I can encourage the other ranks to go forward for other things like the Travelling Scholarship. I'm also the deputy trade specialist officer for registered nurse (adult), all part and parcel of being the DNS's WO.

Coping with married life and children

Nowadays when women sign on into the armed forces for more than a brief period they often have to cope with both their career and creating a family. Nikki Duncan and her husband have twin daughters, aged three in 2013. Asked how she coped with having a family and being in the air force, she replied:

> It doesn't work. I will have done my twenty-two years next January [2014], and I will have to come out. It would work if my husband had a Monday to Friday job, but he's a 'loadie', he flies on C17s, so he's away – he's at Brize Norton. We had a nanny to start with, for the first year, so I had her to fall back on, but now the girls are at nursery full time, it's just hard work. I'd love to stay in, because I love doing it, but not with my husband doing the job he's doing.

The opposite view comes from Sonia Phythian:

> I have a little boy who's just turned five years old. My husband Geoff had completed twenty-three years in the RAF and when Freddy arrived he retired from the Service. We didn't want our family to be split apart by both of us serving in the military. Geoff runs his own business from home to fit around me and Freddy, so although it is still difficult when I go away, Dad is always there for Freddy.

Memorable moments

In many situations humour can become an antidote to stress. Sonia Phythian remembers one particular incident in Afghanistan:

> it was three o'clock in the morning, pitch black and I was with my team in our tent accommodation. The alarm sounded alerting us of a possible attack … we quickly put on our helmets and combat body armour and lay on the hard cold plastic flooring …

> suddenly someone starting giggling and before you knew it we were all laughing fit to burst with tears streaming down our faces! I think the absurdity of the situation … pyjamas and full military kit … coupled with the fact that I was with colleagues whom I now considered close friends, acted as a release mechanism for us all. Thankfully, the alert was a false alarm but it certainly helped us at the time to release some anxiety …
>
> Operational deployments are always a good leveller … they remind you of what is important and what isn't … providing patient care within the operational environment certainly gives you perspective on life and that's a good skill to hold on to.

Of all the situations she has met so far, Rachel Frearson considers her most memorable moments to have taken place during aeromeds:

> The helicopter thing, being shot at, you know! Hoping that the patient lives. There are a few hairy moments but once you get to the other side you're in the aircraft with that patient relying on you, so you have to make sure that you're prepared for it. But that's another thing, pushing you out of your comfort zone, and going on your own, no one's ever expecting you, and you don't know what to expect … Last time I spent a week at the Gateway just waiting to get on a flight, and ended up going on a C17 with just fifteen other people and a tank! Ending up in Bastion, where I was supposed to be, but then flew to Kandahar and waited there for five hours, but nobody came to get me … It was horrendous at the time.

Lee Bond recalls a time when 'I went to pick a young marine up from Zermat, a skiing resort in Switzerland, but I landed at Geneva, which meant I'd got a four-hour train journey to get up to where he was, so it was more like railo-med than aeromed!'

Other memorable times have had Royal connections. 'I have done some other fun things,' enthuses Corporal Anthony Beynon:

> I got to do the Diamond Jubilee Parade in Windsor … fantastic! Just when I got back from being away [in Afghanistan], I had two weeks' leave and then went down to Halton to practise for the parade. I think they only had five or six nurses doing that, but … doing it when you'd just got back, and being able to wear a medal for that parade, it felt so much better. Being part of that was fantastic.

On another memorable aeromed, Rob Morris:

> went out to Boston (USA) to pick somebody up from the royal yacht. A crew member. The plan was to get me out there and back before the royal family arrived. I was travelling to the airport to catch the flight – with very little notice – and the admiral on board rang the ward and spoke to one of the sergeants and said, very posh voice: 'Your chap that's coming out, would he like us to book into a hotel or

would he like to sleep on board?' So I got to sleep on board the royal yacht, in the apartment of the Queen's dresser, so, where the Queen sleeps on board, I slept in an adjoining cabin. Very lovely!

Meanwhile, Kirsty Scott had even closer encounters of the royal kind:

We had Prince Harry out in Afghanistan when I was there. He always ate in the cook-house, might sit opposite you. Exactly like one of the lads. Saw him in the gym a couple of times. We were told not to pester him, obviously, but he was very polite, he'd say hello. He's very good-looking!

For Kim Wilson it was Prince William and his bride riding by:

I did the royal wedding. Route lining. It was an amazing experience, one that I really will remember. We spent a short time practising our drill and we had to do a practice run in London at about 4 a.m.! It was really eerie, with all the roads shut off – it was like a ghost town. On the actual day it was nerve racking, but once we started marching it was an amazing feeling. There were crowds of people lining the streets, shouting praises at us as we were marching past, saying what a great job the armed forces did and how good we looked! It was so noisy and so unreal! When we were in our route-lining position, we stood there for what seemed like ages, at attention, my arm started to go a little numb. But seeing William and Kate and the patriotic crowds made it all worthwhile! And I went to one of the garden parties – and saw the Queen curtain-twitching! She was looking out of the window. That's one thing I never thought I'd see!

Other opportunities

For members of the PMRAFNS, opportunities for adventure and new experience open in many unexpected ways. Anthony Beynon was:

lucky enough to go to Bolivia for three weeks, with the military, doing altitude research, to see what effect the altitude has on your body, because most people will go up to a certain height and just start feeling really unwell, so they have to come back down to sea level to sort themselves out. The research was to see why some people get altitude sickness and some don't, and to see if this can be applied to patients in a critical condition. Quite a few of the doctors who were on this expedition were from CAM [Centre for Aviation Medicine] which is where they do all the altitude testing to go on aeromed. But I think the main reason was to see if we can prevent altitude sickness, because training at altitude is really good. Also because if we can identify how people deal with low oxygen levels then we might be able to apply this to a ventilated patient [during an aeromed].

Rachel Frearson spoke about The Princess Mary's Travel Scholarship Fund, which is available but not as widely used as it could be:

> You apply for it and put your business case forward, how it will benefit the service, then you're given the money. I think there's a £1,500 one and then a £3,000 one, major and minor. They often do a presentation at the symposium of people who have used that.

Rachel wrote an article for the *PMs' Magazine*, after she used her allotment from the fund to work in Thailand in 2007:

> I went for four weeks and worked with patients with HIV, which were often boys who had worked in Bangkok and sent their money back to their families. When you worked in a clinic there, they had a map of the village and the house would be coloured in, that's how you'd identify your patients. There were a lot of diabetic patients there, because they have a diet of predominantly fruit, so they'd be thin as thin, but have diabetes because of the high sugar content of their diet – and because they couldn't afford shoes they have lots of foot ulcers and leg ulcers, and burns from their little bikes …
>
> I did the same sort of thing in India too [2008], in a hospital. They put me on the labour ward, which was like being back in the 1960s, nobody made any cries of pain, babies wrapped in bubble-wrap and so on.

Rob Morris also took advantage of the travel scholarship fund when he and another PM went out to Boston, USA, to visit the military veterans' agency:

> We visited the shop-front – it literally is what would have been a disused shop in the High Street – they took it over and they use it as a walk-in clinic. People could just walk in and say, 'I'm a veteran and I've got this problem …' They had social workers there, and therapists. We went to the veterans' hospital, too, talked to the doctors there. How problems can develop years down the line. It was fascinating to see how they managed this growing population of veterans. Because people don't join the military for life any more, they join for five to ten years – for a bit of fun, to travel, to do something different, get away from home, learn a trade … but then after a few years they want to settle down, not keep getting posted, get married, have children … So there's a growing veterans' population. It was fascinating, something I wouldn't have had the chance to do without the PMs' Travel Scholarship. The opportunities are outstanding.

Sports and charity work

Sarah Perkins' main sporting interest is running:

> I've represented RAF Wittering and MDHU Peterborough at road races and cross country many times. I've completed a number of half marathons in my own time as well as doing the London Marathon last year for the RAF Association. I'm currently training for the Milton Keynes Marathon.

While deployed in Afghanistan, Anthony Beynon:

> set up the CO's cup – which we have over here as well – certainly at RAF Wittering we do it, each section competes against the rest for the CO's trophy. So … I set that up out there and everyone loved it. We did sports – basketball, volley-ball, and then a final event, during which we used a rowing machine, having to complete 500 metres before moving on to press-ups, tricep dips, squats, burpees and finally bastardos which are a burpee combined with a press-up, so while you are down on the floor you complete a press-up before jumping back up again.

One Christmas the denizens of Camp Bastion enjoyed a pantomime written, directed and produced by Kev Mackie, who also acted as master of ceremonies. 'The whole performance was the best we'd done,' Kev recalls:

> You could tell that audience and cast alike were having an absolute ball. Even the jokes that I thought weren't that funny got real belly laughs. Some people were crying with laughter and when the Dame came on, he (she), didn't have to work them very hard at all. By the time the interval came we had really got the room buzzing and singing the songs. The second half flew by and the only person to forget their lines was me, and I had the script in front of me! It only made everyone laugh louder and we were soon doing the finale and receiving a standing ovation. I did the thanks and everything before bringing the cast out to take their bow. Each actor got a huge reception and then when I thought it was nearly over the Dame stopped and did the thanks to me, asking COMKAF [the boss, Commander of Kandahar Airfield] to present me with a T-shirt emblazoned with the panto poster on the back and 'Director' on the left breast. The guys had clubbed together and got the shirt made by the local T-shirt printer. I was truly touched by the gesture. Throwing twelve cast together, plus the fourteen or so helpers had been hard work at times, but I couldn't have done it without their commitment and support and I know they all enjoyed it – even when I was shouting at them for getting things wrong!

Not only did the cast and audience have a lot of fun, they also raised a decent sum of money for the charity Warchild.

In August 2013, military personnel at MDHU Peterborough cycled the distance from RAF Brize Norton in Oxfordshire to Camp Bastion. No, not literally: they used a static bike in the atrium at the entrance to the hospital and completed the 5,661km distance in under twenty-four hours, raising to date nearly £1,800.

What of the future?

It appears that our forces will withdraw from Afghanistan very soon: the final draw-down, scheduled for 2014, may have taken place by the time you read this. What will happen after we leave? Should we have gone in there in the first place? The questions remain and no doubt history will reach its own conclusions. None of us has a crystal ball to predict the future with any certainty. The world seems to be an increasingly volatile place, with, in recent years, the violence of the so-called 'Arab Spring', the troubles in Libya and Mali, in Egypt and in Syria. Who knows what the PMs may be required to deal with in years to come?

Some of them offered their thoughts on the subject. Asked if he thought that peace and progress would continue in Afghanistan after we withdraw, one senior contact replied:

> I don't know. I hope so. The Afghan army and the Afghan police have had a lot of mentoring, a lot of training, restructuring and reorganisation. Most people I've spoken to think the Afghan army lads are really good. Not quite so keen on the police. If you look at the incidents there have been involving the Afghan police you'll understand why. Of course, the army lads get moved around, but the police tend to stay where they live – like our police – so it's very easy for pressure to be applied. What do you do when your family is threatened? They are in a difficult position, some of them.

A more junior PM agrees:

> I think, when we actually leave, things will go back to the way they were. Even now, it's exactly the same as it was [in the early days]. We still get so many injuries through IEDs, and insurgents going into the Afghan police and working beside our British troops … when we leave, there'll be nothing there to protect the civilians.
>
> We worked closely with the Afghan interpreters and they'd do anything to get to England. Most of them don't tell friends or relatives that they're working on Camp Bastion because they're afraid that the insurgents, or the Taliban, might get to hear about it and kidnap their family, hold them for ransom … So they want to know what's the best way to get to England.

A colleague added that for the PMs, 'It's a bit more [about] training now, with Afghan closing, training for contingencies. We're beginning to see more people on call for things, planning for the unknown …'

'As some of the operations overseas come to a close,' says another:

> a lot more of us will be retained for contingency operations. I'm currently on call for a six-month period, to go to … it's called Commando Forward Surgical Group. It's attached to logistics regiment, working alongside the Marines in their medical capability. It's navy-led, but there are often spaces that need filling, so all our RAF nurses who've got aeromed experience, we can bring that alongside, for use in any other conflicts, if they arise.

A senior PM who has seen many changes, not always for the better, comments, 'But you have to remain positive, no point in getting down … so you get on and adapt. I've enjoyed my time, but when the time comes to leave I'll probably be ready – six and a half years to go. I'm in until age fifty-five.'

Another senior officer from the Defence Medical Services Review observes:

> For the branch … and the RAF Medical services … we've hit very interesting times. The Defence Medical Services (DMS) 2020 Review was completed in response to the Strategic Defence Security Review 2010 and provided direction on how the DMS would support Defence delivery. I'm involved with the implementation of the DMS20 recommendations for the PMs and RAF Allied Health professionals. Understandably some of the nurses feel a little unsettled because our manpower figures look different – some specialties have reduced in number and others have increased. There is a lot to consider such as career progression, extension of service, training opportunities and recruitment in order to achieve the new figures by 1 April 2018.
>
> Implementing DMS20 has provided an opportunity to review the structure of the PMs and make sure we have the correct balance of rank and specialty – this is needed and it is good the Review has given us the impetus to 'spring-clean' the Trade and Branch. Op Herrick provided a massive learning experience for the PMs and raised the profile of RAF nurses and medics within the public domain. The public have been able to see through the media, probably in close detail for the first time, the role that RAF medical personnel have within areas of conflict; we've recruited an awful lot of well-qualified people who are keen to 'get out there' and do the job.
>
> But I think we also need to start acknowledging that Op Herrick is now moving into the past as the plan is that the UK military will have left Afghanistan by the end of 2015. Our focus needs to shift to our future role within operations which is now supporting contingency operations rather than enduring commitments. We need to start changing our mind-set and think about the nature of future conflicts and what will be expected of RAF nurses. The next operation will be very different to Op Herrick, particularly with regards to the comfortable and established environment of the Role 3 at Camp Bastion. We need to ensure we are militarily and clinically prepared to provide medical care from a basic field hospital within an austere envi-

> ronment. A lot of doctrine has been written on future conflicts and it's important we read and understand it so we can ensure we are prepared to continue delivering first class medical care … I think all this is very exciting.

With the operational tempo at such a high level, the PMs are probably busier today than they have been since the Second World War. Despite the severity of cuts imposed by government, they continue to be highly motivated and dedicated to their work and to the Service whose uniform they wear with pride.

Squadron Leader (later Wing Commander) Pippa Ward came across some interesting clues to the future: it seems that boffins are inventing space-age protective clothing for nurses and patients. In America (where else?) something going by the tongue-twisting title of the Defence Advance Projects Research Agency has come up with a Star Trek-style tricorder to detect germs and viruses, and a blood-scrubbing agent which, injected into the blood stream, will destroy harmful micro-organisms and thus save personnel from the inconvenience of wearing protective suits. How thoughtful! Other projects include a 'smart shirt' to be worn by fighting troops. This has 'fibre optic cable woven into the material, with sensors and a transmitter which can identify wounds … and alert medics to the soldier's position … using satellite technology.' Sensors can also track a bullet through a human body and even identify its calibre, though it puzzles Pippa that the scientists seem to assume that the injured person won't notice he (or she) has been shot. She adds, 'what is even more worrying is the presumption that medics can read maps! Although technology hopes to make life easier, is there really any substitute for a professional, human and caring member of the PMRAFNS? I think not!'

Valete

Original members of the RAF Nursing Service were all female, all qualified nurses; they held officer status but remained civilians; they wore starched white veils and long skirts; they were not allowed to travel in aircraft while on duty and they were strictly non-combatant. They joined what was considered to be a temporary branch of a temporary service, for the duration of the war only: the First World War.

Nearly 100 years on, men and women may join the PMRAFNS with equal rights and equal opportunities; they bear all ranks from NCO to air commodore; they work alongside colleagues of the navy and army; both sexes might wear trousers, or flying gear, or camouflage battledress and 'bone-dome'; they most definitely fly, in whatever type of aircraft suits their purpose and, what is more, when necessary they carry arms and know how to use them.

They are also members of the Royal Air Force, required to take part in a wide range of service activities, from the rigours of recruit camp to a survival weekend at RAF Cranwell and on to serve under rocket attack in war zones; or they undertake subsidiary roles from duty medic to mess secretary and orderly officer. On the social side, there are dinners and balls, opportunities to take part in expeditions or adventure training; there are sports and charity events. A glance at the annual magazine reveals PMs revelling in activities such as sailing, free-fall parachuting, equestrian team riding, swimming, netball, hockey, mountaineering, deep-sea diving, gymnastics, cricket, squash, Judo, Kung Fu, skiing – the list goes on. They may be chosen to march across the arena representing their service at the Albert Hall during the Festival of Remembrance, and to parade at the Cenotaph next day; or to help line the route on grand state occasions.

As you read this book, they will be out there somewhere, at home and abroad, wearing their air force blue and caring for the sick and wounded. This book celebrates their long and continuing service. It deserves to be widely recognised.

Whatever their experience may have been, in war or in peace, not one of them regrets a single moment of service life. The sentiment of all of them was aptly expressed by Gwen Butler, whose career in the PMs, begun in 1925, took her from early Halton to Palestine and Iraq. During the Second World War she was matron of RAFH Lagens in the Azores and, after becoming the first matron of Nocton Hall, she went on to become senior matron at Halton. On her retirement in 1952, she recalled her twenty-seven years with the Service, adding, 'If I had my time over again I would not change one second of it. I think this is the most wonderful nursing service in the world … I have been thrilled with every minute.'

PS: On the Subject of . . .

Matrons

Why do matrons have such a bad reputation? Whatever the answer, matrons of the PMRAFNS have left their own legends, still being told: the doves and the dragons.

Doves . . .

A PM says: 'Most of the Matrons were very efficient, great organisers, and they cared about people. It might not always have seemed that way to nurses working under them, but . . .'

From the 1930s:

> The two outstanding matrons were Miss Oliver and Miss Clubb. They were both so very human . . . When I returned from Aden I was posted as Matron to Air Ministry in 1939. I have never met a Matron-in-Chief who considered her staff as Dame Emily Blair did. She was most particular that each member be placed in wards or SSQrts to which she was most suited.

From a wartime WAAF: 'Having come under WAAF, RAF and PMRAFNS scrutiny, I found Matron Hards at Ely was a welcome breath of fresh air – far from stuffy, and companionable to a degree, she was a delight to know.'

From the 1960s:

> You didn't have chaps in your room. You could only entertain them in the ante room and they had to be out by eleven o'clock . . . Matron used to go around the corridors making sure no one was having a little snog anywhere. This doctor was absolutely potty about a friend of mine . . . decided he was going to propose. He got hold of her, opened this door and pulled her in, thinking it was a room, but it was the linen cupboard – a boiling hot linen cupboard. Matron was going along knocking on doors, making sure nobody was in there, got as far as the linen room and hears this voice saying, 'Will you marry me?' and the reply, 'I can't marry you – I'm going to faint in this heat!' Matron interrupted, 'Couldn't you find somewhere a bit more romantic than a linen cupboard?'

A senior matron:
By the time the hospital had run down to these few wards, we were all living down in the officers' mess. I remember the CO saying one day, 'Pity the sisters' mess isn't open, you'd have beautiful accommodation.' I said, 'Yes, and I'd live there in absolutely solitary state. Down in the main mess everybody talks to everyone. But in a nursing officers' mess no one's very keen on talking to the matron!'

A card written and illustrated for Scots-born Matron Mary R Gall, on her retirement in 1960, reads:

> Mary Gall – Greetings from the PMRAFNS
>
> Last week to Honkers, next week to Malay,
> Back to Episkopi, off the next day.
> You flew down the Red Sea, called in at Bahrain,
> Your visits to Stations were never in vain.
> One week to Malta, the next week to SHAPE,
> You've kept our flag flying, and cut down Red Tape.
> Sometimes by staff car, and often by air,
> A year at White Waltham and Tavistock Square.
> From Cosford to Changi, from Wales to Kowloon,
> The girls are all hoping we'll meet again soon.
> Wherever you turn up, you're welcome, Miss Gall,
> And now you're for Edinburgh, best of them all.
> You've flown with the air force, touched down at the 'drome.
> Most kindly of Matrons, at last you are home.

So some are human, after all. As for the rest –

Dragons …
From J.G. Kingan, once Commanding Officer of RAF Halton:

> A nurse nick-named 'Tatty', after a character in the radio series ITMA, decided to grace the PMs with her presence, only to discover that, while WAAF officers of RAF Halton lived in the normal mess and mixed socially with male officers, nursing officers of the sisters' mess at PMRAFH Halton were more closely guarded than nuns in a convent. Not that this deterred Tatty. She was sent for by Matron, who observed disapprovingly, 'I hear you have been seen in the company of an officer from the main camp.' Tatty admitted to the relationship, adding that she and the gentleman in question were, in fact, engaged to be married. 'I'm pleased to hear there's nothing untoward in this relationship,' said Matron. 'Congratulations. You

> may go.' Next day, Tatty was ordered to report forthwith to Ely. But she had the last laugh – she married her officer and retired from the service.

The matron of wartime Rauceby Hospital, a big, blonde woman with a passion for bridge, wanted young Sister Sunshine to make up a four. When Sunny said she was too stupid and would rather do embroidery, she was given the task of smocking a dress out of a piece of apple-green silk which matron had brought back from the East. 'For my sins, I had to smock the front and back – and she was a HUGE woman!'

Then there was the PM who refused to hurry even when a German plane flew low over the country road where she was walking: 'Matron says we mustn't run while wearing uniform.'

From a male PM:

> Miss Mangleworzel, matron at Halton, was a very fearsome character – bite the head off a junior doctor fifty yards away … I worked one Christmas Day. The hospital was very quiet. I'd finished my shift and decided to dress up as one of the nurses – student nurse, SEN – hat and everything, dress, even a touch of lipstick. What I hadn't realised was that matron was doing rounds. In she walks, with me in full drag. She stopped and looked at me, dead-pan, and I thought … I'm dead! But she burst out laughing! I got on well with her after that. I was her deputy matron on my next posting. She said, 'I used to think you were such a stuck-up boy in theatres …' But if she was in a bad mood you might as well jump out the window.

Sister Molly Moonlight was happy to be posted to Wegberg to escape the proximity of Senior Sister Gripe. But as luck would have it Gripe was also posted to Wegberg, on the very same day. She gave Molly the choice of travelling alone by train and ferry or going as a passenger in Gripe's car. Not wanting to cause offence, Molly chose the car. Unfortunately the vehicle demanded mechanical attention, which delayed them. The evening before they were due at Wegberg they drove full tilt down to Folkestone, with a stressed-out Molly frantically searching the timetables for a suitable ferry. She found one and they arrived in good time, only to see the ferry just putting out to sea – poor Molly had read the summer timetable, and the winter schedule had just started.

Gripe was NOT amused. 'So what are you going to do now?' she barked.

'Cry,' said Molly – and she did.

Touché!

During some local riots and disturbances in Bahrain, a somewhat unpopular Muharraq matron, who was known to enjoy a drink, came in one day and announced in annoyance that she had been stoned. 'What, drunk again, Matron?' came the riposte.

A sixteen-year-old boy apprentice (now a senior officer) came under matron's constant disapproval. 'I could never do anything right for her,' he recalls. One day when she was showing him how to wrap a bandage she ordered him to cut some tape to hold the bandage in place. 'How long do you want it, ma'am?' he asked politely. 'Too long, or too short?'

Overheard at an annual reunion

Princess Mary came to Cosford when I was there. They were really fussy – if the shade of paint in the decor wasn't right … The dining room at Cosford was painted twice, for instance, and the carpet was too long.

Who was it at Cranwell missed church service because she had to deliver a baby in an airman's married quarter? The mother's main worry was the risk of mess on her carpet – all she could think about was having to face the Families' Officer!

When we were at Ely, Danny Whosit and Imogen Cartilage … she was in charge of maternity and he was consultant obstetrician. They were both very keen on horse-racing bets. On a Saturday morning, or whatever, they'd hope we weren't busy so one of them could go down to the bookie in Ely.

Wasn't it Imogen, at St Athan, stood on a floor polisher and went zussing out, almost out through the door of one of the Nissen huts? She was quite a big girl, wasn't she? And Scottish.

The patients used to help clean the wards in the old days. It was always cleaner when they did it. They'd say to each other 'Don't throw that down there – I've just polished the floor!' … As a junior sister, you had to sweep half of the ward – throw tea-leaves down, I remember – do exactly half, and the ward maid did the other half.

The wards were a damn sight cleaner than they are now, you had to do high dusting around the rails around the beds … Mind you, Matron Millipede … she used to have the officers doing it – she'd dump a tray of cutlery on them – 'Clean that!' she'd say, or 'You do this!' She's not still with us, is she? Don't print this if she is! I remember when I first went into the service, she said, 'Never, ever … neither lend nor borrow!' and she'd never lend anything to another ward, but if she wanted something it'd be, 'Nurse, go and get such-and-such from the other ward,' but if anyone came to her ward on the cadge …

And you opened all the windows – put all the patients in bed, under the blankets, and opened all the windows in the morning, to air the ward, while you were cleaning. Every morning. However cold. Oh – they were all covered up, though!

What do you suppose happened about the brooch – the one Dame Joanna's family gave? You know! Copy of the medical badge, studded with diamonds and rubies. They'd given it to her as a birthday present and after she died they presented it … It was given to all matrons-in-chief when they took office, and on formal occasions, when they were in mufti, they would wear it. Now we've got a male MiC … I wonder what Bob does with it!

When I was at Brampton we used to call them 'bean-stealers' – the married chaps who had their married quarters outside the mess but still came and ate our mess rations for nothing. Some of the younger officers – PAs to the big bods on Support Command staff, formed themselves into the SLIME Club – that's Single Living-in-Members' Executive – and they held gourmet dinners, but only members of the SLIME Club were invited. Some very high-ranking officers found themselves excluded, but … they invited me to join them!

In sisters' mess one breakfast-time, all the cutlery was missing. We were about to call the police when we realised all the cruets were still there – solid silver all of them, so maybe we hadn't been burgled. Then someone spotted the cutlery under the chairs in the maids' dining room. The officers had been in, playing pranks. So we plotted revenge … A gang of us sneaked into the dining room at the officers' mess and somehow managed to cart away two hefty twelve-seater dining tables. Put them in the solarium off the orthopaedic ward. They weren't discovered for three days! So then the officers came and pinched the loo seats out of the sisters' mess, at which point Matron and the CO hit the roof, but other hospitals got to hear about it, and they started … so it spread.

Did you hear that story about the Dame Joanna Tennis Tournament … Ely, I think, 1988 or thereabouts. Dear old 'Gloria' Swansong, who was theatre sister there – straight-faced, not much sense of humour – you must remember her! Well, she was organising the tournament and she got into a bit of a state because the mess stewards had set out a place for Dame Joanna, with a name tag, and were a bit peeved when she didn't turn up! – they didn't realise she'd have been 112!

I remember doing an aeromed to Cyprus. Sitting in the back of this Hercules. Very noisy, very loud – and very full! We were flying over Italy, just had breakfast, and suddenly we just … dropped. Out of the sky. I caught my breakfast on the way back up again as we levelled off. I was absolutely terrified. I remember looking at the air loadmaster, who was normally so cool and contained – he was white as a sheet! Anyway, we got to Cyprus and were on the beach later that day, when the captain – the Flight Lieutenant who'd been flying the aircraft – mentioned the bumpy ride, and I said, 'I'm not flying in a Hercules again, it was just dreadful.' With that, the loadie looked across and said, 'You don't know the half of it. We were actually hit by lightning – and the hold was full of high explosives.' No wonder he'd gone white!'

Were you there at Wroughton when … This Indian pilot had been admitted. Crashed his plane and injured himself. Anyway, Doris was night sister and he asked her … he said could she find out who kept leaving religious tracts and Catholic pamphlets on his side table. Well, she knew the day sister was a very devout Roman Catholic so … after a few discreet enquiries she discovered … The pilot had been asked his religion and he'd said he was a Parsee – Zoroastrian, or something, isn't it? The ward-master had got him down as 'RC'!

The Princess and the Parrot

In the early 1960s, Princess Alexandra was staging through RAF Gan, a tiny island in the middle of the Indian Ocean. Gan being a men-only station, PM Jane Stott was seconded from Changi to escort Her Royal Highness while on the island. The Princess was due to be shown around the camp and to meet everyone, as usual, but they decided that one place should remain out of bounds – the back of the sergeant's mess, where lived a pet parrot whose language was even more colourful than his plumage.

So, the day came, the Princess did the rounds, and then said, 'Isn't there something I haven't seen?' She had heard about the parrot! Reluctantly, they took her to see it and crossed their fingers while she talked to it, 'Pretty Polly …'

'BUGGER OFF!' said the parrot.

A deathly hush; everyone held their breath.

'Good heavens!' said the Princess. 'It speaks English!'

Appendix A

Significant Dates for the PMRAFNS

1918, 1 April: Royal Air Force officially forms.

1918, 1 June: Royal Air Force Nursing Service (RAFNS) created; nurses posted to units in UK. Miss Cruickshank MiC from November.

1919: Former Medical School Unit (wooden huts) becomes RAF Hospital Halton. Many other units close on ending of WW1.

1921, Jan: RAFNS established by Royal Charter as a permanent branch of the RAF.

1922: First PMs to be posted overseas, to Iraq.

1923, 14 June: HRH Princess Mary becomes first Patron; service renamed Princess Mary's RAFNS.

1925: First air ambulance service in UK, based at RAF Halton.

1927, 31 October: Princess Mary gives her name to the new hospital at Halton.

1923–34: PMRAFNS strength around 100.

1930: Retirement of first MiC, Joanna M Cruickshank (later Dame Joanna). She presents a cup for the winner of the annual PMRAFNS Tennis Tournament.

1937: Service has 134 Regular sisters, but as war threatens qualified nurses join a new PMRAFNS Reserve.

1939: The service has 184 Regular nursing sisters and 69 Reserves, plus pool of 200 VAD nurses. By Sept 1939, 6000 volunteers apply for 460 Reserve vacancies.

1941, 25 April: Defence (Women's Forces) Regulations grant emergency commissions; PMs don officers' rank markings but are still addressed by professional titles. Nurses are allowed (for the duration) to remain in PMRAFNS even when married.

1942, Jan: New post of Principal Matron established, to work at Air Ministry.

1943: 1,126 PMRAFNS sisters staff 33 RAF hospitals and 71 SSQs; in addition, nursing sisters work in a welfare capacity at 47 RAF stations.

1944: MBEs awarded to two PMs, the first women to enter Normandy after D-Day. Largest annual number of airborne casevacs: 300,000.

1945: A steady demobilisation of PMRAFNS Reserves in Europe. No major war casualties among PMs; but many honours and awards.

1948: Brief period of parachute training for PMs.

1949, Feb: Women's services fully integrated into RAF. PMs hold commissions and adopt female officer rank, though professional titles continue to be used inside hospitals.

1950: HM George V approves the appointment of Princess Royal, Patron of PMRAFNS, to Air Chief Commandant.

1950–51: Korean war proves the advantages of evacuating casualties by air. PMs attend airborne patients for first time.

1951: RAF Hospitals Halton, Ely, Wroughton and Wegberg approved as 'training schools' for members of the RAF Medical Service.

1950s: Hey-day of sea-trooping and long-haul aeromeds.

1956: PM Daphne Budgen killed on casevac duty when Anson crashes in Germany.

1956–57: Suez crisis; closure of canal obliges troop-ships to go via South Africa.

1959: Formal flight-nurse training begins at Lyneham.

1962, Oct: SRN training introduced: students become Staff Nurses/NCOs of PMRAFNS NCE (non-commissioned element).

1965: Death of HRH Princess Mary, the Princess Royal, Air Chief Commandant PMRAFNS.

1966: Appointment of HRH Princess Alexandra as Royal Patron and Air Chief Commandant of PMRAFNS.

1967, March: Training for SENs offered by all UK RAF hospitals.

1967: Wroughton becomes 'Princess Alexandra's' RAFH.

1969: SENs and Pupil Enrolled Nurses allowed to enlist on local service engagements.

1968–77: Overall reduction in commitment of RAF; closure of most RAF hospitals overseas, and smaller ones at home. Wroughton and Akrotiri staffed jointly with army.

1977: Discontinuation of SRN training at RAF hospitals.

1978: First edition of the PMRAFNS Magazine published.

1980, April 1st: Unified Nursing Service: integration of male nurses into PMRAFNS. Women officers assume male rank titles.

1982: The Falklands War: many casualties brought home by air, tended by PMs; PARAFH Wroughton is initial reception hospital.

1985, 2 January: PMs become part of the tri-service Defence Nursing Services (DNS).

1986, 5 Nov: helicopter crash in Limassol Bay kills three members of the four-man crew, including PMs Fiona Johnstone and Martin Cook.

1987, March: Start of conversion training, for Enrolled Nurses who wish to qualify as Registered General Nurses. RAFH Ely renamed 'The Princess of Wales RAF Hospital'.

1988: SEN training discontinued.

1990–91: The First Gulf War 'operation Desert Storm': PMs on standby at Brize Norton and Akrotiri; at Muharraq, Bahrain, and in Saudi Arabia.

1992: First male Matron, appointed at Wegberg. PMRAFNS Association launched. RAFH Ely closes.

1993: PMRAFNS Trust formed.

1994: Defence Cost Review announces reorganisation and beginning of tri-Service MDHUs.

1995: First male matron-in-chief appointed. PMs called into active service in Bosnia.

1995–96: Opening of MDHUs at Peterborough, Cambs (mainly staffed by PMs), Frimley Park, Hants (mainly army) and Derriford, Plymouth (mainly navy).

1996: 31 March – closure of Halton, Wroughton and Wegberg. TPMH Akrotiri becomes part of Defence Secondary Care Agency. 'Conversion' training ended. RGN training re-commenced on opening of tri-service Royal Defence Medical College, Gosport.

1999: Civil war in Kosovo involves PMs in humanitarian work and movement of personnel closes some wards at Haslar.

2001: Opening of RCDM Birmingham, main defence hospital and receiving hospital for all wounded; employing PMs. Military nurse training also moves to Birmingham.

2001: military operations launched against the Taliban in Afghanistan take PMs out to Kabul, then on to Kandahar and eventually Camp Bastion, Helmand Province.

2003–09: Second Gulf War involves PMs in 'Operation Telic', Iraq.

2007: Air Command created, HQ at High Wycombe.

2008: 90th Anniversary of RAF (and PMRAFNS) celebrated.

2009: Closure of Royal Hospital Haslar.

2010: Strategic Defence and Security Review demands more cuts in armed services to come into effect in next few years.

2011: Tactical Medical Wing, RAF Lyneham, relocates to RAF Brize Norton.

2012: Final closure of TPMH Akrotiri.

2014: Final withdrawal from Afghanistan(?).

Appendix B

Hospitals and Other Medical Units of the RAF: Britain

Earliest hospitals, from 1917

London area (mostly temporary sites)

Hampstead, north London: RFC Hospital, Mount Vernon, opened October 1917; RAF Central Hospital, Holly Hill, 1 April 1918–May 1919; RAF(Voluntary)Hospital, 37 Bryanston Square, January-November 1919; RAF(Voluntary)Hospital, 82 Eaton Square, January 1919–January 1920; RAF Officers' Hospital, 22 Fitzjohn's Avenue, opened April 1919; WRAF Hospitals: 53 Hollycroft Avenue; 13 Parsifal Road; 24 Chesterfield Gardens, November 1919–January 1920

Croydon, Surrey: Convalescent Hospital, Shirley Park, January–November 1919

Finchley, Middlesex: RAF Central Hospital, 1919–25; Officers' Convalescent Hospital, established in Avenue House, closed November 1919; RAF Central Hospital, East End Road, July 1919–June 1925, transferred to Uxbridge

Other areas:

Blandford Camp, Dorset: RAF and WRAF Hospital, September 1918–early 1920; RAF Auxiliary Hospital, October 1918–early 1919 (opened in old workhouse, solely to cope with flu outbreak)

Bolton Percy, Yorks: RAF Convalescent Hospital, Nun Appleton Hall, January–November 1919

Calshot, Hants: SSQ at flying-boat base, First World War

Cranwell, Lincs: RNAS sick bay, 1916–18; RAFSH, 1918–40

Halton, Bucks: RFC Training School, 1917–19; RAF Medical School and Hospital, 1919–27

Hastings, Sussex: 'The Hermitage' Hospital, January-May 1919

Matlock, Derbys: RAF Convalescent Hospital, October 1918–April 1919 (re-opened WW2)

Old Sarum, Salisbury, Wilts: RAF/Army Hospital, December 1918–early 1920

Members of the early RAF Nursing Service also served, singly or in pairs, at First World War WRAF depots at: Middleton Steventon; Saltley College, Birmingham; NARD, Sheffield; Glasgow; Hansworth College, Birmingham; Uxbridge; Shorncliffe; No 5 TDS, Peterborough; Aldborough; Farnborough; and Salisbury

Between the wars, 1920–39

By August 1920 most of the early hospitals had ceased to function and the WRAF was disbanded in April 1920 (it reformed as the WAAF in 1939). Only three RAF hospitals remained, the largest being Halton, with a main hospital and an isolation unit; next came Cranwell, and finally the Central RAF Hospital, Finchley. A few staff nurses worked at individual SSQs at Uxbridge, Middx; Henlow, Beds; Manston, Kent; Flowerdown, near Winchester, and Calshot, Hants.

In 1939, as Britain once again geared itself for war, new RAF stations sprang up, and with them large sick quarters and hospitals – and more hospitals.

From 1939

Birmingham: Royal Centre for Defence Medicine (RCDM) opened at Birmingham's Queen Elizabeth Hospital, April 2001

Blackpool, Lancs: 'Cleveleys' RAF Officers' Convalescent Hospital, June 1943–November 1945; Airmen's Convalescent Depot, 1940–46

Bridgnorth, Salop: RAF Station Hospital, August 1939–November 1947

Castle Archdale, N.Ireland: SSQ in Necerne Castle, 1940s

Catterick, N Yorkshire: Army hospital, became tri-Service Duchess of Kent Military Hospital, unit of the Defence Medical Services; closed April 1999 on relocation to MDHU Northallerton. DMS psychiatric unit remained at Catterick pro tem

Chessington, Surrey: MRU for WOs, NCOs and airmen from June 1950; joint services rehabilitation unit from August 1968; closed 1985, when it combined with Headley Court

Church Village, Pontypridd, S.Wales: RAFGH, September 1942–April 1946

Collaton Cross: MRU, January 1946 (renamed Chessington 1950)

Cosford, Salop: Large SSQ, September 1938, became RAFSH/RAFGH, 1939–77

Cranwell, Lincs: RAFSH, 1918–40

Down Ampney, Gloucs: SSQ at RAF Down Ampney was central air evacuation centre for D-Day casualties and PoWs, 1944–46

Ely, Cambs: RAFGH, 1938/9–1987; Princess of Wales Hospital, 1987–92

Evesham, Worcs: RAFGH, May 1940–March 1946

Halton, Bucks: RAFH, March 1919–27. New hospital, Princess Mary's RAFH, opened October 1927; closed March 1996

Haslar, Hants: One of the oldest military (Royal Navy) hospitals, became a tri-Service unit of the Defence Medical Service in 1996, when it was renamed The Royal Hospital Haslar. Ended its tenure as a military hospital in March 2007 and closed completely in 2009. Military medical care continued from 2005 at MDHU Portsmouth (*qv*)

Haverfordwest, Pembrokeshire, Wales: RAFSH, February 1945–April 1946

Headley Court, Surrey: Officers' MRU, 1949–85; DMS MRU, 1985 to present.

Henlow, Beds: RAFSH, September 1939–48

Hereford: RAFSH, June 1940–November 1947

Hoylake, Cheshire: MRU, 1940–December 1945, moved to Collaton Cross

Innsworth, Gloucs: RAFSH, June 1940–September 1948

Kirkham, Lancs: RAFSH, June 1940–June 1948

Littleport, Cambs: Opened 1939; became annexe to Ely RAFGH, August 1940

Lochnaw, Dumfries: RAFSH, September 1942–October 1945

Locking, Somerset: RAFSH, 1939–49

Loughborough, Leics: MRU, 1942–47

Matlock, Derbys: RAF neurological hospital, October 1939–May 1945
Melksham, Wilts: RAFSH, July 1940–46
Mongewell Park: MRU, 1945–50
Morecambe, Lancs: RAFSH, February 1940–October 1944
Nocton Hall, Lincs: RAFGH, 1947–83; FOPD linked with Ely, 1983–91
Northallerton, N.Yorks: RAFGH, January 1943–November 1947; MDHU within NHS Hospital, opened 1999
Padgate, Cheshire: Large SSQ, 1938; RAFSH, May 1939–57
Peterborough, Cambs: MDHU within NHS Hospital, from February 1996
Portsmouth: MDHU opened at Queen Alexandra Hospital, Cosham, in 2005
Rauceby, Lincs: Annexe for Cranwell RAFGH from 1 April 1940; complete hospital function transferred from Cranwell, 1 June 1940; returned to civilian use, 1945
St Athan, Glamorgan: Large SSQ, 1938; RAFGH, July 1940–49; RAFSH 1949–61
Torquay, Devon: Officers' Convalescent Hospital, September 1939–January 1943. (After damage during two bombing raids, its function transferred to Cleveleys, Blackpool)
Uxbridge, Middx: RAF Officers' Hospital, 1925; WAAF Hospital, February 1940; RAFSH from August 1941; closed 1972
Weeton, Lancs: RAFSH, June 1940–December 1959
West Kirby, Wirral: RAFSH, 1940–December 1957
Wick, Scotland: SSQ (special treatment centre) April 1941; operating theatre open 1943; RAFSH, 1944–45
Wilmslow, Cheshire: RAFSH, July 1940–December 1958
Wroughton, Wilts: RAFGH, July 1941–67; Princess Alexandra's RAFH, 1967–76; Princess Alexandra's Hospital (RAF/Army), 1976–92; Princess Alexandra's RAFH, 1992–96
Yatesbury, Wilts: RAFSH, February 1939–December 1947

PMs have also worked, and continue to work, at SSQs on RAF stations around the UK.

In 2013

UK Armed Forces no longer run dedicated military hospitals. Instead, Ministry of Defence Hospital Units (MDHUs) are embedded within certain civilian or National Health Service hospitals, operating under the direction of Defence Medical Services and staffed by personnel from all three Services.

Five MDHUs currently operate in the UK: Frimley Park Hospital, Surrey; Queen Alexandra Hospital, Portsmouth; Derriford Hospital, Plymouth; the new City Hospital, Peterborough; and Friarage Hospital, Northallerton.

The Ministry of Defence is also responsible for the Royal Centre for Defence Medicine (RCDM), Queen Elizabeth Hospital, Selly Oak, Birmingham, which opened on 2 April 2001.

Appendix C

Hospitals and Other Medical Units of the RAF: Overseas 1922–38 (in order of opening)

The earliest RAF hospitals overseas lay in the Middle East. They were formed from existing military hospitals manned by the RAMC during and immediately after the First World War.

Iraq:

Baghdad, Indian and Isolation Hospitals manned by RAFNS from October 1922

Baghdad/Hinaidi, No 23 Combined Service (RAF/Army) Hospital from October 1922; moved early 1923 to a new site and became RAFBGH Hinaidi, Baghdad; moved again December 1937 to Dhibban/Habbaniya (see 1939–2000, below)

Basra(Basrah), RAF Combined (British and Indian) Hospital opened 1923; reduced to SSQ 1925; closed March 1928 but reopened briefly 1930s to cope with cholera epidemic

Dhibban/Habbaniya, RAFBH/GH moved to Dhibban from Baghdad in December 1937; renamed RAF Habbaniya, May 1938

Karradah, Indian Hospital, opening date not known; closed 1926

Ser Amadia, rest and leave centre for RAF (summers only), 1932–54. PMs from hospitals in Iraq were attached here for short periods

Egypt:

Aboukir, SSQ, 1924–5 (closed because of riots); opened again from 1928–31

Cairo, British Stationary Hospital (RAF/Army), 1920s

Palestine:

Ludd (Lydda/Sarafand), Palestine General Hospital (RAF), 1924–40

Aden:

Steamer Point, army hospital taken over by the RAF, 1 April 1928

1939–2000

Aden:

Khormaksar Beach, Aden Protectorate Levies' Hospital, staffed by PMs 1959–67

Sheikh Othman: PMs stationed here 1941

Steamer Point: No 7 RAFH during Second World War; then RAFGH, closed 1967

Algeria:

Algiers, No 2 RAFGH, November 1943–1946

Azores:

Lagens, SSQ/RAFSH, December 1943–October 1946

Bahamas:

Nassau, SSQ/RAFH, October 1942–February 1946

Bahrain:

Bahrain, RAFH, January 1959–January 1964; became RAFH Muharraq, closed December 1971; RAF War Hospital, December 1990–March 1991 (First Gulf War)

Belgium:

Brussels, No 8 RAFGH, September 1944–1945

Burma:

Kyaukpyu, Ramree Island, No 67 MFH, 1945

Rangoon, No.65 MFH, July–November 1945; became RAFH Mingaladon, closed 1946

Ceylon (Sri Lanka):

Katunayake, Negombo, hospital at staging post, 1950–60

China:

Peking, British Embassy, digital post (one sister only), filled by a PM from 1973

Cyprus:

Akrotiri: Princess Mary's RAFH, 1956–77; renamed The Princess Mary's Hospital (TPMH) and jointly staffed RAF/Army, 1977 to 2012. (On 1 April 1996 it became a Defence Medical Services [DMS] Hospital, part of the Defence Secondary Care Agency)

Regional medical centre

Nicosia, SSQ, current

Troodos, medical centre

Egypt:

Cairo (Abbassia/Heliopolis), No 5 RAFGH, 1942–7

Fayid, RAFGH with families' wing at Abyad, 1947–56

France: Fontainebleau, French civil and military hospital, British wing, 1950s

Germany:

Hamburg, No 53 MFH, 1945–6; became BMH

Rinteln, No 8 RAFH, 1945–53; BMH, 1953–96 with digital post filled by a PM 1990s

Rostrup, RAFH, 1952–8

Wegberg, RAFH, from 16 November 1953, closed 31 March 1996

Gold Coast (Ghana):

Takoradi, RAFH, January 1942–November 1947

Hong Kong:

No 80 MFH, became Static Hospital, September 1945

SSQ opened June 1946, closed same year

Kai Tak, SSQ/Medical Centre, closed 1979

Kowloon, BMH, 1945/6–95, PMs attached 1980s and 1990s

Shek Kong, army medical centre, PMs attached from 1979; closed on handover 1997

Iceland:

Reykjavik, RAFH, March 1942–May 1946

India:

Allahabad, Uttar Pradesh, No 11 RAFGH, 1945–6

Calcutta, W Bengal, No 9 RAFGH, 1 January 1945–1946

Cawnpore, Uttar Pradesh, No 64 MFH, became No 12 RAFGH 1945–6

Chittagong (now Bangladesh), No 61 MFH, December 1943–July 1945

Imphal, Assam, No 60 MFH, January 1944–1945

Karachi (now Pakistan), No 10 RAFGH, April 1945–January 1948

Mauripur (now Pakistan), SSQ on staging post opened January 1948

Worli, Bombay, Second World War transit camp. SSQ opened January 1946, PMs withdrawn July 1947

No 62 MFH moved around the Arakan (area between Calcutta and Burma) 1944–6, locations included Cox's Bazaar, Shillong, Khumbirgram, Comilla, Imphal and Meiktila

Iraq:

Habbaniya, RAFGH, 1938–56; RAFSH 1956–8
Ser Amadia, rest and leave centre, closed 1954

Israel/West Bank:

Jerusalem, St John Ophthalmic Hospital, digital post filled by a PM 1980s

Italy:

Foggia, Apulia, No 4 RAFGH, June 1944–1946
Torre del Greco, Naples, No 1 RAFGH, replaced No 25 MFH, December 1943–May 1946

Japan:

Iwakuni, Honshu Island, British Commonwealth Air (BCAir) Hospital, July 1946–March 1948; RAF base and hospital active again October 1951–March 1955
Miho, Honshu Island, SSQ at RAF base, 1946–8
Okinawa, Ryuku Island, USAF/RAAF base, staging post for RAF casevacs, 1946–8 and 1951–5

Libya:

Benghazi, No 4 RAFGH, March 1943–April 1944
El Adem, SSQ at staging post, 1942–69
Tripoli, No 3 RAFGH, August 1943–January 1944

Malta:

Luqa, No 1 RAF Field Hospital, August 1943; SSQ from May 1946

Pakistan:

Islamabad, British Embassy, digital post filled by a PM 1980s and 1990s

Palestine:

Tel Litwinsky, Jaffa, No 3 RAFGH, February 1944–January 1948

Saudi Arabia:

Al Jubail, medical centre/32 Field Hospital, 1990–1
Dhahran, King Abdul Aziz Airbase Military Hospital; PMs deployed here 1990–1

Singapore:

Changi, RAFGH 1947–72/3; ANZUK Hospital, then UK Military Hospital, 1972/3–5
Seletar, No 81 MFH operated here 1945/6; later an SSQ opened at RAF Seletar

Tunisia:

Carthage, No 1 RAFGH, July-September 1943; No 31 MFH, September 1943–1945

Yugoslavia:

No 31 MFH was here during the late stages of the Second World War

2001–14

Afghanistan:

Med. Centres in Kabul and Kandahar, manned by ISAF including PMs.
War Hospital at Camp Bastion, Kandahar, active 2006–2014?

Cyprus:

The Princess Mary's Hospital, Akrotiri, Defence Medical Services [DMS] Hospital, part of the Defence Secondary Care Agency. Closed 2012

Appendix D

Royal Patrons and Matrons-in-Chief
Royal patrons – air chief commandant PMRAFNS

1923–65 HRH Princess Mary The Princess Royal CI GCVO CBE RRC
1966– HRH Princess Alexandra The Honourable Lady Ogilvy GCVO

Matrons-in-chief

June–Oct 1918 Miss L.E. Jolley (temporary service only)
1918–30 Dame Joanna M. Cruickshank DBE RRC
1930–38 Dame Katherine Christie Watt DBE RRC
1938–43 Dame Emily M. Blair DBE RRC
1943–48 Dame Gladys Taylor DBE RRC
1948–52 Air Commandant Dame Helen W. Cargill DBE RRC QHNS
1952–56 Air Commandant Dame Roberta M. Whyte DBE RRC QHNS
1956–59 Air Commandant Dame Alice Mary Williamson DBE RRC QHNS
1959–63 Air Commandant Dame Alice Lowrey DBE RRC QHNS
1963–66 Air Commandant Dame Veronica M. Ashworth DBE RRC QHNS
1966–70 Air Commandant Pauline Giles DBE RRC QHNS
1970–72 Air Commandant Ann S. McDonald CB RRC QHNS

Directors of RAF nursing services and matrons-in-chief

1972–78 Air Commandant Barbara M. Ducat-Amos CB RRC QHNS
1978–81 Air Commandant/Air Commodore Joan Metcalfe CB RRC QHNS
1981–84 Air Commodore I. Joy Harris CB RRC QHNS
1984–85 Air Commodore April A. Reed RRC QHNS
1985–88 Group Captain M.M. (Miche) Shaw RRC QHNS
1988–91 Group Captain Elizabeth A.I. Sandison RRC QHNS
1991–94 Group Captain Ethnea M. Hancock RRC QHNS
1994–97 Group Captain Valerie M. Hand RRC QHNS/ Air Commodore DDNS 1995–7
1997–2001 Air Commodore Robert H. Williams RRC QHNS/ DDNS (1999–2001)
2001–04 Group Captain Annie Reid OBE ARRC QHNS / DNA
2004–06 Group Captain Wendy Williams RRC QHN / DNA
2006–10 Group Captain Jackie Gross RRC QHN
2010–13 Group Captain Phil Cushen ARRC QHN / DNA
2013– Group Captain Phil Spragg MA MSc QHN

Appendix E

List of PMRAFNS Contributors

Includes ONLY members of the PMRAFNS whose words are quoted in the text. They are listed alphabetically by first name

A. Elizabeth Mansell (Mrs Ogden) PMRAFNS 1943–5; correspondence 1999
Alma Barnard (Mrs Tyack) PMRAFNS 1963–7; interviewed 1999
Angela Scofield (Wg Cdr Rtd) PMRAFNS 1980–98; correspondence and conversation 1999
Ann Golding (Sqn Off. Rtd) PMRAFNS 1960–89; interviewed 1999
Ann Tickle (Mrs Waters) PMRAFNS 1952–7; correspondence 1999
Anne Caird (Mrs Austin) PMRAFNS 1948–51, 1954–5; *PMs Magazine* 1997
Anne M. Taylor (Sqn Off. Rtd) PMRAFNS 1956–71; interviewed 1999
Anne Sumner (Mrs Wynne-Jones) PMRAFNS NCE 1962–3; via audio-tape 1999
Annie Warburton (Sqn Ldr) PMRAFNS 1984–?; interviewed 1999
April Reed (Air Cdre Rtd) PMRAFNS 1955–85, MiC 1984–5; interviewed 1999
Barbara Millar (Mrs Wight) PMRAFNS 1950–4; correspondence 1999
Barbara Rampton (Mrs White) PMRAFNS 1944–7; correspondence 1999
Beryl Chadney, PMRAFNS 1943–7; correspondence 1999
Beynon, P. Anthony, PMRAFNS from 2009, interviewed Feb. 2013
C.V. 'Ronnie' Oxborough (Sqn Ldr Rtd) 1968–1984; correspondence 1999
Christina Watson (Mrs Hunter) PMRAFNS 1941–6; correspondence 1997–9
Christine Bramley (Mrs Bull) PMRAFNS 1954–8; *PMs Magazine* 1999
Clare Woolley (Mrs Fowler) PMRAFNS 1962–70; correspondence 1999
Colin McMillan (Flt Lt Rtd) PMRAFNS 1986–94; *PMs Magazine* 1992
Constance P.I. Bull (Wg Cdr Rtd) PMRAFNS 1966–90; correspondence 1999
Cynthia Mayfield (Mrs Brown) PMRAFNS NCE 1966–9; correspondence 1999
D.M. 'Jane' Stott (Sqn Off. Rtd) PMRAFNS 1953–69; *PMs Magazine* 1997
Dame Joanna Margaret Cruickshank (1875–1958), Matron-in-Chief of PMRAFNS 1918–30; her own writings, including unpublished draft of PMRAFNS History written post-WW2
Debbie Gurney (Mrs Jones) (Sqn Ldr) 1994–?; *PMs Magazine* 1997
Debbie Meikle (Warrant Officer) PMRAFNS from 1983, interviewed Feb 2013
Dilys Palmer (Mrs Bore) PMRAFNS 1940–6; *PMs Magazine* 1993
Doreen A. Elston (Mrs Curston) PMRAFNS 1955–9; *PMs Magazine* 1999
Doreen Francis (Sqn Off. Rtd) PMRAFNS 1945–70; correspondence 1999
Doreen Hunt (Mrs Tomlin) PMRAFNS 1953–8; *PMs Magazine* 1998 and in correspondence 1999
Doreen Smedley (Wg Cdr Rtd) PMRAFNS 1955–83; interviewed 1999
Doris Stanford (Mrs Kent) PMRAFNS 1947–60; *PMs Magazine* 1999 and in correspondence and conversation 1999
Dorothy Hutchins (Sqn Off. Rtd) PMRAFNS 1957–75; correspondence 1999

Dulcie Flower (Mrs Wright) PMRAFNS 1945–8; correspondence 1999
E Therese Saunders (Mrs Ayres) PMRAFNS 1952–6; correspondence 1999
Eileen Adams (Mrs Knapper) PMRAFNS 1951–4; correspondence 1999
Elizabeth E.I. Sandison (Gp Cpt Rtd) PMRAFNS 1964–91, MiC 1988–91; interviewed 1999
Elizabeth F. Chalton (Mrs Walker) PMRAFNS 1955–6; documents lodged at Hendon RAF Museum
Elizabeth Kidman (Sqn Ldr Rtd) PMRAFNS 1974–92; interviewed 1999
Elizabeth Lown (Mrs Armstrong) PMRAFNS 1965–9; memoir lodged at Hendon RAF Museum
Elizabeth Smallwood (Mrs Andrews) PMRAFNS 1941–5; *PMs Magazine* 1993
Ethnea Hancock (Gp Cpt Rtd) PMRAFNS 1961–94, MiC 1991–4; interviewed 1999
Eve Loxston (Mrs Hall) PMRAFNS 1942–6; *PMs Magazine* 1999
Evelyn Addison (Mrs Glen) PMRAFNS 1943–6; correspondence 1999
Frances M. Keech (Mrs Judson, formerly Mrs Warner) PMRAFNS 1943–6; correspondence 1999
Geoff Holliday (Sqn Ldr Rtd) RAFMS/PMRAFNS 1966–96; *PMs Magazine* 1985
Gwen Butler (Wg Off. Rtd) PMRAFNS 1925–52; information from her cousin Mrs Denize 1999
Gwladys N. 'Tommy' Thomas (Mrs McGregor) PMRAFNS 1939–44; correspondence 1999
Helen E. Kell (Sqn Ldr Rtd) PMRAFNS 1971–87; correspondence 1999
Helen Ryan (Flt Lt Rtd) PMRAFNS 1984–1992; correspondence 1999
Helen W. Cargill (Air Cdt Rtd) PMRAFNS 1923–52 (MiC 1948–52); account of her life and career by her sister Jean Macrae, Imperial War Museum
Iris 'Fluffy' Jones (Mrs Bower, formerly Mrs Ogilvie) PMRAFNS 1939–49; unpublished memoir 'Normandy to the Baltic' (*c.*1985) and in correspondence and conversation 1999
Iris M. Jarred (Mrs Bartram) PMRAFNS 1942–6; interviewed 1999
Iris Rawlings (Mrs Kerse) PMRAFNS 1958–66; correspondence 1999
Ishbel McCabe (Mrs Bennet) (Sqn Ldr Rtd) PMRAFNS 1986–91; correspondence 1999
Isobel Hipkin (Mrs Bedford) PMRAFNS 1963–9; correspondence 1999
J.E. 'Beth' Smith (Mrs Hamson) PMRAFNS NCE 1967–8; correspondence 1999
Jackie Gross (Wg Cdr) PMRAFNS from 1984, MiC 2006–10; *PMs Magazine* 1996
Janet Smith (Mrs Campbell) PMRAFNS 1956–60; correspondence 1999
Janice Blood (formerly Hutton, now Mrs Oakman) (Sqn Ldr Rtd) PMRAFNS 1978–96; *PMs Magazine* 1998
Jean Brown (Sqn Ldr Rtd) PMRAFNS 1954–8, 1960–73; correspondence 1999
Jean King (Mrs Flower) PMRAFNS 1956–60; *PMs Magazine* 1998
Jean Ponsford (Mrs Howell) PMRAFNS 1942–5; *PMs Magazine* 1994
'Jenny' Jenkins PMRAFNS 1939–n/k; *PMs Magazine* 1978
Jessie M. Higgins (Wg Off. Rtd) PMRAFNS 1939–68; *PMs Magazine* 1996 and interviewed 1999
Joan Botting (Mrs Peake) PMRAFNS 1940–6; diary and interview transcribed by her son Andrew G. Peake, Imperial War Museum
Joan K. White (Mrs Cool) PMRAFNS 1943–6; correspondence 1999
Joan Metcalfe (Air Cdre Rtd) PMRAFNS 1948–1981, MiC 1978–81; interviewed 1999
Josephine Boase (Sqn Ldr Rtd) PMRAFNS 1967–88; PMRAFNS archive
Joy Harris (Air Cdre Rtd) PMRAFNS 1950–84, MiC 1981–4; interviewed 1999
Joy Knowles (maiden name n/k) PMRAFNS 1940s; correspondence 1999
Joyce F. Kellow (Mrs Wyatt) PMRAFNS 1944–7; correspondence 1999
Judy Cooke (Mrs Owens) PMRAFNS 1962–5; correspondence 1999
Judy Hopkins (Mrs Foote) (Sqn Ldr Rtd) PMRAFNS 1966–82; interviewed 1999
Julia Inkpen (Mrs Jenkins) PMRAFNS 1950–4; correspondence 1999

Kate Crompton (Mrs Wilmot) PMRAFNS 1963–6; correspondence 1999
Kate New, RAFNS 1918–1920, told her story to the editor of the *PMs Magazine* in 1981, when she was 98 years old. She died in 1984, shortly before her 101st birthday
Kathleen Hird (Mrs Bion) PMRAFNS 1948–51; correspondence 1999
Kathleen M. Burrows (Mrs Bennett) PMRAFNS 1945–58; *PMs Magazine* 1999
Kathleen W. Cranston (Mrs Slim) PMRAFNS 1938–40; correspondence 1999
Kathy Mogg (Mrs Ostler) PMRAFNS 1959–1963; *PMs Magazine* 1985 and 1998
Kay Griffiths (Cpl) PMRAFNS from 2009, interviewed 2013
Kevin C. Mackie (Sqn Ldr, later Wg Cdr) PMRAFNS 1990–2013; interviewed 1999
Kim Wilson (Cpl) PMRAFNS from 2007, interviewed Feb 2013
Kirsty Scott (Cpl) PMRAFNS from 2010, interviewed Feb 2013
L.E. Jolley (Temporary Principal Matron) PMRAFNS June-Nov 1918; PRO records
Lee Bond (Warrant Officer) PMRAFNS from 1994; interviewed Feb 2013
Lesley Chew (Wg Cdr) PMRAFNS 1978–?; *PMs Magazine* 1991
Lesley Cornwall-Jones (Mrs Howat) PMRAFNS 1953–5; *PMs Magazine* 1989
Linda Kendall (Mrs McKenzie) PMRAFNS NCE 1964–8; correspondence 1999
Louise Hardy PMRAFNS 1923–46; *PMs Magazine* 1978 and 1979
Margaret 'Jane' Clews, PMRAFNS 1951–5; correspondence 1999
Margaret Crombie (Mrs Price) PMRAFNS 1949–51; correspondence 1999
Margaret Kingston (Sqn Off. Rtd) PMRAFNS 1951–71; interviewed 1999
Marianne Galletly (Mrs Hollowell) PMRAFNS 1941–5; correspondence 1999
Marion Welch (Mrs Lampard) PMRAFNS 1918–30; letters and reports, PMRAFNS archive
Marion Wood (Mrs Donaldson) PMRAFNS 1961–7; correspondence and conversation 1999
Marjorie Eavis (Mrs McCandlish) PMRAFNS 1943–52; *PMs Magazine* 1980
Marjorie Ells (Ellis?) PMRAFNS service dates n/k; *PMs Magazine* 1979
Mary Allen, VAD attached PMRAFNS 1939–45; correspondence 1999
Mary Drew (Mrs Mitchell) PMRAFNS 1941–6; *PMs Magazine* 1994
Mary E.R. Edwards (Mrs Sellors) PMRAFNS 1920–42; reminiscences (1964) PMRAFNS archive
Mary Michal 'Miche' Shaw (Gp Capt Rtd) PMRAFNS 1963–1988, MiC 1985–8; correspondence 1999
Mary Moultrie (Mrs Nicholson) PMRAFNS 1941–5; *PMs Magazine* 1983
Mary Page (Mrs Payne) PMRAFNS 1953–7; correspondence 1999
Mary Williams (Mrs Hancock) PMRAFNS 1944–8; correspondence 1999
Maureen Lumley (Wg Off. Rtd) PMRAFNS 1942–74; in correspondence and conversation 1999
Monica Fern (Sqn Ldr Rtd) PMRAFNS 1963–80; interviewed 1999
Monica Railton Jones (Mrs Chandler) PMRAFNS 1943–52; correspondence 1999
Muriel K. Dunn (Sqn Off. Rtd) PMRAFNS 1951–1972; *PMs Magazine* 1997
Nadine Gay PMRAFNS NCE 1964–7; correspondence 1999
Nicola Duncan (Flt Sgt) PMRAFNS from 1992, interviewed 2013
Noelle Horrocks PMRAFNS 1941–4; *PMs Magazine* 1982
Olive Kirkham (Sqn Off. Rtd) PMRAFNS 1950–1966; correspondence 1999
Pamela Love (Mrs Batchelar) PMRAFNS 1947–51; correspondence 1999
Pat Surridge (Sqn Ldr Rtd) PMRAFNS 1966–94; *PMs Magazine* 1986
Patricia Maslen (Mrs Perry) PMRAFNS NCE 1964–7; correspondence 1999
Pippa Ward (Sqn Ldr) PMRAFNS 1988–?; *PMs Magazine* and correspondence 1999
R.A. 'Annie' Reid (Wg Cdr, DNS[RAF]) PMRAFNS from 1975, MiC 2001–4; *PMs Magazine* 1988
R.A. 'Penny' Penrose (Wg Off. Rtd) PMRAFNS 1950–1980; correspondence 1999
Rachel Frearson (Cpl) PMRAFNS from 2006, interviewed Feb 2013

Rachel Johnson PMRAFNS 1985–1996; *PMs Magazine* 1992
Richard Laurence (Sqn Ldr Rtd) PMRAFNS 1983–2000; interviewed 1999
Rob Morris (Flt Sgt) Med Tech from 1994, PMRAFNS from 1995, interviewed Feb 2013
Robert H. Williams (Air Cdre, Rtd)) RAFMS 1962–76; Med Tech Branch 1976–80; PMRAFNS 1980–2001; MiC/DNS(RAF) from 1995, DDNS from 1999–2001, correspondence and conversation 1999–2000
Rona Black (Mrs McAlpine) PMRAFNS 1941–7; correspondence 1999, and letters from 1940s
Rosemary Partington (Wg Cdr Rtd) PMRAFNS 1957–88; interviewed 1999
Sally Donovan (Mrs Pullan) PMRAFNS 1952–6; interviewed 1999
Sandra Cranswick (Mrs Philpott) PMRAFNS 1966–70; correspondence 1999
Sarah Perkins (Sgt) PMRAFNS from 2003, interviewed Feb 2013
Sharon Smith (Mrs Callcott) (Sqn Ldr) PMRAFNS 1987–?; *PMs Magazine* 1995 and correspondence 1999
Sheila Power (Mrs Bellamy-Knights) PMRAFNS 1967–72; interviewed 1999
Shelagh Firth (Gp Capt Rtd) PMRAFNS 1957–87; correspondence 1999
Shelagh Glenn (Mrs Barber) PMRAFNS 1960–8; interviewed 1999
Sonia Phythian (Wg Cdr) PMRAFNS from 1996, interviewed Feb 2013
Stephen Doyle (Sqn Ldr), QARANC from 1993, PMRAFNS from 2000, interviewed Feb 2013
Susan Armistead (Mrs Sutcliffe) (Sqn Off. Rtd) PMRAFNS 1943–51; correspondence 1999
Susan Pound (Mrs Gray) PMRAFNS 1975–8; correspondence 1999
Sylvia Emery (Mrs Pounds) PMRAFNS 1951–7; correspondence 1999
Terry A. Smith, RAFMS/PMRAFNS 1966–1997; PMRAFNS archive
Tessa Lawless, PMRAFNS 1951–5; *PMs Magazine* 1994 and 1997; and correspondence 1999
Valerie Blackwell (Mrs Cornford) PMRAFNS 1942–5; correspondence 1999
Valerie M. Hand (Air Cdre Rtd) PMRAFNS 1967–71 & 1972–95, MiC 1994–5, DDNS 1995–7; interviewed 1999
Violet Craig (Mrs Gibbons) PMRAFNS 1940–9; *PMs Magazine* 1978
W. Charlesworth, Matron, PMRAFNS WW1; PMRAFNS archive
Wendy Williams (Wg Cdr) PMRAFNS from 1984, MiC 2004–6; *PMs Magazine* 1988
Winifred Gardner (Mrs Penman) PMRAFNS 1945–8; articles lodged at RAF Museum Hendon and correspondence 1999
Zena Cheel (Wg Off. Rtd) PMRAFNS 1961–84; interviewed 1999

Appendix F

Key to acronyms

A&E	Accident and Emergency (department)
A(E)LO	Aeromedical (Evacuation) Liaison Officer
AC	Aircraftman (lowest rank in the RAF)
Aeromed	aeromedical evacuation flight, bringing patients back to home hospital
AMA	Assistant Medical Administrator
AOC-in-C	Air Officer Commanding in Chief
ARRC	Associate of the Royal Red Cross
BATUS	British Army Training Unit Suffield (in Alberta, Canada)
BCAir	British Commonwealth Air Forces in Japan 1946–48
BMH	British Military Hospital
CAS	Chief of the Air Staff
Casevac	original term for casualty evacuation by air
CB	Companion of the Bath
CBE	Commander of (the Order of) the British Empire
CCAST	Critical Care Air Support Teams
CCS	Casualty Clearing Station
CI	(Order of the) Crown of India
C-in-C	Commander in Chief
CO	Commanding Officer
DA(E)LO	Deputy Aeromedical (Evacuation) Liaison Officer
DBE	Dame Commander of (the Order of) the British Empire
DCMH	Departments of Community Mental Health
DDNS	Director of Defence Nursing Services (from 1985)
DGMS	Director General of Medical Services (from 1938)
DMETA	Defence Medical Training Agency
DMS	Director of Medical Services (1918–38)
DNS(RAF)	Director of Royal Air Force Nursing Services (from 1972)
DSCA	Defence Secondary Care Agency
(D)WRAF	Director of the Women's Royal Air Force
(D)WRNS	Director of the Women's Royal Naval Service
EN(G)	Enrolled Nurse (General)
GCVO	Knight Grand Cross of the (Royal) Victorian Order
GS	General service
IED	Improvised Explosive Device
IPTM	Institute of Pathology and Tropical Medicine (at PMRAFH Halton)
IRT	Immediate/Incident Response Team
ISAF	International Security Assistance Force (in Afghanistan)
ITU	Intense Treatment Unit (formerly ICU, Intensive Care …)
ITW	Initial Training Wing
JMC	Joint Medical Command

LAC	Leading Aircraftman
MDHU	Military District Hospital Unit (also called Ministry of Defence Hospital Unit)
MERT	Medical Emergency Response Team
MFH	Mobile Field Hospital
MiC	Matron-in-chief
MO	Medical Officer
MOD	Ministry of Defence
NATO	North Atlantic Treaty Organisation
NBC	Nuclear, Biological and Chemical
NCE	Non-Commissioned Element (students/staff nurses, 1962–77)
NCO	Non-Commissioned Officers
NHS	National Health Service
NSP	Normal safety procedures
OC	Officer Commanding
PARAFH	Princess Alexandra's Royal Air Force Hospital
PECC	Patient Evacuation Control Cell
PMO	Principal Medical Officer
PMRAFH	Princess Mary's Royal Air Force Hospital
PMRAFNS	Princess Mary's Royal Air Force Nursing Service
PMs	Members of PMRAFNS
POWs	Prisoners of War
PQRE	Professionally Qualified and Re-entrant (officers' training course)
QAIMNS	Queen Alexandra's Imperial Military Nursing Service (until 1949)
QARANC	Queen Alexandra's Royal Army Nursing Corps (from 1949)
QARNNS	Queen Alexandra's Royal Naval Nursing Service
QHNS	Queen's Honorary Nursing Sister
RAAF	Royal Australian Air Force
RAF	Royal Air Force
RAFBH	Royal Air Force British Hospital
RAFGH	Royal Air Force General Hospital
RAFH	Royal Air Force Hospital
RAFNS	Royal Air Force Nursing Service (1918–23)
RAFSH	Royal Air Force Station Hospital
RAMC	Royal Army Medical Corps
RCDM	Royal Centre for Defence Medicine (Birmingham)
RDMC	Royal Defence Medical College
RFA	Royal Fleet Auxiliary
RFC	Royal Flying Corps
RGN	Registered General Nurse
RMN	Registered Mental Nurse
RNAS	Royal Naval Air Service
RRC	(Holder of the) Royal Red Cross
SAC	Senior Aircraftman
SEN	State Enrolled Nurse
SERE	Specialist Entrant and Re-entrant (officers' training course)
SNCO	Senior Non-commissioned Officer
SRN	State Registered Nurse
SSQ	Station Sick Quarters
TMW	Tactical Medical Wing
TPMH	The Princess Mary's Hospital (Akrotiri, Cyprus)

UN	United Nations
UNPROFOR	United Nations Protected Forces
u/s	Unserviceable
USAF	United States Air Force
VAD	(Nurse of the) Voluntary Aid Detachment
WAAF	Women's Auxiliary Air Force (1939–49)
WO	Warrant Officer
WRAF	Women's Royal Air Force (1918–20; 1949–)
WRNS	Women's Royal Naval Service
WW1	World War One, 1914–18
WW2	World War Two, 1939–45
YMCA	Young Men's Christian Association

Select Bibliography

Arthur, Max, *There Shall be Wings: The RAF from 1918 to the Present* (London: Hodder and Stoughton, 1993)

Beauman, Katherine Bentley, *Partners in Blue* (London: Hutchinson, 1971)

Bowyer, Chaz, *RAF Operations 1918–1938* (London: William Kimber, 1988)

Bushby, John R., *Air Defence of Great Britain* (Shepperton: Ian Allan, 1973)

Cormack, Andrew and Volstad, Ron, *The Royal Air Force 1939–45: Uniforms*, Men-at-Arms Series (Oxford: Osprey Publishing, 1990).

Escott, Beryl E., *Women in Air Force Blue* (Yeovil: Patrick Stephens, 1989)

Fairbairn, Tony, *Action Stations Overseas* (Yeovil: Patrick Stephens, 1991)

Green, Peter and Hodgson, Mike, *Cranwell: RNAS and RAF Photographs* (Hinckley: Midland Publishing, 1993)

Harfield, Alan, *Blandford and the Military* (Sherborne: Dorset Publishing, 1984)

McBryde, Brenda, *Quiet Heroines* (London: Chatto and Windus, 1985)

Otter, Patrick, *Lincolnshire Airfields in World War Two* (Newbury: Countryside Books, 1996)

Rexford-Welch, S.C. (ed.), *The Royal Air Force Medical Services* (3 vols), part of History of the Second World War/United Kingdom Medical Series (London: HMSO, 1954)

Hancock, Gp Capt. E.M. 'Princess Mary's Royal Air Force Nursing Service', in Ross, Tony (ed.), *'75 Eventful Years': A Tribute to the Royal Air Force 1918–1993* (Canterbury: Wingham Aviation Books, 1993)

Taylor, Eric, *Front-Line Nurse: British Nurses in World War 2* (London: Robert Hale, 1997)

Thetford, Owen, *Aircraft of the Royal Air Force since 1918* (London: Putnam, 1988)

Tunbridge, Paul, *History of RAF Halton* (London: Buckland Publications, 1995)

Woodman, Richard, *The Arctic Convoys, 1939–45* (London: John Murray, 1994)

MTE Journal Editors: Gp Capt. J. Kyle, June 1941–Dec 1942; Gp Capt. G.W. McAleer, Jan 1943–August 1945; Asst Editor: Flt Sgt R.H. Smith, June 1941–August 1945 (Medical Training Establishment and Depot, Royal Air Force, 1946).

Other sources

Air Historical Branch, London
College Library, RAF Cranwell
Community Relations, RAF Coningsby
Imperial War Museum, London
Personnel Records, RAF Innsworth
Public Record Office, Kew
RAF Museum, Hendon
Royal Signals Museum, Blandford, Dorset
PMRAFNS history files, Matron-in-Chief's Office

Contributions (letters, interviews, photos and cuttings) from individual PMs or their relatives, members of RAF Medical Branch, VAD nurses, RAF, WRAF and civilian patients, and family members of same; and the invaluable internet.

Index